CRACK COCAINE

A Practical Treatment Approach for the Chemically Dependent

BARBARA C. WALLACE, Ph.D.

BRUNNER/MAZEL, *Publishers* • NEW YORK

Wallace, Barbara C.
    Crack cocaine : a practical treatment approach for the chemically
dependent / Barbara C. Wallace.
        p. cm.
    Includes bibliographical references.
    Includes index.
    ISBN 0-87630-604-0
    1. Crack (Drug) 2. Cocaine habit—Treatment. I. Title.
    [DNLM: 1. Cocaine. 2. Substance Dependence—therapy. WM 280
W187c]
    RC568.C6W34 1991
    616.864706—dc20
    DNLM/DLC
    for Library of Congress   90-2683
                                                                          CIP

Clients' initials and all other identifying information have been changed in case examples to preserve the confidentiality of patients.

We gratefully acknowledge the following publishers for giving their permission to reprint or adapt material.

Pages 37, 38, 42, 47 & 49. Adapted from B.C. Wallace (1990). Crack addiction: Treatment and recovery issues. *Contemporary Drug Problems, 17,* 1, 79–119. Adapted by permission of Federal Legal Publications, Inc., New York, New York.

Pages 81 & 82. Quotations from H.A. Meyersburg and R.M. Post (1979). An holistic developmental view of neural and psychological processes: A Neurobiologic-psychoanalytic integration. *British Journal of Psychiatry, 135,* 139–155. Reprinted by permission of British Journal of Psychiatry, London, England.

Pages 234–251. Material adapted from B.C. Wallace (1989). Psychological and environmental determinants of relapse in crack cocaine smokers. *Journal of Substance Abuse Treatment, 6,* 2, 95–106. Adapted by permission of Pergamon Press, Elmsford, New York.

Pages 252–271. Material adapted from B.C. Wallace (1989). Relapse prevention in psychoeducational groups for crack cocaine smokers. *Journal of Substance Abuse Treatment, 6,* 4, 229–239. Adapted by permission of Pergamon Press, Elmsford, New York.

Published by
BRUNNER/MAZEL, INC.
19 Union Square West
New York, New York 10003

Manufactured in the United States of America
10   9   8   7   6   5   4   3   2   1

To all those chemically dependent patients who challenged me to grow as a clinician and from whom I learned so much. And for all those who desperately need quality treatment in order to successfully recover from their addiction.

Also, for baby Ramsey and all the children who deserve to grow up in a world free of opportunities to develop chemical dependency.

Contents

viii				*Crack Cocaine*

List of Illustrations

Preface

This book presents an opportunity to share data, clinical observations, theoretical formulations, and illustrative cases that communicate my experiences in treating compulsive crack-cocaine smokers on an inpatient detoxification unit at Interfaith Medical Center in Brooklyn, N.Y. The particular unit on which I worked became a specialized crack unit in the fall of 1986. Julio Martinez, former director of the New York State Division of Substance Abuse Services, visited the facility and enthusiastically helped us to dedicate our new "crack unit" on October 8, 1986—the first of its kind in the New York metropolitan area.

Armed with psychodynamic training, the value of research instilled during a postdoctoral fellowship in narcotic drug research, experiences working with veterans in a methadone maintenance program, and prior experience at Interfaith Medical Center working with the intravenous-heroin-patient population, I set out with enthusiasm to tackle the challenge of crack-cocaine treatment. My response after a couple of weeks in a "crack unit" was, "Please give me back my heroin addicts!"

What I was responding to were clinical impressions that intravenous-heroin users easily connect with feelings, talk about their depression, and readily cry and express feelings in individual sessions, and were as a group rather sedate throughout detoxification as they were gradually given lower doses of methadone. Their oral rage and self-destructiveness created special treatment challenges.

In contrast, the crack-cocaine smoker was arrogant, aloof, and not inclined to discuss or connect with feelings. As a group, crack-cocaine smokers appeared to the clinical staff as grandiose, inflated, and generally very narcissistic. When we were in transition to becoming primarily a crack unit and still had a mixture of intravenous-heroin users being treated alongside crack-cocaine smokers, therapy groups were difficult because the crack patients felt superior to the hard-core intravenous-heroin addicts and could not identify with them or with their experiences. As a group, they were very energetic and gregarious, utilized manic defenses, and laughed, joked, and enjoyed pranks and high-energy antics while on the detoxification unit. These "clown theatrics" often threatened to undermine the integrity of the unit as a therapeutic milieu. Also, the crack patients were younger in general and included many 17- to 24-year-old patients (25% of the crack patient population I treated).

Modifications in treatment were necessary with the crack-patient population in recognition of their psychological characteristics. The treatment is essentially a tale of tailoring treatment to the needs of a diverse group of patients who usually have in common an overreliance on narcissistic defenses and deficits in the regulation of affect, self-esteem, and behavior in interpersonal relationships.

Treatment of the crack patients required the best of my clinical skills, challenging me to engage them emotionally in treatment and to convince them of the severity of their addiction and how they had to proceed in order to overcome it. Empathy was essential despite their aloofness and arrogance. The challenge and excitement lay in transforming this aloofness and grandiosity into involvement in the treatment process. A variety of clinical interventions evolved in response to this challenge.

I left Interfaith Medical Center in August 1988 in order to enter academia, where I would have more time for writing about my experiences. Having worked with over 300 crack-cocaine patients on an individual basis (assessment, individual sessions, group sessions) and with over 200 others in community meetings and therapy groups (co-led with another therapist), I had ample clinical data to share through journal articles and oral presentations on crack treatment.

During the spring of 1989, I gave a series of three oral presentations to the staff at the Smithers Alcoholism Treatment and Training Center in New York City, which had been struggling to cope with an increase in patients presenting with crack-cocaine usage. The motivation to write this book evolved in response to their enthusiastic reception of my ideas and the feeling on the part of several "seasoned" staff members that I had integrated and clearly stated their own clinical sense of what seemed to work and why it seemed to work with these difficult patients. More specifically, a woman approached me after one lecture in particular and said, "It sounds like a book."

Thus, this book elaborates on these oral presentations, shares data and research findings compiled with patients while working on the detoxification unit, and attempts to convey in clear, precise language what I feel is a practical treatment approach that was developed for use with crack-cocaine smokers. However, the approach also extends to the treatment of the chemically dependent in general.

There are no longitudinal follow-up data or outcome-evaluation studies that validate the effectiveness of the treatment approach espoused here. The state of the art regarding crack treatment involves the fact that only a few outcome-evaluation studies specifically involving crack populations are available in the literature. The limited data that do exist on the subject generally show only preliminary findings of what might be promising with no hard evidence that current approaches investigated actually work. On the other hand, the approach to crack treatment advanced in this book has benefited from analysis of patients' psychosocial data (Wallace, 1987) and of data on relapse episodes (Wallace, 1989a). This body of data led to modifications and refinements in the treatment model. Hence, research findings have affected the evolution and refinement of this treatment approach, although a grant-funded evaluation is clearly needed and shall be pursued in the future.

The intended audience for the book includes those striving to upgrade their clinical skills for work with crack smokers, as well as anyone seeking to understand the kind of treatment those addicted to crack require in order to recover from the addiction. The book articulates a well-justified "yardstick" against which promising or future crack-treatment models should be measured. It attempts to describe a comprehensive and intensive model of crack treatment that permits matching patients to particular interventions as part of a cost-effective and practical process of assessment of individual treatment needs. For those who need to design, implement, and evaluate treatment programs for crack smokers, the book should prove to be a valuable adjunct.

Acknowledgments

This book would not have been possible without the positive, nurturant, working environment at Interfaith Medical Center. I must also acknowledge the vision of Jochanon Weisenfreund, M.D., (director of the Department of Psychiatry) who—in responding to the critical treatment needs of the Brooklyn, N. Y., community—created the crack unit. Also deserving of recognition are Maryann Elberth, who provided empathic leadership as a unit chief, and other supportive staff members at Interfaith Medical Center who were instrumental in producing the kind of working environment that allowed me to grow as a clinician in response to the needs of the chemically dependent. Despite Interfaith Medical Center's financial and other problems as an inner-city hospital serving a poor community, it must be acknowledged as a vital institution striving to provide desperately needed quality treatment to its surrounding community.

All of the research findings that came out of my work on inpatient detoxification units were accomplished in cooperation with Interfaith Medical Center. I thank Dr. Weisenfreund for his support of my research efforts and this book project.

I must also acknowledge the loving support and guidance of my family and friends, who provided needed strength and encouragement for my pursuits. In a similar vein, I must thank my editor and all those who read and gave me feedback on various parts of this work, helping me to produce what I hope is a clear and practical approach to the treatment of the chemically dependent.

Introduction

A conservative estimate in the middle 1980s suggested that as many as eight million Americans use cocaine regularly, and that 5–20% of them have developed a serious dependence on cocaine (Cregler & Mark, 1986). The 1988 National Household Survey on Drug Abuse found that the number of heavy crack and cocaine users rose significantly from 1985 to 1988; there has been a 33% increase since 1985 among those using crack or cocaine once a week or more; among those using crack or cocaine on a daily or almost daily basis, such usage rose by 19% (National Institute of Drug Abuse, *New York Times*, Aug. 1, 1989, p. A14). A recent Senate Judiciary Committee set the figure of cocaine addicts at 2.2 million, which is in contradistinction to earlier reports by the National Institute of Drug Abuse (*New York Times*, May 15, 1990, p. A20). The introduction of crack cocaine has created an epidemic. Crack-cocaine smoking has replaced heroin use as the main illicit drug problem confronting this nation (DeLeon, 1989). Crack cocaine, in particular, has led to an increased demand for treatment, which is often unavailable because of long waiting lists (Martinez, 1989). Pressure on treatment programs to increase their services to the large and growing body of cocaine users remains strong (Dougherty & Lesswing, 1989), while efforts to expand treatment facilities continue (Martinez, 1989).

The characteristics of crack-cocaine smokers may necessitate modifications in treatment programs (Rainone, Kott, & Maranda, 1988; Wallace, 1987) designed to address the needs of heroin addicts and alcoholics. Crack smokers may even require treatments that are different from those utilized with intranasal cocaine users (Kleinman, Miller, Millman, et al., 1989), or they may have to be modified in light of crack-population characteristics (Washton, 1989; Washton & Gold, 1987; Spitz & Rosecan, 1987; Stone, Fromme, & Kagan, 1984). Hence, the crack-cocaine epidemic presents a considerable treatment challenge.

OVERVIEW OF THE BOOK

In order fully to appreciate the nature of the treatment challenge, several dimensions of the problem must be understood. A biopsychosocial model of crack addiction permits a comprehensive survey of the multiple interacting variables that explain the development and maintenance of crack addiction (Donovan & Marlatt, 1988). Biological, social, and psychological variables merit examination as dimensions of the crack problem.

Understanding the current crack-cocaine epidemic requires consideration of social factors that have contributed to an atmosphere that fosters widespread experimental and recreational use of chemicals. As an important biological factor, the unique neurochemical actions of cocaine on brain functioning must be appreciated in order to understand the nature of the treatment challenge. Chapter 1 covers these social and biological factors. However, another dimension of the treatment challenge involves the accurate diagnosis of the severity and stage of a user's progression in crack smoking. Related issues include the effect of psychopathology on the treatment of crack addiction, the possible role of psychological factors in creating a susceptibility to developing crack addiction, and research findings on crack smokers' characteristic psychopathology. All of these psychological factors involve issues of diagnosis and are discussed in the second chapter. A third chapter provides research findings on crack smokers' ($n = 245$) psychosocial functioning, rounding out the discussion on the nature of the treatment challenge. Part I thus highlights how a biopsychosocial model of crack addiction permits appreciation of numerous issues and subtle complexities that require the attention of the clinician. Acknowledgment of the social environment, neurochemical changes in brain function, psychopathology, and psychosocial factors as interacting variables behind the mystery of widespread crack addiction remains critical for effective treatment of the crack-cocaine-dependent population. In this way, the first section of the book justifies the importance of utilizing a biopsychosocial model of crack addiction while providing an overview of the nature of the treatment challenge.

Part II covers theoretical issues and implications for clinical technique. Chapter 4 explains the theoretical rationale for the use of pharmacological adjuncts, and Chapter 5, that for psychoanalytic approaches, recognizing the effect of childhood histories of disturbed object relations with parents and how they may predispose experimental and recreational crack users to the development of addiction. The rationale behind utilizing behavioral approaches and appreciating the social environment is covered in Chapter 6. This part of the book moves the field of chemical dependency toward the development of integrated theoretical models that permit recognition of the role of interacting multiple variables and provide a sound rationale for treatment. Chapter 7 provides case histories that illustrate the necessity of utilizing a biopsychosocial theory of addiction that integrates pharmacological, psychoanalytic, and behavioral approaches.

The third part of the book covers crack-treatment models. Here, Chapter 8 reviews "what works" for crack and cocaine patients in treatment. Chapter 9 presents an analysis of promising treatment approaches and models of intervention in need of modification to improve their efficacy with crack populations.

Part IV furnishes a description of clinical technique in the assessment phase. Chapter 10 covers the elements of an effective clinical interview, and Chapter 11 presents strategies for engaging the ambivalent crack addict in the treatment process.

The last section of the book (Part V) describes clinical techniques of value in the treatment phase with the chemically dependent and diverse populations of patients sharing the common feature of having experienced childhood trauma. Chapter 12 reviews obstacles to effective treatment and how clinicians can avoid certain pitfalls that can sabotage treatment. Chapter 13 explains the need for a multifaceted technique to address the multideterminants of relapse by presenting research on the process of relapse in crack patients. This chapter is adapted from Wallace's (1989a) work, "Psychological and Environmental Determinants of Relapse in Crack Cocaine Smokers." And a final chapter (14) draws on the work "Relapse Prevention in Psychoeducational Groups for Compulsive Crack Cocaine Smokers" (Wallace, 1989b) to provide treatment practitioners with a detailed description of what they can actually do and say to prepare patients to avoid relapse. This section shows the importance of utilizing a multifaceted clinical technique with the chemically dependent, combining psychodynamic and cognitive-behavioral elements, educational directives, and metaphor. The recommended multifaceted clinical technique logically arises out of appreciation of the need to address the various determinants of relapse and numerous variables to which our integrated biopsychosocial theory drew our attention.

I

CRACK:
THE NATURE OF
THE TREATMENT
CHALLENGE

1

Societal Demand, the Art of Drug Distribution, and the Pharmacology of Crack

Why has crack-cocaine smoking become so widespread across the United States? How have individuals of all races, classes, and income levels, and even children and adolescents, become users of crack cocaine? This chapter seeks an answer to this question through a review and analysis of several interacting factors. We shall explore how societal demand for chemicals, the art of drug distribution, and the pharmacology of crack all help to explain how people begin crack use, persevere in its use, and end up driven to pursue compulsive crack smoking despite severe personal deterioration and numerous negative consequences.

SOCIETAL DEMAND FOR CHEMICALS

In the 1960s, experimental and recreational use of marijuana, amphetamines, and LSD constituted a social ritual for adolescents and young adults. Drug usage continued to represent the primary way in which leisure time was spent well into the 1970s and 1980s for a generation of adolescents and young adults who grew up having internalized the societal value that the experimental and recreational use of chemicals was a normal and relatively safe behavior. The media must also be recognized as a powerful social and cultural force that conveys the message that alcohol is an essential vehicle for transporting oneself to the level where fun or a good time occurs. It is in this kind of atmosphere that older generations accepted values promoting the use of alcohol, as did a maturing generation the drug-use values of the 1960s, to be joined by more recent recruits into the contemporary drug culture, all searching for a regular supply of chemicals.

Societal demand for a steady, certain supply of chemicals remains a fundamental reality in our culture. In support of this reality, the past two decades

3

have seen an increasing growth in domestic marijuana production and in the production of methamphetamine and other designer drugs in chemical laboratories throughout urban and suburban America. By engaging in the manufacture of various chemical substances, people not only ensure a consistent supply for themselves, but also a profitable livelihood in light of the constant demand.

A willingness to experiment with new chemicals promoted as relatively safe characterizes our cultural predisposition toward newly available substances on the illicit drug market. Many long-time, regular users of a chemical substance readily welcome a new and different high. Some persons consider themselves "chemical connoisseurs" and willingly experiment with virtually any new chemical thought not to be too dangerous. Others actually seek out those drugs described as dangerous or lethal, joyfully anticipating the promise of an especially good high.

INTRANASAL COCAINE USAGE: AMERICA'S FAVORITE NEW DRUG

The intranasal use of cocaine in the 1970s and 1980s reflected cocaine's status as America's favorite, new, relatively safe drug. In many respects, there may not be any truly "new" drugs, merely old chemicals reintroduced or revitalized.

Cocaine is such a drug, boasting a long history predating the Incan empire in Peru. It is derived from the plant *Erythroxylum coca*, which is grown in South America. Cultivated there for thousands of years, its past and present social functions, according to Grinspoon and Bakalar (1985), "suggest the wide variety of possible cultural definitions of drug use" (p. 16). The European cultural view of the use of cocaine for medicines and for pleasure began to evolve with the isolation of the principal alkaloid in 1860 by Albert Niemann. The white crystalline powder extracted from Peruvian coca leaves experienced its first wave of popularity in the United States after being used by Sigmund Freud (1974) and promoted in his 1884 paper, "On Coca." Freud hailed cocaine as a stimulant like caffeine and recommended it for a variety of illnesses and symptoms, including fatigue, nervousness, morphine addiction, and alcoholism. It was not until the deleterious effects of the continued use of high doses became apparent—psychosis, paranoia, compulsive use, inability to terminate use—that cocaine was restricted to medical circles. It was still valued as an anesthetic for mucous membranes, such as in surgery involving the eyes or nose (Grinspoon & Bakalar, 1985, pp. 19, 22, 29).

Growth in the importation and availability of cocaine hydrochloride (the salt or powder form, which can be utilized intranasally or intravenously, as it is soluble in water) during the 1970s and 1980s met the need for an energizing and chic new drug. Lasch (1979) describes our contemporary society as one in which societal and family dynamics have combined to create a culture mainly composed of narcissists. The glamour of cocaine and its pharmacological effects coincide with the needs of the narcissist. For those who attempt to ameliorate painful feelings, emptiness, boredom, and low self-esteem, cocaine represents an attractive and seductive drug because of the feelings of euphoria, grandiosity, and confidence it provides—especially to those wishing to emulate the life-styles of the rich and famous users of cocaine. As America's favorite new drug, it no longer remains the special toy of the media, stars, or even of those mostly middle- and upper-middle-class white males who were its initial users (Washton & Gold, 1987). Intranasal cocaine usage grew to include people of all races and backgrounds in clubs and bars, and at parties, where anyone with the desire, and the money, could try the new drug. Cocaine powder was also sprinkled on marijuana joints and placed in cigarettes.

Clayton (1985) asserts that there was indeed an epidemic of cocaine use in the United States in the late 1970s and early 1980s, concluding that "if the price of cocaine remains low or drops even lower and the purity remains high or goes even higher, this society may experience an epidemic of cocaine use without historical equal in terms of magnitude and coverage" (p. 30). Even more prophetic were the words of Wesson and Smith (1985), who felt that "if the drug were more readily available at a substantially lower cost, or if certain sociocultural rituals endorsed and supported the higher dose patterns, more destructive patterns of abuse could develop" (p. 150). The prophecy became reality.

A NEW SOCIOCULTURAL RITUAL: COCAINE FREE-BASE SMOKING

It was as early as 1974 that free-basing (smoking the base in a small pipe) first appeared in California as a new ritual in the drug community. Siegel (1985) describes compulsive-use patterns developing in those utilizing the smoking or inhalation method; between 1978 and 1982 a dramatic change in compulsive use was observed, with such users becoming predominantly smokers of cocaine free-base. By 1980, this new sociocultural ritual was being reported throughout the United States (Siegel, 1982, 1987).

The smoking, or free-basing, of cocaine provides a more potent "rush," a more intense euphoria, and a considerably more powerful high than does inhaling cocaine powder. After only a few minutes, however, the euphoria subsides and is followed by an irritable craving for more free-base cocaine. The result is that users continue free-basing until they or their drug supplies are fully exhausted—often after several days of smoking (Inciardi, 1987, pp. 465–466).

Thus, the new sociocultural ritual of free-basing carried a higher potential for addiction, as reflected in loss of control and compulsive usage. Nonetheless, this ritual continued to gain in popularity, because of publicity surrounding comedian Richard Pryor's accidently "setting himself on fire" while admittedly smoking cocaine. This incident sparked the curiosity of recreational users of intranasal cocaine and those connoisseurs ever searching for a new high.

For most users, the only deterrent to carrying out the new ritual was the lack of knowledge of exactly how to go about it. The demand for instructions was met by the availability in "head shops"—drug paraphernalia shops that masquerade as tobacco or variety stores—of kits and booklets on how to prepare one's own free-base cocaine. The kits attempted to guide individuals through the process of converting cocaine hydrochloride (the salt or powder, which is not efficiently smoked) to its free-base form, chunks or rocks of a more stable nature. The cocaine alkaloid must be derived or chemically "freed" from the cocaine hydrochloride salt or powder form. The difficulty of following written directions and the volatility of chemicals such as ether that were typically involved in the preparation of free-base cocaine made the task rather difficult (Hopkins, 1989). The use of baking soda or ammonia instead of ether is less dangerous, but still creates some challenge for the novice.

CRACK: A PACKAGING AND MARKETING BREAKTHROUGH

The skills of anyone who knew how to "cook up" or prepare free-base cocaine became invaluable in the drug culture, with users teaching one another. Even simpler for novice users, however, was to be able to purchase precooked preparations. Drug dealers met that need with the manufacture and distribution of "rock" on the West Coast and "crack" on the East Coast. The introduction of "rock" and "crack" as precooked free-base cocaine constituted a packaging and marketing breakthrough.

Reports of the smoking of rock on the West Coast (Smith & Wesson, 1985) spread in 1985. The initial reports of crack-cocaine usage in New York City were released to the media in November 1985 (Hopkins, 1989). Wetli (1987) asserts that in 1986 the smoking of cocaine had become more widespread and popular because of the introduction of rock and crack.

Packaging and marketing techniques include selling crack in relatively inexpensive vials, permitting those with as little as $20, $10, $5, or even $3, to purchase an exciting high. To assure their customers of their availability, drug dealers, like doctors, wear beepers to alert them to a need for their services. Possessing an array of demographics—street-level gangs, family networks, urban and suburban outlets—dealers soon realize their potential to become entrepreneurs through the production and distribution of crack. As a result of the breakthrough of crack into the drug marketplace, the practice can be characterized as part of a booming cottage industry that guarantees profits. albeit with the risk of arrest and incarceration.

Even though the packaging, marketing, and distribution of crack have permitted the evolution of some of the most vicious capitalists that the United States has ever seen, others caution that only those at the top of drug empires reap substantial economic rewards. Low-level crack dealers actually earn very little while working long hours as "sellers" or as "lookouts" to watch for the police. Frequently, the development of dependency on the very substance the seller is dealing—smoking the crack that was meant to be sold or using the money from sales to purchase crack for one's own use—quickly erodes any profit. Some argue that the myth of wealth or easy money from crack distribution inspires the entrance of new workers into the drug-distribution network, whereas in reality the low-level drug worker's earnings are small and life-style is correspondingly bleak (Kolata,1989, November 26, pp. 1, 42).

Perhaps when dealers become users, they fall victim to the allure of crack cocaine, become addicted, and deny the reality of the deterioration characterizing their life-style. Loss of profits because of one's addiction to crack, injuries inflicted as punishment for failing to pay drug suppliers, and the desire to promote the myth of a glamorous and profitable life may follow as likely scenarios in the life of a dealer who has become an addict. This dimension of the crack trade, which involves "addict workers," tempers somewhat the depiction of all crack dealers' becoming entrepreneurs. However, there remain compelling case examples of drug dealers who not only accumulate enormous wealth through the crack trade, but also develop elaborate techniques for laundering their profits (Holmes, 1989, pp. 1, B4). Depending on the extent to which the dealer may utilize crack cocaine, either a considerable amount of money can be amassed or it can be squandered on an expensive habit.

Halfon (1989) reminds us not to neglect an important factor that may explain the motivation to develop a drug economy. For Halfon, inextricably linked to the evolution of booming cottage drug industries is the loss of services and the poverty that characterized the 1980s. He links his observations of the gap between rich and poor in the 1980s, and the gutting of our programs for the underprivileged, to the evolution of a drug economy centered on the packaging, marketing, and distribution of crack cocaine.

Pre-Packaging for the Most Efficient Route of Administration

Crack is immediately and completely absorbed when smoked (Wetli, 1987); thus the smoking of free-base cocaine or crack constitutes the most efficient way to deliver the drug to the brain. Moreover, smoking or inhalation permits the fastest delivery of the most concentrated dose of cocaine. When inhaled or smoked, it takes cocaine a mere six to seven seconds to get to the brain, whereas intravenous injection takes two to three times longer, and the much more inefficient intranasal method some two to three minutes to do so. Thus the initial effects of smoked cocaine are more intense and are felt more rapidly than with comparable intravenous doses (Jones, 1987, pp. 57–58). Even the experienced intravenous cocaine user would be impressed by such a rapid, intense, euphoric rush. As a result, when packaged as a smokable form of cocaine, crack easily found a-market of users demanding more of this intense high.

Testimony to the marketing genius of prepackaging cocaine for the most efficient route of administration—in small, firm chunks that provide a potent dose that is easily smoked in a cigarette, marijuana joint, glass pipe, or stem (glasslike straw with a screen holding the crack in place as it burns)—is afforded by the large numbers of individuals who not only try crack, but persevere in its use.

State-of-the-Art Drug-Dealing Methodology

Packaging techniques for crack also reflect "state of the art" drug-dealing methodology, where dealers strive to ensure product purity and to avoid product tampering (Hopkins, 1989). The lower-level drug sellers who may have tampered with the product (securing the actual crack for their own use), as well as those desperate addicts who sought to sell chips of soap or white bread as crack in old crack vials, undermined the buyers' confidence in crack sold on the street. However, the creativity and energy of crack entrepreneurs emulates some of the very best acceptable models of American capitalist ventures.

According to Hopkins (1989), an update on drug-dealing methods in 1989 reveals yet even more innovative packaging and distribution techniques. Heat-sealed, clear plastic straws containing crack and "gun clips" of ten small vials of crack serve to guarantee product purity and prevent tampering. Crack can also be compressed into wafer and pill shapes—antacid and aspirin "look-alikes" that would have to be analyzed in a laboratory to prove that they were crack cocaine. Professional analysis, however, has shown such crack wafers and pills to be 95 percent pure cocaine (Hopkins, 1989), validating the production expertise of drug entrepreneurs (chunks of street crack have been found to be 35 to 100 percent pure, according to Wetli, 1987). Hopkins explains that although the user must still break apart and smoke these pill look-alikes, this state-of-the-art drug packaging permits a user, such as an adolescent attending school, to avoid detection by carrying crack in a pill bottle. Partly because of the success of innovative packaging and marketing strategies on the part of drug-dealing entrepreneurs, crack continues to proliferate, as does the involvement of users.

There are no signs of abatement in the crack epidemic. Instead, the methodology of crack dealers improves and expands. Crack is even prepared in microwave ovens. And children have become drawn into drug dealing as providers of labor and carriers of drugs (Hopkins, 1989).

CRACK: AMERICA'S BIGGEST DRUG PROBLEM

Nationwide growth in the population of those who are probably addicted to crack justifies William Bennett's (director of Federal Drug Policy) declaration that crack is "our biggest and most immediate problem" (Berke, 1989). Crack smoking has become widespread notwithstanding the myth propagated by the media that it is an inner-city, low-income, largely minority problem. This is the result of the use of hidden undercover cameras in crack houses in three areas and interviews with crack users there. Such cameras and interviewers are not permitted in the crack or base houses in affluent suburban neighborhoods, which are usually in the basements of homes or in apartments. Many middle-class communities are "still asleep" to the widespread local availability of crack (Hopkins, 1989). Cocaine-distribution networks have also spread into rural states in the Midwest and South. Thus, the availability of crack in all areas—urban, suburban, and rural—engenders continuing growth in the population of crack addicts.

Crack use by the middle class has been increasingly recognized. According to some estimates, as many as 70% of New York City's drug users may be affluent. Doctors, nurses, accountants, professors, Wall Street executives, air traffic controllers all have fallen victim to the crack epidemic (Elmer-DeWitt, 1989, Nov. 6, *Time*, p. 95). The growing involvement of adolescents, and even children as young as 12 and 13 years of age, in crack smoking, and in crack-related sexual and criminal behavior, has been documented (Inciardi, 1990; Inciardi & Pottieger, 1990).

The magnitude and severity of widespread crack use can be seen in the plight of hospital-emergency-room patients presenting with medical or psychiatric complications arising from crack (chest pain, heart attack, brain seizures, strokes, violent or erratic behavior, paranoia, psychosis, anxiety, and depression) as well as of victims of the violence associated with the drug trade. Helping professionals in emergency-room and hospital settings who treat the most debilitated of the crack addicts find themselves not only burned out, but also turned off by patients who steal, trade sex for crack or crack money, and engage in drug dealing—to list a few behaviors suggesting the severe personal deterioration suffered by crack smokers (Gross, 1989).

What drives these crack smokers to continue their compulsive behavior to the point of such severe personal deterioration? How can crack smoking be pursued despite gunshot wounds, heart attacks, and crack-induced psychosis? Regardless of class, race, or income, what drives crack smokers to exhausting their financial and personal resources to obtain the drug? How can crack smokers, particularly adolescents, be reduced to exchanging sex for crack when they no longer have anything else of value to offer (Inciardi, 1990)? How can affluent crack smokers go through trust funds, savings accounts, and charge-card credit lines or take out second mortgages on their homes (Elmer-DeWitt, 1989)? Why do crack smokers, regardless of income, sell possessions such as jewelry, cars, clothing, and stereos? An understanding of crack's pharmacological actions in altering the brain's neurochemistry provides further insight into the nature of the problem.

THE PHARMACOLOGY OF COCAINE

We must appreciate the pharmacological actions of crack in order to understand more fully the nature of the problem and why its use is producing a growing body of addicts nationwide. Certainly, if it were not for the art of drug dealing, the potent smokable crack would not be widely available for experimental use by a willing public socialized to casually try any new, relatively safe chemical. But even without the efficient and potent delivery of cocaine to the brain of the user (as with crack), cocaine hydrochloride (salt, powder, intranasal and intravenous form) remains highly addictive, despite earlier misconceptions regarding its addictive potential.

Cocaine's pharmacological effects include euphoria, increased energy, enhanced alertness and sensory experience, and elevated feelings of self-esteem and self-confidence (Daigle, Clark, & Landry, 1988, p. 189). Once tried, it is cocaine's pharmacological actions that "keep the user using" (Cohen, 1987, p. 8). Because of these pharmacological actions, the user feels as though it is imperative to repeat the self-administration of cocaine again and again. This repetitive process provides for intense conditioning (see Chapter 6) to continue drug-seeking behavior (Cohen, 1987, pp. 6–7). Essentially, cocaine euphoria serves as a positive reinforcer (in laboratory animals and humans), which motivates the user to continue ingesting cocaine (Daigle, Clark, & Landry, 1988, p. 189).

Animal Studies: Cocaine's Reinforcing Properties

Animal research reveals that cocaine is the only drug for which laboratory animals will continually bar-press without stopping for food or rest, and for which they will also pass up females in heat. Animals persist in cocaine self-administration despite its accompaniment by a punishment, such as an electric shock. Animals will choose a higher dose of cocaine with an electric shock instead of a lower dose not accompanied by shock. Laboratory research shows cocaine to be the most reinforcing of drugs, with animals consistently self-administering it until they drop dead; this was not found to be true in heroin or alcohol studies. These animal studies are important because they predict the addictiveness of cocaine in humans (Johanson, 1984; Geary, 1987; Rosecan & Spitz, 1987). They also provide a model of the reward value and addictive properties of cocaine (Nunes & Rosecan, 1987). In humans, cocaine serves as a remarkably powerful reinforcer of behavior (Herridge & Gold, 1988). As a result, in the real-life laboratory of the contemporary crack culture, humans are like laboratory animals—punishments and negative consequences associated with crack fail to prevent crack smokers from continuing their habit. And as Wetli (1987) reports, cocaine may cause sudden death by a variety of mechanisms, regardless of the route of ingestion.

Cocaine's Impact on the Brain Reward Center

The brain-induced euphoria that cocaine produces constitutes an immediate and powerful reward. Repetitive self-administration results in a conditioning whereby the reward or euphoria leads to an increase in those behaviors that preceded or led to the reward or euphoria. Episodes of drug-seeking behavior and self-administration (smoking crack) became more frequent (see Chapter 6). The frenetic and obsessive pursuit of the drug—despite the effect on health, work, family, and finances—reflects how voluntary behavior becomes controlled by cocaine. This kind of behavior occurs because of cocaine's powerful influence on the reward center in the brain.

Thus, one hypothesis holds that the cocaine reward is mediated in animals and humans alike through an intense euphoric, mood-elevating effect. (Geary, 1987, p. 33). Cocaine's action in the dopaminergic synapse may mediate cocaine's rewarding properties. Whereas the rewarding properties of food and water are conveyed to the central nervous system over networks of sensory nerves, cocaine can powerfully and directly activate the brain's central circuits of goal-directed behavior. It is in this way that motivation for cocaine can come to dominate motivation for food, water, and sex. Cocaine's provision of a shortcut to the pleasure of reward is based on neural mechanisms involving the dopaminergic system, which explains its powerful reinforcing action (Wise, 1984). What humans experience as euphoria when using cocaine probably reflects the activation of reward circuits in the brain. Since the behavior of obtaining and using cocaine is so powerfully rewarded by this euphoria and activation of brain reward circuits, this behavior is repeated despite often compulsive, self-destructive cocaine-use patterns (Herridge & Gold, 1988, p. 234).

Thus, cocaine provides a much more powerfully rewarding experience than naturally occurring rewards (food, water, sex) and socially constructed rewards (money, paycheck); cocaine's euphoria may therefore come to dominate as the most important reward for which individuals structure and organize their behavior. The motivation to secure and use cocaine may become a user's primary preoccupation to the point of physical dehydration and malnutrition, as well as job loss as a result of the drug's direct and powerful influence on the brain's reward center.

The Neurochemical Actions of Cocaine

The euphoria of acute cocaine administration may be attributed to its neurochemical actions that block the reuptake of dopamine, producing a short-duration overload. However, cocaine also interferes with the reuptake of norepinephrine and serotonin. When these neurotransmitters are available to act at the synapse for a longer time, a message of more intense stimulation—or euphoria occurs (Trachtenberg & Blum, 1988). Our understanding of cocaine neurobiology remains partial and incomplete at this point (Nunes & Rosecan, 1987, p. 48).

With regard to its effect on the dopaminergic system, cocaine rapidly blocks the reuptake of dopamine into dopaminergic nerve terminals and facilitates the release of dopamine. In addition, cocaine activates tyrosine hydroxylase. There is an acute increase in dopamine availability and neurotransmission, and in the number of dopamine receptors, along with an increased dopamine receptor sensitivity. With chronic cocaine use, there is a reduction in dopamine concentrations, with the net effect of decreased amounts of dopamine. The neurochemistry of cocaine and its impact on norepinephrine also involves the blocking of norepinephrine reuptake while facilitating the release of norepinephrine. With chronic use, receptor sensitivity also results in this system. Here, the net effect is decreased amounts of norepinephrine (Gold, Washton, & Dackis, 1985). Among the numerous other neurobiological systems affected by cocaine are endorphins and other polypeptides, aminobutyric acid (GABA), acetylcholine (ACh), calcium, and phenylethylamine (Nunes & Rosecan, 1987). In this way, cocaine's powerful psychoactive properties may involve multisubstrate pathways and even opioid peptides may serve as substrates for cocaine's rewarding effects; cocaine's acute and chronic effects are likely due to activation and alteration of multiple neurotransmitter systems (Trachtenberg & Blum, 1988, pp. 320–321). Collectively, these neurochemical changes in the brain of the user following from cocaine's pharmacological effects have important consequences.

COCAINE RECONCEPTUALIZED: A UNIQUELY ADDICTING DRUG

Rosecan & Spitz (1987) reconceptualize cocaine as a uniquely addicting drug, based on its neurochemical actions. They stress that while the cocaine addict in some ways resembles the alcoholic or the heroin or amphetamine ad-dict, there are important differences. When used over time, cocaine is power-fully addicting, justifying the assertion that it is our most addictive drug and unique among those substances abused by drug users. Acute tolerance, re-bound depression or the "crash," and "craving" have specifically been attrib-uted to dopamine depletion and receptor supersensitivity that follows from chronic cocaine use (Nunes & Rosecan, 1987, p. 64). The neurochemical changes produced by chronic cocaine use also explain the withdrawal syn-drome, which includes lethargy, depression, oversleeping, and overeating in ad-dition to the eventual craving for more cocaine (Rosecan & Spitz, 1987, p. 12).

Users actually experience a neurochemically based need for more cocaine, which, after chronic use, manifests itself as an all-consuming cocaine craving (Rosecan & Spitz, 1987, pp. 12–15). With chronic or repeated doses, the neuro-chemical mechanisms produce cravings that can interact with the conditioning or learning mechanisms (Jones, 1984), helping to produce a severe addiction. This happens because each time that the discomfort of cocaine craving is allevi-ated by the administration of more cocaine, repetitive trials establish cocaine administration as a form of negative reinforcement. When negative reinforce-ment occurs, the cocaine user learns to terminate or avoid dysphoria or craving by taking more cocaine. Positive reinforcement takes place when the reward of the cocaine's euphoria leads to the likelihood of cocaine use increasing in the future. Thus, negative reinforcement, in addition to the positive reinforcement provided by cocaine's euphoria, ensures that the continued use of cocaine is ef-fectively sustained (Daigle, Clark, & Landry, 1988, p. 189) and the develop-ment of addiction proceeds. Gawin (1989) explains that cocaine produces physiological changes in parts of the brain that regulate psychological pro-cesses; thus, cocaine only affects parts of the brain that are psychological.

In susceptible individuals, the need for cocaine can supplant other interests and become an addiction. While many individuals appear to use cocaine safely or "recreationally," the "cumulative neurochemical changes produced, com-bined with a progressive psychological reliance on the drug, can lead even the most casual user to compulsive use" (Rosecan & Spitz, 1987, p. 15). In this way, addiction develops either as an attempt to reverse the unpleasant effects (re-bound depression, the "crash") or because of the intense craving for the cocaine euphoria that users typically describe (Nunes & Rosecan, 1987, p. 55). But so far we have only covered the new view of cocaine's addictive potential. Once we enter the realm of crack, an even greater potential for addiction exists.

Crack: The Most Addictive Form of Cocaine

Since crack is much more potent than intranasal cocaine, the chemical dis-ruptions it produces in the brain are more deleterious. This has led Rosecan et al. (1987) to assert that crack is the most addicting form of our most addicting drug. Because crack possesses such a high addictive potential, whereas intranasal cocaine users may progress from recreational to compulsive use over months or years, escalation to compulsive crack smoking may easily occur within days to weeks. Rosecan et al. (1987) explain that the depletion of brain neurotransmitters and a supersensitivity of their receptors presumably are accelerated by crack because it is so potent. The neurochemical changes produced are responsible for the rapidity with which compulsive use develops. In addition, personality changes and psychiatric disorders involving symptoms of depression, irritability, social withdrawal, and paranoia are seen much sooner with crack than with cocaine. Also, the withdrawal syndrome (oversleeping, overeating, depression, and craving for more drug) is more pronounced and prolonged with crack. In their view, this explains why crack use constitutes the new cocaine epidemic. Moreover, crack users are difficult to treat because their addictions are usually quite severe by the time they enter treatment. Typically, they have suffered major disruptions at work and in their marriages and families when finally seen by professionals in treatment. (Rosecan et al., 1987, pp. 300–301).

The potency and neurochemistry of crack, therefore, are important factors that explain the etiology of compulsive crack smoking, the potentially rapid development of crack addiction, and the obsessive pursuit of such smoking among the severely addicted despite gunshot wounds and crack-induced seizures. In this way, crack addicts are "on a mission" to seek, secure, and smoke as much crack as possible, despite negative consequences and punishments.

CONCLUSION

In this chapter, we have seen that a more thorough understanding of how crack use has become such a widespread and pressing problem that—going beyond the classic white, middle-class male intranasal cocaine user—includes women, adolescents, and minorities, from all classes, and from all geographical regions of the country requires recognition of several interacting factors. Societal demand for chemicals, the art of drug distribution, and the pharmacology of crack all help to explain how users begin and persevere in crack use, and end up driven to continue compulsive crack smoking despite severe personal deterioration and numerous negative consequences.

2

DSM-III-R: Diagnosing Cocaine Dependence and Other Psychopathology

The challenge of treating the crack-cocaine smoker cannot be appreciated unless diagnoses of the degree of the substance use and of any additional psychopathology have been made. This chapter covers the accurate diagnosis of the degree and severity of cocaine use, the incidence of mood (affective) and personality disorders in cocaine-using populations, and the implications of the incidence of psychopathology for understanding the etiology of addiction.

COCAINE USE AND THE DSM-III-R

The 1987 revision of the third edition of the *Diagnostic and Statistical Manual of Mental Disorders* (DSM-III-R) of the American Psychiatric Association (APA) includes important changes (since the 1980 DSM-III) that affect the diagnosis of patients using cocaine or crack on axis I. The 1980 DSM-III permitted only the diagnosis of cocaine abuse. Recognition of the development of a dependence on cocaine was introduced with the 1987 revised edition. DSM-III-R no longer views evidence of physiological tolerance and withdrawal as necessary in order to diagnose the dependence syndrome. These changes permit recognition of the very serious state of dependence on a psychoactive drug, or addiction, and that it can be based on other significant criteria (involving maladaptive and pathological behavior) without evidence of tolerance or physiological manifestation of a withdrawal syndrome.

However, prior to discussing dependence on psychoactive substances such as cocaine or crack, it is important to recognize the recreational use of drugs in our society that will not qualify for a DSM-III-R classification. DSM-III-R substantiates society's general regard of the recreational use of substances to modify mood or behaviors under certain circumstances "as normal and appropriate" (APA, 1987, p. 165). This includes the nonpathological moderate use of alcohol.

Recreational Use of Illicit Chemicals

However, beyond DSM-III-R's rational discussion of the recreational use of alcohol, which may not be considered maladaptive or pathological behavior, there are the realities of contemporary society. A large subculture made up of individuals of various ages, races, and income levels incorporates experimentation with and recreational usage of various psychoactive substances into the fabric of its social life. Thus, a contemporary clinician needs to maintain the conceptual category of recreational use of chemicals when proceeding with the assessment, diagnosis, and treatment of psychoactive substance-use disorders.

Ideally, society will move beyond a philosophy born in the 1960s that sanctions the experimental and recreational use of illicit chemicals, as well as alcohol, as representing normal behavior. Many patients referred for diagnosis and treatment present a pattern of illicit chemical use, particularly of marijuana, that may only qualify for classification as experimental or recreational. However, such cases also include experimental or recreational uses of other chemicals—among them cocaine, and perhaps even crack. Provision of secondary prevention education and a clinical assessment of the meaning and role of chemical use in a person's life remain essential for these individuals; anyone who has begun to use a substance as potentially addictive as crack cocaine must be educated as to the potential effects of the continuation of the practice—primarily the risk of escalation to compulsive or chronic use.

On the other hand, clinicians must be aware that a user's protestations that drug usage is only experimental or recreational may be an attempt to deny the severity of addiction. Thus, clinical knowledge and utilization of the categories of experimental and recreational chemical use remain important in making essential differential diagnoses. A clinician must be able to determine whether or not one is in an experimental or recreational stage of chemical use, or has moved into a category of abuse or dependence. The distinction between experimental and recreational use of chemicals based on the DSM-III-R categories of psychoactive substance abuse and dependence can help to link individuals to appropriate treatment interventions. More intensive treatments are appropriately reserved for those presenting psychoactive substance abuse and dependence syndromes. For genuine cases of experimental or recreational use of chemicals, educational and preventative interventions emerge as necessary but sufficient.

Psychoactive Substance Abuse and Dependence

Within DSM-III-R, the pathological use of any psychoactive substance may be diagnosed as either dependence or the residual category of abuse. When clinicians make the diagnosis of psychoactive substance dependence, DSM-III-R permits specification of the severity of the dependence as either mild, moderate, or severe. In addition, dependence may be in partial or full remission (APA, 1987), as in the case of the cocaine-dependent patient whose prior alcohol dependence is in full remission (no alcohol use in past six months), or the recovering cocaine patient who has had a few relapses in the past six months, justifying a diagnosis of cocaine dependence in partial remission.

The symptoms of dependence and abuse are the same across all nine categories of psychoactive substances—alcohol, amphetamines, cannabis, cocaine, hallucinogens, opioids, phencyclidine (PCP), sedatives, hypnotics (APA, 1987). However, the category of cocaine or crack and the criteria for ascertaining the nature of a patient's psychoactive substance use remain of interest here. The DSM-III-R categories of dependence and abuse specify criteria that must be met in order to make a proper diagnosis.

Crack-Cocaine Dependence

DSM-III-R provides nine criteria for cocaine or crack-cocaine dependence and requires that the individual meet at least three of these criteria to qualify for the diagnosis of dependence syndrome. Also, the symptoms of the disturbance must have persisted for at least one month or have occurred repeatedly over a longer period of time. This second qualification permits recognition of the binge pattern (episodic or biweekly and monthly use) common in cocaine and crack users, and the fact that this may constitute a dependence syndrome. The criteria necessary to diagnose dependence clearly suggest pathological and maladaptive patterns of behavior associated with chemical use, the most important being loss of control and continued use despite knowledge of negative consequences (APA, 1987).

The first criterion involves taking cocaine or crack in larger amounts or over a longer period than intended (APA, 1987, p. 167). A typical example from patient reports is that of the crack smoker who intends to consume only $40 worth of crack on a Friday evening, planning to return to his wife and children well before 11:00 p.m. Instead, he spends all $300 in his wallet on a binge that ends Saturday morning. This criterion begins to suggest loss of control.

A second criterion involves persistent desire, or one or more unsuccessful efforts to cut down or control crack-cocaine use (APA, 1987, p. 168). Whether these failures represent neurochemically based drug cravings, a desire triggered by conditioned environmental stimuli associated with crack smoking (a drug associate, a song, one's bedroom, the sight of drug paraphernalia), or a yearning for the psychoactive effects of the drug (euphoria, energy, confidence), the person reports a persistent desire to smoke crack. Also, the average crack smoker meeting the criteria for crack-cocaine dependence reports several failed attempts to cut down or control crack smoking. Both the woman who promises herself that she will stop getting high altogether and the student determined to

smoke only one vial of crack so he or she can go to sleep and be able to attend
school in the morning lack control and typically fail in their efforts.

Also reflecting loss of control, the third criterion is spending a great deal of
time on activities focused on either getting crack, smoking it, or recovering
from its effects (APA, 1987, p. 168). The person who must spend time hustling
on the street for money to buy crack, the one who steals money to purchase
crack, and the one who compulsively smokes crack "for hours on end" all typ-
ify this maladaptive behavioral pattern.

A fourth criterion, indicative of the deleterious effects of compulsive crack
smoking, involves frequent intoxication or withdrawal symptoms from crack
that prevent the fulfilling of major obligations (at work, school, or home). Also
the performance of such duties as driving or handling machinery is hazardous
when one is intoxicated. Examples include the individual who fails to go to
work or school because he or she is still high, having stayed up all night smoking crack (APA, 1987, p. 168); one who goes to work still high or as withdrawal
sets in, is irritable and depressed, and falls asleep on the job; and the mother
attempting to care for her children while she is on crack or in withdrawal.

The fifth criterion covers discontinuation of normal social activities. Important social, occupational, or recreational activities are given up or reduced because of crack-cocaine smoking (APA, 1987, p. 168). This probably reflects the
possible anhedonia, or loss of pleasure, that the crack addict experiences, as
well as the all-consuming nature of one's efforts to secure and compulsively use
crack. Drug-seeking behavior and compulsive crack smoking predominate as
the central activities in life. Many compulsive crack-cocaine smokers completely discontinue working, whether voluntarily or through dismissal. Money
once spent on other recreation now is reserved for crack, as is nearly all available leisure time. This again validates the maladaptive pattern of behavior that
dominates the user's life and stems from crack smoking.

Criterion 6 not only reflects loss of control, but also the persistence of crack-
related pathological, maladaptive, and destructive behavior. Crack smokers
who meet this criterion continue their substance use despite knowledge of having a recurrent social, psychological, or physical problem that is caused or exacerbated by crack cocaine (APA, 1987, p. 168). For example, social
problems—such as a wife's dispute with her husband who is intolerant of her
crack smoking and is threatening to ask the Bureau of Child Welfare to inter-
cede in the care of the children—fail to deter a woman from crack smoking. Depressed over the subsequent loss of her children, she will continue to smoke
even though she realizes her "crash depression" following smoking only makes
her problems worse, while effectively delaying the recovery necessary for her to
regain child custody. The male addict who has had a seizure from smoking
crack resumes compulsive smoking upon discharge from the hospital despite

the knowledge that the seizure was caused by crack. These are just two examples of the pathological and maladaptive pattern of behavior associated with continued crack smoking among those dependent on cocaine.

A seventh criterion requires evidence of marked tolerance. According to this criterion, the crack smoker must report that there has been at least a 50% increase in the amount of crack cocaine required to achieve the desired euphoric effect. Alternatively, the crack smoker must demonstrate tolerance by reporting that there has been a markedly diminished effect with continued use (smoking) of the same amount of crack (APA, 1987, p. 168). As a result of tolerance, many crack-cocaine smokers report an inability to get high anymore even though they have continued compulsively self-administering crack—usually at the same dose at which they previously experienced euphoric and stimulating effects. Typically, the amount of crack smoked increases astronomically over the course of an addict's crack usage. Crack smokers report gradually escalating from $50 daily doses to $100–200, and even $500, daily doses in order to achieve, sustain, and prolong the desired effects.

The eighth possible criterion refers to withdrawal symptoms, which can follow cessation of prolonged (several days or longer) and heavy crack-cocaine smoking. They may also follow a reduction in the amount of crack cocaine used (APA, 1987, p. 168). The symptoms of withdrawal from crack cocaine include a dysphoric mood, marked by depression, irritability, and anxiety. In addition, the individual may experience either fatigue, insomnia, or hypersomnia, as well as possible psychomotor agitation. The withdrawal symptoms persist for more than 24 hours after the person's last dose of crack, thus extending beyond those unpleasant rebound effects ("the crash") of tremulousness, irritability, and feelings of fatigue and depression. It is at this point that withdrawal can be said to be occurring (APA, 1987, p. 143).

And, finally, the ninth criterion directly relates to the manifestation of withdrawal symptoms and involves the smoking of more crack cocaine to relieve or avoid withdrawal symptoms (APA, 1987, p. 168). The all-too-familiar compulsive self-administration of crack, as users smoke for hours or days on end, substantiates the repetitive use of crack to avoid the crash and more prolonged withdrawal symptoms. Some crack smokers admit that the avoidance of withdrawal by taking more crack partly explains their compulsive-use patterns.

A crack smoker meeting even three of these nine criteria has a considerable addiction to crack or presents the dependence syndrome. The nature and severity of the dependence—as reflected in these criteria and examples—further clarify the nature of the treatment challenge posed by crack addiction. The difference between crack-cocaine dependence and the less severe cocaine abuse must be understood by the clinician, who must make a differential diagnosis.

Crack-Cocaine Abuse

Following DSM-III-R, crack-cocaine abuse permits recognition of those less severe cases of crack smoking that have not met the criteria for dependence. For those users who have not engaged in smoking crack for periods as long as a month and have not had numerous binges, a diagnosis utilizing the residual category of cocaine abuse may be in order. Usually, these are crack-cocaine smokers who have only recently started smoking crack and so clearly fail to meet even three criteria for dependence. Within the category of abuse, DSM-III-R emphasizes that these individuals are less likely to show any marked physiological signs of withdrawal, and have not felt the need to take more of the substance to relieve or avoid withdrawal symptoms (APA, 1987, p. 169).

Clearly, the overall picture reflects a much less severe but still maladaptive pattern of crack-cocaine smoking. An example might be the person who smokes crack on perhaps one weekend a month. Although the consequences of this once-a-month binge might be a Monday morning absence from school or work or a day of prolonged sleeping, this is the only symptom (APA, 1987, p. 169). This individual has never attempted to stop or cut back, but also has not spent inordinate amounts of time in securing or using the drug.

This person, who may have considered himself or herself a recreational user of crack cocaine, officially crosses the line into abuse when a single maladaptive behavior (crack-related absence from work, a day of prolonged sleeping), occurs repeatedly. Of importance to the clinician are the indications for treatment that arise from a diagnosis of crack-cocaine abuse. Obviously, less intensive treatment interventions should be considered. Only suicidal or homicidal ideation or acute toxic reactions such as paranoid psychosis would justify the more intensive inpatient interventions usually reserved for those presenting with cocaine dependence. More typical would be referrals for outpatient treatment and/or advice to join an anonymous self-help group. The bottom line is that the diagnosis of cocaine abuse or cocaine dependence is of critical importance in helping the clinician determine the nature and severity of crack use and in making decisions on short- and long-term-treatment plans.

This discussion of the criteria for dependence and abuse has focused specifically on crack cocaine, including examples reflecting the experience of crack-cocaine smokers. However, the point must be made that the same criteria apply to the use of alcohol, amphetamines, cannabis, cocaine, hallucinogens, opioids, PCP, sedatives, and hypnotics. Overall, the modifications reflected in DSM-III-R permit the field of chemical dependency to achieve uniformity in its approach to the diagnosis of psychoactive-substance use. DSM-III-R can function as an important tool in discerning the progression of drug use or the severity of addiction.

SEQUENCE OF STAGES IN CHEMICAL USE

The notion of users navigating through a series of stages in the use of chemicals, suggesting a sequence of stages in chemical use, arises from our discussion. In the first stage, the experimental phase, the curious novice utilizes a drug for the first time. Beyond those first few experimental uses of crack cocaine lies the next phase of recreational use. The recreational user continues to use the chemical substance, usually because of a desire to repeat the psychoactive effects that are recalled from the experimental phase. It is rather easy to cross the line into the official DSM-III-R diagnostic category of abuse when those first signs of maladaptive behavior begin to repeat themselves—forming a pattern of oversleeping, lateness, or absences from work, for example. As the number of maladaptive behaviors increases, signs of loss of control are evidenced, use continues despite knowledge of negative consequences, and the symptoms extend beyond a one-month period, the line between abuse and dependence has been crossed.

Hence movement from experimental use to recreational use to a maladaptive pattern of abuse and to an even more maladaptive and pathological pattern of dependence or addiction summarizes the possible stages in the sequence of chemical use that may face the clinician. The clinician must be able to discern and diagnose each of these stages. In the real world of recreational chemical users, many may cross the line into abuse on occasion, but never proceed to the state of dependence or addiction. Many recreational users of chemicals may consider themselves controlled users of substances, accepting absences from work, symptoms resulting from cessation of chemical use, and periods of dysfunction as the price they must pay for "a good time." And unknowingly, they have actually crossed the line into abuse.

"You Dare Smoke Crack": Providing Preventative Education

An acronym or mnemonic of value in education and prevention efforts with patients is shown in Figure 2.1. We can ask patients: "Do you DARE smoke crack?" We can then educate them to the idea that smoking crack is analogous to their taking of a dare, which involves considerable risk, since Dependency may follow abuse, Abuse may follow recreational use, Recreational use may follow experimental use, and Experimental use may lead to a sequence in crack-smoking behavior with severe and negative consequences. In view of this possibility, patients may rethink their position on the experimental and recreational use of drugs, especially when we avoid scare tactics and are realistic and balanced in our view of how specific risk factors may predispose patients to movement from experimental and recreational phases to phases of abuse and dependency.

SEQUENCE OF STAGES TOWARD DEVELOPMENT OF DEPENDENCY

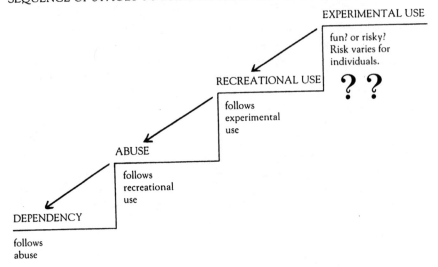

KEY FEATURES OF USE IN EACH STAGE

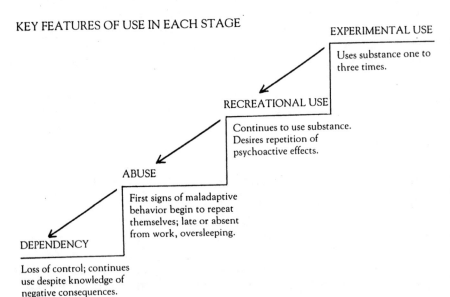

Figure 2.1. DARE Model of Chemical Dependency, showing sequence of stages toward the development of chemical dependence and the key features of use in each stage. Acronym or mnemonic DARE reminds us of the advancing stages of chemicals where dependency follows abuse, abuse follows recreational use, and recreational use follows experimental use. Within prevention efforts we ask, "you DARE smoke crack?" and answer this question with a graphic reminder of the inherent risk.

It is also important to counter denial with explanations of the movement beyond an experimental phase. The nature of this movement varies a great deal. Some may advance rapidly over the course of one to several months, while others may proceed very gradually over one to three years. Individual differences and the nature of an individual's affective and personality functioning, ego strength, and defensive functioning may also determine the development of abuse or a dependence syndrome. Indeed, multiple factors may affect the course of advancing stages in the severity of chemical use. Some of the most effective efforts at secondary prevention involve spelling out in detail how an individual patient's affective and personality functioning may place that patient at particular risk for possible loss of control and movement toward dependence. Also effective as a form of secondary prevention education are explanations of how these factors interact with the chemical actions of cocaine, which may produce compulsive drug-taking behavior. Such detailed explanations may go well beyond scare tactics or sensationalized descriptions of the actions of drugs. As a part of preventative educational efforts, the use of visual graphics can be learning aids. The visual graphic (see Figure 2.2) of a staircase depicting either the regressive movement toward personal deterioration that continues to advance with chemical use or the progressive movement that can be initiated with abstinence toward positive goals and self-actualization may also be of value.

Aside from prevention efforts, it is crucial that the treatment practitioner understand that the nature of the problem varies depending on whether or not the user presents in an experimental or recreational stage of chemical use, as opposed to abuse or the most severe stage of dependence or addiction. In order more fully to appreciate the nature of the treatment challenge presented by the crack dependent, crack smokers' psychological functioning must also be assessed by clinicians.

AFFECTIVE AND PERSONALITY DISORDERS IN THE CRACK DEPENDENT

Psychopathology may modify patients' response to treatment, treatment outcome, the symptom picture, and the course of an addictive disorder in terms of how rapidly addiction develops (Meyer, 1986). Questionnaire instruments such as the Addiction Severity Index (ASI) have been developed to ascertain the level of psychiatric disturbance a patient presents (McLellan, 1986), while the structured clinical interview for the DSM-III-R administered by interviewers also facilitates the making of DSM-III-R diagnoses (Spitzer & Gibbon, 1987). However, the traditional clinical interview and DSM-III-R diagnostic categories provide an efficient means of ascertaining the presence of diagnosable psycho-

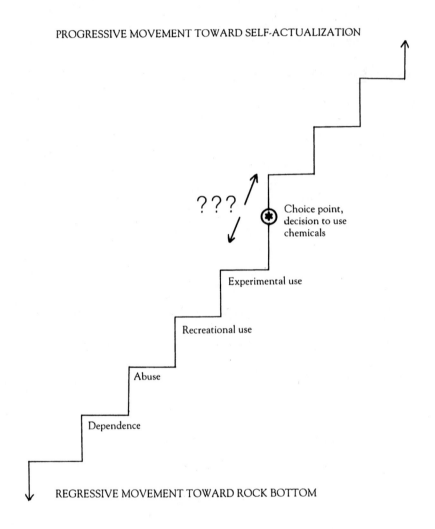

PROGRESSIVE MOVEMENT TOWARD SELF-ACTUALIZATION

???

Choice point, decision to use chemicals

Experimental use

Recreational use

Abuse

Dependence

REGRESSIVE MOVEMENT TOWARD ROCK BOTTOM

Figure 2.2. Progressive or Regressive Movement in DARE Model of Chemical Dependency. Model depicts either the progressive movement up a staircase toward positive growth and realizing one's potential, or the regressive movement downward toward a rock bottom that follows from dependence. The choice point or decision to use chemicals represents that moment when patients decide either to initiate regressive, destructive movement by using crack or to avoid chemical use and pursue progressive movement toward positive goals and ideals.

pathology. Axis I of the DSM-III-R permits the diagnosis of clinical syndromes such as mood disorders, while axis II permits the diagnosis of personality disorders that usually are first evident in childhood or adolescence but persist into adulthood. Psychopathology not meeting DSM-III-R criteria for a disorder is also noteworthy. Clinicians should attempt to determine how this psychopathology interacts with the axis I diagnosis of crack-cocaine dependence. The formulation of short- and long-term-treatment goals are directly informed by the presence of psychopathology.

Psychopathology: Disagreement, Confusion, and Scant Data

Dougherty and Lesswing (1989) characterize the literature on the psychological features and psychopathology of cocaine users as "rather scant." As a result, conjecture and misconceptions exist about the etiology and treatment of cocaine use (p. 45). Moreover, there is no consensus on the relationship between psychopathology and the etiology of drug dependence (Blume, 1989). One prominent view on this relationship involves Rosecan and Spitz's (1987) explanation that some persons are at risk for the development of an addiction because of their psychological predisposition. Cocaine users may self-medicate painful emotional states or address painful life problems (loss of love or employment), underlying insecurities, and defects in self-esteem. Also, cocaine may be used to enhance one's performance (athletic, sexual, social, work), but while it may improve performance acutely, it impairs it chronically. "In this way, users can become psychologically dependent on cocaine long before the physical dependence sets in" (Rosecan & Spitz, 1987, p. 13).

Confusion over the relationship between psychopathology and cocaine use evolves from the old question of the chicken and the egg: Which came first? Meyer (1986) points out that axis I and axis II psychopathology may serve as a risk factor for the development of an addictive disorder, psychiatric symptoms may develop in the course of chronic drug use, and some psychiatric disorders emerging as a result of drug use persist into the period of abstinence (p. 7). The development of a cocaine-induced panic disorder that appears to be precipitated by cocaine use and persists when such use has been terminated (for months or years) has been reported (Louie, Lannon, & Ketter, 1989). Meyer (1986) also suggests that addicts' behavior and psychopathological symptoms may become meaningfully linked over time, and that some psychopathology is found no more frequently in addicts than in the general population, suggesting that there is no relationship between psychiatric disorders and the addictive disorder (p. 7).

Another apt summary of the possible relationship between cocaine and psychopathology cites the possibility that the agonist effects of cocaine and cocaine withdrawal probably precipitate depression or that cocaine is used to self-medicate a premorbid disorder (Kleinman, Miller, Millman, et al., 1990). Mirin, Weiss, and Michael (1986) similarly observe that individuals experiencing withdrawal from Central-Nervous-System stimulants present with depression, anxiety, guilt, and low self-esteem, but it is unclear whether these symptoms can be attributed to withdrawal or to the unmasking of an underlying primary mood disorder, or are a response to the social, financial, and occupational problems that follow chronic drug use (pp. 57–58). Cocaine abusers who self-medicate mood disorders and behavioral disorders such as residual attention-deficit disorder (ADD) (Khantzian, 1985) may have been at risk for the development of cocaine dependence because of their constitutional or biochemical predisposition (Rosecan & Spitz, 1987, p. 14).

Thus, even a discussion of psychological factors implicates an interaction of cocaine's pharmacology with a person's biological factors and baseline psychological functioning. With chronic cocaine use, both the individual user's biochemical functioning and characteristic psychological functioning may change. Unfortunately, research does not adequately recognize, attempt to untangle, and control for these confounding and static variables, and so current data must be seen as limited in fully resolving the relationship between cocaine dependence and psychopathology. Despite confusion, disagreement, and scant data, a review of the available data on cocaine- and crack-using populations and an analysis of psychopathology clinically observed in the crack-cocaine dependent may shed light on the etiology of crack dependence and the nature of the treatment challenge presented by compulsive crack smokers.

Research Studies with Cocaine Users in Treatment

Using a structured diagnostic interview, Gawin and Kleber (1986) report that the majority (54%) of cocaine patients ($n = 30$) presented an axis I mood disorder; specific breakdowns show that 13% presented major depression with melancholia; 20%, dysthymic disorder; and 17%, cyclothymic disorder; one subject presented with ADD. Cocaine seemed to be utilized to alleviate dysphoria (Gawin & Kleber, 1986). Supporting this work, Weiss and Mirin (1986) reported a study of 30 cocaine patients where 53.3% presented with an axis I mood disorder; 9% had unipolar depression and 7% had a cyclothymic or bipolar disorder. With regard to such findings, Gawin and Kleber (1986) make an important point that erroneous assessments of major depression or bipolar disorder may be made if the symptoms of the cocaine "crash" and their time course are not sufficiently acknowledged. For many individuals, chronic cocaine use is depressogenic; this may be related to the neurochemical changes produced by such use, which resemble those seen in depression, according to preliminary studies (Rosecan & Spitz, 1987, p. 14). Because of these possible factors, diagnoses of mood disorders should be deferred unless a clear corroborating history or longitudinal assessments during periods of no cocaine usage permit such a diagnosis (Gawin & Kleber, 1986). Beyond their appreciation of mood disorders diagnosable on axis I, Kleber and Gawin (1984a) have also emphasized that cocaine may serve narcissistic needs, compensate for interpersonal failures, help cope with boredom and feelings of an inner emptiness, and manage psychiatric disturbance.

Wallace (1987) reports data on patients presenting with cocaine dependence. Findings show that 39% of patients (*n* = 31) met criteria for either major depression (in remission or recurrent) or dysthymic disorder, while another 16% presented with depression not sufficient to meet the criteria for a mood disorder. Deferred diagnoses reflect Wallace's (1987) caution in diagnosing mood disorder unless a clear corroborating history was available. Wallace argues that such data document the possible role of psychiatric symptoms in the etiology of drug dependence.

It is interesting that with relatively small samples (average *n* = 30) Gawin and Kleber (1986), Weiss and Mirin (1986), and Wallace (1987) find somewhat similar rates of DSM-III mood disorders, 54%, 53%, and 39%, respectively (54% for Wallace when including those presenting with some depression not meeting DSM-III criteria). Findings of over a 50% rate of mood disorder may be significant. According to Rosecan and Spitz (1987), this represents a greater incidence of mood disorders than that typically reported in other substance abusers (p. 14). Overall, these data support the idea that cocaine's euphoria may have addressed underlying dysphoria and depression, which characterize the majority of cocaine patients. However suggestive and mutually reinforcing, data based on such small samples remain troublesome.

Regarding axis II disorders (personality or developmental disorders), Mirin and Weiss (1988) found that cocaine patients (*n* = 128) presented with borderline personality disorder (14%), antisocial personality disorder (16%), histrionic personality disorder (21%), and narcissistic personality disorder (24%). Wallace (1987) also reports (again with a rather small sample, *n* = 31) that 45% of cocaine patients presented with a personality disorder; specifically, clinical interviews and observation of patients in treatment revealed patterns of antisocial personality disorder (13%), borderline personality disorder (10%), narcissistic personality disorder (10%), dependent personality disorder (10%), and passive-aggressive personality disorder (6.5%). This kind of evidence of personality disorders remains important because an axis II diagnosis correlates with psychopathology and substantially influences treatment prognosis (Meyer, 1986). Wallace (1987) recognizes narcissistic psychopathology—beyond DSM-III-R diagnosable personality disorders—as characterizing crack patients in particular; often this narcissism does not meet the criteria for a narcissistic personality disorder.

Since crack smokers may differ in their characteristics and treatment needs from intranasal users of cocaine, data on populations of largely crack smokers remain important in clarifying the role of psychopathology in the treatment of this population. Kleinman, Miller, Millman, et al. (1990) found in a sample ($n = 76$) that heavily used crack (but included intranasal users) that when using the relatively new structured clinical interview for DSM-III-R—which has only preliminary reliability studies—47% had an axis I depressive disorder. Specifically, over one quarter (28%) presented a current (within the last 30 days) major depressive syndrome and another 12% had a major depressive episode at some time in their life; 6% presented with a dysthymic disorder. Regarding axis II diagnoses, the majority (58%) presented an axis II personality disorder, with the predominant diagnoses of antisocial (21%), passive-aggressive (21%), borderline (18%), and self-defeating (18%) disorders. Another 42% presented no axis II personality disorder, while 42% had two or more axis II disorders.

Additional analysis by Kleinman, Miller, Millman, et al. (1990) suggests that clients diagnosed as having a depressive disorder are more likely than others to have used crack or smoked free-base cocaine they cooked themselves, as opposed to using intranasal cocaine, in the last 30 days; this finding may support a self-medication hypothesis. As the number of years of cocaine use increases, the trend indicates that the likelihood of having a depressive disorder also increases. In addition, persons with an axis I diagnosis also began use of tobacco, marijuana, and cocaine at a significantly earlier age than others. The authors conclude that these data suggest a self-medication hypothesis but the data make no major contribution to the resolution of the chicken-or-egg issue. They conclude by hypothesizing that cocaine may be both a trigger of psychological disorders and a form of self-medication for psychological disorders. Also of interest, those with no DSM-III-R psychopathology were more likely to be married (Kleinman, Miller, Millman, et al., 1989).

Wallace's (1990a) data on a predominantly crack-smoking sample show ($n = 61$) that only one quarter (25%) presented a mood disorder; specifically, 7% presented major depression, either in remission or recurrent; 18% presented a dysthymic disorder; and another 16% presented some depression not meeting the criteria for a diagnosis. Considered together, a total of 41% experienced depression or dysphoria. Wallace also utilized a clinical interview in addition to observations of patients during treatment to arrive at axis II diagnoses; patients presented dependent personality disorder (8%), narcissistic personality disorders (5%) antisocial personality disorder (5%), and borderline personality disorder (3.3%), to name predominant trends. Only one third (32.8%) of patients received a diagnosis for a personality disorder. Deferred diagnoses constituted the majority (43%) of axis II diagnoses. Here again, Wallace placed emphasis on the fact that narcissistic traits of grandiosity, a very fragile self-esteem, and a well-hidden, painfully low self-esteem characterize many crack patients, but may fail to meet the criteria for DSM-III-R diagnostic categories (Wallace, 1990a).

With a large (n = 100) sample of cocaine patients, Dougherty and Lesswing (1989) provide no systematic information on axis I diagnoses of mood disorders, but augment research findings on axis II personality disorders. Their report fails to identify the predominant route of administration of cocaine among their inpatient population. They argue that their use of standard measures (Minnesota Multiphasic Personality Inventory, Millon Clinical Multiaxial Inventory, Rorschach, Beck Depression Inventory) fails to substantiate the hypothesis that cocaine abusers self-medicate underlying primary mood disorders. Dougherty and Lesswing's (1989) investigation revealed that on the Minnesota Multiphasic Personality Inventory, 90% had abnormally elevated profiles involving signs of characterological disturbance. Two thirds showed poor frustration tolerance and impulse control; difficulties with anticipating consequences and learning from experience; a hedonistic orientation with needs for excitement, stimulation, and immediate gratification; rebelliousness and anger; and defenses involving acting out, externalization, and rationalizing. On the Millon Clinical Multiaxial Inventory, 88% had a DSM-III axis II personality disorder, with most (over 50%) showing either a mixed personality disorder, borderline personality disorder, or narcissistic personality disorder. Rorschach findings showed a high degree of narcissism, underlying anger and negativity, increased cognitive slippage, and reduced reality testing, consistent with a history of heavy drug abuse; normal-range levels of dysphoric/depressive experience also prevailed. The Beck Depression Inventory suggested minimal to mild symptoms of self-reported depressive symptoms (p. 46).

Dougherty and Lesswing (1989) not only interpret their findings as providing no significant evidence that cocaine abusers were self-medicating an underlying primary mood disorder, but describe patients as energized rather than dysphoric or depressed. They speculate that this observed trait of high energy/activity reflects a characterological psychodynamic regarding the drug of choice, supporting the work of Wurmser (1974). They also emphasize the importance of their findings of "character defects" and axis II personality disorders (pp. 46–47). The presence of axis II personality disorders receives recognition as highly significant, since they affect assessment, treatment planning, and prognosis (Blume, 1989).

DeLeon's (1989) observation that even psychometrically sound and replicable methods using standard testing instruments may be less sensitive than clinical interviews may apply to an analysis of Dougherty and Lesswing's (1989) data. Or alternatively, larger samples using standardized instruments may provide a more accurate picture of cocaine patients' characteristic psychopathology.

Summary Interpretation of Research

Perhaps the best characterization of the body of data arising from all of these studies relates to the reality that multiple, complex, and varied relationships may exist between cocaine or crack use and psychopathology. The population of cocaine and crack patients emerges as a heterogenous group. Perhaps anyone with any set of characteristics could become addicted to crack or cocaine because these substances are so addictive. Each of the "snapshots" provided by these research studies when viewed separately suggest findings and trends of some significance.

Consistent with the summary of data that Rosecan and Spitz (1987) provide, it seems safe to assert that certain individuals, because of psychological or constitutional factors, appear to be predisposed to cocaine dependence, whereas more systematic research is needed to define the specific elements that result in excessive use of cocaine (Rosecan & Spitz, 1987, p. 14).

An additional summary interpretation may be that, together with the patient, treatment professionals must attempt to put together the "pieces of the puzzle" as to the relationship between any psychopathology—diagnosable via DSM-III-R or failing to meet formal criteria—and cocaine or crack use. Clinical experience suggests that in the real world of assessing and treating crack patients, numerous and unique puzzles are tentatively assembled and used as a guide in short- and long-term-treatment planning. A continuum of psychopathology from mild to severe characterizes crack smokers, who emerge in clinical practice as a diverse group.

Deficits in Self-Regulatory Capacities

Taken as a whole, all of the data reviewed may inadvertently support the following argument: Data showing characterological defects, narcissism, and DSM-III-R documentable mood and personality disorders in the cocaine dependent support a self-medication hypothesis that does not limit itself to difficulties patients have in regulating mood or dysphoria. Here, the concept of self-medication extends to include patients' difficulties with regulating self-esteem, as well as their behavior. This view follows that of Khantzian (1985), who clearly describes a predisposition to become dependent on chemicals owing to recurrent painful affect states that relate to defects in the ego and self-capacities, leaving such persons ill equipped to regulate and modulate feelings, self-esteem, relationships, and behavior. In the present view, deficits in self-regulatory capacities that include regulation not only of affective states, but also of self-esteem and behavior, may have predisposed patients toward becoming dependent on chemicals.

Following Khantzian (1985), the most important symptom found in cocaine and crack patients may be recurrent painful affective states that relate to defects in ego and self-capacities. This may account for the high rates (approximately 50%) of mood disorders found in the majority of research studies (Gawin & Kleber, 1986; Weiss & Mirin, 1986; Kleinman, Miller, Millman, et al., 1990). However, the range of mood disorders (39%, Wallace, 1987; 25% Wallace, 1990a; minimal to mild symptoms on the Beck Depression Inventory, Dougherty & Lesswing, 1989—with respectively larger samples) suggests diversity within and across cocaine and crack populations. Sample demography may account for some of this diversity in mood disorders, following DeLeon's (1989) report that "psychopathology is evident across demography but consistently worse for . . . whites" (p. 181). Where samples are largely made up of white subjects (80%, Gawin & Kleber, 1986), greater affective disturbance emerges, while somewhat lower rates of affective disturbance are seen in samples comprised largely of African-Americans and Hispanics. Studies show 47% with mood disorders in a sample made up of 61% black and 18% Hispanic (Kleinman, Miller, Millman, et al., 1990); 39% in a sample 77% black and 7% Hispanic (Wallace, 1987); and 25% in a sample 92% black (Wallace, 1990a). Rates of mood disorders decrease as the proportion of black subjects in samples increases. With a more racially balanced sample that is 61% white and 37% black, Dougherty and Lesswing's (1989) advantage of a large sample size supports minimal mood disturbance. However, Wallace's (1987, 1990a) use of clinical interviews and findings of depression and dysphoria not meeting DSM-III diagnostic criteria for a mood disorder suggests that subtle, but significant, disturbances frequently exist in patients, supporting the observations of Khantzian (1985).

Patients may use cocaine to address an inability to regulate or modulate feelings, self-esteem, or their behavior in interpersonal relationships. Clinical observation suggests that patients also lack an ability to identify, label, or process feelings. A self-report of depression may not appear on an instrument such as the Beck Depression Inventory—as Dougherty and Lesswing (1989) report—if a patient does not know how to identify feelings. Also, high energy—as Dougherty and Lesswing also observe—may reflect a manic defense against a depression or recurrent painful affective state that patients are unable to regulate or modulate without resorting to a manic defense. Narcissism that others report (Kleber & Gawin, 1984; Wallace, 1987; Wallace, 1990a; Mirin & Weiss, 1986; Dougherty & Lesswing, 1989) may serve defensive purposes against a well-hidden, painfully low self-esteem or painful feelings associated with memories of narcissistic injuries to the self; such individuals lack an ability to regulate and modulate their self-esteem or painful feelings, which may also lead to a plummeting of self-esteem and defensive reliance on grandiosity and inflation. All of these characteristics suggest deficits in self-regulatory capacities.

Thus, the overall variety found in the reporting of axis II personality disorders and other character defects in research studies may reflect deficits in self-regulatory capacities that patients possess in, one, several, or all areas—feelings, self-esteem, relationships, behavior. In this way, it makes sense that a formal diagnosis of narcissistic personality disorder ranges, in reports based in various samples, from 24% (Mirin & Weiss, 1986) to 10% (Wallace, 1987) to 5% (Wallace, 1990a); while total presence of axis II personality disorders ranges from 88% (Dougherty & Lesswing, 1989) to 58% (Kleinman, Miller, Millman, et al., 1990) to 33% (Wallace, 1990a). Varied and diverse patterns of deficits in self-regulatory capacities could explain these findings. However, some differences in the prevalence of axis II personality disorders could relate to different sample demographics, such as racial composition, as discussed earlier. Wallace (1987, 1990a) still emphasizes, in work with largely African-American crack smokers, the importance of subtle narcissistic problems that fail to meet diagnostic criteria and to indicate deficits in self-regulatory capacities.

This view permits an explanation of the tremendous diversity in both DSM-III-R mood and personality disorders and in psychopathology not formally diagnosable via DSM-III-R found in research studies. In a broad sense, then, crack and cocaine patients self-medicate primarily recurrent painful affective states. However, these states are linked to a varying range of defects in the ego and self-capacities of patients. Cocaine use may medicate or address even more prominent and detectable problems in the regulation and modulation of self-esteem or behavior in interpersonal relationships. The clinical assessment of both DSM-III-R documentable psychopathology and more subtle, but significant, psychopathology emerges as crucial in uncovering patients' deficits in self-regulatory capacities that may have contributed to the development of addiction and may have been exacerbated by chemical use, and that require remediation in treatment. Thus, psychopathology further complicates and informs the nature of the crack-treatment challenge. A clinical interview that relies on DSM-III-R diagnostic categories, but also on patient material and input in the assessment process, may permit efficient detection of both the diagnosable and the more subtle, but significant, psychopathology that is so important in treatment planning. Individual differences and unique patient characteristics are best detected in this way, permitting the design of treatment plans tailored to the individual patient.

BEYOND DSM-III-R: THE PREDOMINANCE OF NARCISSISM

A predominance of narcissistic traits that do not meet DSM-III-R criteria for a personality disorder can be observed in crack smokers when they are newly abstinent, as in inpatient detoxification settings (Wallace, 1987; 1990a). This draws clinical attention to deficits in the regulation of self-esteem that require remediation through treatment. Following the work of Levin (1987), narcissistic traits or psychopathology may reflect a vulnerability or susceptibility that may have played an etiological role in the development of addiction to chemicals such as crack. Levin discusses the treatment of alcoholics, asserting that his clinical research and treatment recommendations extend to the chemically dependent in general. Of interest here is his discussion of narcissism in the newly abstinent or newly sober patient.

What this book is suggesting is neither that all alcoholics suffer from narcissistic personality disorders, which is clearly contrary to fact, nor that all psychopathology is narcissistic pathology, as the more radical of the self psychologists maintain. Rather, narcissistic problems often play a decisive role in the etiology of alcoholism, and the alcoholic process inflicts deep and lasting narcissistic wounds which frequently eventuate in a regression, if a fixation did not already exist, to at least some degree of pathological narcissism. This, we maintain, is the usual final outcome of severe alcoholism, and treatment must address itself to its remediation. Helping the alcoholic find a way to maintain a reasonably constant, sufficiently high level of self-esteem and a reasonably secure self-cohesion without resort to alcohol is the key issue in treatment. . . (p. 75)

The kind of severe personal deterioration that characterizes crack smokers (who have compulsively smoked more and more crack despite negative consequences and punishments) may eventuate in a regression to a level where narcissistic psychopathology predominates—if a fixation did not already exist. Narcissistic problems may have characterized crack smokers' baseline personality functioning. Or narcissistic wounds related to the trauma of crack-related personal deterioration may characterize the personality functioning of newly abstinent crack smokers.

This view of the trauma produced by crack-related behaviors and severe crack-related personal deterioration as resulting in narcissistic injuries finds credence in the work of Bean-Bayog (1986). She recognizes two types of situations—pathological states and stress or trauma—where character is unable to carry out its functions of "maintenance of homeostasis, regulation of self-esteem, preservation of ego identity, maintenance of automatic barriers to overstimulation from internal and external or internal sources, and containment of fluctuation in affect" (p. 335). This assertion forces us to recognize that the deficits in self-regulatory capacities possessed by crack and cocaine patients—as evidenced in the research studies reviewed above—may have followed from the trauma of addiction, despite our earlier discussion of these deficits as possibly predisposing patients to the development of an addiction.

In contrast to the author's earlier assertions, Bean-Bayog (1986) focuses on the damage to character produced by the traumatic effects of alcoholism, and recognizes that as a response to trauma, the alcoholic sustains narcissistic injuries of stigma and social degradation that are handled by "narcissistic defensive

maneuvers, devaluation of others, and reassuring grandiose self-congratulation"
(p. 342). Other responses include denial, magical thinking, lowering of expectations, depression, guilt, and personality disruption. Bean-Bayog rejects the con-
ventional model of treatment of alcoholism that sees the drinking as a
symptom of underlying character disturbance. She advocates a view of alcoholism as traumatic and as producing psychopathology. She states that the implications of her view are that the trauma of alcoholism must be stopped, a
recurrence prevented, and damage from trauma repaired and healed. "Finally,
any underlying or antecedent character problem should be treated to prevent
vulnerability to recurrence of the trauma in the future" (p. 344). Thus, despite
her emphasis on trauma as producing a failure in maintaining self-regulatory
capacities, she also recognizes the crucial role of antecedent or underlying character problems in constituting a vulnerability to recurrence of the trauma of addiction, or relapse. It can only be assumed that any preexisting character
problems could also have played a role in the etiology of the first occurrence of
an addiction. Most important, we are forced to recognize the significance of the
trauma of addiction, and that, regardless of our ability to definitively solve the
mystery of the relationship of psychopathology and addiction, the addictive
behavior must be stopped, damage from the addiction repaired, and relapse
prevented through efforts that include remediation of any underlying
psychopathology.

What remains most striking in most newly abstinent chemically dependent
patients is narcissism. Injuries to the self of the crack smoker or chemically dependent patient must be healed, whether from the trauma of addiction or
rooted in long-standing character problems. The severity and implications of
narcissistic psychopathology may vary, as well as its etiology. However, the concept taken from Levin (1987) of characteristic narcissism found in the newly abstinent having its origin in either a fixation point or a regression to a level of
narcissistic functioning permits both chicken and egg etiologies.

If we integrate the perspective of Levin (1987) and Bean-Bayog (1986) and extend their view of the alcoholic to crack smokers or the chemically dependent
in general, we derive the following working hypothesis. The newly abstinent
patient, as a consequence (1) of the trauma of addiction, or (2) of a regression
to a state of pathological narcissism induced by the trauma of addiction, or (3)
of both the trauma of addiction and a subsequent regression in personality
functioning, as well as of a long-standing psychopathology (usually narcissistic),
fails in maintaining psychic homeostasis, regulating self-esteem, preserving ego
identity, maintaining automatic barriers to overstimulation from internal and
external sources, and containing fluctuations in mood. If we consider all three
of these possible scenarios as capturing the psychological and emotional state
of newly abstinent chemically dependent patients when they present themselves for treatment, we may account for the diversity in personality and affec-

tive functioning found in the research studies of cocaine patients reviewed above. This working hypothesis also permits us to recognize that the answer to the question of what came first, psychopathology or substance abuse, emerges as a complicated and varied response that depends on the individual patient.

CONCLUSION

This chapter has attempted to guide the helping professional through the task of arriving at an accurate diagnosis of crack-cocaine dependence or abuse, as clearly distinct from possible cases of the experimental or recreational use of chemicals. An approach to understanding the advancing stages of chemical use toward the most severe state of dependence is captured in the DARE model of chemical dependency, which provides visual graphics of value in preventative education for those who are in danger of escalating from experimental or recreational use to abuse and dependence. The chapter also reviewed research studies revealing the incidence of mood and personality disorders in cocaine-using populations. Interpretation of these data supports a view of crack-cocaine patients as either possessing deficits in self-regulatory capacities that predisposed them to the development of chemical dependency, or having experienced the trauma of crack dependence with a resulting failure in the ability to maintain self-regulation successfully.

To appreciate the nature of the treatment challenge, the psychopathology characteristic of the newly abstinent crack smoker—whatever its origin—must be recognized as a significant dimension of the treatment challenge. More important than attempting to answer the difficult question as to what came first—substance abuse or psychopathology—is the necessity to understand the importance of an individualized assessment of patients to ascertain the unique dimensions of the substance-use problem and its severity, the role and meaning of any additional DSM-III-R diagnosable psychopathology, and the implications of more subtle psychopathology not meeting DSM-III-R criteria (such as narcissism) for treatment planning.

3

Psychosocial Characteristics of the Crack Dependent

This chapter reviews data available on a relatively large African-American (92%) sample ($n = 245$) of crack smokers (Wallace, 1990b), providing insight into the psychosocial characteristics and functioning of persons presenting such severe addiction to crack that they met DSM-III-R criteria for crack-cocaine dependence and qualified for inpatient hospitalization on a detoxification unit (see Table 3.1). While the data (Wallace, 1990b) may have limitations in generalizing to those individuals presenting with crack-cocaine dependence and possessing similar demographics, an analysis of the data may support the thesis advanced by Levin (1987) and extended to newly abstinent crack smokers in Chapter 2: characteristic narcissism has its origin in either a fixation point or a regression to a level of narcissistic functioning. In addition, the data on the psychosocial characteristics of an inner-city sample of crack smokers may reveal the kind of general life problems or crack-related problems that may be typical of individuals who have advanced to crack dependence. Media stereotypes may be debunked by taking a close look at the actual psychosocial characteristics of a relatively large sample of crack-cocaine smokers treated by Wallace (1990b) in an inpatient detoxification unit from 1986 to 1988 during the height of the crack epidemic.

DYSFUNCTIONAL FAMILY HISTORIES IN CHILDHOOD

Characteristics of crack smokers suggest the possibility that those who smoke experimentally and recreationally have risk factors that may have predisposed them to the development of the abuse and dependency syndromes. Data on a large sample of crack-cocaine smokers in treatment (Wallace, 1990b) seem to support the hypothesis of a preexisting fixation point in crack smokers, following Levin's (1987) conceptualizations as discussed in the previous chapter. A crack smoker's baseline

36

TABLE 3.1
Background Data*

	Men No.	(N = 158) (%)	Women N	(N = 87) (%)
Ethnicity				
Black	143	(90.6)	83	(95.4)
Hispanic	10	(6.3)	3	(3.4)
White	4	(2.5)	1	(1.2)
Other	1	(.6)	—	—
Education				
High-school dropout	76	(48)	47	(54)
High-school graduate/GED	52	(32.9)	27	(31)
HS/GED and two years college	22	(13.9)	11	(12.7)
College graduate	6	(3.9)	2	(2.3)
Missing	2	(1.3)	—	—
Employment Data				
Unemployed	48	(30.4)	51	(58.6)
Unemployed over one year and history of crack-related loss of a job	46	((29.1)	21	(24.1)
Currently unemployed but employed within past year	35	(22.2)	7	(8)
Currently employed	18	(11.4)	5	(5.8)
Currently employed and history of crack-related loss of a job	4	(2.5)	1	(1.2)
SSI	7	(4.4)	2	(2.3)
Patterns of Crack Use				
Crack only (some marijuana)	129	(81.7)	64	(73.5)
Crack and alcohol	10	(6.3)	7	(8)
Crack and intranasal heroin	6	(3.8)	8	(9.2)
Crack and intravenous drugs	9	(5.7)	1	(1.2)
Crack and methadone maintenance	4	(2.5)	5	(5.8)
Crack and pills	—	—	2	(2.3)

*Adapted from Wallace (1990b). Reprinted by permission.

personality may have included a fixation point for narcissism that was rooted in a childhood narcissistic injury to the self. Psychosocial data on this sample (Wallace, 1990b) provide evidence of exposure to dysfunctional family dynamics in childhood. Fixation points for an inability to regulate self-esteem, and for a defense of inflation and grandiosity in response to a painfully low self-esteem, may be rooted in painful experiences in dysfunctional families. In this regard, data show (Wallace, 1990b) that the vast majority (91%) of crack smokers are adult children of dysfunc-

TABLE 3.2
Crack Smokers as Adult Children of Dysfunctional Families*
(N = 245)

Dysfunctional Family Pattern	Men (N = 158)		Women (N = 87)	
	N	(%)	N	(%)
Alcoholic father	41	(25.9)	24	(27.6)
Alcoholic mother	22	(13.9)	23	(26.4)
Alcoholic stepfather	10	(6.3)	5	(5.8)
Exposed to alcoholism and domestic violence	24	(9.8)	16	(6.5)
Report domestic violence	28	(17.7)	21	(24.1)
Parental abandonment: father	27	(1.0)	14	(5.7)
Parental abandonment: mother	99	(3.7)	3	(1.2)
Parents separated	30	(12.2)	20	(8.2)
Physically abused	16	(6.5)	17	(6.9)
Sexually abused	3	(1.2)	14	(5.7)
Emotionally abused	9	(3.7)	9	(3.7)

*Adapted from Wallace (1990b). Reprinted by permission.

tional families. Specifically, 51% of crack smokers are adult children of alcoholic families with other dysfunctional family dynamics experienced in childhood relating to domestic violence (20%), parental abandonment (22%), parental separation (20%), physical abuse (14%), sexual abuse (7%), and emotional abuse (7%). Table 3.2 shows specific breakdowns on dysfunctional family dynamics. The data argue strongly for the probable existence of fixation points for narcissistic psychopathology in the majority of crack smokers (91%) in this rather large sample (Wallace, 1990b).

The finding that 51% of patients are adult children of alcoholics reinforces Washton's (1989) finding that 41% of cocaine patients present a history of alcohol or drug problems in parents or grandparents. Thus, for both Washton's largely white, middle-income sample and Wallace's (1990b) largely African-American lower- and lower-middle-income sample, a history of dysfunctional family dynamics involving familial alcoholism may be significant. Washton states that what appears to be transmitted "from one generation to the next (biologically and/or psychologically) is probably a nonspecific vulnerability to chemical dependency rather than an alcohol-specific or cocaine-specific predisposition" (p. 26).

However, the present interpretation of data showing that 91% of crack smokers are from dysfunctional families and 51% are from alcoholic families (Wallace, 1990b) suggests that psychopathology associated with these childhood experiences constituted a risk factor for the development of an addictive disorder. Patients' susceptibility to developing an addiction may be related to the psychological and emotional consequences of exposure to an alcoholic parent or dysfunctional family system. Painful affective states are usually associated with memories of traumata experienced in dysfunctional families in childhood, and with childhood narcissistic injuries that provide the basis for fixation points for patients' adult manifestation of narcissistic psychopathology. An associated low self-esteem, or difficulties in regulating self-esteem as well as affective states, may characterize adult children of dysfunctional families.

CRACK-RELATED DETERIORATION: ADDING INSULT TO INJURY

Crack-related psychosocial deterioration may even add insult to preexisting narcissistic injuries rooted in childhood traumata experienced in dysfunctional families. This supports a second, alternative hypothesis—arising from the work of Levin (1987)—that the predominance of narcissistic psychopathology observed in the newly abstinent patient may reflect a regression to "at least some degree of pathological narcissism" (p. 75). The process of experiencing severe crack-related personal deterioration may certainly inflict the kind of "deep and lasting narcissistic wounds" of which Levin speaks. Adult crack-related trauma and narcissistic injuries following the experience of crack dependence may induce a regression to a level characterized by the use of grandiosity and inflation as a defense against a painfully low self-esteem.

Bean-Bayog's (1986) approach of focusing on a failure in self-regulatory capacities as a consequence of the trauma of addiction (as discussed in Chapter 1) actually supports the current author's view: the narcissistic injury and trauma following from the experience of severe crack-related deterioration may add insult to those preexisting narcissistic injuries crack smokers sustained as children in dysfunctional families. In this way, we can begin to answer Meyer's (1986) question as to which came first, the chicken or the egg. Apparently, the reality of crack smokers' childhood histories and the incidence of crack-related trauma and severe crack-related deterioration permit the possibility that psychopathology both may precede and follow drug use. The view of Bean-Bayog, together with Levin's view of characteristic narcissism found in the newly abstinent having its origin in either a fixation point or a regression to a level of narcissistic functioning, permits both chicken and egg etiologies, as well as the concept that trauma following from crack use adds insult to preexisting injury.

CRACK-RELATED CHANGES IN EMPLOYMENT PATTERNS

Crack-related changes in individuals' characteristic employment patterns may be experienced as a narcissistic injury to the self, and may also be traumatic as a result of the instability that follows a significant change in employ-ment status. Psychosocial data show that one third of men (32%) and one quarter (25%) of women experienced crack-related loss of employment (Wallace, 1990b). For patients presenting with the dependence syndrome, it is no surprise that despite crack-related loss of employment, patients have continued to smoke crack in spite of the fact that it resulted in lateness, absences from work, and warnings from superiors. The brain-driven compulsion to smoke crack took precedence over these problems and eventually resulted in loss of employ-ment. Patterns of sporadic employment also characterize the sample (17%). These individuals were unemployed at the time of detoxification but had been employed within the past year. They were able to secure employment, but their crack smoking prevented maintaining a job beyond the first payday. Typically, a binge results in an unexplained absence during a probationary period and sub-sequent dismissal or in a failure to return to work because of feelings of shame. Since many of the patients in the sample have been smoking crack for two to three years, it is no surprise that 85% are unemployed (Table 3.1 presents spe-cific breakdowns). Persons capable of working as evidenced by a history of sta-ble employment but who do not work, adolescents who fail to enter the job market, and those who have lost jobs, all because of crack, end up with radi-cally restructured lives once they become compulsive crack smokers.

As one patient on the inpatient detoxification unit who had been referred to the treatment unit by several friends openly reflected, "black Wall Street" was being treated on the unit in response to the crack epidemic gripping the New York metropolitan area. This was a reference to the messengers, mailroom em-ployees, business-school-educated computer operators, executive secretaries, word-processing employees, and college graduates working in white collar jobs in banking, insurance, and brokerage houses. In addition to people employed (or newly unemployed) in these positions, school teachers, subway conductors, bus drivers, sanitation workers, maintenance workers, and fast-food-service em-ployees were among those who entered inpatient detoxification and are a part of the sample. Seasonally employed laborers, self-employed carpenters, and the frequently unemployed also found themselves, as a result of their crack use, in that state of unemployment that seems to represent the culmination of a path of deterioration so commonly observed in the crack dependent (Wallace, 1990b).

However, crack smokers are not a monolithic group and many continue to be employed. Among the men in the sample, 11.4% were still employed at time of detoxification, and among women, 5.8% were still employed. The diversity within the sample regarding employment status must not be overlooked. Not all crack smokers fall asleep on the job, are frequently late or absent, or arrive at work appearing to be high. Employers often see no outward signs of crack use, despite a dependence syndrome that justifies inpatient detoxification.

Whatever the specifics of a patient's crack-related deterioration in psychosocial functioning, as reflected in changes in the pattern of employment, the data (Wallace, 1990b) support the hypothesis that such changes can constitute significant narcissistic injuries to the self. Also, these changes in employment may be experienced as traumatic, and contribute to the kind of regression to a level of pathological narcissism that Levin (1987) asserts could explain the narcissism observed in newly abstinent patients—such as those undergoing treatment during a two-week detoxification.

PATTERNS OF CRACK-COCAINE SMOKING

Patterns of crack-cocaine smoking also highlight the fact that crack smokers are a diverse group with varied use patterns. The patterns of smoking found in the sample (Wallace, 1990b) shed light on how maladaptive behavioral symptoms common to the dependence syndrome develop among crack smokers. Deterioration, debilitation, and attendant feelings of shame seem concomitant to the kind of heavy-crack-smoking patterns seen in the sample (Wallace, 1990b).

A Predominance of Daily Smokers

The data show that over half (51.4%) of the patients are daily users, 20.9% utilize crack three to five times per week, and 6.9% use it twice a week. As Table 3.3 shows, the vast majority (72.2%) of compulsive users smoke crack daily or three to five times a week, a pattern that begins to reveal the severity of most patients' addictions prior to entering inpatient detoxification. Our understanding of the neurochemical actions of crack cocaine and of how users easily engage in compulsive-use patterns explains how, for the majority of patients, crack is smoked on such a frequent basis. Both positive and negative reinforcement as discussed in Chapters 1 and 6 explain how, in addition to crack cocaine's pharmacological actions, conditioning phenomena permit crack smokers to escalate to daily, or nearly daily, use patterns.

Binge Use Constituting Dependence

Within the sample, patterns of smoking crack three to five days a week can involve an "every other day pattern" or a binge that lasts from three to five days. Siegel (1987) describes binge use as a potentially toxic variation of compulsive use; this "pattern refers to continuous periods of repeated dosing during which users consume substantial amounts of cocaine" (p. 185). A minority of crack smokers (5.7%) in Wallace's (1990b) sample engage in binges that take place over several hours as opposed to several days. A Friday night binge may

TABLE 3.3
The Frequency and Dose of Crack Smoking

Frequency of Crack Smoking	(N = 245) N	(%)
Daily	126	(51.4)
3–5 times per week	51	(20.9)
Twice per week	17	(6.9)
Once per week ("weekends")	6	(2.5)
Bimonthly (payday)	8	(3.2)
Missing data	37	(15.1)

Dose Smoked in Dollars	Daily Users (N = 126)		3–5 Times per Week (N = 51)	
	N	(%)	N	(%)
<$50	33	(26.2)	20	(39.2)
>$50–100	27	(21.4)	19	(37.3)
>$100–200	36	(28.6)	8	(15.7)
>$200–300	17	(13.5)	3	(5.9)
$400–500	3	(2.4)	1	(1.9)
>$500	4	(3.1)	—	—
Missing data	6	(4.8)	—	—

*Adapted from Wallace (1990b). Reprinted by permission.

end sometime on Saturday. Among patients in the sample, these binge patterns of compulsive smoking involve 2.5% of patients smoking crack once per week (usually on weekends) or 3.2% smoking bimonthly (corresponding to paydays).

External Controls Affect Crack-Smoking Patterns

Wallace (1990b) suggests that, based on clinical observation and case histories, external controls may operate in limiting crack use even though users contend with severe cravings. While crack cravings may be so intense and uncontrollable that "the crack user will lie, steal, or even commit acts of violence in order to obtain more of the drug" (Rosecan, Spitz, & Gross, 1987, p. 300), many crack users are charming and conniving as they borrow money, use money reserved for household bills, or impatiently wait for payday in order to get high (Wallace, 1990b). In this way, for a minority of crack smokers (3.2%), payday serves as an external control limiting crack use. But when that day comes, these users lose all control, although they usually promise themselves to stop after spending a certain amount of money. However, the binge may not end for perhaps six, 12, or even 24 hours, when all of their money is gone or they fall asleep from exhaustion. They then continue their compulsive crack smoking whenever money again becomes available, usually on payday. Soon they may begin borrowing against their check before payday when their craving for crack becomes so intense that they cannot wait until the end of the week to satisfy it. For others, binges begin to last two or three days, or longer, also signaling movement toward more severe addiction (Wallace, 1990b).

Competing Rewards Set Limits on Crack Use

Limits may also be set on crack use when smokers are able to acknowledge rewards that compete with the crack-cocaine euphoria. Positive reinforcers such as a paycheck, a home, a car, or the love of children or a spouse may compete with the memory of the euphoria. Rewards such as these and fear of their loss thus may intervene in limiting, controlling, or stopping crack use. Among bimonthly "payday" crack smokers, it is usually the feared loss of a job, spouse, or home that has led to entrance into the hospital for treatment. Thus, a variety of external controls other than payday may place limits on crack use in many crack smokers because they serve as rewards that effectively compete with the desire for the crack-induced euphoria (Wallace, 1990b).

Escalation to Frequent Crack Use

On the other hand, clinical observation and patient self-reports support the contention that most daily and almost daily crack smokers were once weekly or bimonthly binge smokers. Within the sample, many patients have not been able to set limits on their crack use, and have gradually increased the frequency of their smoking over months or years. Changes in the frequency of crack smoking suggest an escalation from bimonthly to weekly, then to biweekly, then to several times per week, and finally to daily crack use. However, this escalation is not inevitable since the data show the part that external controls and competing rewards can play in determining the frequency of smoking, in placing limits on crack use, and in facilitating termination of crack smoking. The desire to avoid a withdrawal syndrome (depression, crack craving, oversleeping, overeating) may also explain why some smokers increase their frequency of crack use (Wallace, 1990b). The time between episodes of crack use may become progressively shorter as smokers use crack again and again to avoid the dysphoria and to satisfy crack cravings. Alleviation of dysphoria by smoking more crack serves as a form of negative reinforcement that can strengthen the response of crack smoking (see Chapter 6).

Diversity again emerges as the hallmark of this sample (Wallace, 1990b) of crack-cocaine smokers. Individual patients respond to awareness of external controls, competing rewards, and feelings of anxiety over the possible loss of valued rewards or possessions in a variety of ways. Some seem not to respond at all, pursuing compulsive crack smoking to satisfy cravings and as a consequence of conditioning phenomena as they escalate from infrequent to more frequent crack use. Others may try to limit crack use, but their efforts fail in the face of a compulsion to smoke more crack, and they also escalate the frequency of their smoking. For still others, the fear of losing certain rewards or possessions is sufficient motivation to limit crack use to weekends or paydays, and escalation of use does not proceed, as seen in the diverse data on frequency of crack smoking (Wallace, 1990b). Myths of compulsive, out-of-control crack smokers who steal to feed their costly habit bow to a much more complex reality of diverse and somewhat constrained crack-smoking patterns, as indicated by these data.

Diversity in Self-Administered Doses

Information on the dose or amount of crack smoked when a patient gets high further clarifies the nature and severity of crack smoking among those meeting the criteria for crack-cocaine dependence. Dose information is reported as money spent per day on crack. The majority of patients in the sample report purchasing either $5 or $10 vials that contain chunks or pellets of crack. This crack packaging is not based on weight, but on a drug dealer's estimate of a reasonable street dose to be sold for a particular price—in contrast to cocaine powder for intranasal use, which is usually sold by the half gram, gram, or eighth of an ounce. Washton (1989) argues that on a weight-for-weight basis, crack is actually twice as expensive as cocaine powder (p. 15). For patients in Wallace's (1990b) sample, a report of smoking a $100 dose of crack per day would mean smoking the contents of either 20 $5 vials or ten $10 vials.

Since daily smokers of crack (51.4%) and those who smoke three to five times per week (20.9%) make up the majority of the sample (72.3%), an analysis of the average dose of crack needed to get high seems worthwhile. Results indicate that, among daily users (n = 126), most spend an average of $100–200 on crack per day (28.6%). Equal numbers of daily crack smokers average less than $100 per day (47.6%) and over $100 a day (47.6%). In contrast, the vast majority (76.5%) of smokers who use crack three to five times per week (n = 51) average less than $100 to get high, whereas a minority (23.5%) spend an average of over $100 per day (Wallace, 1990b).

These data suggest that the severity of crack dependence as reflected in the average dose smoked is somewhat greater for daily users than it is for those who smoke three to five times per week. This characteristic is consistent with crack smoking that advanced from infrequent to more frequent patterns; here an escalation toward a higher dose also seems to accompany escalation to a higher frequency of smoking. It follows that those who smoke more frequently (daily versus three to five times a week) would also have a more severe addiction, as reflected in the average dose self-administered when getting high. In this way, daily smokers spending an average of $100 or more a day are among those with the most severe cases of crack-cocaine dependence (Wallace, 1990b).

Whereas only 23.5% of three-to-five-times-per-week smokers use an average crack dose worth over $100, 47.6% of daily users average over $100 when they get high. Thus, more daily users require a high dose (over $100) when smoking crack. These daily users may have achieved a higher tolerance, requiring a larger dose to achieve the same effects (Wallace, 1990b).

Overall Evidence of Severe Dependence

In accordance with Washton's (1987) characterization of crack addiction, crack smoking has led—in these cases of high-dose, frequent smoking—to a "tenacious addiction," as reflected in the data on dose and frequency of crack use. Wallace's (1990b) data also dispel the myth that crack provides a "cheap" high. For those who smoke crack daily and three to five times per week, their habit is extremely expensive. This analysis of the dose regularly consumed by the crack smoker also "provides another measure of addiction severity" (Washton, 1989a, p. 84).

Data on dose are significant because "in general the more cocaine the applicant is using, the more difficult it will be for him/her to break the cycle of compulsive drug use" (p. 84). Since the majority of crack smokers in the sample are daily users (51.4%), and half of these (47.6%) are high-dose users (over $100 per day), it may be particularly difficult for these individuals to break the cycle of compulsion. For those presenting this most severe manifestation of addiction to crack (smoking daily or three to five times a week), the treatment challenge may be more difficult, and the risk of relapse during recovery may also be greater (Wallace, 1990b). The higher the dose typically smoked per day, the more frequent is the self-administration of crack. Here, the response of crack smoking can be thought of as a deeply ingrained habit or as a strongly established operant or response. When crack smoking begins to suggest a chain-smoking pattern—as in the case of high-dose-per-day smokers and daily smokers who may also be high-dose smokers—negative reinforcement (see Chapter 6) also serves to strongly establish the response of smoking more crack to alleviate the dysphoria, crash depression, irritability, and cravings that follow once the brief crack high and stimulant effects have passed.

Other Drug-Use Patterns

Data show that some patients frequently attempt to manage the crash depression, dysphoria, and withdrawal from crack with marijuana, alcohol, and other drugs. However, the majority of patients (78.4%) in the sample report primarily smoking crack only, although some in this group also smoke marijuana;

a specific breakdown is not available. Another 21.6% of patients report that, in addition to their crack addiction, they use alcohol, intranasal heroin, intravenous heroin and cocaine, and methadone (in and outside of maintenance programs) to an extent that qualifies as an addiction-dependence syndrome in addition to their crack dependence.

Washton (1989a) observes that free-base crack smokers tend also to use other drugs in larger quantities in order to counteract the extremely negative aftereffects of high-dose cocaine use. Unique for this sample are the high rates of crack smoking in combination with marijuana smoking only. Most crack smokers seem to avoid withdrawal symptoms by taking more crack. The allocation of all available funds for more crack may explain the largely singular use of crack. This finding is likely related to the fact that most users were daily crack smokers and the majority of the patients are unemployed—which probably facilitated compulsive crack smoking while decreasing the need to utilize a sedative-hypnotic (alcohol or pills) in order to sleep or to come down from crack in preparation for work or to carry out some other obligation. However, these remarks are clearly speculative (Wallace, 1990b). Recent reports suggest that more crack smokers are using heroin to help them come down and to help perpetuate the euphoria of crack (*New York Times*, Nov. 12, 1989, p. 46).

Consequences of Crack-Smoking Patterns

In summary, the kinds of high-frequency and high-dose compulsive patterns of crack smoking found among patients in the sample show to some extent how crack-related psychosocial deterioration characterizes crack smokers' lives. Daily or nearly daily smokers of high doses of crack must easily fail to meet major role obligations and obviously soon deplete their financial resources to pay for such high-level crack consumption. It requires little imagination to foresee a range of negative experiences that befall crack smokers of this kind. Trauma and narcissistic injuries to the self easily follow that might lead to a regression to a level of functioning characterized by pathological narcissism. Individuals smoking such large quantities of crack on such a frequent basis must certainly undergo significant personal deterioration likely to be experienced as traumatic, painful, and a cause of shame. A defense of grandiosity and inflation may emerge as a last, relatively harmless defense for a patient who undergoes severe crack-related deterioration in psychosocial functioning as a result of such compulsive smoking patterns.

PATTERNS OF HOMELESSNESS ATTRIBUTABLE TO CRACK ADDICTION

Unemployment as one of the key characteristics of crack smokers with such high-frequency and high-dose compulsive patterns has several painful conse-

TABLE 3.4
Crack-Related Homelessness*

	Men		Women	
	N	(%)	N	(%)
Asked to leave their household	Total N	38	Total N	7
And end up homeless	19	(50)	4	(57.1)
And enter detoxification	6	(15.8)	—	—
Other outcome	13	(34.2)	3	(42.9)
Crack-related loss of apartment	Total N	13	Total N	6
And live with family	9	(69.2)	6	(100)
And end up homeless	4	(30.8)	—	—
Crack-related homelessness with other/unknown etiology				
(Left on their own, started living in crack houses, streets)				
	Total N	14	Total N	5
Circumstances of the crack-addicted homeless				
Total experiencing homelessness	Total N	37	Total N	9
Shelter-system involvement	17	(46)	4	(44.5)
Living on street	8	(21.6)	3	(33.3)
Living here and there				
(from sofa to sofa of family, friends)	12	(32.4)	2	(22.2)

*Adapted from Wallace (1990b). Reprinted by permission.

quences. Crack smokers who are unemployed often drain family finances or fail to contribute to them. Discord and conflict frequently follow unemployment, as do requests for crack users to leave home. Within the total sample ($n = 245$), 18.7% of patients were actually asked to leave their household. Table 3.4 shows patterns of crack-related homelessness found in Wallace's (1990b) sample.

Of those patients asked to leave their homes ($n = 45$), 51.1% became homeless. Being expelled from one's home may also shock patients and motivate them to seek treatment. Thus, another 13.3% of these patients entered detoxification as a result of their newly homeless status, while many others continued compulsive crack smoking after leaving home (Wallace, 1990b).

Financial problems and an inability to pay bills also may lead to loss of apartments. In the sample, 7.8% of patients lost their apartment; according to patients, it was crack related, in that they used their rent money to feed their crack habit. Of these ($n = 19$), 21.1% ended up homeless and 78.9% moved in with extended-family members. Thus, within the African-American community, the family network often provides support for crack users who have lost their homes because of crack use (Wallace, 1990b).

The incorporation of crack users into relatives' households is not always successful. Of those patients in the sample who became homeless ($n = 46$), 30.4% spent an average of two months moving from couch to couch among the homes of friends, acquaintances, and family, and nearly half (45.7%) relied on public shelters, averaging four months in the system. Another 23.9% spent an average of 1.5 months living on the streets. Regardless of the etiology, a total of 19% of crack smokers in the sample ended up homeless. This finding highlights the degree of psychosocial deterioration following from compulsive crack smoking that a user can actually experience. Thus, the crack epidemic contributes to the homeless population. Although it affects fewer than one fifth of the patients in the sample, homelessness is a relatively low rung on a ladder all too frequently descended by compulsive crack-cocaine smokers who exhibit the dependence syndrome (Wallace, 1990b). To end up living on the street, in a shelter for the homeless, or as a begrudgingly accommodated intruder on someone's couch certainly represents a kind of trauma and injury to the self. This experience of trauma, humiliation, and shame may eventuate in the defensive use of grandiosity and inflation, as seen in the characteristic defensive armor of crack smokers entering detoxification.

CRACK SMOKERS' INABILITY TO CARE FOR CHILDREN

Stories of the abuse and abandonment of infants and children, explanations of the damage done to fetuses in the womb, and speculation as to what happens to children of crack smokers behind closed doors are among the most provocative factors when discussing the dimensions of a crack smoker's life. The data on this sample of crack smokers (Wallace, 1990b) shed some realistic light on these issues to balance speculation and myth. Crack-related deterioration in mothers' ability to care for children reveals a shocking decline in psychosocial functioning compared with a precrack level of functioning. Among women with children in the sample ($n = 70$), over one third (34.3%) report that the Bureau of Child Welfare has become involved in their children's lives as a result of the mother's crack use and the neglect or abuse that followed, placing 30% of the children with relatives and 4.3% in foster care. Another 15.7% of these children are being cared by for relatives without formal bureau involvement. Thus, among crack-smoking mothers, the majority (52.9%) have become dysfunctional as a parent and no longer care for their children (Wallace, 1990b), as seen in Table 3.5. Loss of one's role and function as a mother entails one of the most profound insults and narcissistic injuries to the self of a mother.

The data also suggest that the African-American family system seems to be helping to ameliorate a crisis in child care created by the crack epidemic. When patients repeatedly leave their children with relatives while they spend hours or days compulsively smoking crack, the relatives often take over child care completely—sometimes with little or no choice in the matter. When no concerned relative or agency intervenes, children remain with crack-smoking parents (Wallace, 1990b).

Only 44.3% of crack mothers are still caring for their children. Although some proudly proclaim that they took good care of their children, never spend-

TABLE 3.5
Crack-Related Deterioration in Psychosocial Functioning*

Child-Care Patterns	Men (N = 82)		Women (N = 70)	
	N	(%)	N	(%)
Total with children				
Caring for children, no BCW involvement (for men, child is usually with the mother)	73	(89)	31	(44.3)
BCW involvement and not crack related	2	(2.4)	1	(1.4)
BCW involvement and children with relatives	—	—	21	(30)
BCW involvement and children in foster care	3	(3.7)	3	(4.3)
No BCW involvement and children cared for by relatives	4	(4.9)	11	(15.7)
Pregnant (three additional women also have other children included above)	—	—	3	(4.3)

Familial Discord	Men (N = 158)		Women (N = 87)	
Crack-related arguments with partner or family members	37	(23.4)	18	(20.6)
Marital conflict, problems with lover, or separation from partner	33	(20.8)	14	(16.1)
Domestic violence	12	(7.6)	19	(21.8)
Criminal activity				
Volunteer drug dealing	30	(19)	3	(3.5)
Prostitution	—	—	3	(3.5)
Stealing from household, selling possessions, shoplifting, hustling, pickpocketing	27	(17.1)	9	(10.3)

*Adapted from Wallace (1990b). Reprinted by permission.

ing money allotted to the children's needs for crack, the quality of that care remains suspect given the denial characteristic of crack smokers, as well as their fears of Bureau of Child Welfare involvement. These fears are realistic since treatment professionals who suspect child abuse or neglect are obliged to report this information to Child Welfare. However, other patients who are still caring for their children enter detoxification because they have observed a deterioration in their own parenting behavior (Wallace, 1990b). Thus, once again, we enter the realm of misconception if we fail to appreciate the diversity to be found among crack-cocaine smokers. Crack smokers as parents are undeserving of mass generalizations as to their neglect and abandonment of children. On the other hand, such parents are certainly creating dysfunctional family dynamics that are likely to place their children at risk for a range of potential emotional, psychological, and behavioral problems. But the nature of their dysfunction defies a particular stereotype as many crack smokers persevere in ensuring the performance of essential functions as a parent.

Crack smoking among pregnant women and the consequences for the developing fetus are critical issues (Chasnoff & Schnoll, 1987). Within the year prior to detoxification, two patients had had infants taken away from them at birth when cocaine was detected in the infants' systems. They hoped to regain child custody as a result of finally following judges' mandates to seek treatment. Another six patients detoxed in response to pregnancy; three of these women already had children. Thus, 11.4% of crack mothers in the sample were in a position to expose fetuses to crack cocaine. Pain, humiliation, and trauma follow from the loss of an infant's custody shortly after its birth. Clinical experience suggests that these mothers sustain significant narcissistic injuries to the self from such trauma, and defensively use denial, grandiosity, and inflation while continuing compulsively to smoke crack—and to self-medicating their depression over separation from the child—to disguise their inner experience. Yet other mothers seem relieved to be free of parenting responsibilities while pursuing crack smoking. However, such reactions still usually thinly veil such a stance as defensive in nature; guilt, shame, longing, and sadness usually reside deep inside. Clinical management of these feelings of guilt, shame, and depression related to past child care and loss of contact with infants and children are central issues that must be sensitively addressed in these women's treatment.

The fact that only 11.4% of crack mothers exposed infants to crack cocaine in the sample (Wallace, 1990b) balances myths of widespread exposure of infants to crack use by minority women. A 1986 estimate is that 10% of women in an average obstetrics practice may be using cocaine (Yonekura, 1989). Chasnoff provides data showing that in a sample of 715 women, a total of 14.8% tested positive for either alcohol, marijuana, cocaine, or opiates. To further debunk myths of high rates of substance abuse among minority women, Chasnoff found that among white women, 15.4% tested positive, whereas among black women, 14.1% tested positive when blind urine samples were taken. Also, in private-sector hospitals, the positive urine rate was 13.1%, whereas in the public sector, 16.3% tested positive; Chasnoff points out that these differences are not significant (Yonekura, 1989). The extent to which the predicaments of minority women are exploited and utilized to fuel myths of neglect and criminal behavior is revealed by these data.

CRACK-RELATED FAMILIAL DISCORD

Since personality changes (depression, irritability, social withdrawal, paranoia) and withdrawal symptoms (crack craving, depression, oversleeping, overeating) characterize crack smokers (Rosecan, Spitz, & Gross, 1987), they often provoke arguments, creating conflict and familial discord. Such arguments frequently focus on financial problems related to crack and unemployment, dysfunction as a spouse or parent, or demands for money for crack by partners in a state of withdrawal and drug craving. Thus, the majority (54.3%) of crack smokers in the sample report some kind of familial discord that is directly related to their crack smoking, according to patients. This familial discord specifically involves crack-related arguments with partners and family members (22.5%), conflict with lovers or partners and/or a resultant separation (19.2%), and domestic violence (12.7%). In the view of patients, compared with any preexisting familial discord, crack either creates or exacerbates relationship problems, justifying the reporting of these events as crack related (Wallace, 1990b).

Criminal Involvement

Patients in the sample (Wallace, 1990b) were not systematically asked about crack-related criminal involvement. In the context of a clinical interview or the short-term individual psychotherapy conducted on an inpatient detoxification unit, exploration of such activities as prostitution or exchanging sex for crack does not occur. Only when such information is volunteered or elicited in response to questions on source of income to support crack is it available for data analysis.

Drug dealing represents another feature of the crack smoker's life-style, an activity that often is necessary to support costly crack habits. Among men in the sample ($n = 158$), 19% admitted involvement in drug dealing. Commission of minor crimes that usually go unreported includes stealing from one's household, hustling, pickpocketing, shoplifting, and selling one's own possessions (14.7%). Among women, 4% say they have been involved in prostitution (Wallace, 1990b). Rates of prostitution and informally exchanging sex for crack actually are probably much higher for women in the sample, as suggested by the work of Inciardi (1990) on adolescent female crack smokers.

High Levels of Sexual Activity

According to Washton (1989b), a dual addiction to sex and drugs is rampant among patients addicted to cocaine (p. 32). Inciardi (1990) acknowledges the concern that with crack use in particular, the high level of sexual activity that may be resulting from the exchange of sex for the drug presents a greater potential for transmission of the human immunodeficiency virus (HIV) and other sexually transmitted diseases. Participation in staff rounds and discussion with medical staff concerning patients' medical status and treatment support speculation that the patients in Wallace's (1990b) sample are very active sexually, often without protection. Reports of high rates of syphilis, in particular, and of gonorrhea, as well as less frequent reports of herpes and vaginal warts, indicate the highly active sex lives of both men and women who had spent considerable time in the crack culture, including indulgence in unprotected sex with people who have crack to share or in the general promiscuity of crack-using environments. This represents yet another manifestation of the kind of severe crack-related deterioration that patients experience.

More common in a clinical interview is for patients to acknowledge painfully that they have undergone "personal deterioration," a familiar and polite "catch-all" admission that encompasses such behavior as heightened sexual activity, the selling of personal possessions, stealing from family and friends, and hustling or selling stolen goods—all activities about which patients do not feel very good nor proud. Other patients experience feelings of control, power, and confidence related to skills developed in connection with prostitution or hustling; these skills give some patients a sense of self-efficacy. For some, it is only deep inside that the feelings of pain or shame lie—feelings that are not worth accessing early in treatment. Working through such feelings of shame may not be appropriate until these painful affects arise naturally or reach consciousness, or until their remaining unconscious jeopardizes the maintenance of abstinence (see Chapter 11). However, these kinds of experiences and underlying feelings may be the basis for the utilization of narcissistic defensive functioning. Overall, recognition of diversity within the population of crack smokers and appreciation of individual differences and experiences among them remain essential in assessing the nature and extent of crack-related deterioration in psychosocial functioning.

CRACK USE: A WELL-KEPT SECRET

Where overwhelming evidence of psychosocial deterioration does not exist, one must appreciate that because of media stereotypes of violent and abusive crack addicts, many crack smokers may conceal their drug use and related problems. Trying hard to appear "normal," many crack users—both in treatment and not yet participating in treatment—may be barely "getting over" as a parent, spouse, or employee, presenting facades more or less of stability. However, a gradual pattern of psychosocial deterioration may characterize crack smokers' lives behind closed doors where financial problems, unexplained absences from work, and familial discord substantiate the negative impact of the crack smoking (Wallace, 1990b). The only outside-world hint of crack-cocaine smoking may be a pattern of failing to achieve self-actualization, a lack of attention to personal appearance, or lateness or absences from work. We can be assured that not only is crack smoking widespread, but that across the nation users smoke crack in private, remaining all too aware of, if not paranoid about, the possible repercussions of disclosure of their behavior.

CONCLUSION

This chapter's review of data on a relatively large sample of crack-cocaine smokers (Wallace, 1990b) shows variety in the frequency and dose of crack-smoking among users even when they present with the dependence syndrome. Overall, the tremendous diversity that characterizes crack smokers in this sample highlights the fact that they are not a monolithic group. The data also assist clinicians in understanding the narcissism observed in newly abstinent crack-cocaine smokers. The kind of humiliation, insult, and narcissistic injuries to the self caused by traumatic and severe crack-related deterioration explains a regression to a level of narcissistic functioning and the patients' use of defenses of inflation and grandiosity. Together with a possible preexisting fixation point rooted in narcissistic injuries to the self acquired in dysfunctional families in childhood, the narcissism observed in crack smokers emerges as having a rational basis.

This view of a predominance of narcissism in the crack dependent must be tempered by arguments that cocaine induces grandiosity, in addition to the entire range of pathological emotions in humans (Nunes & Rosecan, 1987). However, what remains compelling is that crack-related personal deterioration may be so painful that grandiosity and inflation exacerbate denial and combine as a necessary defensive armor for individuals already left sensitive, fragile, and vulnerable by childhood traumata in dysfunctional families.

Alternatively, it remains essential to recognize that some crack smokers may not have sustained a significantly negative impact from dysfunctional family dynamics, nor do they experience a regression to a level of pathological narcissism as a result of crack-related trauma. For some patients, even in the face of loss of employment, child custody, and housing, and of familial discord, a response of resiliency emerges. Narcissistic traits are not necessarily characteristic of all compulsive crack smokers who have undergone crack-related psychosocial deterioration. Genuine regret, sincere motivation for change, and an ability to connect with painful feelings about crack use without resorting to the occasional use of grandiosity and inflation may also occur. In this way, the present author's appreciation of the predominance of narcissism and of a childhood history of dysfunctional family dynamics must not promote a monolithic and stereotypical view of crack-cocaine smokers. Diversity again remains the hallmark of such populations.

A response of resiliency may also follow for most crack patients among those who exhibit grandiosity and inflation early in abstinence; with empathic and supportive treatment, many such patients may make the transition from overreliance on narcissistic defensive functioning and denial to an ability to connect with and process feelings and to face the helping professional with regard to the addiction. However, it is only by understanding and appreciating the roots and function of the narcissism observed in the newly abstinent chemically dependent person that a clinician can be empathic, supportive, and optimally effective in helping them to recover from their dependency.

The data also show how many patients who present with crack dependence also must cope with various life problems as a result of being newly unemployed, being homeless, having lost child custody, or having had significant conflicts with spouses or family. General life problems may be a powerful predictor of treatment outcome (Stoffelmayr et al., 1989). Thus, the data (Wallace, 1990b) serve as well to characterize the nature of the treatment challenge posed by the crack dependent by describing the kind of general factors or level of functioning many crack smokers possess at the time they seek treatment. In conclusion, crack smokers are not a monolithic group even when it comes to crack-related or general life problems—11% are still employed, 28% smoke crack only once a week or twice a month (usually on payday), 81% are still domiciled, 44% of crack mothers still care for their children, and 46% of patients still have positive family relationships.

It is likely that the degree of psychosocial deterioration patients present relates to their precrack level of functioning and corresponds to the severity of the addiction. Future, more elaborate analysis of these variables needs to be undertaken in research studies. But most important, psychosocial data and information on general life problems represent additional pieces of the puzzle that patients present and that clinicians must consider in order to understand the development of crack dependence, the nature of the treatment challenge, and issues in treatment planning. Despite the limitations in trying to generalize these findings on an inner-city African-American sample (Wallace, 1990b) to other crack smokers, it is likely that diversity and a more complex reality than captured by media stereotypes also characterize other samples of crack-dependent patients with different demographics.

II

THEORY AND IMPLICATIONS FOR CLINICAL TECHNIQUE

4

Pharmacological Approaches

A biopsychosocial model of crack addition assists in the identification of probable etiological factors in the development of an addiction. Biological, psychological, and social factors may prove to be etiological factors from which corresponding treatment interventions logically arise. In this way, we may arrive at a theoretical rationale for specific kinds of treatment interventions. This approach follows Marlatt (1988), who asks, "Is it possible to match treatment modality with specific etiological factors. . . ?" (p. 476). The selection of specific treatment modalities that address biological, psychological, or social etiological factors may logically follow from a consideration of etiology. Knowledge of etiology therefore may facilitate matching patients to specific treatments. One of the guiding principles behind the use of a biopsychosocial model of addiction is that careful assessment determines which specific treatment interventions are necessary for individual patients (Donovan & Marlatt, 1988). However, before considering assessment (Chapter 10) and the process of matching patients to treatment modalities, we must present the theoretical rationale for the use of treatment interventions.

A discussion of the theoretical rationale for utilizing pharmacological adjuncts with crack smokers follows from recognizing biological variables that may play a role in the etiology of crack addiction. In Chapter 1, we saw that the pharmacological and neurological actions of crack cocaine on the human brain are partly responsible for the development of compulsive crack smoking and, therefore, for the development of addiction, or crack dependence. Using our knowledge of etiological factors as a rationale for treatment, it follows that the neurochemical disruptions created in the brain of the crack user suggest the necessity of using pharmacological adjuncts in the treatment of the addiction.

WHY USE PHARMACOLOGICAL ADJUNCTS?

It cannot be assumed that all patients will require the use of pharmacological adjuncts. However, for crack patients presenting with crack dependence and

sharing many common features, routine consideration of pharmacological adjuncts may be important to maximize the chances of a successful recovery. Having noted in Chapter 3 the kind of daily or nearly daily high-dose crack
smoking we observed as predominating among the patients in Wallace's (1990b)
sample, we can appreciate how chronic or compulsive crack smokers likely have
instigated neurochemical changes in their brain function, and also have probably neglected their diet and nutrition. Even though scientific knowledge of
brain neurochemistry and of brain and cocaine interactions is limited, a rationale for utilizing pharmacological adjuncts exists in the literature. The use of
different strategies in restoring and addressing neurochemical disruptions in
brain function caused by crack cocaine reflects the state of the relatively new
and experimental treatment modality of providing chemotherapies, medications, or pharmacological adjuncts to crack and cocaine patients. Nonetheless,
a biopsychosocial model of crack addiction appreciates the importance of experimental pharmacology and the rationale for treating crack dependence with
pharmacological adjuncts. However, we must also recognize that the variety of
approaches to utilizing pharmacological adjuncts, diverse strategies, hypotheses, and research approaches all reflect the need for more research in this experimental field. The urgency of the crack-cocaine epidemic necessitates that this
research be done and that patients benefit from available knowledge by receiving safe and promising treatments as suggested by research findings.

Pharmacological Adjuncts as Relapse Prevention

The provision of pharmacological adjuncts can actually be thought of not
only as a treatment intervention, but also as a form of relapse prevention.
Pharmacological adjuncts may assist patients in maintaining abstinence. For
example, early departure from a range of treatment modalities (inpatient, outpatient, residential) may reflect patients' exercising their right to sign out of facilities (often against medical advice) or to terminate participation in treatment
in order to satisfy powerful cravings for crack. The field of chemical-dependency treatment may improve treatment outcome by assessing patients for the
provision of pharmacological adjuncts, while keeping pace with experimental
research findings that prove which adjuncts are best for which kinds of patients. Several perspectives on and approaches to the use of pharmacological
adjuncts prevail in this field, which is admittedly in its infancy, and merit
examination.

Use in Specific Phases of Recovery

Herridge and Gold (1988) recognize that pharmacological adjuncts may play
a specific role in the early withdrawal phase when a patient is attempting initial

abstinence from crack cocaine, and another role in the next two to three months of early abstinence. They challenge the widely held belief that "in the early phase of cocaine withdrawal the symptoms are mild and do not require treatment" (p. 238). However, they also argue the importance of an alternative view, which recognizes that drug craving in particular—which is a "powerful brain-driven force that tends to make patients behave in whatever way will insure the acquisition and ingestion of cocaine" (p. 238)—justifies the use of pharmacological adjuncts in the withdrawal phase. This first phase may last up to four days, and also includes symptoms of agitation and anorexia, followed by fatigue, exhaustion, depression, hyperphagia, hypersomnia, and diminished craving. The use of pharmacological adjuncts in this early phase of withdrawal may be critical to prevent patients from signing out of treatment and resuming their use of crack cocaine.

Following the conceptualization of Herridge and Gold (1988), we might view the use of pharmacological agents as for either the four-day withdrawal period or the second phase following withdrawal, which may last up to ten weeks. While mood and sleep normalize in the second phase, a powerful craving for cocaine may still arise, especially in response to stimuli associated with cocaine use. There remains a great danger of relapse during this second phase in which crack cravings may spontaneously reoccur or may be triggered by environmental cues. Since antidepressants require three weeks to take effect, Herridge and Gold recognize the value of the antidepressant desipramine in reducing cravings in the second phase (p. 238), citing reports that it can reduce cocaine cravings and facilitate abstinence (Tennant, Rawson, & McCann, 1981).

Gawin (1989) refers to the four-day withdrawal period as the "crash," while Herridge and Gold (1988) call it the withdrawal period. Gawin likens the crash to a hangover characterized by agitation. Also, Gawin views the first phase of a crash as followed by what he refers to as a one- to ten-week withdrawal phase; this is the same "up to ten week" second phase to which Herridge and Gold refer, although their terminology differs. Within Gawin's system, after the four-day crash terminates, anhedonia gradually begins to appear and cravings begin to become a problem. At this point, the withdrawal and anhedonia characteristic of this second phase involve a biological component, according to Gawin. Patients feel boredom in association with the anhedonia, do not experience normal pleasures, and find life to be empty, shallow, and pale (Gawin, 1989).

Based on animal research studies with rats, Gawin follows a strategy whereby the provision of antidepressants is geared toward normalization of the brain reward center, which, as explained in Chapter 1, is deleteriously affected by crack use. Gawin sees the administration of antidepressants during the one- to ten-week withdrawal phase as facilitating the discontinuation of cocaine use, decreasing cravings, and permitting the achievement of abstinence. In addition, Gawin recognizes, as do Herridge and Gold, the great danger of relapse in re-

TABLE 4.1
Phase-Specific Pharmacological Approaches

Researcher	Setting	Phases Recognized	Length of Phase	Adjunct Administered
Herridge and Gold (1988)	Inpatient	1. Withdrawal	1 to 4 days	Bromocriptine
		2. Second phase	1 to 10 weeks	N/A
Gawin (1989)	Outpatient	1. Crash	1 to 4 days	Desipramine
		2. Withdrawal	1 to 10 weeks	Desipramine

sponse to conditioned cues, so he cites an indefinite time period of a third phase, which he calls the extinction phase—suggesting that extinction to conditioned cues goes on indefinitely. Although Herridge and Gold and Gawin use different terminology and language, they describe a period of initial abstinence lasting up to four days and a second period of continuing symptoms that lasts up to ten weeks.

During the early initial period of withdrawal, Herridge and Gold (1988) recommend the use of bromocriptine. For the second period of prolonged abstinence (or avoiding relapse), Gawin recommends the use of desipramine, whereas Herridge and Gold concur in recognizing the potential value of this particular approach during the second phase after the initial withdrawal.

Individual Classes of Agents vs A More Complete Approach

Trachtenberg and Blum (1988) refer to four classes of medications and nutritional/neurochemical agents that are in current use: antidepressants (desipramine, imipramine, trazodone, phenelzine, lithium); antipsychotics (chlorpromazine, fluphenazine); antiparkinsonian agents (bromocriptine, amantadine, levodopa); and amino acids (tyrosine, tryptophan), and aminoacid, vitamin, and mineral mixtures. Instead of advocating the use of just one class of agents, Trachtenberg and Blum suggest a more complete approach and aim to address neurochemical changes involving the functioning not only of dopamine, but also of norepinephrine, serotonin, opioid peptides, GABA, and acetylcholine. They also recognize that chronic cocaine use results in alterations to the number and affinity of transmitter receptors as well as the anatomical connections involving these neurons (Banerjee et al., 1979; Borison et al., 1979; Chanda, Sharma, & Banjeree, 1979; Taylor, Ho, & Fagen, 1979). Moreover, Trachtenberg and Blum appreciate that these profound alterations can require prolonged recovery (Gold & Washton, 1987; Nunes & Rosecan, 1987).

Trachtenberg and Blum recognize that most contemporary approaches focus on only some of the alterations in brain neurochemistry when treatments ad-

TABLE 4.2
A More Complete Pharmacological Approach

Researcher	Goal	Systems Addressed	Adjunct Administered
Trachtenberg and Blum (1988)	To address neurochemical changes in all systems affected by cocaine	Dopamine Norepinephrine Serotonin Opioid peptides GABA Acetylcholine	*Tropamine (a nutrient containing elements to address each system)

dress only single neurotransmitter systems and presume that there is an adequate supply or prompt restoration of all the other neurotransmitter systems. Trachtenberg and Blum, therefore, argue for a more complete approach that focuses on each of the modified neurotransmitter systems. They advocate precursor amino-acid loading and enkephalin/endorphin elevation to facilitate the restoration of critical neurotransmitter deficits known to occur in cocaine abusers. They note evidence suggesting that Tropamine (Matrix Technologies, Inc.), an example of precursor amino-acid loading, effectively reduces cravings (Blum et al., 1988); they suggest a potential role, in particular, for pharmacological adjuncts that address multiple neurochemical changes—and thus provide a more complete approach to restoration of cocaine-induced neurochemical changes. The use of such adjuncts also constitutes an important relapse-prevention effort in their view.

Psychotropic Medication for Psychiatric Illness

Another prominent perspective involves the use of psychotropic medication to address preexisting or coexisting psychiatric illness. From this perspective, Rosecan and Nunes (1987) discuss the use of antidepressants, lithium, methylphenidate (and other stimulants), bromocriptine, and amino acids. The use of medication in chronic cocaine abusers follows the rationale that they suffer a greater prevalence of mood disorders (depression, manic depression, and cyclothymia) than other substance abusers. While Rosecan and Nunes recognize that accurate diagnosis of affective illness is difficult to make with active cocaine users or those in withdrawal, they cite the fact that chronic cocaine use may intensify preexisting affective illness, that cocaine may be depressogenic for some patients, and that neurochemical changes produced by chronic cocaine use appear similar to the changes found in depression as part of the rationale behind the use of medication. According to their perspective, lithium is indi-

TABLE 4.3
Medication-for-Psychiatric-Illness Approach

Rosecan and Spitz's (1987) Approach

Disorder Addressed	Medication/Pharmacological Adjunct Administered
1. Cyclothymia/manic depression	1. Lithium
2. Major depression	2. Antidepressants
3. Paranoid psychosis that does not remit within 24 hours of last · cocaine use	3. Antipsychotics
4. Refractory cases of cocaine; relapse problem	4. Bromocriptine
5. Unclear indication for use	5. Amino Acids

cated in the treatment of cyclothymia or manic-depressive illness. Where evidence of major depression exists, the use of antidepressants is indicated. Methylphenidate or other stimulants are indicated for ADD, and antipsychotic (neuroleptic) medication is indicated for the treatment of paranoid or other psychosis that does not resolve within 24 hours of cessation of cocaine use. They recognize that, from a psychiatric perspective, the only indication for the use of bromocriptine involves refractory cases of cocaine abuse where relapse is a problem; and the indication for the use of amino acids is unclear from this medication of preexisting or coexisting psychiatric illness perspective. Most important, Rosecan and Nunes (1987) validate that craving may have neurochemical correlates that involve the depletion of neurotransmitters and receptor supersensitivity (pp. 258–260).

AN INTEGRATED PERSPECTIVE AND RATIONALE FOR THE USE OF PHARMACOLOGICAL ADJUNCTS

As we saw in Chapter 2, data on the presence of mood disorders in cocaine users are fraught with problems. Diversity in the prevalence of psychopathology may best characterize research findings on the presence of mood and personality disorders. With chronic cocaine use, which best characterizes the use patterns of compulsive crack-cocaine smokers, the neurochemical disruptions tend to be even more deleterious. Also, with crack smokers, craving that may be neurochemically based has usually been a factor in the escalation from recreational-use patterns to cocaine abuse or dependence. Cravings tend to be a more common problem for crack smokers—with an associated high risk of relapse—than are documentable mood disorders.

If we integrate the perspectives of Herridge and Gold (1988), Trachtenberg and Blum (1988), and Rosecan and Nunes (1987), we may arrive at a rationale for the use of pharmacological adjuncts with crack-cocaine smokers. Most patients meeting the criteria for cocaine dependence have engaged in chronic crack smoking at a dose and frequency that may be quite high, as the data of Wallace (1990b) presented in Chapter 3 suggest. For these patients, a critical treatment intervention may be the provision of pharmacological adjuncts that facilitate achieving a stable state of abstinence. Following Herridge and Gold, it seems logical to incorporate the concept of a stage of withdrawal lasting up to four days and a second phase of ten weeks or two to three months when chances of relapse are greatest.

The author suggests the following phases of recovery from crack.

1. *Early abstinence/withdrawal phase.* This phase involves the initial period, in which patients are either in a state of withdrawal, or the period in which they may undergo a formal detoxification. This is a period of early abstinence from drugs. The first period can be seen as lasting up to 14 days. Chances of departure from treatment and immediate relapse to chemical use are very high during this time.

2. *Phase of prolonging abstinence.* This second phase involves the period after initial withdrawal when individuals attempt to prolong the time for which they are able to remain abstinent and avoid relapse. It lasts up to the first six months following the cessation of drug use. This period is typically marked by at least one "slip" or relapse episode, especially when relapse-prevention education is not an intensive part of treatment. Treatment efforts may effectively reduce chances of relapse during this period when patients are very vulnerable.

3. *Pursuing lifetime recovery.* Beyond the first six-month period of prolonging abstinence, a third period extends to include anywhere from one to several years or a lifetime of recovery. During the first year of recovery in particular, a danger of relapse to crack or the development of an addiction to other drugs exists. A risk of relapse following from the spontaneous reemergence of cravings, or cravings arising on the anniversaries of past large cocaine use (New Year's Eve) or in response to an individual's conditioned cues for chemical use (a reward for hard work, a celebration) make the first few years of recovery rather hazardous as well. Decisions regarding the avoidance of social drinking and recreational drug use are critical for recovering individuals in this phase. Treatment that decreases the likelihood of engagement in compulsive, destructive behaviors of any kind is important. Recovery must be pursued for the rest of one's life because a great chance of relapse exists when one is under a great deal of stress, as when a loved one dies, a job is lost, at retirement, or in response to any significant stressor. Reengagement in anonymous self-help groups or support in therapy can prevent a relapse—even after years since last chemical use or contact with treatment professionals—at these stressful times. Education informs patients to reengage in treatment as prevention against relapse when

major life stress occurs, regardless of the number of years of abstinence one has under one's belt.

Pharmacological adjuncts should be conceived as addressing cocaine-induced neurochemical changes in the early abstinence/withdrawal phase when intense cravings may lead to relapse, or alternatively, as facilitating the process of recovery by decreasing cravings after the immediate period of withdrawal. Patients should be viewed as either attempting early initial abstinence in the first days following crack use, or as attempting to prolong periods of abstinence, after having gone through the period of early initial abstinence or a withdrawal phase. We should also recognize the task of pursuing lifetime recovery and the kind of psychiatric symptoms or risk of relapse patients face even in this period. The role, kind, and purpose of an adjunct might vary, depending on the phase of abstinence a patient is navigating.

Following Trachtenberg and Blum (1988), a more complete approach that focuses on each of the modified neurotransmitter systems and involves precursor amino loading and enkephalin/endorphin elevation may be worthy of implementation to reduce craving and foster relapse prevention. We get from their conceptualization the notion that an approach to just one neurotransmitter system may be incomplete. Even more important, we get the clearly stated concept that the use of pharmacological adjuncts constitutes relapse prevention. From the perspective of Trachtenberg and Blum, a consideration of side effects suggests that desipramine and amantadine may be the most ethical drugs to use, and also the most successful in reducing cravings. However, each operates better in a situation where the stores of dopamine, norepinephrine, and serotonin are near normal levels. The provision of neurotransmitter precursors can promote the attainment of nearly normal neurotransmitter levels and promote the effectiveness of desipramine and amantadine (p. 329). Thus, a more complete approach, or one combining agents from different classes, emerges as an important contribution on how to utilize pharmacological adjuncts as part of an overall strategy of relapse prevention.

If we follow the perspective of Rosecan and Nunes (1987), a careful assessment may reveal cases where a preexisting or coexisting mood disorder requires specific psychotropic medication. Even where the use of an antidepressant such as desipramine (or imipramine or trazodone) is indicated to treat major depression, evidence suggests that amino-acid precursor loading with L-tyrosine improves the effectiveness of antidepressant medication, and thereby supports the assertion of Trachtenberg and Blum that a more complete approach combining agents from different classes should be used by professionals. The idea that individualized assessment should be utilized is consistent with the goals of a biopsychosocial model that strives to match individual patients to treatment tailored to address their needs. It logically follows that some cases may indicate the use of medication to address a bipolar disorder or residual ADD.

TABLE 4.4
Suggested Pharmacological Approach for the Crack Dependent

Phase Length and Name	Features of Crack Smokers in Each Phase	Pharmacological Approach for Phase
Phase I Day 1–14 (Withdrawal Phase)	• Intense cravings • Crack dreams • High risk of relapse • Risk of departing treatment • Psychotic reactions or psychiatric history for psychosis, bipolar disorder, ADD, Major depressive illness	• Pharmacological adjuncts to address several systems. • Assessment for medication
Phase II First three months to six months (Prolonging Abstinence)	• Intermittent cravings: some spontaneous, others in response to environmental and internal emotional cues • Preexisting psychopathology	• Antidepressants • Assessment for other psychiatric medication
Phase III Six months onward (Lifetime Recovery)	• Intermittent cravings: some spontaneous, others in response to environmental and internal emotional cues (anniversary dates of past cocaine use, personal cues) • Underlying psychopathology and/or brain-based anhedonia from cocaine use?	• antidepressants(?) • Continuing assessment or psychiatric medication

However, because of the problems with diagnosing mood disorders in cocaine-using or newly abstinent patients, a stronger rationale for the use of pharmacological adjuncts may be to address neurochemical disruptions in brain chemistry and the cravings they produce. Hence the standard for selecting pharmacological adjuncts for the initial period of abstinence, or the phase of withdrawal, is to restore a neurochemical balance in the brain of the user, which was disrupted by chronic crack smoking. When an individual moves beyond early initial abstinence, withdrawal is no longer an issue, and a more accurate diagnosis of mood disorder becomes possible; in the second or third week of abstinence, a rationale for the use of psychotropic medications may be to address mental disorders. Although, even in this phase where periods of abstinence are prolonged and relapse prevented, the use of antidepressants may reduce cravings and address anhedonia, as Gawin (1989) suggests; but, in combination with other classes of drugs (amino acids), greater efficacy in accomplishing this goal is likely with antidepressants (Trachtenberg & Blum, 1988).

IMPLICATIONS OF THEORY FOR TREATMENT

Following this analysis, it may be that a straightforward pharmacological plan involves the provision of amino acids, nutritional supplements, or a combination of agents from various classes to patients while they are in withdrawal, the purpose being to address the craving for crack cocaine and the neurochemical disruptions in brain function. The use of amino acids, vitamins, or a combination of agents can also serve as preparation for the provision of antidepressant medication down the road—when the goal is to prolong the period of abstinence, and also to avoid relapse; at this time, assessments of mood disorders in patients are more clearly a reflection of preexisting or coexisting psychiatric illness. By this time, amino acids will have restored neurotransmitter levels to more normal levels, facilitating the action of antidepressants.

A cautionary note is in order here, as this discussion must remain in the realm of speculation since the field of experimental pharmacology is still in its infancy. Decisions on the utilization of pharmacological adjuncts or chemotherapies remain with medical professionals who must continue to conduct research to find which strategies ultimately will prove most effective with which kinds of patients.

However, what emerges as most important is the view of Herridge and Gold (1988), who suggest that professionals may be remiss in assuming that the withdrawal syndrome associated with cocaine is so benign that pharmacological interventions are not necessary. Indeed, with crack in particular, the neurochemical disruptions created in the brain of the crack smoker may be so deleterious, and neurochemically based crack cravings may be so intense that treatment professionals may be safer in assuming that restoration of brain chemistry should be pursued through the use of safe pharmacological adjuncts that require very little indication for use other than a diagnosis of crack dependence. This may be crucial in the early initial period of abstinence or withdrawal so that cravings will not lead to departure from treatment and relapse to crack use.

Limitations of Pharmacological Adjuncts as a Treatment Tool

It might be debated that in later phases, beyond withdrawal, or when patients are attempting to prolong abstinence, nonpharmacological interventions or a range of behavioral and other interventions might best address spontaneous cravings and cravings that occur in response to conditioned environmental stimuli. The use of pharmacological interventions in preparation for such cravings might be judged as inappropriate and as reinforcing the concept that chemicals can be used for self-regulation. It is crucial, instead, that treatments strengthen patients' ability to regulate their behavior and spontaneous impulses, feelings, and cravings. In fact, evidence suggests that the experience of poorly regulated feelings may precede the occurrence of cravings in a chain of events that characterizes a relapse episode (Wallace, 1989a). An inability to identify, label, process, or manage feeling states may be a significant factor in patients' lives. A relapse or return to chemical use may be a response to negative feeling states and represent an attempt to seek relief or assistance in managing them; environmental cues are not always responsible for triggering cravings or instigating a relapse episode—internal states can do this as well.

The anhedonia that characterizes early stages of recovery after the period of withdrawal (Rawson, 1989; Gawin, 1989) may be a result of neurochemical events in the brain brought about by cocaine use, as Gawin suggests; or anhedonia may be one among many defensive and/or emotional states that result when an individual has yet to learn how to identify, label, process, and manage negative feelings states and to function emotionally without the use of stimulant chemicals. Since chemicals have provided feelings of pleasure and accompanied sexual activities, "partying," and other pleasurable recreational pastimes, an individual may appear unable to experience pleasure. A posthedonistic period of compulsive crack smoking that is followed by anhedonia may reflect a rebound phenomenon, a brain-based phenomenon, a return to a baseline personality unable to process and experience feelings in a normal fashion, or an interaction of these probable processes. Practically speaking, the individual may not "know how to" have sex, to relax, or to feel without crack cocaine, having developed a psychological dependence on this substance that accompanied such activities on innumerable occasions. This alternative explanation of what appears as an anhedonia may be plausible.

Education and therapeutic support and direction in managing these states and learning to identify, label, feel, and process emotions and cravings without resort to crack smoking or self-medication strategies may be a viable treatment intervention in the second phase of recovery—beyond initial withdrawal—when the goal is to prolong the period of abstinence. Indeed, we may deceive patients by suggesting that long-term provision of a chemical or medication is a solution to their emotional and behavioral problems. Self-medication may have been in response to the very symptoms of anhedonia, depression, and anxiety that reemerge (perhaps exacerbated by a year of not feeling emotions in a natural drug-free state) after achieving abstinence from crack cocaine.

On the other hand, not evaluating patients for the provision of antidepressant medication can constitute an ethical neglect of some patients' needs or a failure to recognize disruptions to the brain's reward center, as Gawin (1989) suggests. Only careful, individualized assessment of a patient's history, past and current functioning, mental status, and responses throughout treatment can determine when a strategy is to be recommended and for whom. According to Gawin, individual metabolism as it interacts with desipramine in the first few days of administration is the best single predictor of who has a good chance of responding positively to its further administration on an outpatient basis, and for whom an inpatient setting is required when desipramine's actions are not likely to help in securing abstinence.

CONCLUSION

This chapter has reviewed the theoretical rationale for the use of pharmacological adjuncts with the crack-cocaine-dependent person. Our knowledge of the etiology of chronic compulsive crack smoking in cocaine-induced disruptions in brain function that create the need for more cocaine directs the selection of pharmacological adjuncts to rectify neurochemical imbalances in brain function and receptor sensitivity. Pharmacological adjuncts might be best used during early initial stages of abstinence or for the withdrawal syndrome that has the critical feature of the intense crack cravings that seem to be neurochemically based following chronic crack smoking. The use of pharmacological adjuncts may also be logical following a relapse or a return to chronic crack smoking. This is in accordance with the logic that chronic crack smoking leads to deleterious changes in brain neurochemistry and that crack cravings that may be neurochemically based may lead to a resumption of compulsive smoking.

Ideally, treatment should strive to provide patients with the best possible chances of successfully establishing a stable state of abstinence while reducing the chances of relapse. The use of safe pharmacological adjuncts in early initial abstinence, or withdrawal, might be a critical element of treatment. While an individualized assessment determines whether a patient requires psychotropic medication for a preexisting or coexisting psychiatric or mood disorder, antidepressants are utilized to address cocaine-induced neurochemical disruptions and to reduce crack cravings in the second phase of prolonging abstinence after the first phase of withdrawal.

Given the infancy of the research on the use of pharmacological adjuncts as treatment for cocaine abuse and cocaine dependence, practitioners must keep pace with experimental research findings. Pharmacological adjuncts that are safe, have a sound rationale for their use, are ethical, and promise to play a role in reducing cravings and promoting the successful recovery of patients must emerge from double-blind, controlled, placebo studies with a sufficient number of subjects. Unfortunately, mostly open trials and studies with as few as one or eight subjects are the basis of much of our understanding in this nascent field. Fortunately, some quality research is currently under way (Gawin, 1989) and foreseen down the road (Rawson, 1989).

It is important that medically supervised provision of appropriate pharmacological adjuncts be appreciated as relapse prevention. While Trachtenberg and Blum (1989) led the way in asserting that the use of pharmacological adjuncts serves to prevent relapse, the field of chemical dependency must follow in recognizing that crack-cocaine dependence and the associated high risk of relapse must be stridently addressed. If patients are successfully to negotiate the very first, initial phase of withdrawal and make progress toward prolonging the period of abstinence into a stable period of recovery, the dysphoria and withdrawal of the initial phase must be respected as a difficult challenge that often leads to patient relapse and a return to crack use.

Pharmacological adjuncts may be crucial in permitting patients to achieve initial abstinence and in going through the period of withdrawal. Only these patients will remain as candidates for prolonging abstinence in a second phase beyond withdrawal. To avoid relapse and proceed toward a stable recovery, pharmacological adjuncts may play a valuable role in helping patients attain a state of abstinence. Thus, the concept of the provision of pharmacological adjuncts (in specific phases of recovery) as relapse prevention emerges as a central notion in designing effective crack-cocaine treatments.

5

Psychoanalytic Approaches

This chapter provides a theoretical rationale for the utilization of a psychoanalytic approach with the crack-cocaine-dependent person. Crack-cocaine smokers may have been placed at risk for escalation to dependence on crack as a consequence of exposure to a range of dysfunctional family dynamics in childhood. Implications for treating crack-cocaine smokers are also discussed.

ADULT CHILDREN OF ALCOHOLIC AND
DYSFUNCTIONAL FAMILIES

A number of authors have discussed the kinds of emotional and psychological problems that characterize many of the 28 million adult children of alcoholics (ACAs) in the United States (Cermak, 1988). Researchers emphasize problems with intimacy, trust, control, and difficulty in identifying or expressing feelings (Ackerman, 1987; Woititz, 1983, 1985; Black, 1981, 1985; Wanck, 1985; Cermak & Brown, 1982). The ACA self-help movement, professionally led groups for ACAs, and creative therapeutic approaches have literally blossomed into a national phenomenon in recognition of the range of emotional and personality problems these people possess (Cutter & Cutter, 1987; Downing & Walker, 1987; Wegscheider-Cruse, 1986; Tuchfeld, 1986; Gravitz & Bowden, 1986; Brown & Beletsis, 1986; Seixas & Levitan, 1984; Cermak & Brown, 1982).

Black (1985) expands her discussion of the characteristics of ACAs to include children from a vast array of dysfunctional families. According to Black, the problem in a dysfunctional family may be alcoholism, physical abuse, sexual abuse, overeating, or mental illness—to name a few. Adult children from dysfunctional families (ACDFs) may require professional treatment or the support of self-help groups in an effort to address therapeutically the consequences of their childhood development.

A Consequence of ACA Status: A Susceptibility to Alcoholism

Within the literature, there is substantial discussion of the danger that ACAs themselves will enter into a pattern of abuse of and dependence on alcohol (Cermak & Brown, 1982; Black, 1981). In fact, the alcoholism rate for ACAs is four times greater than the rate for the general population (Goodwin et al., 1973). Moreover, the path of recovery from alcoholism seems more precarious for ACAs, since they suffer higher relapse rates than alcoholics without ACA status (Wanck, 1985). Studies emphasize a genetic predisposition for the development of alcoholism in children of alcoholics, particularly sons of alcoholics (Goodwin, 1976, 1979; Goodwin, Shulsinger, Hermansen, et al., 1973). However, the role of environmental factors remains important (Cloninger, 1983). Levin (1987) points out that "children of alcoholics are at extremely high risk for alcoholism, although this is not necessarily, and certainly not exclusively on a genetic basis" (p. 56). Blum (1988) summarizes some of the remarkable progress being made in researching the causes of alcoholism, citing findings that ACAs were found to have lower plasma beta-endorphin levels (p. 1).

Growing Recognition of a Risk for Chemical Dependency

A few authors discuss the predisposition of ACAs for entering into a pattern of abuse of or dependence on other chemicals (Washton, 1989a; Anderson, 1986; Black, 1985; Mirin, Weiss, & Michael, 1986). Data on crack smokers suggest that the abuse of chemicals or a predisposition for the development of chemical dependency may be yet another problem characterizing ACAs and ACDFs; among the psychosocial characteristics possessed by crack-cocaine smokers, we saw in Chapter 3 that ACA (51%) and ACDF (91%) status were most striking (Wallace, 1990b). In Wallace's sample of crack-cocaine smokers, dysfunctional family dynamics include alcoholism, domestic violence, parental abandonment or separation, and physical, sexual, and emotional abuse. Clinicians and researchers must recognize the ACA's and ACDF's risk for involvement with chemicals other than alcohol.

Unraveling Etiological Roots of Addiction

A number of authors recognize that even where biological predisposition is carefully considered in the etiology of addiction, considerations of psychopathology remain important for treatment planning (Levin, 1987; Allen & Frances, 1986; Hesselbrock, 1986a). Marlatt (1988) notes that various conflicting theoretical positions have been put forth to explain the antecedents and determinants of addiction, along with corresponding recommendations for treatment. Among these, "some approaches favor a disease model of etiology, whereas others focus more upon acquired psychosocial factors" (Marlatt, 1988, p. 475). Perhaps most comprehensive are those approaches that utilize a "multivariate model of etiology, in which addiction is defined as a 'biopsychosocial' disorder" (Marlatt, 1988, p. 475). Thus, our consideration of acquired psychosocial factors in this chapter may unravel just one dimension of the etiology of addiction within a biopsychosocial model of crack addiction.

OBJECT-RELATIONS THEORY

For the newborn infant and throughout a child's development, the most important objects remain those human beings who provide nurturance and perform the primary caretaking function. Object-relations theory traces the psychological and emotional implications of our history of interpersonal relations with our primary caretakers. Kernberg (1975, 1976, 1986) articulates an object-relations theory and clinical psychoanalysis that integrate important aspects of Freudian psychoanalysis, the British school of object relations, and American ego psychology while also outlining treatment recommendations. Some of Kernberg's (1976) early theoretical formulations, particularly his concept of internalized memories of interactions with parental figures in the form of self–object–affect units, permit the author to describe the probable impact of childhood trauma in dysfunctional families.

In this regard, Kernberg states that "(o)bject-relations theory may refer to the general theory of the structures in the mind which preserve interpersonal experiences and the mutual influences between these intrapsychic structures and the overall vicissitudes of expression of instinctual needs in the psychosocial environment" (p. 56). It therefore includes "all the vicissitudes of the relationship between the intrapsychic and the interpersonal fields" (p. 56). He further asserts that his theory is useful in understanding various processes of internalization, regressive types of character pathology with problems of identity, chronic types of marital conflicts, the depth and stability of internal relations with others, the capacity for tolerating guilt and separation, the working through of depressive crises, and the extent to which the self concept is integrated (pp. 58–59). Kernberg's theory may help us to understand the consequences of crack smokers' having internalized interactions with far-from-ideal parental figures in dysfunctional families, and the task of managing the trauma of crack addiction by an individual left with a regressive type of character pathology as a consequence of childhood object relations.

Internalization of Object Relations

For Kernberg (1976), internalization is a broad concept that encompasses the subordinate concepts of introjection, identification, and ego identity (p. 76). Introjections occur earliest in development on a most primitive level, and involve the reproduction and fixation of an interaction with objects in the environment. A cluster of memory traces results that is made up of an image of the object, the image of the self in interaction with the object, and the affective coloring of both the object-image and self-image. This affective coloring or valence takes place under the influence of a libidinal or aggressive drive. Introjections may have a positive valence or coloring such as the loving mother–child interaction engendered by a drive of libidinal gratification. Or, alternatively, a mother–child interaction may take place under a negative valence or coloring where an aggressive drive prevails. In this very early stage of internalization processes, self-images occurring under a positive affective valence fuse, as do those under a negative affective valence; object images of the same affective valence also fuse together. This fusion contributes to the process of differentiation of self- and object-images, and is seen in early infancy (pp. 29–30).

Identification, the second higher-level form of introjection in Kernberg's (1976) scheme, requires that the young child be able to perceive the role aspects of interpersonal interactions. On this level, the cluster of memory traces involves the image of the object adopting a role in an interaction with the self, the image of the self more clearly differentiated from the object (compared with the earlier level), and the affective coloring of the interaction where the affect is more differentiated and less intense than on the earlier level. Identification as a process of higher-level internalization of object relations first appears in the last quarter of the first year of life, but becomes more fully developed during the second year of life. The best example or evidence of identification as a process of internalization of object relations is the imitation of the mother's behavior by the young child (pp. 30–31).

Within Kernberg's system, ego identity represents the highest level in the organization of internalization processes and captures the overall organization of identifications and introjections. Although very primitive, distorted object-images continue to exist in the unconscious mind, most primitive identifications in normal development are gradually replaced by selective, partial identifications. As development proceeds, only those aspects of object relations are internalized that are in harmony with the individual's identity formation; here we identify with people whom we love and admire in a realistic way, culminating in the establishment of a well-integrated ego identity (pp. 31–34).

Self–Object–Affect Units

A pathological outcome that may occur in the course of development as a consequence of conflict-laden or severely disturbed early object relations is intimately related to the pathological development of splitting, as Kernberg (1976) points out. Kernberg also elucidates how splitting interferes with the successful integration of self- and object-images. In such cases of fixation, primitive identifications or "nonmetabolized" early introjections remain and may come to the surface. We observe these not as "free floating" internal objects but as crystallized ego structures (p. 34).

We can think of the structure or organization of these primitive identifications (or "nonmetabolized" early introjections) as involving memory traces of interactions composed of an image of the self, an image of the object, and the associated affective valence with related libidinal or aggressive drive. Kernberg's (1976) self–object–affect units (S-O-As) capture these internalized object relations or internalized memories of interactions with parents. S-O-As may come to the surface as crystallized ego structures.

As Kernberg elaborates, "Affects organize internalized object relations into the overall structures of the mind and, simultaneously, organize aggression and libido as the major drives" (p. 114). Regarding aggression, he says, the "inward direction of aggression is normally elaborated in stable internalized object relations. . . , thereby guaranteeing the successful neutralization of aggression. The failure of this adaptive intrapsychic channeling of aggression may be considered, in broad terms, one reason for self-destructiveness in man" (p. 115).

The legacy of unmetabolized S-O-As also relates to the outcome of narcissism. For Kernberg, narcissism cannot be analyzed separately from internalized object relations or affect dispositions. "The development of normal and pathological narcissism always involves the relationship of the self to object-representation and external objects, as well as the struggle between love and aggression" (p. 116) where libidinal or aggressive impulses accompany either positive or negative affects. In summary, self–object–affect units are "primarily determinants of the overall structures of the mind (id, ego, and superego)" (p. 57) and affect our expression of aggressive and libidinal drives. The importance of S-O-As or internalized object relations, their quality, the consequences for the expression of aggression or self-destructiveness, and their significance for one's overall psychological and emotional functioning cannot be overemphasized. How do we most often become aware of the presence of S-O-As as crystallized ego structures?

Transference Manifestations

For Kernberg (1976), "Active transference dispositions consistently reveal the activation of units of self- and object-representation linked by a particular affect disposition" (p. 79). From the perspective of the clinician, early conflict-laden object relations may be activated prematurely in the transference in connection with ego states that are split off from each other (p. 21). Splitting of the ego serves the essential function of protecting patients against anxiety. In this way, splitting represents not only a defect in the ego, but also an active defensive operation (p. 23). Transference states based on traumatic or conflict-laden interactions with parental figures may arise. When they do, they may reveal contradictory ego states that can be understood as the oscillatory activation of split-off ego states that have their origin in "nonmetabolized" or unintegrated internalized object relations (pp. 21–23).

Kernberg's conceptualizations help us to appreciate the dynamic nature of transference states or the spontaneous dynamic emergence of an S-O-A that has its origin in very early object relations. These transference states—or the appearance of autonomous affective complexes, to utilize Jung's (1969) language—or the acting out of an S-O-A involves the activation and presence of an old interpersonal dynamic from very early childhood. Kernberg's work permits recognition of the fact that aggressive and libidinal drives may also accompany the emergence or activation of an S-O-A. Thus, the manifestation of transference states represents an opportunity to witness the effects of far-from-ideal object relations.

A Range of Character Pathology

Within Kernberg's (1976) theory, either psychotic, borderline, neurotic, or higher-level character pathology such as narcissistic personalities may result, depending on when the fixation or failure in development occurs. The earliest fixation during the first month of life can result in autistic psychosis. When the fixation takes place during the second to sixth or eighth month of infancy, the symbiotic psychoses of childhood, adult schizophrenia, or depressive psychoses may follow. Fixation during the sixth or eighth month of infancy up to the third year of life, and/or regression to the stage of object relations occupying this period, brings about borderline personality organization. When a fixation or failure occurs in a stage lasting from three and a half years of age to age six or seven, the neuroses and the higher-level character pathology (hysterical, obsessive-compulsive, narcissistic, depressive-masochistic) result.

Transference manifestations of unmetabolized S-O-As vary, depending on the age at which the fixation transpired and the resulting personality organization. Splitting is characteristic of borderline personality organization, which may be contrasted with the higher defensive organization and use of repression characteristic of nonborderline character pathology and symptomatic neuroses. Kernberg goes on to explain that in borderline patients, ego states are actively kept apart (p. 65). In fact, borderline patients cannot differentiate between present and past object relations. They actually confuse transference phenomena and reality and cannot differentiate the analyst from the transference object (p. 161). In contrast, one does not observe in neurotic patients or in normal individuals "the preservation of primitive, past internalized object relations in such an unaltered condition."

In fact, within treatment, narcissistic personalities may "have difficulty evoking not only real people in their past but their own self-experiences with such people" (Kernberg, 1976, p. 73). Other manifestations of adult character pathology, such as the experience of emptiness (p. 74), persist in these cases as a consequence of experiencing far-from-ideal object relations in childhood.

In Kernberg's theory, the final outcome of internalization processes, or of pathological identification processes with parental figures, is character pathology (p. 79). He asserts that the character structure represents the automatized, predominantly behavioral aspects of ego identity (p. 73). Furthermore, he explains that, within psychoanalytic treatment, character traits of patients reveal how pathological object relations have been internalized and become "frozen" into a character pattern (p. 79). Thus, adult character permits observation of the impact of far-from-ideal object relations in childhood.

Adult character pathology varies, as does the response of the clinician when confronted with different manifestations of far-from-ideal object relations in treatment. Kernberg acknowledges that developments and modifications in psychoanalytic technique provide clinicians with an armamentarium of psychotherapeutic tools. Careful diagnosis of patients so we can appreciate the nature of their character pathology and the degree of its severity can "improve our capacity for optimal individualization of psychological treatment" (p. 157). Kernberg's classification of character pathology may permit such careful diagnosis. He recognizes that three main levels of instinctual fixation can be encountered by clinicians—high, intermediate, and low (p. 141).

Higher-Level Character Pathology

Kernberg (1976) explains that at the higher level of organization of character pathology, patients have a relatively well-integrated but punitive superego. A well-integrated ego and an ego identity have been achieved, along with a stable self-concept. Use of repression as a defense appears excessively in response to unconscious conflicts. Character defenses (fixed patterns of behavior) involve those mostly of an inhibitory or phobic nature, which are reaction formations against repressed instinctual needs. Partial inhibition of the expression of sexual or aggressive drives prevails. Ego constriction follows from the excessive use of neurotic defense mechanisms, yet overall social adaptation is not seriously impaired at this high level of character pathology (pp. 143–144). These adult manifestations of far-from-ideal object relations, when the consequences are relatively mild, remind us of how the kind and quality of internalized S-O-As capturing interpersonal relations with parental figures affect the expression of aggressive and libidinal drives and the very structure and functioning of the ego, id, and superego.

Intermediate Character Pathology

At the intermediate level of organization of character pathology, Kernberg (1976) explains that the superego is even more punitive and in addition it is not well integrated. This results in the person feeling demands from the superego to be great, powerful, and physically attractive. Demands for moral perfection also abound. Dissociated expressions of unacceptable sexual and/or aggressive needs and a "structured impulsivity" in certain other areas may prevail. The dissociation of contradictory ego states, or some use of splitting as a defense may occur, along with projection and denial, although repression is still the main defensive operation of the ego at this stage. Oral or pregenital features are present, representing a regression from oedipal conflicts. Object relations are stable, a capacity for deep involvements with others exists, along with a tolerance for the conflict that may characterize these relationships (pp. 144–145).

Lower-Level Character Pathology

At the lower level of organization of character pathology, Kernberg (1976) points out that superego integration is minimal. A primitive form of projection occurs. The ego and superego structures are not delimited and the ego uses primitive dissociation or splitting as its central defensive operation. Splitting involves the alternation of contradictory ego states and is reinforced by the use of denial, projective identification, primitive idealization, devaluation, and omnipotence. Individuals on this lower level lack an integrated self-concept, lack empathy for objects, maintain object relations of a need-gratifying or a threatening nature, and experience identity diffusion. Ego weakness prevails and can be seen in lack of anxiety tolerance, lack of impulsive control, and chronic failure in the area of work (pp. 145–147).

A Continuum of Outcomes: Normality

Kernberg (1976) emphasizes that we must appreciate the possibility that normal object relations may have been attained. For Kernberg, when we approach the end of the continuum, we move toward an outcome of normality—"a well-integrated, less severe and punitive superego, realistic superego demands, an ego ideal and ego goals which permit an overall harmony in dealing with the external world, as well as with instinctual needs" (p. 151) prevail.

Clearly, an outcome as a result of experiencing a dysfunctional family dynamic may include the achievement of a normal adult character capable of healthy expression of libidinal and aggressive drives and of maintaining harmony in spite of external stressors. Thus, resiliency in the face of life's stressors and the trauma of crack addiction remains a possible outcome even among those individuals exposed to dysfunctional family dynamics in childhood. This view of a continuum of outcomes permits appreciation of the diversity to be found in the real-world samples of crack-cocaine smokers and ACDFs.

Repetition of S-O-A Dramas

Kernberg's (1976) theory may also be extended to behavioral manifestations commonly observed in ACDFs even where the criteria for DSM-III-R diagnoses of mental disorders, or mood and personality disorders, are not met. Kernberg's conceptualizations permit understanding behavioral manifestations suggesting the role of unintegrated and unmetabolized S-O-As. Many adults create transference dramas with their adult partners, playing out interpersonal dramas captured in their internalized S-O-As from childhood. Having internalized memories of how mother and father interacted, some adults now play out a drama in which they are one or the other of their parents (perhaps both at different times) from childhood and somehow get their partner to play a reciprocal role. A drama with a spouse or lover amazingly repeats dynamics directly derived from unconscious or conscious memories of how one's parents once interacted. These internalized object relations provide a script for behavior when the child who witnessed these events becomes an adult "actor."

Other individuals have taken on the role of the powerful parent (object in the internalized S-O-A) and have placed their children in the role their own childhood self once played. A child may be neglected, abandoned, or physically abused by an adult crack smoker, just as that crack smoker's parent once mistreated the crack smoker as a child. The role reversal permits mastering the old trauma and anxiety from childhood in a maladaptive fashion while damage is done to a new generation.

In this way, the legacy of partial, incomplete, and unintegrated identifications with parents dictates aspects of adult behavior for many ACDFs. Chaos and discord likely characterize the interpersonal relationships of many of these adult children as they tend to poorly regulate their own interpersonal behavior, reflecting the activation of transference states, complexes, or S-O-As from childhood. Many patients experience the conscious shock of recognition that they are living their parents' lives and doing to their children things that were done to them as children, or treating their spouses the way a parent treated the other parent; yet they feel little or no control over stopping the drama by themselves.

Compulsive Behavior in ACAs/ACDFs

ACAs/ACDFs may present problematic symptomatology that may only be neurotic, suggest mild character pathology, and fail to meet criteria for personality or mood disorders. However, their characteristics may leave them susceptible to the development of compulsive, destructive behavioral patterns, as well as chemical dependency. Clinical work with and observations of ACAs/ ACDFs suggests that compulsive behavioral patterns not involving the use of alcohol or psychoactive chemicals are prominent. Compulsive behaviors such as overeating, overexercising, going on shopping sprees, and workaholism also manifest in ACAs/ACDFs in response to stimuli that threaten to activate dysphoric states. It is as if patients anticipate the dreaded experience of a recurrent painful affective state and engage in compulsive behavior to ward off and prevent its emergence or activation. Clearly, this highlights how ACAs/ACDFs not only may discover that chemicals relieve the discomfort of dysphoric states and assist in self-regulation of self-esteem and painful affective states, but also that engagement in some compulsive behavior prevents the emergence of the dysphoria or the experience of a plummeting self-esteem. The price paid for engaging in a compulsive behavior often includes coming to terms with destructive and negative consequences of acting or making decisions in a state where one is effectively cut off from one's feelings and emotions and cognitive decision making and reality testing are deficient. However, where one was able to avoid painful affective states, the negative consequence of being overweight, "burnt out" from workaholism, or in debt may seem like fair compensation for temporary relief from dysphoric states.

Interpreting Manifestations of Narcissism in the Newly Abstinent

How can we interpret the predominance of narcissism in the newly abstinent in light of Kernberg's (1976) formulations? We may recall Levin's (1987) view that the predominance of narcissism observed in the newly abstinent reflects either a fixation or a regression to pathological narcissism. Following Bean-Bayog (1986), we are reminded that character is unable to carry out its functions when in a pathological state, or in the face of stress or trauma. The stress and trauma of crack addiction may induce a regression to a state of pathological narcissism. On the other hand, before the trauma of addiction, individuals' underlying character probably varied from lower, intermediate, and higher levels of character pathology to normality. We can utilize Kernberg's proposed classification of three stages (and a fourth possibility of a normal adult character outcome) to outline the kind of fixation points and adult character patients possessed before they became addicted. The nature or severity of narcissism observed in the newly abstinent may be a function of having possessed either a higher, intermediate, or lower level of character pathology prior to addiction. The crack smoker's level of prior pathology, if any, will probably dictate how the person will handle the stress and trauma of crack addiction; in the newly abstinent, therefore, we will probably observe a range of outcomes reflecting resiliency and varying degrees of management of trauma, as well as regression varying in severity. This permits appreciation of the diversity of underlying character structures and narcissistic pathologies that may confront the clinician when treating the newly abstinent crack smoker.

Implications for Treatment

Beyond managing the varying manifestations of narcissism in the newly abstinent (see Chapters 10, 11, 14), the underlying and long-standing character pathology of patients may still require remediation to reduce the susceptibility of relapse. Assessment and appreciation of a patient's pathology will determine clinical technique in treatment. In terms of technique, Kernberg (1976) states that with patients at the higher level of character pathology, psychoanalysis may be utilized; with those at an intermediate level, psychoanalysis is still the treatment of choice unless there are contraindications; and finally, with those at the lower level of organization of character pathology, psychoanalysis is usually contraindicated in favor of a modified procedure (pp. 152–153).

Thus, Kernberg feels that the range of adult character pathology he describes can be treated, although the prognosis and length of treatment vary depending on the level of character pathology. For Kernberg, a process of human growth involves "to a great extent reshaping of the internal world on the basis of interpersonal experience" (p. 75). It therefore remains possible for a professional in the course of treating a person with character pathology to avoid taking on the kinds of unhealthy reciprocal roles and attitudes that the pathological structure of patients normally evokes in interpersonal relationships. In this way, a patient's internal world can be reshaped in the course of interpersonal experience occurring in the context of "a neutral psychoanalytic relationship" (p. 75). It is actually within the course of psychoanalysis that "the distorted images of the past are changed gradually into a more realistic perception of the parents and an understanding in depth of their values and frailties" (p. 75). With this understanding of how a legacy of having internalized conflict-laden object relations with parental figures in dysfunctional families affects adult character and personality functioning and how the internal world can be reshaped through psychoanalysis, hope exists for remedying the psychological and emotional consequences of childhood development in dysfunctional families—perhaps thereby gradually reducing the chances of relapse or involvement in self-destructive or compulsive behavior.

A NEUROBIOLOGICAL–PSYCHOANALYTIC APPROACH

The process of working through distorted images of the past and arriving at a realistic perception of parents may be more difficult where patients, such as those with narcissistic personalities, have difficulty evoking real people from their past. These individuals may not be able to recall their own self-experiences with parental figures, as Kernberg (1976) explains.

The only identifiable symptom for some patients may be a spontaneously recurring aggressive impulse, painful affective state, or bodily tension. The origin of recurrent tension, painful affective states, or aggressive impulses may lie in an interaction between one's very young, preverbal self and a far-from-ideal parental figure. Yet, the only coded memories we can readily access as adolescents or adults involve verbally coded or describable experiences. More difficult to access are memories prior to a verbal period. How can we comprehend the nature of a patient's experience when the only describable symptoms relate to emptiness, bodily tension, or physiological distress?

Meyersburg and Post (1979) help to clarify the nature of internalized object relations and symptoms of bodily tension or physiological distress, attempting a neurobiological–psychoanalytic integration in providing a holistic developmental view of neural and psychological processes establishing memories of internalized object relations:

> During the early months, the striatal and limbic systems subserve the tasks of integrating and storing emotional and perceptual experiences. As neocortical structures evolve, and as language capabilities supervene, they not only take over these functions but also tend to modulate and re-integrate the memory experiences stored in the more basic structures. Severely painful emotional loading of early experiences may establish memories which have disruptive potentialities, not only by facilitating dysphoric responses to a repetition of the earlier stimuli but possibly by exerting a delaying or inhibiting influence on the subsequent development and maturation of neural structure. . . . The dysphoric tone of these experiences is not *affective* in the usual sense associated with adult emotion, but is *organismic*, since the neural base for more differentiated experience does not yet exist. Hence, "memories" of these experiences will replicate the dysphoric tone of the primary episode as well as the general state of being which prevailed at that time. Some memory traces will consequently be inchoate, and possessed of immense organismic distress. Since they lack roots of a cognitively decipherable sort, they constitute a terrifying enigma. (p. 144)

Individuals possessing a legacy of far-from-ideal object relations with parental figures may experience a recurring dysphoria, organismic distress, or bodily based tension that seems inchoate, unaware of the relationship of these symptoms to very early childhood trauma in dysfunctional families. Patients may feel unable to articulate or describe their experience when dysphoria or a bodily based tension recurs. This kind of confusing experience may support the discovery that chemicals are extra-reinforcing when they address or alleviate bodily tension or dysphoria. A recurrent spontaneous dysphoria that seems out of a patient's control can seemingly justify the use of chemicals. At least initially, the use of chemicals may permit patients to continue a behavior and provide them with a measure of control over their affective and bodily experience. Compulsive behaviors such as the use of drugs, overeating, overexercising, going on a shopping spree, or workaholism may provide a sense of control, when such behaviors temporarily avert the emergence of anxiety or a dysphoric state that threatens to occur spontaneously.

A Lowered Threshold for Dysphoria

Meyersburg and Post (1979) have likened the spontaneous recurrence of the anxiety that may be associated with a traumatic memory of separation to the kindling phenomenon observed in laboratory animals. Unintegrated physiological activity may spontaneously take place, they say, in the following way:

> (S)ome animals, after long-term repetitive kindling stimulation, undergo what has been termed "spontaneity" . . . that is, they develop overt seizures in the absence of applied electrical stimulation. We suggest that similar activation of neural centres and memory traces important for behavioral end-points occurs, analogous to but distinct from the production of seizures. For example, separation of an infant from his mother, occurring in a particularly stressful way or in a conflictual context, may lead to the enhancement of the infant's separation dysphoria and to the setting-up of lowered threshold activity in the associated neuronal circuitry. Thus, when the individual at some later time is restressed by another separation, a resurgence of the original dysphoric pattern of reaction may supervene . . . just as a more chronically kindled animal may develop spontaneous reactivation of the kindled centres . . . so it may also be possible for the child or adult, spontaneously or following stress, to regress to a previous level of functioning independent of the recurrence of a particular stressful external situation. (pp. 148–149)

Meyersburg and Post effectively describe the mechanism by which a child or adult might regress to a previous level of functioning as a result of childhood trauma, permitting activation of an S-O-A, transference state, or inchoate dysphoria state. Childhood trauma may have established a lowered threshold for the experience of a dysphoric pattern of reaction. The notion that a trauma, such as a particularly stressful or conflictual separation from a mother early in development, enhances separation dysphoria and sets up a lowered threshold activity in the associated neuronal circuitry remains consistent with the notion of a prior fixation point being established through traumatic experiences in dysfunctional families. The individual with such a fixation point—or for whom the threshold or tolerance for stress has been lowered—is quite vulnerable to later stressors and may spontaneously experience dysphoric reactions or regress to some degree of pathological functioning.

Meyersburg and Post's views, therefore, permit an understanding of how the stress of addiction, or of being newly abstinent, or the physiological and psychological symptoms of withdrawal from chemicals such as alcohol or crack cocaine, may induce a regression to a previous level of functioning. We arrive at a deeper understanding of Levin's (1987) assertion that the narcissism in the newly abstinent reflects an infliction of narcissistic wounds (as a result of the addiction), which result in a regression to at least some degree of narcissism, if a fixation did not already exist. Although Meyersburg and Post provide an example of separation dysphoria stemming from an infant's separation from its mother, numerous scenarios are imaginable as legitimate avenues by which a lowered threshold for dysphoric reactions can become established. Traumatic interpersonal events—including overstimulation, abandonment, disappointments, and exposure to unpredictable, inconsistent, and unempathic parenting behavior—might all result in fixation points and a lowered threshold for the emergence of dysphoric reactions. In this way, a variety of parental stimuli may be damaging and constitute object relations sufficiently traumatic to result in significant consequences for functioning later in life. A range of consequences may follow as a result of possessing a lowered threshold for the experience of dysphoria, or a tendency to regress to a previous level of functioning under stress.

Disturbing Memories: Motion Pictures in the Mind

In addition to a spontaneously reoccurring organismic distress, bodily tension, aggressive impulse, or painful affective state, patients may be able to access memories of traumatic interpersonal relations with parents. Sometimes this suggests a temporary regression in the service of the ego, a structure that maintains contact with, and can still test, reality. In fact, some patients are able to recognize, or can become aware of, what can be cognitively relabeled a "motion picture in the mind" (Wallace, 1987). Some ACAs/ACDFs can close their eyes and recall vivid memories of traumatic interactions or animated family scenes that can be acted out in the mind. These memories can provide a starting point in treatment with ACAs/ACDFs, even though earlier, preverbal memories may not be describable or accessible except as symptoms of a recurrent dysphoric state. These vivid, animated memories sometimes spontaneously recur, or may be evoked by such stimuli as the recollections of another patient during group therapy.

In other cases, the regression cannot be said to be in the service of the ego;

the ego as a complex (Jung, 1969) or structure may be temporarily displaced and its functions such as an ability to test reality temporarily suspended. The spontaneous emergence of traumatic memories may meet the criteria for the post-traumatic stress disorder (PTSD) in the severely physically or sexually abused. Vivid memories may seemingly be relived in present reality or flashbacks spontaneously reoccur. Also, patients presenting dissociative disorders may suffer from recurring vivid memories of physical abuse or sexual abuse as scenes that haunt. In these cases, the appearance of autonomous complexes (Jung, 1969), or spontaneously reoccurring transference states, capturing memories of traumatic interpersonal interactions, temporarily displace the ego, and the regression to a previous level of functioning or fixation points remains a dreaded experience.

Adolescents and the Extra-Reinforcing Effect of Chemicals

Adolescents with a lowered threshold for dysphoric reactions may easily discover the extra-reinforcing properties of chemicals. Reports of children as young as 12 years of age smoking crack (Inciardi & Pottieger, 1990) suggest that even children's substance abuse may reflect the discovery that the emotional and psychological consequences of exposure to dysfunctional family dynamics and a lowered threshold for dysphoric reactions with which they may have been coping for years (and with which they still struggle on a daily basis) can be better managed with chemicals. The current stress of dysfunctional family dynamics (an incestuous parent, an alcoholic parent, physical or verbal abuse, domestic violence) may trigger powerful reactions of anxiety or dysphoric states. Some children and adolescents experience the effects of chemicals as alleviating a state of desensitization that was an adaptation to dysfunctional family dynamics, a lowered threshold for dysphoric reactions, and a tendency to regress to a previous level of functioning in the face of stress.

As a consequence of their threshold for dysphoric reactions being lowered earlier in development, some individuals probably relied on avoiding the expression of all affects or impulses, or on becoming desensitized to stimuli that triggered strong reactions of fear, anxiety, or anger with accompanying aggressive impulses. In a state of desensitization to stimuli, children express no overt emotional or behavioral reaction to stressful dysfunctional dynamics in the home. Their lack of feeling and emotional reactivity may also appear as an anhedonia. For some adolescents still at home, as well as for some adults in general, a resulting protective wall prevents them from expressing any affects or impulses. The gradual learning and rehearsal of an ability to regulate or modulate affects or impulses fails to take place throughout childhood and adolescent development as a result of the construction of a protective wall or the entering into a state of desensitization to stimuli. Emotional reactions occur and old painful affects persist, but behind a wall.

In a related vein, Barclay-McLaughlin (1989) describes a similar state of desensitization in individuals living in communities that have felt the impact of the crack war. Residents of crack-war-zone communities marked by daily gun fights and murders also use a protective wall or become desensitized. In effect, dysfunctional community dynamics might be said to prevail and may contribute to, or further compound, a susceptibility to experience chemicals as extra-reinforcing.

Chemicals may be experienced as extra-reinforcing when they temporarily relax a defensive stance, allowing feelings normally walled up to find expression. For these individuals, stimulants might provide a feeling of vitality and energy normally lacking when a defensive armor or wall serves as a barrier for the expression of affects and impulses. Sedatives might also appeal to the novice as a way temporarily to relax a rigid stance. Chemical use may serve to medicate underlying feelings of tension, anxiety, depression, or recurrent organismic distress and dysphoria.

In this way, the conceptualizations of Meyersburg and Post (1979) expand our understanding of how an individual possessing a fixation point or a history of stressful object relations with parental figures may be susceptible to the development of an addiction. By virtue of possessing a lowered threshold for the experience or resurgence of dysphoria, an inherent predisposition for finding any chemical used on an experimental basis to be extra-reinforcing exists. Chemicals may be experienced as extra-reinforcing when they allay bodily tension and dysphoria.

PTSD in Adolescent Crack Smokers

Adolescents who present with PTSD following the violence and trauma associated with the crack culture (as Pinto of Samaritan Village in New York reports: Kolata, 1989, Aug. 11, pp. A1, A13) may also reflect the consequences of a lowered threshold for dysphoric reactions and anxiety in face of significant stress. As a result of childhood exposure to far-from-ideal object relations, adolescents exposed to violence and sex in the crack culture may respond poorly to this stress and lack the kind of integrated ego structure necessary to avoid PTSD. The same individuals who are vulnerable to the development of PTSD in adolescence (in the crack war or in Vietnam) are probably those who are vulnerable to the development of dependence on chemicals; the extra-reinforcing effects of chemicals, as well as the inability to manage traumatic stressors by an ego suffering deficits stemming from a childhood in a dysfunctional family, reflect the consequences of internalized object relations determining id, ego, and superego functioning.

Also, Kernberg's (1976) formulations help us to spell out how adolescents' weak egos may fall back upon splitting when faced by a traumatic stressor such as witnessing a killing in a crack war or in Vietnam. Meyersburg and Post's (1979) work helps us to understand how even prior to the experience of trauma in the crack culture, these adolescents probably had a lowered threshold for the experience of dysphoria, and were probably already prone to experiencing spontaneously reoccurring affects and bodily tensions and to regression when confronted by stress, as a legacy of the trauma of growing up in a dysfunctional family.

Many adolescents from dysfunctional families may have carried a predisposition for such symptoms and phenomena, and no stress as yet may have been sufficient to stimulate dysphoric reactions or a regression. Yet, their earlier fixation and possibility for regression to a level where splitting as a defect in the ego and defensive operation prevail have laid the groundwork for a susceptibility to the development of PTSD or spontaneously reoccurring dysphoria. As Ackerman (1987) states, the stress of childhood may be particularly noticeable during the stresses of adulthood up until the mid-30s (pp. 42–43); here we suggest that the incredible stress of witnessing violence in the crack war makes apparent, perhaps for the first time in one's lifetime, the long-lasting impact of the stresses of childhood in a dysfunctional family. Thus, many adolescents may not be able to integrate or manage traumatic or graphically violent experiences, facilitating the spontaneous reemergence of such memories as symptoms of PTSD.

Implications for Treatment

What are the implications for treating patients who present a spontaneously reoccurring dysphoria, a lowered threshold for the experience of dysphoria in the face of stress, and a resulting tendency to regress to fixation points? Patients who have discovered that chemicals provide relief from recurrent dysphoria, bodily tension, or feelings of boredom, emptiness, or painful affect require therapeutic assistance to learn how consciously to recognize, identify, label, and process these recurrent states without resorting to chemicals for their temporary management. Learning coping skills, receiving therapeutic support, and gradually learning how to respond to and regulate these states without chemicals must be part of treatment in order to minimize the chances of relapse to chemicals or to some compulsive or destructive behavior.

Because some patients' thresholds for dysphoric reactions were lowered earlier in development, and some developed a reliance on avoiding the expression of all affects or impulses, patients will need therapeutic assistance in learning how to lower a defensive armature or wall so that they can express feelings and impulses. The relaxation of an inhibition of affect and impulses must be gradually achieved, as defensive desensitization is replaced with an ability not only to experience affects and impulses, but also to modulate and regulate their expression.

Those who can see motion pictures in the mind, or can consciously recall vivid memories of traumatic events that transpired in dysfunctional families when they were children or adolescents, must be assisted to describe these events verbally and to process the painful affects they felt at the time of the traumas. In this way, the unconscious may be made conscious and contents that young egos could not integrate may become integrated into consciousness. Issues of timing and the kind of skilled and empathic responses on the part of the therapist that are crucial to this process suggest that the very best clinical skills are needed in work with chemically dependent ACDFs. Long-term treatment may be necessary, as well.

When adolescents or children still reside in dysfunctional families (or dysfunctional communities that are crack war zones), helping professionals must provide them with consistent and nurturant object relations and an opportunity to internalize and identify with positive role models. Assistance in interpreting and coping with dysfunctional family (or community) dynamics must also be provided. These adolescents must learn to regulate and modulate affects instead of relying on defensive strategies or chemicals to cope. Empathic responses and interpretations on the part of clinicians should emphasize how behaviors and defenses may reflect an attempt to adapt to dysfunctional dynamics, but surviving this period without defensive armature, inhibitions, phobias, or maladaptive coping responses may be accomplished with therapeutic support.

Prevention of the development of chemical dependency, or some other compulsive behavior designed to ward off the emergence of dysphoric states, may therefore rest on providing treatment to adolescents and children who must cope with dysfunctional family stress and trauma. More generally speaking, prevention efforts of this kind with these children emerges as critical in light of this review of psychoanalytic (Kernberg, 1976) and psychoanalytic–biological theory (Meyersburg & Post, 1979). The high risk of developing adult character pathology, chemical dependency, and destructive compulsive behaviors may be reduced through the provision of treatment.

KOHUT'S SELF PSYCHOLOGY

Kohut (1971, 1977) recognizes certain narcissistic problems in those presenting with personality disturbances that have their root in the kinds of traumatic experiences with parental figures discussed thus far. Kohut's self psychology may utilize a different terminology in conceptualizing the consequences of childhood trauma, but his work assists in further developing a psychoanalytic rationale for specific treatment interventions with crack smokers. A thorough review of Kohut's (1971, 1977) conceptualizations is by no means attempted here. Rather, the way in which his theory may be extended to the situation of children growing up in dysfunctional families and help clarify how such children may develop a predisposition for finding chemicals extra-reinforcing is attempted.

Normal and Pathological Development

Regarding the trauma responsible for narcissistic personality disturbance, Kohut (1971) begins by discussing the normal situation where some unavoidable shortcoming in maternal care occurs. This results in the end of the previous image of perfection destroyed by the maternal (or paternal) shortcoming. One consequence is the establishment of a grandiose and exhibitionistic image of the self, the grandiose self. This permits the compensatory feeling that "I am perfect," diminishing the trauma of maternal shortcomings. The second consequence is the giving over of the perfection known before the maternal shortcoming to an admired omnipotent (transitional) self-object, the idealized parent imago. This permits the feeling of "You are perfect, but I am part of you," to preserve a part of the original experience of narcissistic perfection, as Kohut (1971) explains. Usually, the grandiose self and idealized parent imago (self-object) are integrated into the adult personality. However, if above and beyond those normal and unavoidable shortcomings, the child suffers severe narcissistic traumas, then the grandiose self does not merge into the relevant ego content but is retained. When corresponding traumatic disappointments in the admired adult occur, the idealized parent imago is retained and does not become the tension-regulating psychic structure needed by patients (pp. 25–28).

For Kohut, when disappointment in or the traumatic loss of the idealized parent imago takes place, disturbances in the narcissistic sectors of the personality follow. Instead of development proceeding with the internalization or acquisition of permanent psychological structures that can fulfill the function that the idealized self-object once fulfilled, the child does not achieve optimal internalization. With a psyche left fixated on an archaic self-object and a hunger for objects upon whom a dependency can be developed, such persons strive to substitute objects for the missing segments of the psychic structure. These objects "replace the functions of a segment of the mental apparatus which had not been established in childhood" (p. 46).

Kohut explains that very early traumatic disturbances or traumatic disappointments in the relationship to the archaic idealized self-object may result in a psyche that lacks the ability to maintain narcissistic equilibrium on its own—or is unable to reestablish equilibrium after it has been disturbed. Kohut describes the trauma patients suffered in terms of a severe disappointment in a mother "who, because of her defective empathy with the child's needs (or for other reasons) did not appropriately fulfill the functions (as a stimulus barrier; as an optimal provider of needed stimuli; as a supplier of tension-relieving gratification, etc.) which the mature psychic apparatus should later be able to perform (or initiate) predominantly on its own" (p. 46). According to Kohut, "(A)n unusual vulnerability of the psyche in early latency, and its regressive response to traumas occurring at that period, is, of course, not only a function of that present moment but is also determined by the child's earlier traumatic experiences" (p. 45).

For children who grow up in dysfunctional families, narcissistic injuries to the child's developing self likely occur, while traumatic disappointments are equally likely correlates of this traumatic experience. These kinds of traumatic disappointments or disturbances to the process of internalizing object relations and developing optimal psychic structure may arise both early in development, and later in the latency period of childhood, when parents continue to behave in a dysfunctional manner.

The work of Kohut (1971) also extends our discussion toward consideration of those much more subtle but significant traumas that may characterize childhood interactions with parental figures. Certainly, traumatic disappointments in the once-admired parental figure go hand in hand with the experience of being physically or verbally abused, or witnessing parental alcoholism or domestic violence. However, nothing so overtly traumatic may be necessary to produce a traumatic disappointment in a parental figure in order for the foundation for later narcissistic personality disturbance to be laid. Parental failure may involve understimulation, insufficient gratification, or permitting overstimulation, as Kohut suggests.

In addition, Kohut helps clinicians to appreciate the effect of receiving insufficient or inconsistent mirroring on the child's developing self and psychic structure when living in a dysfunctional home. For Kohut, it is in the "normal phase of the development of the grandiose self in which the gleam in the mother's eye, which mirrors the child's exhibitionistic display, and other forms of maternal participation in and response to the child's narcissistic-exhibitionistic enjoyment, confirm the child's self-esteem and, by a gradually increasing selectivity of these responses, begin to channel it into realistic directions" (p. 116). Kohut also explains that "the most significant relevant basic interactions between mother and child lie usually in the visual area: the child's bodily display is responded to by the gleam in the mother's eye" (p. 117). We can utilize his formulations in estimating the nature of the impact on the child's development of self-esteem and psychic structure when a mother or parental figure is not able or consistently available to provide this important mirroring function. A dysfunctional family environment not only offers opportunities for experiencing disappointments in the parental figure, but also probably fails to afford the experience of healthy mirroring as one of the most important and basic interactions between caregiver and developing child.

Consequences for Adult Functioning

The patients Kohut discusses suffer specific disturbances in the realm of the self and of those archaic objects cathected with narcissistic libido (self-objects) that are still in intimate connection with the archaic self (i.e., self-objects are objects that are not experienced as separate and independent from the self). Essentially, this state of affairs reflects the fact that these archaic configurations have not become integrated with the rest of the personality. As a result, the adult personality and its mature functions are deprived of energies invested in the ancient structures. A second consequence may be that the adult, realistic activities of these patients are hampered by the intrusion of the archaic structures (Kohut, 1971, pp. 3–4).

Kohut specifically articulates how symptoms of narcissistic disturbance involve subtly experienced, yet pervasive, feelings of emptiness and depression, which may alternate with feelings of aliveness and happiness (pp. 16–17). Very important is the psyche's inability to regulate self-esteem or maintain it at normal levels (p. 20). A narcissistic vulnerability to perceived emotional abandonment or fear of loss of the object also prevails, while a well-hidden inhibition or phobia may exist (pp. 20, 22).

Regression and Transference States

Kohut recognizes the importance of and specifically studies transference phenomena (mirror transference, idealizing transference). For example, he speaks of a regression when a form of narcissistic transference has spontaneously established itself. He also recognizes the importance of identifying events (usually narcissistic injuries) that precipitate the regression.

A Susceptibility to Addiction

A consequence of narcissistic personality disturbance involves a susceptibility to addiction, as Kohut (1971) explains. He views narcissistic problems as central to the psychopathology contributing to an alcoholic's or addict's reliance on a chemical. Resulting deficits in self-regulatory capacities—regulation of tension or self-esteem—permit the use of chemicals to perform self-regulatory functions. As Kohut points out, traumatic disappointments and the fact that the child does not gradually internalize experiences of being optimally soothed (having been overstimulated or understimulated instead) leave the individual fixated on aspects of archaic objects, which are then found in the form of drugs. Their vulnerability permits them to utilize the psychoactive effects of drugs to replace a defect in the psychological structure (p. 46).

Implications for Treatment

In sum, Kohut's (1971) views permit us further to build a rationale for treatment by substantiating that deficits in self-regulatory capacities characterize those who are addicts. Childhood experiences may have been sufficiently traumatic not only to have established an adulthood pattern of functioning characterized by the breakthrough of ancient, archaic material from an earlier era, but also to have created an overall pattern of narcissistic disturbance characterized by poor regulation of tension and self-esteem, and occasional depression, emptiness, and boredom. Moreover, Kohut also directly links deficits in the self's capacity to perform regulatory functions to addiction.

Providing substantial hope, Kohut believes that beyond the assessment of psychopathology, clinicians can also furnish treatment that promises to improve patients' self-regulatory functions. Object relations become actively established in psychoanalysis and the massive identifications with the analyst that arise in treatment are worked through as a consequence of "the spontaneous establishment of transferences and minute processes of [transmuting] reinternalization" (Kohut, 1971, pp. 165–166). Psychoanalytic therapy not only allows transferences to develop spontaneously (including the relationship to archaic, narcissistically cathected objects), but also, through the working-through process, permits the "projected or otherwise mobilized structures to be transformed and gradually reinternalized (transmuting internalization)" (p. 165).

Also of interest to clinicians treating the crack dependent, Kohut covers how traumatic states can be dealt with in psychoanalysis. Persons presenting with narcissistic personality disorders have insufficiently developed basic neutralizing psychic structures, and so "are easily hurt and offended, they become quickly overstimulated, and their fears and worries tend to spread and to become boundless" (p. 230). Kohut explains that, as a result, within psychoanalysis there will be long periods where the analyst must "participate empathically in the psychic imbalance from which the patient suffers; he must show understanding for the patient's painful embarrassment and for his anger that the act that has been committed cannot be undone" (p. 231). Kohut also explains that the genetic roots of the patient's intense rage and self-rejection may become clear through psychoanalysis when relevant memories emerge. These memories will tend to refer to situations in which "the child's legitimate claim for the approving attention of the grownups had not been responded to, but in which the child had been belittled and ridiculed at the very moment when he most proudly had wanted to display himself" (p. 232).

An impulse expressed or displayed before an unempathic parent may become inhibited and a phobia around its expression may persist into adulthood as a consequence of parental failure to respond appropriately to the child's exhibitionistic display. Treatment addresses not only the psyche's inability to regulate self-esteem and manage states of psychic imbalance, but also well-hidden inhibitions or phobias that may emerge as rooted in childhood memories of being responded to poorly by far-from-ideal parental figures.

Kohut emphasizes that the presence of the analyst and the analyst's response to patients' traumatic states are crucial, for they may bring about quick relief for the flooded mental apparatus of the patient and may contribute to the understanding the patient gains about the causes of the states of mental imbalance and the nature of the recurrent traumatic states (p. 237). From Kohut's perspective, management of traumatic states in analysis initiates development toward the building up of psychological structures. The patient also learns to "initiate the handling of these increasingly familiar tension states without the aid of the analyst" (p. 238), perhaps imagining the presence of the analyst or repeating the analyst's words. Kohut further points out that these gross identifications are eventually replaced by truly internalized attitudes, and even by independent personality manifestations such as humor, that were there in a rudimentary and latent from but had no prior chance for development (p. 238). His work suggests that the analyst may play an important role by serving as a mirror for patients. Clinicians need to mirror patients properly and empathically, as well as tolerate exhibitionistic displays and the expression of impulses perhaps long inhibited.

Since many patients with a narcissistic personality disturbance may have developed a reliance on chemicals to perform self-soothing and self-regulatory functions, Kohut's theory can direct clinical technique with the chemically dependent who are also ACDFs. Even where the manifestations of narcissism in the newly abstinent chemically dependent patient reflect a regression in response to the trauma and shame of crack-related deterioration and not a preexisting, full-blown narcissistic personality disorder, Kohut's theory helps us to understand the kind of empathic role clinicians must play in assisting patients in performing self-regulatory functions without the use of chemicals.

ACKNOWLEDGING DIVERSITY IN DYSFUNCTIONAL-FAMILY EXPERIENCES

Ackerman (1986, 1987) recognizes the tremendous diversity of experience to be found among ACAs. He emphasizes that variables that have an impact on an ACAs emotional and psychological status include "the degree of alcoholism experienced, the type and kind of alcoholic in the family, the child's perception of the experience, the child's resilience to stress, the gender of the alcoholic and of the child," the child's age when exposed to alcoholism, positive offsetting factors, and cultural factors (p. 2). For example, Ackerman (1987) acknowledges that adult children from homes in which two parents were alcoholic are more susceptible to alcoholism at earlier ages. The range of consequences involves the fact that, as children of two alcoholics, they probably experience more emotional and physical neglect. Stressing the variety of consequences, Ackerman presents empirical data showing that daughters of two alcoholic parents appear to be more deleteriously affected than sons of two alcoholics. Ackerman also documents that the most frequently reported childhood experiences with an alcoholic parent involve verbal belligerence, abusiveness, and embarrassment.

We can generalize Ackerman's findings to the experience of children in dysfunctional families. When one or both parents are inconsistent, abusive, or traumatically disappointing, and when certain offsetting factors are present or absent (child's age, child's perception of the experience, gender of child and parent, child's resilience to stress, and positive offsetting factors), a variety of consequences can be seen as following from the childhood experiences.

Tuchfeld (1986) similarly recognizes variability in both the extent of parental alcoholism and in the effects of parental alcoholism on children, viewing the home environment of ACAs as similar to those environments that result in disturbed and fixed character development. However, Tuchfeld points out that severe psychological problems may not result; education clarifying the impact of childhood experience in alcoholic homes may constitute sufficient treatment for many ACAs. Steinglass, Bennett, Wolin, and Reiss (1987) highlight the stability found in many alcoholic homes. In a similar vein, different types of family systems exist in alcoholic families with varying degrees of psychological consequences for the children. According to Flanzer (1986), forms of violence exacerbate the negative impact of alcoholism in the family. In this regard, he recognizes that "alcohol abuse and family abuse often intensify one another in a deadly spiral" (p. 33). Family violence may take the form of sexual abuse, incest, child abuse and neglect, and spouse abuse (p. 33). Flanzer emphasizes that men and women drinkers are equally likely to be abusers.

For dysfunctional families in general, we can also assume that disturbed and fixed character development may occur, but also that severe psychological problems may not follow. Education may be sufficient for some, but for others, psychotherapy with certain modifications may be necessary. Also, variety in the nature of the dysfunctional family system and the corresponding effects on children must be acknowledged. And finally, multiple trauma at the hands of both mothers and fathers, who may be not only alcoholic or drug addicted, but also physically, sexually, or emotionally abusive, must be acknowledged, as well as the correspondingly more severe and deleterious results for children developing within such systems.

TABLE 5.1
Consequences of Far-From-Ideal Object Relations in Childhood

Theorist	Trauma	Outcome
Kernberg (1976)	Early conflict-laden or severely disturbed object relations	Early introjections and primitive identifications not integrated into an ego identify.
		Nonmetabolized or unintegrated internalized object relations persist.
		Transference states, oscillatory activation of ego states (S-O-As) observed in patients.
		Psychotic, borderline, neurotic, and narcissistic disorders develop.
		High-, moderate-, and low-level character pathology seen in adulthood.
Meyersburg and Post (1979)	Separation of infant from mother in stressful way	Infant's separation dysphoria enhanced.
		Lowered threshold activity set up in associated neuronal circuitry.
		Later, when restressed by another separation, a resurgence of original dysphoric pattern may supervene.
		Spontaneously or following stress, individual regresses to a previous level of functioning.
Kohut (1971)	Childhood narcissistic trauma. Unempathic mirroring by mother	Unintegrated, archaic structures are retained (grandiose self, idealized parental imago).
		Narcissistic injuries precipitate a regression/narcissistic transference.
		Adult personality and its mature functions are deprived of energies invested in the ancient structures.
		Adult realistic activities are hampered by the breakthrough and intrusion of archaic structures.
		Poor tension regulation results, as well as feelings of emptiness, depression that may alternate with feelings of aliveness, and happiness; and fluctuations in self-esteem/inability to regulate self-esteem.
		Traumatic reactions reflect inability to maintain/restore psychic balance.

POOR EARLY OBJECT RELATIONS.
- Unintegrated internalized object relations (Kernberg, 1976).
- Lowered threshold for tolerating dysphoria (Meyersburg & Post, 1979).
- Unintegrated archaic configurations (Kohut, 1971).

↓ (results in)

POOR SELF-REGULATORY CAPACITIES.
- Character pathology (Kernberg, 1976).
- Transference states based on internalized S-O-As (Kernberg, 1976).
- Vulnerability to stress and regression (Meyersburg & Post, 1979).
- Narcissistic injuries precipitating a regression (Kohut, 1971).
- Adult activities hampered by breakthrough and intrusion of archaic structures, feelings of emptiness, boredom, and fluctuations in self-esteem (Kohut, 1971).

↓ (results in)

EXTRA-REINFORCING IMPACT OF CHEMICALS.
- Chemicals perform self-regulatory functions (Chapters 2 and 5).
- Chemicals are extra-reinforcing when they regulate self-esteem, affective states, dysphoric states, tension (Chapter 5).

↓ (results in)

ADVANCEMENT THROUGH STAGES OF CHEMICAL USE.
- The extra-reinforcing impact of chemicals facilitates experimental users' advancing to recreational use, abuse, and dependence syndrome (Chapter 2).

↓ (results in)

THE TRAUMA OF ROCK BOTTOM AS NARCISSISTIC INJURY.
- Addiction is experienced as trauma (Bean-Bayog, 1986) as users hit a personal rock bottom.
- Personal deterioration and the loss of employment, housing, and child custody are experienced as narcissistic injuries (Chapter 3).

↓ (results in)

THE PREDOMINANCE OF NARCISSISM IN NEWLY ABSTINENT PATIENTS.
- Regression and/or fixation to pathological narcissism is seen (Levin, 1987).
- Narcissistic injuries add insult to prexisting injury (Chapter 3).
- Denial, grandiosity, inflation, arrogance, aloofness, splitting prevail (Levin, 1987; Wallace, 1987).

↓ (results in)

THE NEED FOR TREATMENT AND REMEDIATION
OF UNDERLYING PSYCHOPATHOLOGY.
- Pathology and lack of self-regulatory capacities constitute risk factors for relapse to chemical use or involvement in some other compulsive behavior (Chapter 5).
- Vulnerable patients need treatment and relapse prevention education.
- Assessment determines kind of treatment to which patients are matched (Chapter 10).
- Deficits in service-delivery system bar many from gaining access to desperately needed treatment (Chapters 8, 9 and 15). Many regress toward never-ending levels of rock bottom (see Figure 2.2) as their psychosocial deterioration worsens (Chapters 3 and 7).

Figure 5.1. The Pyramid of Problems for the Chemically Dependent.

CONCLUSION

This chapter has reviewed contemporary approaches to ACAs and ACDFs. Table 5.1 summarizes the consequences of far-from-ideal object relations with parental figures in dysfunctional families during childhood development from the perspectives of Kernberg (1976), Meyersburg and Post (1979), and Kohut (1971).

The theories of Kernberg, Meyersburg and Post, and Kohut were utilized in this chapter in an effort to understand the probable consequences of childhood development in dysfunctional families. The relationship between childhood trauma and the risk of developing chemical dependency and other destructive compulsive behaviors was established. The chapter's analysis has emphasized an appreciation of how etiological factors, psychopathology, and chemical use interact in creating the need for treatment (see Figure 5.1).

The psychoanalytic approach articulated in this chapter suggests that character pathology, dysphoria, bodily tension, anxiety, depression, and less resiliency in negotiating stressors may be integral aspects of adult character, personality, and affective functioning that have evolved out of a history of disturbed object relations with parents in dysfunctional families. Chemicals may be experienced as extra-reinforcing, promoting a reliance on them to perform self-regulatory functions and to medicate recurrent tension, anxiety, and affective states.

Implications of a psychoanalytic approach for treatment include recognizing that the remediation of underlying deficits in self-regulatory capacities constitutes a form of relapse prevention that may not only reduce the chances of relapse to crack but also the risk of involvement with a new chemical and engagement in destructive compulsive behaviors.

6

Behavioral Approaches

At this point, it is important to consider the theoretical rationale for the utilization of cognitive-behavioral interventions. If we appreciate the etiology of crack addiction in conditioning phenomena and in exposure to a social environment saturated with an inexpensive crack product, then certain clinical interventions may arise as logically necessary. More specifically, a rationale for treatment emerges out of an appreciation of principles of operant and classical conditioning and other learning experiences in a social environment.

OPERANT CONDITIONING

In Chapter 1, we discussed Cohen's (1987) view that the pharmacological actions of cocaine make the user feel as though it is imperative to repeat its self-administration again and again. As Cohen explains, it is with the repetitive self-administration of cocaine that intense conditioning to continue drug-seeking behavior occurs (pp. 6–8). Here, we must elaborate on the way in which operant conditioning (also known as instrumental conditioning) explains how patterns of compulsive crack-cocaine smoking both develop and are maintained as an enduring intractable behavior.

Treatment

Positive Reinforcement

Extension of Skinner's (1953, 1961) operant-conditioning paradigm to the crack-smoking situation permits an analysis of how conditioning takes place. Cocaine's pharmacological actions allow its euphoria to serve as a positive reinforcer. In Chapter 1, we referred to Daigle, Clark, and Landry's (1988) explanation that the cocaine euphoria is a positive reinforcer for both laboratory animals and humans, motivating the continued ingestion of cocaine (p. 189). Within Skinner's (1953, 1961) operant-conditioning paradigm, a positive reinforcer serves as a stimulus that increases the probability that the operant, or response to the environment that immediately preceded presentation of the reinforcer, will occur again. The crack euphoria acts to strengthen the response

97

or behavior that preceded its delivery. Since euphoria serves as a reward that follows the behavioral response or operant of the self-administration of crack, crack euphoria effectively strengthens the behavior of self-administration of crack. The reward or positive reinforcement of crack euphoria thus increases the frequency of those behaviors that preceded the reward. In this way, smoking behavior and the behavior of seeking out and procuring crack increase as well.

Thus, with cocaine—the most reinforcing of all drugs as seen in self-administration studies with laboratory animals discussed in Chapter 1—the behavior of self-administering cocaine becomes a strongly established response. When self-administered by laboratory animals, the response becomes such a centrally activated reward involving brain reward centers that the animals will bar-press for more cocaine without stopping for food, rest, or a female in heat (Johanson, 1984; Geary, 1987).

In humans, the behavior of seeking out and smoking crack also increases in frequency because of the reward of an intense euphoria. The self-administration of crack becomes such a strongly established response as a result of its direct action on the brain's reward center. We recall from Chapter 1 that, because of its ability to powerfully and directly activate the brain's central circuits of goal-directed behavior, a motivation to acquire cocaine can dominate that for food, water, or sex (Wise, 1984). Crack smoking persists despite such punishments as gunshot wounds, incarceration, or crack-induced seizures, heart attacks, psychosis, and personal deterioration. These negative consequences of crack smoking or involvement in the crack culture are delayed; for punishment to be effective, it must be immediate. In contrast, the crack euphoria is immediate, permitting development of a strong operant or response to smoking crack. Kalish (1981) explains that operant conditioning remains stronger when the delay in delivery of the reinforcer is short, as in the case of the euphoria that rapidly follows the smoking of crack. Crack's direct actions on the brain's reward center further permit the experience of an immediate reward or pleasurable sensation from crack euphoria. The operant-conditioning paradigm clarifies the way in which a compulsive self-administration pattern easily follows from the experience of smoking crack, readily producing a dependence.

Effects of Tolerance and an Inconsistent Crack Supply

Washton (1989a) points out that in the case of chronic users, "a point is reached where the drug no longer produces any pleasurable sensations at all—only unpleasant ones—but the compulsion to recapture the vividly remembered, illusive high propels a continuing futile chase for paradise lost" (p. 23). These comments highlight the strength of the operant or response to smoking crack as a result of the positive reinforcement of euphoria. Such a strong operant or response is not easily extinguished. Washton's comments correctly are made within the context of a discussion on the development of tolerance, where the user must self-administer larger and larger doses of crack to achieve the desired effect. Washton also notes that during prolonged binges, subsequent doses of cocaine produce decreasing euphoria because of the development of tolerance (p. 23).

The effects of tolerance—where only an increase in the size of the dose will produce the desired effect—and the reality that crack smokers often cannot afford to feed a costly crack habit can combine to create a partial reinforcement schedule. Within operant conditioning, such a schedule involves a situation in which a reward or reinforcement does not always follow the performance of a behavior, such as smoking crack, as when users who cannot always finance a prolonged binge are forced to smoke varying doses of crack, thus forming an inconsistent pattern of dosage. That is, a user who in one crack-smoking session may not be able to acquire a dose sufficient to achieve the desired effect, at a later session may be able to procure a larger dose of crack that does produce the reward of euphoria, feelings of confidence, and stimulation. At this point, a user would again experience positive reinforcement, and having to return to smoking a much smaller amount of crack could result in feelings of frustration because the dose would not achieve the desired effect.

The operant or response of self-administration of crack becomes further strengthened by this partial or intermittent reinforcement schedule. Behaviors learned under such conditions are even harder to extinguish—as demonstrated by animal research (Capaldi, 1967). The operant or response of smoking crack achieves maintenance as a behavior that has been even further strengthened (see Figure 6.1).

As we saw in Chapter 3 through data on a large sample of crack smokers (Wallace, 1990b), variations in smoking patterns prevail in the real world of users seeking treatment. Some patients respond to the development of tolerance through increasing doses of crack on a regular basis, while others are bound by external limits such as finances or an unwillingness to perform criminal acts. Clinical observation and patient self-reports suggest that some of the crack dependent who seek treatment have stopped experiencing crack as pleasurable, perhaps because of tolerance. Among these are users with limited finances who smoke low doses of crack after having smoked much higher doses in the past; their resulting lack of euphoria and stimulation probably relate to the development of tolerance because of the inability to purchase subsequently larger and larger doses. Other patients, who describe smoking increasingly high doses of crack without getting high or experiencing euphoria, probably enter treatment when they have reached a "point where their reward circuits become tolerant to all pleasurable stimulation" (Washton, 1989a, p. 24). However, clinical observation and patient self-reports also suggest that many patients entering treat-

Treatment

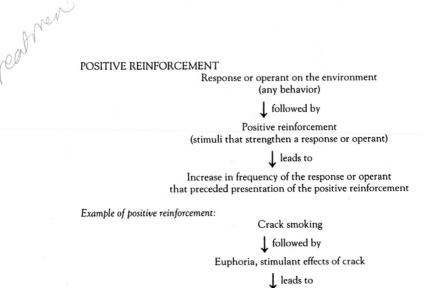

POSITIVE REINFORCEMENT
Response or operant on the environment
(any behavior)

↓ followed by

Positive reinforcement
(stimuli that strengthen a response or operant)

↓ leads to

Increase in frequency of the response or operant
that preceded presentation of the positive reinforcement

Example of positive reinforcement:
Crack smoking

↓ followed by

Euphoria, stimulant effects of crack

↓ leads to

Increase in frequency of crack-smoking behavior

Figure 6.1. Operant Conditioning in the Development and Maintenance of Addiction: Part I

ment have continued to experience euphoria in recent crack-smoking sessions, although the sensations may not be nearly as pleasurable or intense as they remembered from their initial experience with crack smoking. These clinical observations and patient self-reports highlight the interaction of the effects of tolerance with the crack smokers' often inconsistent crack supply. As a result, a partial reinforcement schedule is established for the delivery of the positive reinforcement of crack euphoria. Consequently, the crack-smoking behavior further increases.

Operant-conditioning principles provide a partial explanation of the development and maintenance of crack dependence. The role of negative reinforcement within the operant-conditioning paradigm furnishes an additional explanation of the development and maintenance of crack addiction.

Negative Reinforcement

Not only do human crack smokers act in order to secure a reward or positive reinforcement, but negative reinforcement also serves to establish behavior.

NEGATIVE REINFORCEMENT
                    Presence of unpleasant or aversive stimuli

                              ↓ followed by

                         Some response that is made
                              (a behavior)

                                ↓ leads to

                         Removal of a negative reinforcer
                       (unpleasant or aversive stimuli ends)

                                ↓ leads to

             Strengthening probability that response will occur again
                      (occurrence of behavior increases)

Example of negative reinforcement:
                    Presence of crash symptoms, dysphoria, cravings

                              ↓ followed by

                    Response or behavior of smoking more crack

                                ↓ leads to

                         Removal of negative reinforcer;
                    crash symptoms, dysphoria, cravings end

                                ↓ leads to

             Strengthening probability that smoking crack will occur again;
                    occurrence of crack-smoking behavior increases.

Figure 6.2. Operant Conditioning in the Development and Maintenance of Addiction: Part II

Within the operant-conditioning paradigm, removal of aversive stimuli following a response increases the probability that the response will occur again. Extending this conception to the scenario of chronic cocaine or crack use, the "crash," dysphoria, cravings, and irritability constitute unpleasant or aversive stimuli—and the cocaine or crack user soon learns that the self-administration of more crack can terminate or remove these aversive stimuli. Thus, negative reinforcement, as well as positive reinforcement, helps to establish the behavior of repetitively self-administering cocaine or crack as a strong, enduring response (see Figure 6.2). As a result of both positive reinforcement, where crack's euphoria serves as a reward, and negative reinforcement, where further smoking promotes relief from crash symptoms, we can better appreciate how the self-administration of crack becomes an addictive behavior.

Implications of Operant Conditioning for Treatment

If we are to appreciate the role of operant conditioning in the etiology and maintenance of an addictive disorder such as crack-cocaine dependence, we must recognize the necessity for and logic of clinical interventions that take this etiology into consideration. We must not underestimate the task a crack smoker faces in discontinuing the practice when crack has served as a negative reinforcement that has relieved not only crash symptoms, but perhaps also feelings of depression, boredom, anxiety, low self-esteem, and stress from interpersonal interactions. As a strong response or deeply ingrained habit, crack smoking may be difficult to surrender as an addictive behavior established through positive and negative reinforcement.

A consideration of operant conditioning in establishing crack addiction suggests a dual strategy in helping crack smokers successfully recover from addiction. Clinicians must acknowledge the extent to which an individual patient who may harbor negative feelings such as depression and low self-esteem experiences other rewards in life as sources of positive reinforcement. Do other rewards effectively compete with the positive reinforcement that the crack euphoria provided? Treatment may have to systematically manage and address this reality both by providing an alternative mechanism for managing aversive feelings and by instituting alternative sources of positive reinforcement in crack smokers' lives that effectively compete with the memory of the crack euphoria. Specifically, clinicians can assist crack smokers by (1) helping them manage dysphoric internal states, and (2) directing them toward recognizing alternative constructive sources of positive reinforcement that promise satisfaction and may compete with the memory of the crack euphoria (an apartment, a career, reunion with children).

Alternative Means of Managing Aversive States

For patients experiencing the crash or in a state of withdrawal, pharmacological adjuncts (as discussed in Chapter 4) can help them to manage the dysphoria, cravings, and irritability to which they would normally respond by self-administering more crack as a form of negative reinforcement. Very early in abstinence or during the withdrawal phase, as well as throughout recovery, therapists can assist patients in learning how to manage and regulate painful affective states, feelings of low self-esteem, and behavior in interpersonal relationships. Through therapeutic assistance with managing feelings, self-esteem, and behavior, patients may avoid resorting to crack-cocaine smoking as a form of negative reinforcement that formerly had reliably relieved aversive feelings.

Identifying Sources of Positive Reinforcement

Helping professionals can assist crack smokers in identifying alternative sources of positive reinforcement. Therapists may motivate them by outlining how they can structure their treatment and recovery so as to secure such reinforcement. These sources of positive reinforcement must be viable rewards that can effectively compete with the memory of the crack euphoria—such as being reunited with one's children maintaining a relationship with a spouse, returning to gainful employment so as to acquire the secondary reinforcer of money, or receiving training for a career. The process of identifying these sources of motivation—some of which may have been lost or jeopardized as a result of crack smoking—can begin very early in patient–therapist contacts (see Chapter 10). These positive reinforcements may be able to compete successfully against the euphoria, excitement, and false sense of confidence felt when high as a result of the pharmacological actions of crack. Treatment practitioners are on target when structuring clinical interventions and treatment programs that prepare and motivate patients for the realistic attainment of sources of positive reinforcement. The empathic responses from and approval of a therapist can serve, as well, as a form of secondary reinforcement that assists patients in the process of behavioral change and learning how to identify, label, and manage painful affective states. Residential therapeutic community (TC) settings also provide sources of social approval that can help crack smokers achieve satisfying behavioral change.

Crash Reminders as Aversive Stimuli

The recall of negative drug-related experiences in order to counter the selective recall of the cocaine euphoria represents another technique arising out of an appreciation of operant-conditioning principles. Kertzner's (1987) treatment method includes challenging patient recall of cocaine's euphoria with reminders of the crash, which constitute a type of aversive stimuli. In a similar vein, Washton (1987) counters selective recall of drug-induced euphoria by keeping negative drug-related associations alive, thus inspiring patients to pursue recovery in order to prevent the actual reliving of the unpleasantness recalled through imagery. Thus, a consideration of operant conditioning, and, more specifically, positive and negative reinforcement, not only helps clinicians to appreciate how crack dependence has developed and been maintained, but also assists in providing a rationale for specific treatment interventions

CLASSICAL CONDITIONING

Within the pattern of repeated or chronic crack smoking, opportunities for classical conditioning (Pavlov, 1927), otherwise known as Pavlovian conditioning, also arise. Pavlov acknowledged that the administration of a drug had parallels with the classical-conditioning paradigm. According to that paradigm, when a neutral stimulus undergoes repeated pairing with a stimulus that elicits a reflex or other response, after repeated pairings, a presentation of the neutral stimulus alone may elicit what now emerges as a conditioned or learned response. Neutral stimuli such as drug paraphernalia, a crack-smoking den, a best friend with whom one always gets high, a contemporary song, or white chunks of crack are repeatedly paired with the stimulus of crack and its pharmacological actions when a chronic user smokes crack. This unconditioned stimulus of crack elicits the response of euphoria, confidence, and stimulant effects. Following the repeated pairings of these neutral stimuli (drug paraphernalia, smoking buddy, crack house) with the stimulus of crack and its pharmacological actions, the mere sight of one of these previously neutral, but now conditioned, stimuli results in evoking what we now properly call a conditioned response.

Conditioned Craving and Anticipation of Euphoria

The conditioned response elicited by conditioned stimuli may be thought of, in this case, as a state of anticipation or readiness to experience the euphoria, confidence, and stimulant effects of crack. This conditioned response may include intense cravings, and actually result in the procuring and smoking of crack. The drug paraphernalia, sight of one's "smoking buddy," and the crack house are all now classically conditioned stimuli capable of evoking a conditioned response. These conditioned stimuli may also be thought of as environmental cues that trigger the conditioned response of a state of anticipation, readiness to experience, and intense craving for the euphoria, confidence, and stimulant effects of crack.

The classical-conditioning paradigm explains how this state of anticipation results from the numerous pairings of once neutral stimuli (paraphernalia, crack-smoking buddy, crack house) with crack smoking. Virtually any idiosyncratic stimulus that was repeatedly paired with crack-cocaine-smoking sessions may acquire the power to evoke that response as a result of classical conditioning. Classical conditioning and the way in which any array of stimuli can evoke crack use becomes important in explaining the development and maintenance of drug-using behavior (see Figure 6.3).

Development of More Frequent Crack-Smoking Behavior

The development of gradually more frequent, compulsive, or chronic crack smoking may involve to some extent the role of classically conditioned stimuli. If we consider the recreational crack smoker, classically conditioned stimuli sufficiently and repeatedly paired with the stimulant and euphoric effects of crack within just a few prolonged crack-smoking sessions may later evoke anticipation of and craving for crack's euphoric and stimulant effects. This occurs as recreational users continue to run into drug associates, see crack paraphernalia, walk past crack spots, or experience a Friday or Saturday evening or a payday as previously neutral stimuli that, as a result of repeated pairings with crack-

CLASSICAL CONDITIONING
I. Prior to learning or conditioning:
Component A:

Unconditioned stimulus (UCS)

↓ leads to

Unconditioned response (UCR)

Example of A:

Crack's pharmacological actions (UCS)

↓ leads to

Euphoria, stimulant effects (UCR)

Component B:

Conditioned stimulus (CS)

↓ leads to

Natural response to neutral stimuli

Example of B:

Crack pipe, crack stem, drug-smoking buddy, crack house (CS)

↓ leads to

Normal, visual attention to stimuli

II. The learning or conditioning process:

Conditioned stimulus (CS)

+ (paired repeatedly with)

Unconditioned stimulus (UCS)

Example of II:

Crack pipe, crack house (CS)

+ (paired repeatedly with)

Crack's pharmacological actions (UCS)

III. Evidence of learning or conditioning:

Conditioned stimulus (CS)

↓ leads to

Conditioned response (CR)

Example of III:

Sight of crack pipe, crack house (CS)

↓ leads to

Anticipation of, or readiness to experience,
euphoria, stimulant effects of crack
(Individual is vulnerable to relapse, may seek out
crack's euphoria and stimulant effects, and smoke crack)

Figure 6.3. Classical Conditioning in the Development and Maintenance of Addiction

cocaine use, may now call forth the conditioned response of anticipating and
securing the euphoria and stimulant effects of crack. In this way, a recreational
crack smoker can experience a desire to smoke crack in response to these conditioned cues and escalate toward a pattern of abuse. With gradually more frequent crack-smoking sessions and the loss of control and other crack-related
problems, the dependence syndrome appears. This scenario may result from
more frequent crack smoking in response to the presence of classically conditioned stimuli in the environment.

Maintenance of Crack-Smoking Behavior and Relapse

Even a user who intended to control, cut down, or stop crack use altogether
would be likely to find that anticipation of crack's euphoria and stimulant effects, a desire to use crack, and the actual response of crack smoking to satisfy
one's anticipation of euphoria might easily follow as a response to an array of
environmental cues. These environmental cues were once neutral stimuli, but
are now conditioned stimuli capable of eliciting the conditioned response of
seeking out crack. In this way, relapse or the effective maintenance of crack-
smoking behavior may persist in response to an array of environmental and idiosyncratic cues. Once a crack smoker encounters these conditioned stimuli or
environmental cues, the conditioned response of seeking out the anticipated
crack euphoria arises. Also, a person determined to stop smoking crack may
easily relapse upon encountering these classically conditioned cues in the environment. Such stimuli or cues play a profound role not only in effectively
maintaining crack-smoking behavior, but also in triggering relapse in an individual desperately trying to maintain an abstinent state.

Implications of Classical Conditioning for Treatment

The etiology of crack addiction, as well as its maintenance, involves the role
of classically conditioned stimuli that evoke the response of craving, anticipating, and seeking out crack's euphoria and stimulant effects. Our knowledge of
this etiological factor remains critical for the design of clinical interventions. In
this regard, Pavlov (1927) demonstrated the process of extinction of a conditioned response. He viewed the gradual disappearance of a conditioned response by eliminating the association between the conditioned and
unconditioned stimuli as a process of extinction. For the crack-smoking scenario, extinction of a conditioned response may proceed as follows: The
strength of the conditioned response (anticipation of crack's euphoria and stimulant effects) decreases when the conditioned stimulus (paraphernalia, crack-
smoking buddy, crack den) is repeatedly presented without being paired with
the unconditioned stimulus (crack and its pharmacological actions). In this
way, the conditioned response (anticipation and readiness to experience crack's

euphoria and stimulant effects) begins to decrease. Extinction as a concept within the classical-conditioning paradigm, as well as other concepts from this paradigm, has been extended to the field of chemical dependency in an attempt to design effective drug treatment.

Earlier Approaches to Narcotic Addiction

Prior to the cocaine epidemic of the 1980s, a number of authors had studied the role of classical conditioning in triggering both conditioned craving and withdrawal in chronic opioid-using populations (Wikler, 1948, 1977; O'Brien, 1976; Childress, McLellan, Ehrman, & O'Brien, 1984b) and in alcoholic populations (Blakey & Baker, 1980). Wikler (1948) recognized as early as the 1940s that Pavlovian or classical conditioning could explain observations of heroin addicts' behavior; heroin addicts evidenced mild withdrawal symptoms in response to just the discussion of drug usage at group-therapy sessions. Later, Wikler described the sickness or withdrawal symptoms triggered by a return to a drug-ridden environment that resulted in an individual's craving for and use of heroin. O'Brien (1976) has reported similar cases involving a return to the drug-using environment after a long period of abstinence from heroin.

Any clinician who has worked with a heroin-using population and taken histories that include relapse episodes is familiar with the kinds of incidents that Wikler (1948, 1977) was among the first to report in the literature. All clinicians and researchers have attempted to extend their knowledge and appreciation of heroin addicts' experiences with conditioned craving and withdrawal to their work with cocaine addicts and crack smokers during the current epidemic. The research drawn upon involves both animal and human studies with narcotics.

Animal Studies

Animal studies have expanded our knowledge of how Pavlovian or classical conditioning occurs with narcotics such as heroin, facilitating the conceptual design of effective drug treatments. Conditioned responses resembling the effects of drugs were first reported by Pavlov (1927) in dogs that had been given morphine; the dogs produced a conditioned response similar to the unconditioned effects of the morphine. Thompson and Ostlund (1965) demonstrated the role of environmental cues in relapse, revealing that rats addicted to morphine more readily relapsed when placed in the same environment in which the original addiction had developed. Ternes (1977) showed that monkeys that had repeatedly injected morphine in the presence of music later experienced withdrawal symptoms and relapse after a period of abstinence when again exposed to the environmental cue of that same music. These animal studies have shed considerable light on how classical conditioning affects human drug users.

Human Studies

A number of fascinating investigations with human subjects experienced in the intravenous use of heroin have elucidated how classical conditioning occurs with the self-administration of narcotics. Studies show that human subjects exhibit both druglike and drug-opposite responses as conditioned responses, depending on the circumstances (O'Brien et al., 1988, p. 396).

Druglike conditioned responses.   O'Brien et al. (1988) explain that druglike conditioned responses include the conditioned euphoria that can be seen in needle freaks and with the injection of a placebo solution. The conditioned response resembles the actual effects of the drug in these druglike conditioned responses. Euphoria in response to self-injection, and even physiological signs such as pupillary constriction, have been observed in studies of human subjects injecting a saline solution, suggesting that euphoria was a conditioned response (O'Brien et al., 1988, pp. 398–399). These druglike effects were evoked by the conditioned stimuli of preinjection rituals and the act of self-injection. Studies suggest that in most subjects the opioidlike conditioned response of euphoria is rather quickly extinguished; after extinction of these druglike conditioned responses, withdrawal-like conditioned responses are elicited by the same conditioned stimuli that previously produced opioidlike effects (O'Brien et al., 1988, p. 400).

Drug-opposite conditioned responses.   Drug-opposite conditioned responses include conditioned withdrawal and conditioned tolerance (O'Brien et al., 1988, p. 396). Conditioned withdrawal results because of the thousands of pairings that occur between environmental stimuli and the at-least-daily experience of withdrawal in the typical heroin addict. When exposed to the conditioned stimulus of an environmental cue, the person begins to show signs of withdrawal, such as nausea, diarrhea, and tearing (O'Brien et al., 1988, p. 397). These symptoms of withdrawal from heroin represent a conditioned withdrawal in response to conditioned stimuli, such as a prior heroin-using environment, a needle, or heroin. In order to appreciate how this conditioned withdrawal is a drug-opposite response, we must understand how the homeostatic changes that take place in the body of the heroin addict before an injection of heroin in the person's typical drug-using environment relate to the concept of tolerance.

Conditioned tolerance relates to those homeostatic responses that occur physiologically within an individual in response to stimuli that suggest that heroin is about to be injected (sights, sounds, smells). These homeostatic responses counter the drug effects (O'Brien et al., 1988, p. 398). This conditioned response is the opposite of the unconditioned response, or normal actions of the drug (Siegel & Ellsworth, 1986). It can be thought of as an anticipatory compensation by the body (Siegel, 1988, p. 7). For this reason, Siegel refers to this as conditioned tolerance, which O'Brien et al. (1988) describe as compensatory pharmacological conditional responses (Siegel, 1988, p. 7). One can conclude, therefore, that a complete account of tolerance requires an appreciation of environmental influences, and that an explanation relying on pharmacodynamic principles to explain tolerance is insufficient (Siegel, 1988, p. 5). Individuals who have undergone repeated episodes of withdrawal sickness in a specific environment can experience withdrawal-like symptoms via either the conditioned withdrawal paradigm or by way of a conditioned tolerance mechanism (O'Brien et al., 1988, p. 398).

In an attempt to maintain homeostasis at all costs, the human body anticipates, by virtue of experiencing the conditioned stimuli, that heroin is about to be injected, and drug-opposite effects take place in the body in anticipation of and as preparation for returning it to a state of homeostasis once the injection induces its pharmacological effects. As Siegel explains, when these predrug cues are followed by the usual pharmacological consequences, the compensatory conditioned response (opposite of drug effects) normally serves to attenuate the drug effect; with repeated pairing of the environmental conditioned stimuli (sights, sounds, smells) and the pharmacological unconditioned stimuli (actions of heroin), the drug's effect becomes increasingly attenuated. In this way, a diminished response to the drug can be thought of as tolerance (Siegel, 1988, p. 8).

This view of tolerance can also explain how heroin addicts may accidentally overdose. Research by Siegel (1984) shows that overdoses usually occur when addicts inject a typical dose in an environment different from the one in which they usually do so. The new or different environment lacks those environmental cues or conditioned stimuli that in the past reliably led to a conditioned response opposite to the effects produced by the drug. Without exposure to those cues or stimuli, the heroin addict is not physiologically ready for essentially the same dose of heroin, and so experiences the dose, without the conditioned response of drug-opposite effects, as a very strong dose capable of producing an overdose (Siegel, 1984). One can assume that an individual is at risk for overdose when heroin is administered in an environment that has not previously been paired extensively with the drug, and thus does not elicit the compensatory pharmacological conditioned response that attenuates the drug's effect (Siegel, 1988, p. 9).

Siegel (1988) asserts that both the tolerance and withdrawal symptoms are manifestations of homeostatic mechanisms that correct for pharmacological disturbances caused by a drug. As he further explains, the feedback mechanisms that mediate tolerance when the drug is administered are expressed as withdrawal symptoms when the drug is not administered. In this way, we can see how O'Brien et al. (1988) correctly classify classically conditioned withdrawal as a drug-opposite effect. The anticipation of the actions of heroin contributes not only to tolerance, but also to the elicitation of withdrawal symptoms (Siegel, 1988, p. 12). Thus, some withdrawal symptoms are not due to alterations in feedback mechanisms induced by past drug administration (Siegel, 1988, p. 12), as in the case of an active heroin addict entering withdrawal caused by the need for another intravenous dose of heroin. Instead, some withdrawal symptoms, according to Siegel, are actually preparation symptoms that result from drug-opposite or drug-compensatory conditioned responses (p. 12); these withdrawal symptoms are not those seen shortly after the initiation of abstinence for days or weeks, but those seen after a substantial period of abstinence (Siegel, 1988, p. 12). Where withdrawal is a conditioned response to conditioned stimuli in the environment, "it is the anticipation of the drug, rather than the drug itself, that is responsible for the symptoms" of withdrawal (Siegel, 1988, p. 13). Overall, this work emphasizes the importance of learning factors above those purely physiological factors traditionally recognized as playing a role in substance abuse (p. 18). Conditioned withdrawal and conditioned tolerance emerge as drug-opposite effects—or conditioned responses—that result from anticipating presentation of the drug after exposure to classically conditioned stimuli in the environment. How does this body of knowledge gained from research with heroin addicts inform the design of treatments for cocaine and crack users?

Extinction with Cocaine Users

Childress et al. (1988a) utilize this contemporary understanding of classically conditioned responses not only in their approach to opioid dependence, but also in response to cocaine dependence. Their approach involves identifying the kinds of conditioned responses patients present that seem important in relapse to drug use, finding stimuli that reliably elicit these responses, and developing extinction (nonreinforced exposure) procedures to eliminate or reduce patients' conditioned responses (p. 25). Extinction procedures are added to treatments addressing a range of psychosocial problems. Childress et al. (1988a) report pilot work assessing conditioned responses in abstinent cocaine patients ($n = 16$). This work reveals increased physiological and subjective arousal, increased craving, and reductions in peripheral skin temperature in response to drug-related stimuli (p. 29). The use of an extinction protocol in which cocaine-dependent patients are exposed to 15 hours of cocaine-related audiotapes, videotapes, and objects leads to a virtually complete reduction of cocaine craving by the 15th hour of exposure (p. 35). However, physiological arousal persists and may require further extinction (p. 36). Ongoing treatment and outcome studies must determine the benefits of extinction and the importance of conditioned drug-related responses in relapse (p. 37).

In evaluating their work, Childress et al. (1988a) feel that cocaine craving is by far the most common subjective response to cocaine "reminder" stimuli, although reports of increased arousal, and even of a crash or withdrawal-like feelings, can also occur (p. 39). Conditioned druglike responses, or feelings of actually being high, were relatively uncommon responses to their experimental stimuli (p. 38). (The present author has received clinical reports of conditioned druglike responses upon awakening from vivid dreams of smoking crack; patients actually feel high momentarily.) Childress et al. find that conditioned craving emerges as an extremely prevalent, yet poorly understood, response to drug-related stimuli and that it can occur independently of conditioned withdrawal responses (p. 40). Childress et al. also recognize the problem of generalizing their extinction training to the "real world" and have attempted to use realistic individualized drug "reminders" (p. 40).

Childress and colleagues (1988b) report more substantial findings utilizing their extinction protocol with a sample of 29 cocaine-dependent patients. Results showed that skin-temperature reductions were significantly greater in response to cocaine-related stimuli than to neutral stimuli; these findings are similar to their earlier findings with heroin patients (pp. 76–77). Of the patients' responses to experimental conditioned stimuli, or cocaine reminders, craving was the most common, and was reported two to there times as often as either high or withdrawal/crash responses (p. 78). As a result of 15 extinction sessions over two weeks during inpatient treatment, in addition to a standard drug-treatment program, craving was gradually reduced. The less frequent responses of a high and crash/withdrawal were typically extinguished by the sixth hour (p. 79). Unfortunately, by the 15th hour, physiological arousal to cocaine reminders was still evident for half of the patients in the extinction group. Also, despite the extinction of craving in response to the extinction stimuli in the study, "most patients have reported episodes of craving in response to *real-world* cocaine 'reminders' during the two-month period following hospital discharge" (p. 79).

By way of conclusion, Childress et al. (1988b) attribute the fact that approximately two thirds of patients in the sample relapsed to cocaine use at least once during the two-month follow-up to the incomplete extinction of physiological arousal and incomplete generalization of extinction for subjective craving (p. 79). They interpret their findings that cocaine abusers experience conditioned craving and arousal to cocaine reminder stimuli even after detoxification and extinction trials as indicating just how intense and persistent these conditioned responses may be. This also reveals just how vulnerable the cocaine abuser may be long after detoxification (p. 80). Childress and colleagues speculate on how to improve treatment outcome by the use of the sight of real cocaine, in vivo exposure to drug locations, home-environment extinction sessions, and other behavioral techniques. Of the techniques they are considering, Childress et al. cite the training of *cognitive or behavioral alternatives* in response to cocaine reminders, as well as encouraging the patient actively to cope with the arousal triggered by these stimuli (p. 80). They conclude by acknowledging that this approach is compatible with extinction and that "patients could practice coping techniques in response to the repeated, non-reinforced presentation" of cocaine "reminders" (p. 80).

Siegel (1984) also has added an extinction protocol as an adjunct treatment. This involves providing patients who present with cocaine dependence a vial containing a chemical that smells like "street" cocaine—the idea being that repeated sniffing of the aroma without the actual use of cocaine will result in extinction of the craving for cocaine (Siegel, 1984b, 1988).

Avoidance of the Drug Environment

Siegel (1988) recommends beyond the utilization of extinction procedures the actual relocation of addicts to a different environment after treatment in order to avoid classically conditioned environmental cues triggering the conditioned response of craving or withdrawal and the experience of relapse. He cites work on the experience of Vietnam veterans (Robins et al., 1975; O'Brien et al., 1980), which shows that a return to an environment very different from the one in Vietnam where they used drugs permitted these soldiers to avoid a relapse to heroin use, resulting in an astonishingly high rate of remission of substance abuse once they returned to the United States.

However, it is possible to appreciate the role of classically conditioned stimuli in selecting clinical interventions without literally recommending that patients avoid such stimuli or drug reminders by relocating geographically. Clinicians should not promote the concept of "the geographical cure" (Cinque & Elberth, 1986), or moving elsewhere to avoid an environment containing classically conditioned cues that could trigger a relapse. The danger of the "geographical cure" concept rests in promotion of the idea that a move to a new location can replace long-term aftercare treatment, providing the illusion that a potential for relapse or underlying problems with drugs no longer exists. However, a return to the original drug-using environment or a similar environment is often inevitable and a danger of relapse persists. In fact, because of generalization, stimuli similar to the classically conditioned drug stimuli may also evoke the response of cocaine craving or of actual crack smoking.

Although there is wisdom in the anonymous self-help philosophy of "avoiding people, places, and things," there is the reality of often unavoidable encounters and the necessity of utilizing support systems to avoid relapse. Clinical confidence in (1) relapse-prevention education, (2) the teaching of alternative behavioral responses, and (3) remedying underlying psychological and emotional characteristics that may have made patients vulnerable to an addiction, and continue to contribute to a vulnerability to relapse, argues for clinicians' recommending active involvement in supportive therapeutic treatment rather than to move in pursuit of the deceptive geographical cure.

Classical Conditioning Principles in Designing Interventions

It is possible to appreciate the role of classically conditioned stimuli in selecting clinical interventions without exposing patients to actual cocaine, drug-related stimuli, or cocaine reminders that have been repeatedly paired with cocaine. In addition, it may be impossible or impractical to take a patient to a crack house or neighborhood and have the process of extinction occur. A less literal interpretation of the role of classically conditioned stimuli may involve designing treatment interventions that reflect an appreciation of the role of the processes of extinction. The speculation of Childress et al. (1988b) on the future use of cognitive strategies and behavioral alternatives approaches this idea. Cognitive and educational interventions may prepare patients to anticipate the impact of classically conditioned stimuli in triggering the response of crack smoking. Behavioral rehearsal of alternative behavioral responses, or of how patients can practically avoid exposure to evocative and dangerous stimuli, might also occur.

Promoting a Natural Process of Extinction

Assessing patients and the nature of their immediate environment for such classically conditioned and evocative stimuli as crack-smoking persons in the same home or an immediate neighborhood environment highly saturated with crack might result in recognizing how classically conditioned stimuli preclude the likelihood that initial abstinence can be achieved on an outpatient basis. Inpatient or residential treatment might emerge as essential in such cases. Natural processes of extinction might be fostered by visits home or by passes from a residential TC where repeated, gradual exposures to old environments containing classically conditioned stimuli occur, while receiving the support of an escort who provides an external control. This approach affords residents repeated opportunities to talk about feelings, cravings, and desires evoked on such passes. Residents of TC programs may gradually internalize controlled alternative behavioral responses to classically conditioned stimuli. Moreover, a natural process of extinction of the power of old conditioned stimuli to evoke the response of crack smoking takes place.

More explicit relapse-prevention education can be effective in helping vulnerable patients become aware of the role of classically conditioned stimuli, to be sensitive to the need to avoid such stimuli during early phases of abstinence, and to learn alternative behavioral strategies when confronted with them. Through cognitive-behavioral strategies, crack smokers may learn how to manage conditioned stimuli and effectively engage in alternative behaviors that permit avoidance of relapse. Thus, a number of approaches may be valid in appreciating the role of classical conditioning in the development and maintenance of addiction.

SOCIAL–ENVIRONMENTAL FACTORS

Chapter 1 discussed how the social environment in which crack was introduced as a packaging and marketing breakthrough attracted recreational users of illicit chemicals, naive experimentalists, and chemical connoisseurs willing to try the new crack cocaine. Since crack was an inexpensive, easily available product that could be incorporated into the popular sociocultural ritual of smoking, this experimental use easily advanced to regular, recreational use in social settings. While escalation to compulsive-use patterns has a lot to do with crack's neurochemical actions and behavioral conditioning, the social environment certainly plays a role in promoting its continued use, and that of chemical substances in general. This social environment must be negotiated by patients when they leave the outpatient treatment setting, or when they return to the real world after inpatient or residential treatment. Thus, the role of social–environmental factors must be acknowledged in the etiology and maintenance of chemical use.

Clinical Interventions That Take Into Account Social-Environmental Factors

Treatment interventions must be designed that not only acknowledge the etiology of crack as involving social–environmental factors, but also address the part these factors play in maintaining addiction or in contributing to a return to the use of crack or other drugs. How are patients going to manage in an environment that promotes the social use of illicit chemicals and alcohol? For one thing, they may be provided with cognitive-behavioral or educational interventions that teach them to structure the use of leisure time, reward themselves with other than a chemical reward, socialize and experience intimacy without chemicals, and engage in alternative behavioral responses when facing stimuli that support chemical use. Any beliefs that they can still engage in the selling of illicit chemicals for profit or can participate in social activities with drug users must be challenged in treatment and replaced with an understanding of their vulnerability to dangerous practices and behaviors that could lead to a return to crack smoking. Chapters 11 and 12 present clinical interventions that exemplify the interventions that arise from an appreciation of the etiology of crack addiction in certain social–environmental factors.

Other Social–Cultural Factors

Some crack smokers have self-medicated feelings of boredom, alienation, and low self-esteem that may have had their origin in other significant social–cultural factors. Certain of these factors operate most strongly in the socialization experiences of minorities and women—two groups for which this form of cocaine becomes an equal-opportunity drug, in contradistinction to cocaine powder, which was mostly utilized by middle- and upper-middle-class white males. Feelings of boredom, alienation, and low self-esteem may have their origins in interactions and experiences within a social–cultural environment that not only fails to encourage them to realize their potential, but actually hampers them from doing so.

Experiences in Dysfunctional Society

These feelings of boredom, alienation, and low self-esteem, may be distinct from those feelings characteristic of people evidencing a narcissistic psychopathology. On the other hand, it might be argued that many crack patients, such as women and minorities, presenting with a history of such feelings have actually suffered narcissistic injuries as a consequence of a socialization process—beyond the boundaries of the family—that does not include expectations of their success. Harris-Offut (1986) asserts that America is a dysfunctional family. We can extend this concept and observe societal scapegoating of the minority or female members of the larger American family system, the projection of low or negative expectations for these unfortunate family members, and the sustaining of narcissistic injuries as a result of dysfunctional family dynamics.

Socialization processes for minorities and women have included messages as to their inferior status; formal and informal segregation patterns and treatment by society's institutions serve to socialize them as to their perceived worth in the larger societal context. In effect, society has mirrored to women and minorities an abundance of negative images with associated low expectations. And the media, by continuing to present stereotypical, distorted images, have been the primary mechanism by which this mirroring process has taken place.

Far-from-Ideal Object Relations with Societal Authorities

Narcissistic injuries to women and minorities may also be rooted in a history of object relations with significant representatives and authorities in such societal institutions as schools—object relations that may be so painful that they may be the basis for low self-esteem or a continuing unconscious collusion in fulfilling low or negative societal expectations. This may be a very significant dynamic for many minorities and women who receive such negative reflections not only from the media, but also from authorities they encounter in the educational system and workplace.

If an environment has not fostered the development of individuals in such a way that they can feel confident to take advantage of life's opportunities, then to some extent the etiology of crack addiction may rest in a history of painful and damaging interactions with significant persons in the social environment. A school system contributing to the alienation of students and high dropout rates, unemployment rates that reflect discriminatory hiring practices, or dissatisfaction with the lower wages paid to women and minorities might all be viewed as social–environmental factors that are among the numerous interacting variables that collectively contribute to the development of an addiction.

Implications for Treatment Practitioners

Treatment facilities and professionals must be sensitive to these societal dynamics that affect women and minorities and must structure treatment facilities and programs in such a way that they do not duplicate the subtle projection of low and negative expectations for these groups. Dysfunctional societal dynamics and far-from-ideal object relations with treatment-program leaders should not prevail; instead, equal opportunities for realizing one's potential and for full participation must be made available. The present lack of treatment for pregnant addicts and women with children reflects how programs can unconsciously devalue women and inadvertently fail to allow them opportunities for full participation. It is the residential TCs and inpatient programs that may face the greatest challenge in not recreating institutional patterns and practices that repeat dysfunctional societal dynamics. Group dynamics that easily emerge within these residential settings can replicate society's larger dysfunctional dynamics to the detriment of women and minorities.

Treatment practitioners can play the most important role by treating patients with respect while making sure to avoid projecting low or negative expectations in clinical technique, attitudes, and behavior. Helping professionals must provide an unbiased mirror for patients into which they can trustfully gaze and find a sensitive, realistic evaluation of themselves and the complex nature of their addiction.

Patients can leave treatment with an enhanced sense of self, a knowledge of behaviors in which they must engage to facilitate their recovery, and a cognitive reframing of their addiction, its etiological roots, and how successful recovery can be pursued. Treatment including these elements may constitute the best preparation for women and minority patients for subsequent educational, vocational, and employment opportunities in a social–environmental context that may not have significantly changed by the time they complete that inpatient or residential treatment.

CONCLUSION

The patient reentering the social–environmental context after being treated for crack dependence will be different, it is hoped, as a result of treatment and clinical interventions. Effective clinical interventions must arise out of a rationale that recognizes the role of behavioral conditioning and experiences in a social–environmental context as etiological factors in the development and maintenance of crack addiction. This chapter has covered the way in which behavioral principles underlying both the operant-conditioning and classical-conditioning paradigms provide a rationale for specific treatment interventions. In addition, our understanding of the social–environmental context permits clinicians to be sensitive and empathic providers of interventions that prepare patients to negotiate high-risk situations and avoid relapse. A detailed discussion of clinical interventions recommended for use with crack-cocaine smokers is presented in Chapters 10, 11, and 14.

7

Case Examples: Support for a Biopsychosocial Theory of Crack Dependence

Our discussion in Chapters 4-6 covered the multiple etiological factors that play a probable role in the development and maintenance of crack-smoking behavior, highlighting the need to utilize a biopsychosocial model of crack addiction. Such a model directed our search for the likely etiological roots of addiction in biological, psychological, and social factors.

In Chapter 4, we considered the theoretical rationale for the use of pharmacological adjuncts in light of the etiology of compulsive crack smoking as related to neurochemical disruptions in brain function. Chapter 5 covered psychoanalytic approaches that provide the rationale for the use of psychoeducational and therapeutic interventions to remedy the psychological consequences of childhood development in dysfunctional families. These experiences can leave individuals susceptible to escalation from experimental and recreational crack use to crack dependence, supporting an etiology of crack dependence in acquired psychosocial characteristics. Our review of behavioral principles of conditioning and the influence of other social–environmental factors in Chapter 6 also supported an etiology for the development and maintenance of compulsive crack-cocaine smoking patterns. More specifically, we saw that operant conditioning explained the experience of the crack euphoria as a form of positive reinforcement, the further smoking of crack to alleviate the dysphoria of withdrawal as a form of negative reinforcement, and the role of classical conditioning in creating conditioned stimuli in the environment capable of evoking the response of resumption of crack smoking.

A biopsychosocial theory of crack addiction emerges that incorporates biological, psychoanalytic, and social learning perspectives as discussed in Chapters 4, 5, and 6, respectively. This integrated theory may receive further support through case examples that show the need to recognize the role of multiple interacting variables from biological, psychological, and social realms in order adequately to account for the development and maintenance of crack-smoking behavior.

ILLUSTRATIVE CASES

Case of I.N.

I.N., a 34-year-old, African-American male, and a college graduate, lost a prestigious white-collar job as a result of crack usage, when he began coming to work late with a disheveled appearance and body odor. Although he was warned about these signs of crack use, I.N. was unable to discontinue crack smoking and was fired. Unemployment and continued crack smoking led to I.N.'s foster father's asking him to leave the home. A godmother permitted I.N. to live in her home for three months, kicking him out once, taking him back for a few weeks, and finally sending him away—demanding that he get treatment for his crack addiction. I.N. then stayed in shelters for a year and a half until he entered the hospital for detoxification. He reported that his foster father and godmother remained potential support systems if he would seek treatment. I.N. currently engages in sporadic employment in an unskilled job, returning to the shelter at night.

I.N. used no drugs in high school, but began smoking marijuana in college at the age of 18, averaging one joint every two weeks—which had increased to an average of two joints a day by the age of 25; he then discontinued marijuana smoking because of its side effects. In 1981, I.N. began snorting intranasal cocaine and from 1982 to 1984, was paying a dealer from $50 to $100 a week for relatively pure cocaine. His cocaine use became heavy in 1984 after the death of his foster and the loss of his job. He experienced a major depressive episode at this time, but was able to find an even better white-collar position. In early 1985, I.N. tried crack for the first time and began to use it regularly, and by early 1986, was spending $60–70 on crack during the week and $100 on payday, altogether averaging getting high three times per week. In 1986, with his job and home gone, I.N. was forced to decrease his crack smoking to $20 per day. In response to the intense depression engendered by his predicament, he augmented his crack habit with alcohol—two pints of wine, gin, or vodka a day.

I.N.'s mother had been an alcoholic and he never knew his real father. As a result of his mother's alcoholism, I.N. was placed in foster care at an early age. "It upset me, hurt me," he said, to discover at the age of eight that his foster parents were not his real parents. His first foster mother died when he was 15. I.N. took her death "very hard," admitting that he had always been a "momma's boy" and had spent a lot of time with her while his foster father worked very hard. The foster father soon remarried, and I.N. eventually became close to this second foster mother, whom he considered a good friend and adviser, even though she was an alcoholic and was very aggressive when drunk. She also died, but after he had become an adult. A brother who grew up with him in this household is married, affluent, and solidly upper middle class; he stays away from I.N. because of I.N.'s severe deterioration.

Clinical assessment at the time of inpatient detoxification suggested that I.N. presented with a recurrent major depression related to the deaths of his foster mothers, the loss of excellent employment, and homelessness. This extremely intelligent man, who was grateful for the chance to leave the shelter system and embrace the hope that detoxification provided, readily accepted a referral to a TC. Because he would be on a waiting list, I.N. suggested that his foster father might permit him to live at home instead of in the shelter for one week. However, the father refused after a family session on the detoxification unit, feeling unable to manage the high levels of stress involved in permitting someone no longer trusted into the home. I.N.'s two weeks in inpatient detoxification did not reassure this skeptical but practical man, although he was glad to learn that his foster son was alive, and prepared to receive long-term treatment.

Analysis from a Biopsychosocial Theoretical Perspective

A narcissistic injury at the age of eight (discovery that he was a foster child), the death of his foster mother when he was 15, and exposure late in adolescence to a second alcoholic mother all may have predisposed I.N. to depressive reactions in adulthood and to using cocaine to self-medicate depression upon his second foster mother's death. In addition to a vulnerability to the extra-reinforcing effects of cocaine, crack, and alcohol as medications for depression, I.N. finally found in crack a chemical sufficiently compelling pharmacologically to lead to his downfall. The case permits tracing how the growing availability of more and better-quality cocaine powder in the 1980s permitted I.N. to do what most of his contemporaries were also doing—recreationally using cocaine in early adulthood just as they had used marijuana in college. However, the death of his second foster mother in 1984 led to a major depressive episode; his prior experience at the age of 15 of a foster mother's death and narcissistic injury at the age of eight had predisposed him for a regression and dysphoric reaction in face of this major stressor. As a result, I.N. began to use greater quantities of cocaine to self-medicate the depression.

The availability of crack in the social environment in early 1985, a character left susceptible to crack as extra-reinforcing, and crack's pharmacological actions all explain the etiology and maintenance of an addiction that was so intractable that employment and housing were lost. This case outlines the classic time frame in which the recreational use of cocaine and transition to smoking crack occurred in the 1980s. This case also strikingly depicts the kind of severe personal deterioration that may follow compulsive crack smoking, affecting the college educated and what should be in this generation a stable African-American middle class.

Case of N.R.

A 34-year-old African-American female with three daughters, N.R. attended college for two years. She was fired from a job after six years for falling asleep at work as a result of exhaustion from all-night crack smoking. Since losing that job three years ago, N.R. has lost three more jobs for the same reason, and has been unemployed for the past four months. She is separated from her husband, who had severely beaten her for smoking crack and neglecting her cooking and cleaning tasks. Prior to her crack use, N.R.'s husband had been patriarchal, protective, and loving. N.R. and her children have lived with her mother since the loss of her apartment as a result of her failure to pay the rent, the money having been used for crack. She decided to enter detoxification because of her mother's resentment over having to care for the children for long periods of time while N.R. was smoking crack.

Her history of drug use began when she briefly experimented with marijuana at age 17. N.R. began intranasal cocaine use at age 29, using small amounts infrequently, eventually increasing to $100 worth of the drug every payday (every two weeks). A little over three years ago, she began free-basing $25 doses of cooked cocaine. After trying crack "out of curiosity," N.R. tried to stop because she was afraid of any drug on which she could spend up to $200 in one day—but even after a hospital emergency-room visit for treatment for chest pains and rapid heart beat, she was unable to discontinue crack smoking. She averaged $50–100 of crack on an every-other-day basis. Six months prior to this detoxification, N.R. had her first detoxification at another facility and remained drug-free for three and a half months. An argument with her estranged husband triggered feelings of depression and contributed to a relapse. She had resumed even more compulsive $100-per-day crack use before entering this second detoxification.

As a child, N.R. recalls standing in fear as her parents engaged in frequent arguments that usually led to violence. As a result of marital conflict, her father left when N.R. was seven. Her stepfather was an alcoholic who typically slept when intoxicated and was generally a positive paternal figure.

Clinical assessment at the time of her second two-week detoxification suggested that N.R. presented a dysthymic disorder in addition to cocaine dependence. Her depression involved her emotional reaction to separation from her once-loving husband, the effects of her husband's battering of her prior to leaving their marriage, low self-esteem over the loss of jobs and her husband, and disappointment over her relapse. N.R. resisted a recommendation to enter a TC, evidencing considerable denial of the severity of her addiction.

Analysis From a Biopsychosocial Theoretical Perspective

This case dramatically illustrates that the pharmacological imperative to smoke more and more crack (Cohen, 1987) overrides logic and reason—N.R. was driven to smoke more crack despite an emergency-room visit, damage to finances, loss of employment, and loss of her spouse. The necessity of addressing a $100 daily crack habit with pharmacological adjuncts during a sorely needed detoxification can be seen in this case. Even though a first detoxification with the use of pharmacological adjuncts assisted her in achieving three and a half months of abstinence, N.R. still relapsed in response to depression, as will many vulnerable recovering patients. The learning involved in having experienced relief from the dysphoria of the crack "crash" by the negative reinforcement provided by smoking more crack also may have contributed to N.R.'s use of crack when overwhelmed by feelings of depression. The tension, anxiety, and fear she had felt as a child in a dysfunctional family (arguments, domestic violence, departure of her father, stepfather's alcoholism) likely left N.R. susceptible to experiencing the effects of chemicals as extra-reinforcing when they assisted her in the regulation of dysphoric states. Together with the availability of crack in a social environment, this case illustrates the role of the multiple interacting factors toward which a biopsychosocial theory points as contributing etiological factors in the development and maintenance of crack addiction.

Case of K.R.

A 21-year-old African-American male who dropped out of high school, K.R. decided to enter inpatient detoxification in order to get out of the men's shelters, in which he had been sleeping for the past month and a half. K.R. had lived with his mother before entering the shelter system, but she asked him to leave after he stole various items to support his crack habit. Unemployed for the past year and a half, K.R. has been doing some drug dealing. Previously, he had worked for two years as a semiskilled laborer.

At the age of 13, K.R. began smoking an ounce of marijuana a day, beginning early in the morning and continuing throughout the day. He began sniffing cocaine at age 16, using $20–50 doses on a daily basis, escalating to $300 of intranasal cocaine per day every day. At age 20, K.R. started smoking crack, using $50–60 doses on a daily basis. Involvement in crack distribution had permitted K.R. to escalate to the use of $500–600 worth of crack per day in the month prior to entering detoxification.

When K.R. was a child, his father never lived in the home and he was raised by an alcoholic mother who drank almost every day. K.R. recalls the changes in his mother's personality; she would variably be nice or argumentative or even violent. As a result of his mother's extreme inconsistency and lack of availability to perform mothering functions, K.R. received little attention. He asserts that he was a mother to himself, deciding to leave home at age 15. Dropping out of high school, K.R. lived on his own and worked to support himself. His counterdependent and emotionally distant stance served to protect K.R. from feeling the abandonment and anxiety he experienced every time his alcoholic mother abandoned her children emotionally when intoxicated. Instead he abandoned his mother by leaving home (Wallace, 1990a). Reliance on the chronic use of chemicals assisted K.R. to compensate for the chaotic object relations internalized through interactions with unavailable, inconsistent, and violent parental figures.

K.R. not only had a history of engaging in aggressive/assaultive behavior and drug dealing, but also experienced identity diffusion. K.R. presented with an antisocial personality disorder, and yet responded positively to the limits and rules on the inpatient detoxification unit as an opportunity to internalize controls and learn that he can avoid resorting to expression of aggressive impulses when under stress. K.R. also responded affirmatively during detoxification to interpretations that his history of heavy, compulsive marijuana use dating back to age 13 suggests his struggle to survive in a chaotic, unpredictable home, with an inconsistent alcoholic mother. Clinical assessment suggests that relationship patterns reflect an inability to commit to and sustain a long-term relationship. Although K.R. has two children by two separate mothers, he is uninvolved with either woman, and seems destined to repeat his father's pattern of being unavailable to his children (Wallace, 1990a).

By the end of this first experience with inpatient detoxification, K.R. accepted a referral to a TC. He was very motivated to change his behavior, having benefitted from the positive experience of tolerating limits in detoxification and participating in individual and group psychotherapy. Arriving at his appointment at a TC two weeks after leaving detoxification, he was refused admission because of a minor physical condition noticeable in his appearance, and asked to get medical clearance. He did obtain a medical explanation of his minor symptoms, but the TC still refused to admit him, although he had shown commitment and perseverance in going to this facility for appointments on several occasions.

Unable to enter the treatment to which he had been referred, K.R. returned to working as a semiskilled laborer for a private company, and after about one month, he began using his pay to return to crack smoking. He initially spent $40–50 per day, smoking on a daily basis, but within three weeks, quickly escalated to $300 of crack per day as he continued to work. This relapse occurred approximately three months after K.R. completed his first detoxification. He returned for a second detoxification following three weeks of compulsive crack smoking and a renewal of conflict with his mother over crack-related behaviors.

The case of K.R. highlights the inadequacies in TC residences that lack medical personnel, forcing them to take a very cautious approach to patients with any potential medical problems. These TC inadequacies contributed to K.R.'s relapse episode. Having faced the stress of rejection by the TC and the confusion of a change in plans, K.R. showed some resiliency in trying to resume stable employment and a drug-free life-style.

Analysis from a Biopsychosocial Theoretical Perspective

A relapse to crack smoking reflects the way in which money may represent a conditioned stimulus capable of evoking such a response in vulnerable, newly abstinent patients. The rapid escalation in the frequency and dose of crack smoking during the relapse, and the more gradual increase prior to K.R.'s first inpatient detoxification, indicates the likely role of neurochemically based cravings and conditioning in fueling the development of compulsive crack-smoking patterns. The development of self-medication strategies with marijuana at age 13 suggests the role of dysfunctional family dynamics (mother's alcoholism and violence, father's absence) with which K.R. coped on a daily basis throughout childhood and adolescence. His personality and ego-identity problems also reflect the legacy of these dysfunctional family dynamics and the way in which he was ill prepared for the challenge of assuming responsibilities as a partner and father. A biopsychosocial theory again emerges as necessary in accounting for the role of multiple variables in establishing K.R.'s severe and intractable crack dependence.

Case of W.K.

W.K., a 32-year-old African-American female with one daughter, graduated from high school and has worked as an unskilled laborer in a service industry for a number of years. She decided to move in with her mother in response to financial uncertainty caused by crack smoking. Within this extended household, W.K. has two cousins who smoke crack. Her boyfriend of several years also smokes crack and represents a negative influence. Recurring episodes of missing and stolen items in this household occupied by several crack smokers have created substantial stress, contributing to W.K.'s decision to seek treatment and independent housing. Her mother blames her for any missing items, and verbally abuses her.

A drug history began with marijuana smoking at the age of 14, which was discontinued by age 17. W.K. had been drug-free for over a decade when she tried crack one year prior to entering inpatient detoxification. Initially, she averaged $10 of crack once a month. After three months of this pattern, W.K. escalated over the next two months to $200 crack binges with her boyfriend. The month before entering detoxification, W.K. was averaging $100 of crack per binge, with a binge typically occurring once or twice a week.

As a child, W.K. was exposed to domestic violence that frequently resulted in serious injuries to her mother. She tried to protect her mother, attempting to intervene in parental fights. Her father left the home when W.K. was nine. W.K. was her father's favorite child and she missed him desperately. After her father left home, W.K. was verbally and emotionally abused by her mother, whose attacks focused on W.K.'s brown skin color, which stood in contrast to the mother's very light skin (Wallace, 1990a). W.K. explains that her mother is emotionally unstable and probably has problems stemming from her own childhood. Since initiating crack smoking and moving in with her mother, W.K.'s mother has resumed her vicious verbal abuse of W.K., which causes W.K.'s self-esteem to plummet and promotes the use of more crack to escape painful feelings. Most painful of all, this new adult "round" of verbal and emotional abuse takes place in front of W.K.'s child, perhaps damaging this young child's perception of and respect for W.K. as a mother.

W.K. presents a dysthymic disorder related to intense regrets over the decision to move in with her mother again, persistent verbal and emotional abuse during this period of reunion, and disappointment in herself related to initiation of crack smoking; she is tearful when recalling events of the past year. Assessment also suggests that as a result of childhood experiences, including her father's departure from the home and verbal and emotional abuse by her mother, W.K. has low self-esteem, devalues herself, and as an adult settles for mistreatment and devaluation in unsatisfying relationships (Wallace, 1990a). She accepted a referral to an outpatient clinic, which provided individual psychotherapy, and she explored a number of issues, such as the internalization of low expectations for herself. W.K. became gainfully employed again. However, after a couple of months, she returned to intermittent low-dose crack use while remaining in outpatient treatment, trying to utilize therapeutic support to avoid relapse episodes and restructure her life.

Analysis from a Biopsychosocial Theoretical Perspective

Review of this case permits appreciation of how the availability of crack in the social environment affords individuals who have functioned well without chemicals an opportunity to experiment with this new drug. The way in which members of family systems and peer groups can casually enter into addiction in communities saturated with crack also emerges out of this case. The addictive potential of this drug can lead casual experimentalists to gradually experience tolerance and increase their doses toward the development of dependence syndromes, in view of the pharmacological actions of crack and conditioning. Here, too, a vulnerability for escalation to crack dependence may still partially rest in a character left vulnerable to the extra-reinforcing functions of crack as a consequence of childhood development in a dysfunctional family (domestic violence, parental separation, emotional abuse). Poor self-regulatory capacities in maintaining self-esteem interact with crack's psychoactive effects in promoting a regular drug-use pattern.

Case of N.F.

N.F., a 33-year-old, divorced African-American male with two children, graduated from college and earned a graduate degree that ensures consistent white-collar employment—although disruptions in work have occurred as a consequence of crack smoking. The end of his marriage a year and a half earlier led to a period of depression and N.F. initiated crack smoking through informal social contacts he sought out in an effort to avoid the isolation of an empty apartment. As a result of financial problems stemming from crack use, N.F. lost his apartment six months prior to entering our facility, moving in with his parents and sleeping on their couch.

Brief experimentation with marijuana at age 23 was followed by abstinence from drugs until N.F. began using crack when his wife divorced him. A pattern of three-day binges once a week, during which he smoked $100 of crack per day, typified N.F.'s crack-smoking pattern. His detoxification at our facility represented a second attempt to initiate abstinence. He had detoxed for the first time three months prior to his second detoxification; he remained drug-free only during the first three weeks of outpatient treatment, relapsing and failing to return to outpatient treatment.

As a child, N.F. was physically abused by a stern and demanding immigrant father who had been physically abused by his own father. N.F.'s father stressed academic achievement and established tasks that N.F. had to perform before he entered kindergarten. Hours were set aside in which N.F.'s father would train and test N.F. in the performance of age-inappropriate tasks that any four- or five-year-old child would be developmentally and cognitively unable to perform successfully. When N.F. reliably failed to perform these age-inappropriate cognitive tasks correctly, he was beaten by his father. N.F. survived these beatings and cognitive dilemmas, but developed a passive-aggressive personality disorder (Wallace, 1990a). Once in school, N.F. was taunted and teased by children for being neither African-American nor like other immigrant children from his father's native island; N.F. felt ostracized.

Inhibition of both affect and the expression of aggressive impulses remains as a legacy of this childhood abuse (Wallace, 1990a). An adult workaholic pattern also persists, wherein N.F. strives to anticipate and satisfy the whims of male authorities, while incapable of saying "no" to their requests for task performance at work. As a result of his divorce, N.F. experienced a major depressive episode, which led to a pattern of self-medication with crack. His passive-aggressive personality disorder and inability to be emotionally available and responsive in an intimate relationship had contributed to marital conflicts (Wallace, 1990a). N.F. accepted a referral to an outpatient clinic, hoping to regain a former level of competence through a return to work.

Analysis from a Biopsychosocial Theoretical Perspective

This case again highlights how an individual exploring the contemporary social environment during the height of the crack epidemic was likely to encounter opportunities for experimentation with crack cocaine. Support for the addictive pharmacological actions of crack, the role of reinforcement and conditioning, and a person's susceptibility to addiction rooted in character functioning as factors in the etiology of crack dependence can also be derived from this case. Formation of character occurs within the context of dysfunctional family dynamics (emotional abuse, physical abuse). Subsequent adult character and personality react profoundly to the stress of separation from a spouse, manifesting a major depressive episode for which crack's euphoria provided relief—establishing the effects of crack as extra-reinforcing.

Case of A.N.

A.N., a 26-year-old African-American female and mother of two sons, graduated from high school and received training that prepared her for entry-level employment in private industry. She stopped working within the past year because of drug usage. A.N. decided to enter inpatient detoxification because she observed herself being uncharacteristically short-tempered with her children. Three weeks prior to her entering inpatient detoxification, one son began staying with her mother and her second son with her mother-in-law in response to her growing impairment from crack. A.N. had separated from her husband two years previously because of her disappointment in him as a mate. Her husband also uses crack.

Alcohol use began at age 16, while brief experimentation with marijuana did not continue. At age 20, A.N. experimented with intranasal cocaine use, but discontinued this practice. One year before entering inpatient detoxification, she began smoking crack. A.N. initially smoked $10 worth of crack once every two weeks, while also resuming use of alcohol, and then escalated to her present pattern of smoking $100 of crack per day four to five days a week. She discontinues use when she has no money. In addition to alcohol, she recently also initiated intranasal heroin use to ameliorate the effects of crack, averaging a $10 bag over two days once every two weeks. At other times, A.N. takes Valium and other pills ("downs") to temper the effects of crack. Entrance into detoxification represented her first experience with treatment.

A.N. had been exposed to an alcoholic mother who actively drank throughout A.N.'s childhood. She thus assumed the role of the responsible child who took on the tasks of caring for her younger siblings and cleaning the house. However, she was verbally and physically abused by her mother as her heroic efforts were still deemed not good enough. A.N. was also exposed to domestic violence that resulted in her mother's being "bruised and bloody." A.N. was the child who would run for assistance in managing these violent confrontations. She experienced childhood sexual molestation as well, which she attributes to her mother's disorganization and poor judgment in failing to protect her.

At the time of detoxification, A.N. presented with a dysthymic disorder. Her depressed mood reflected a long-standing experience of recurrent painful affective states and low self-esteem rooted in her childhood history, compounded by more recent disappointments in her husband and marriage. A.N. decided against entering a residential TC postdetoxification so that she could return as the primary caretaker of her children. She did, however, decide to move out of her apartment in an attempt to escape the crack environment. Attempting a geographical cure, she moved to a state where crack remains unavailable as yet. Six months after leaving inpatient detoxification, A.N. was still drug-free, but had not sought out an outpatient aftercare treatment regime. Her change of environment does not constitute sufficient treatment for her serious crack addiction or adequate relapse prevention.

Analysis from a Biopsychosocial Theoretical Perspective

A.N.'s case permits further appreciation of the kind of multiple and tragic dysfunctional family experiences (maternal alcoholism, emotional abuse, physical abuse, sexual abuse) crack smokers survive, and how, despite such histories, patterns of achievement frequently preceded the use of crack. The case also shows the all-too-familiar pattern of social experimentation with virtually any new drug available and popular socially among members of this post-1960s generation. Most drugs used in this manner presented no real problem and were often abandoned after brief experimentation. However, upon use of crack, with its addictive potential and unique and intense pharmacological actions, people such as A.N. escalate to more frequent (bimonthly to nearly daily) use and higher doses ($10–100) of crack.

What also emerges from this case as quite striking is the way in which a character and personality impacted by childhood trauma may present a vulnerability that interacts with other factors in the development and maintenance of crack addiction. For those who suffer recurrent painful affective states and low

self-esteem, or for those with a regressive character that, in response to interpersonal stress (disappointment in husband), reexperiences painful affects from
childhood, crack may be experienced as a form of self-medication that serves
temporarily to regulate affects and self-esteem. The case also reveals deterioration in psychosocial functioning (employment, child care), the use of other
chemicals (alcohol, narcotics, sedative-hypnotics) to modulate the pharmacological actions of crack, and how external controls (availability of money) and
competing rewards (children) place limits on crack use and contribute to the
termination of crack smoking.

Case of M.E.

A 30-year-old male African-American, M.E. is a high-school graduate and is
married with two children. He works for a federal service industry in a supervi-
sory position, earning an excellent income after a decade with this company.
He maintains pride in the upward mobility and level of responsibility he has
achieved at work.

The decision to enter inpatient detoxification followed signs of crack-related
financial difficulties, such as an inability to pay bills. M.E. realized he was placing his family in jeopardy by neglecting important financial obligations. A pattern had recently developed on his job where he regularly took advances
against his bimonthly paycheck for weekend and midweek use of crack, arousing the suspicion of his supervisor.

With regard to drug use, M.E. had a history of off-and-on marijuana use that
began in adolescence, which, he stated, was "never a problem." He has also occasionally sniffed cocaine with male peers, averaging $50–100. He began smok-
ing crack approximately two years ago, escalating to $100 worth of crack during
weekend smoking sessions with his male peer group. M.E. explained that his
drug use got to the point where "I spent everything I had. Every time I got
money, I spent it. I knew I needed help." He came to this realization just two
weeks before entering detoxification (Wallace, 1990b).

During M.E.'s childhood, his father was an employed alcoholic who would
become very drunk on weekends and verbally abuse his wife, arousing fears on
the part of M.E. and his two sisters that he would become violent. As a child,
M.E. also suffered an illness that required several operations, resulting in periods of isolation from his peers. At the age of 15, he faced the death of his
mother, but developed a sense of independence and completed high school as
she would have wished.

During his first inpatient detoxification and treatment, M.E. recognized that
he was repeating his father's pattern; he took his wife for granted, abused crack
on weekends, and neglected to spend time with his children. He also has low
self-esteem and depends on drug use with peers in order to feel accepted. M.E.

admitted his need to please his friends and worried about the fact that he might incur their displeasure by not being able to get high with them after his two-week inpatient detoxification. Also, he acknowledged that a lack of friends and isolation as a child may have left him overly solicitous with his current drug-using peers. M.E. did not express a broad range of affect in treatment, appearing pleasant and agreeable on a consistent basis. His self-percept was as a nice guy whom everyone likes.

After detoxification, M.E. failed to go to Cocaine Anonymous or Narcotics Anonymous meetings, nor did he keep an appointment for outpatient individual and group psychotherapy. M.E. felt that he "could handle it on my own." He observed that he was not doing anything with his spare time and had few leisure activities. After three months of avoiding old peers, M.E. responded to feelings of boredom and irritability by getting high, using $100 worth of crack. Feeling depressed over this relapse, in addition to experiencing the crash depression from crack, he continued compulsive crack smoking for another week, missing work and jeopardizing his job. A return to inpatient detoxification followed, as well as a renewed appreciation of the importance of aftercare treatment (Wallace, 1990b).

M.E. presents, in addition to crack-cocaine dependence, traits of an avoidant personality disorder that does not meet the full criteria for a personality disorder. Moreover, his feeling that he could handle his crack problem on his own and his failure to enter aftercare treatment reflect characteristic narcissism and denial in the newly abstinent; these factors contributed to his relapse episode, as did the feelings of boredom and irritability.

Analysis from a Biopsychosocial Theoretical Perspective

This case suggests how the conditioning involved in using crack to alleviate feelings of dysphoria, depression, and the "crash," as well as feelings of boredom, irritability, and loneliness, can not only promote crack smoking, but also contribute to relapse; when negative feelings such as boredom or depression recur, the negative reinforcement of having used crack to alleviate crash symptoms or negative feeling states in the past can result in renewed crack smoking. Also evident in this case are processes in the social environment whereby peer groups have moved from marijuana smoking and intranasal cocaine use to crack smoking; those susceptible to the influence of the peer group thus move on to use crack, as well. A susceptibility to the influence of peers and a need to please them and gain their acceptance may rest partly in childhood experiences (paternal alcoholism, childhood illness, death of mother) that contributed to low self-esteem. The internalization of far-from-ideal object relations with the father and the impact of dysfunctional family dynamics can also be seen in this case when M.E. observes that he is repeating his father's pattern of behavior—

but abusing crack instead of alcohol, with an even more deleterious effect on general functioning and family life. From the perspective of yet another case example, multiple variables interact as etiological influences in the development and maintenance of crack-smoking behavior, supporting a biopsychosocial theory.

Case of I.K.

I.K. is a 28-year-old married African-American woman with three children. She dropped out of high school but obtained a license as a service-industry worker, having worked for the past year in that capacity. I.K. was separated from her husband, who angrily reacted to her spending inordinate amounts of family money on crack by battering her severely. He left her, and asked the Bureau of Child Welfare to intervene in the children's lives. After the children had spent some time in foster care with strangers, I.K. pressed for their placement with a close family friend, who continues to care for them. Prior to entering inpatient detoxification, I.K. escaped severe depression over the loss of custody of her children by smoking even greater quantities of crack cocaine. She decided to detox in an effort to get her three children back. I.K. is also at risk of losing her apartment as a consequence of crack smoking.

I.K.'s first experience with drugs began at age 27, when she began using intranasal cocaine, and eventually she tried smoking crack. I.K. had been smoking crack for one year prior to detoxification. After two months of crack smoking, she tried to stop on her own, but was unable to do so. It was after eight months of I.K.'s crack smoking that her husband became enraged over her use of household money for crack, although she considered her spending on the drug to be "under control." In response to her subsequent loss of child custody, I.K. "went crazy," smoking crack "every day, all day." She resorted to shoplifting to support her habit, continuing this pattern for three months until entering inpatient detoxification for the first time.

I.K. was the younger of two children. As a result of frequent arguments, her father left the home when she was six years old. Her mother drank alcohol, but remained pleasant, according to I.K.—although she frequently was beaten by her mother for oppositional behavior. When I.K. was 14 years old, her mother died and she was raised by an aunt. The development of problems at school reflected her difficulty in adjusting to the death of her mother.

At the time of her first detoxification, I.K. was very anxious and depressed about the possible loss of her apartment and was concerned over getting custody of her children, hoping there would be an apartment to which her children could return. Her depression failed to meet DSM-III-R criteria for a mood disorder and an axis II diagnosis was deferred. She was referred to a TC for aftercare treatment. However, although she intended to follow up on the referral, she returned to her apartment instead because of fear of losing it. She resumed work as a licensed service-industry worker, frequently visiting her children in their foster home with her family friend. Because of feelings that she was struggling financially, I.K. decided to make "fast money" and began extracurricular work as a "cooker" in a crack house. After two weeks of exposure to the process of producing crack cocaine and frequenting this crack environment, I.K. relapsed to chronic crack smoking. A pattern of drinking alcohol and snorting heroin to temper the effects of crack also developed. She discontinued her service-industry work during this period and eventually lost her apartment after six months of renewed crack smoking. Shoplifting and hustling to support her crack habit led to an arrest and several days in jail. I.K. experienced jail as absolutely intolerable, which motivated her to consider seeking a second inpatient detoxification. She articulates feeling finally "ready" for long-term treatment in a TC. However, her expressed concerns over the initial restrictions and confinement of such a community raise doubts as to her ability to sustain commitment to this aftercare treatment alternative.

Analysis from a Biopsychosocial Theoretical Perspective

The case highlights how exposure to the conditioned stimuli of crack and the crack environment may trigger the conditioned response of renewed crack smoking and relapse. This scenario follows even for persons such as I.K., who are determined to resist temptation. Newly abstinent vulnerable patients may unwittingly set themselves up and eventually relapse to crack use, as I.K. did when planning only to make some "fast money." The narcissism and denial characteristic of the newly abstinent also contribute to poor judgment in deciding to expose oneself to such provocative stimuli (crack, crack environment). Exposure to her mother's drinking behavior, which probably qualifies as alcoholism (although not coded in research as such), an oppositionalism that provoked frequent beatings, and the death of her mother may have contributed to an adult character prone to escalation to the dependence syndrome and denial of the severity of the addiction.

We can also see in this case how crack can cause marital conflict, domestic violence, and separation from one's spouse, and even lead to the loss of child custody. Most important, the case illustrates how the intense depression and anguish following the loss of child custody may be responded to by heavy self-medication with the smoking of more crack. Women such as I.K. may naturally resort to self-medication of depression with more crack as a consequence of their learning through negative reinforcement that smoking more and more crack alleviates the dysphoria of the "crash" that follows when coming down from a crack high. Thus, while the case provides an opportunity to see the way in which crack can lead to the loss of child custody and the placement of children with family or friends in the extended African-American family system, it also furnishes support for the necessity of drawing on a biopsychosocial theory of crack addiction.

Case of E.I.

E.I., a 26-year-old, single African-American man, dropped out of high school and has worked for approximately six years at the same blue-collar-level job in a white-collar establishment. At work, he was reprimanded for crack-related lateness a few weeks before entering treatment. The use of accumulated vacation time permitted E.I. to enter treatment without informing his superiors of his drug problem. He decided to undergo detoxification after failing to pay his rent for over two months and stealing a small amount of money from his mother in order to purchase crack. E.I. admits to shame, embarrassment, and depression over having to admit to his mother the nature of his crack use and related financial problems. A former girlfriend's whereabouts are also a source of anxiety for E.I., as this woman could either be in treatment or out on the streets still compulsively smoking crack.

A drug history began with the use of marijuana at age 15, which he discontinued when he began smoking crack a year and a half ago. E.I. also began drinking beer at age 14, averaging a quart a week and escalating by age 17 to the point where he was able to drink three quarts of beer on his own. Prior to initiating crack smoking, E.I. averaged four or five quarts of beer per day—a quart in the morning, another at lunch, and two or three after work. When he began crack use, he stopped his heavy consumption of beer in order to save his money for crack. E.I. had briefly smoked cocaine (powder) in cigarettes before trying crack. Initially, he smoked $10 worth of crack once per week, which increased to $20–30 crack every day as he tried to accompany his girlfriend on her crack-smoking sprees. Prior to entering detoxification, E.I. had averaged $30–70 worth of crack on a daily basis, and consumed a quart of beer every other day.

During childhood, E.I. was exposed to an alcoholic father who drank daily, became cantankerous, and initiated domestic disputes that culminated in weekend violent beatings of E.I.'s mother that seemed to occur "all the time." E.I. felt scared, as these beatings often resulted in the drawing of blood, a need for stitches, and the calling of the police. He was the youngest of five children and recalls his parents' separation when he was approximately eight years of age because of the violence and his father's alcoholism. E.I.'s father visited the children infrequently, and E.I. admits to having had no father–son relationship. An older brother in the household became involved in intravenous drug use and would terrorize E.I. by beating him up in an effort to teach him how to fight. E.I. was also forced to help his brother inject intravenous drugs. Feeling scared in response to his brother's terrorism, E.I. learned to hide his feelings. A romance at the age of 18 was also experienced as very traumatic as his girlfriend proved to be unfaithful and in the process taught E.I. to "hold back a lot" in intimate relationships.

E.I. left detoxification serious about involvement in outpatient treatment and a return to work. A diagnosis was deferred on axis II. E.I. presented with a depressed mood and intense shame over his secret crack addiction, but no mood disorder was sufficient to meet DSM-III-R criteria.

Analysis from a Biopsychosocial Theoretical Perspective

This case suggests the probable role of crack's pharmacological actions and neurochemically based cravings in promoting an increase in the frequency of crack smoking (weekly to daily) and in the dose of crack smoked ($10 to $70). The case also shows how individuals who are still employed, but limited in financial resources and ashamed and unwilling to steal from their family, both may lose control (escalate to dependence, fall behind in paying bills) and experience external controls (supervisor's warning at work, fear of loss of job, fear of loss of mother's support) as setting limits on crack use and as a source of motivation for entering treatment.

Also, the case illustrates how a son of a violent alcoholic began to develop an alcoholic drinking pattern, and how a vulnerability to crack addiction largely replaced alcohol use. Whereas drinking often permits a more or less functional work pattern, crack use leads to much more dysfunctional behavior, as the reprimand for lateness at work and the crack-related financial problems suggest. Clearly, the pharmacological imperative to smoke more crack can create a serious addiction and jeopardize any sense of stability in an individual's life. Members of a generation that smokes crack therefore may experience more psychosocial dysfunction than their own alcoholic parents, as this case suggests. But for this generation, childhood experiences in dysfunctional families (alcoholism, domestic violence, father's absence) may have left them vulnerable to the extra-reinforcing impact of new chemicals such as crack. Thus, another case supports our use of a biopsychosocial theory.

Case of J.B.

A 27-year-old Hispanic woman with two children, J.B. had dropped out of high school. She left her husband and apartment six months before entering inpatient detoxification. Her husband had introduced her to drug use, and by leaving him she hoped to escape continuation of her own drug problem. J.B. entered treatment to undergo detoxification from crack and intranasal heroin, deciding to remain on 30 mg of methadone. At a social-service agency where she sought information about setting up an apartment with her children, professional workers detected her drug problem and called in the Bureau of Child Welfare. Her two children were placed with her parents by the bureau three months prior to her detoxification. She entered a methadone-maintenance program as one of her first attempts to regain custody of her children after this event. Arguments with her parents, with whom she now lives, motivated her to enter detoxification for her continuing problem with crack and intranasal heroin. The most recent crisis in her life was precipitated by a court decision to the effect that she cannot go near her children, creating an immediate housing problem and emotional turmoil for J.B..

J.B. first began intranasal heroin use at the age of 23. At age 26, she began snorting cocaine. Her intranasal heroin habit was initially $10 a day. She stopped using heroin for one year when pregnant, but soon afterwards began intravenous heroin use, averaging $80–90 per day. She started using crack just five months prior to entering her first inpatient detoxification, initially at the rate of $40–50 of crack two to three times per week. Currently, she smokes $100–150 worth of crack on an every-other-day basis. J.B. continues to snort $10 of heroin once per week despite being on 30 mg of methadone within a maintenance program for the past three months.

As a child, J.B. was the oldest daughter with three siblings. Her father was an alcoholic up until recent years. He would return home after spending large amounts of money while out drinking, to be beaten up by J.B.'s mother who was larger than her husband. He became severely depressed as a consequence of the humiliation of the beatings by his wife. J.B. resented her mother for these beatings and reacted with oppositionalism, whereby she did the opposite of whatever her mother directed her to do. This rebellious pattern led to drug use and an early marriage she did not want. Her father's alcoholism permitted sexual abuse by a family relative when J.B. was nine, as a result of her father's irresponsibility and poor judgment when drunk. When, as an adult, she told her father about this incident, he said that the rape was probably her fault, compounding the hurt and pain of this traumatic event. J.B. adds that the birth of her younger siblings also led to a loss of attention and hurtful feelings, contributing to her doing virtually anything to get parental attention. J.B. left detoxification prematurely when she received notice of court proceedings covering a motion that she might not be able to see her children at all.

Analysis from a Biopsychosocial Theoretical Perspective

The case illustrates the way in which the availability of crack in the social environment permitted its experimental use by even relatively "hard core" intravenous heroin addicts. The compelling and intense nature of the crack-smoking high and the compulsion of users to increase the frequency and dose of crack smoked may be so powerful that crack use emerges as the dominating addiction and preferred high, as the case suggests. Even for someone who negotiates adolescence without using drugs, the experimental use of chemicals in an individual left susceptible to the development of addiction as a consequence of childhood trauma in a dysfunctional family may still lead to an addiction later in adulthood.

When a person in the same household utilizes drugs and introduces a spouse to drug-taking behaviors, the influence of the environment is critical in the development and maintenance of drug-use patterns. The case also shows how many people may need to leave the environmental and interpersonal influence of a dominating spouse who actively uses drugs. However, where a severe addiction has already developed, even when the wife, as in this case, achieves independence from the direct influence of a drug-taking husband, she must still struggle to overcome her addiction.

Multiple interacting variables captured within a biopsychosocial theoretical perspective again explain the complex nature of addiction. The case also highlights the fact that among individuals being maintained on methadone in formal programs, the use of crack-cocaine smoking has also become popular. In addition, this case reveals how loss of child custody and the involvement of child protective services typically follow as a consequence of escalating drug addiction in women. As is also apparent from this case, continuing crises in crack smokers' lives often precludes their continuing or active involvement in treatment.

Case of D.C.

D.C., a 26-year-old male Hispanic, decided to undergo inpatient detoxification after his wife and two children left him because of his crack use. D.C. dropped out of high school, but is a licensed independent contractor. He received three years of specialized course work and training. Marital conflict over the past year focused on D.C.'s difficulty in acquiring contracts for work, financial problems, and difficulties in communicating with his wife. Crack played a role in his financial problems and marital conflict. He and his wife nearly came to blows, resulting in his wife's decision to leave him.

A drug history began at age 19 with the smoking of marijuana a few times a week, but he soon decided to stop the practice, without any problems, and he never attempted the intranasal use of cocaine. Seven months prior to entering detoxification, D.C. began smoking crack. The stress associated with the approaching end of a work contract and related marital conflict led to an increase in crack smoking to his current pattern of $100–150 per day. D.C. was self-medicating feelings of depression and frustration related to loss of work and to arguments with his wife, whom he perceived as nagging him.

D.C. was the youngest of three children. During D.C.'s childhood, his father became ill and unable to work, and financial difficulties ensued. Since D.C. had always been spoiled, this period of financial difficulty was stressful. He often lacked money for lunch and had to walk to school instead of taking the bus. His father finally died from his illness a year and a half prior to D.C.'s entrance into detoxification. One effect of his father's death was a decline in D.C.'s grades and school performance during training for his present line of work, forcing him to take longer to complete his studies. A sister who is a medical doctor was financially and emotionally supportive of D.C. during this difficult period.

D.C. responded to therapeutic support provided during detoxification, which enabled him to cope with what was initially experienced as the devastating departure of his wife. Recognition of long-standing marital conflicts—admittedly exacerbated by his crack use, and from which he escaped by smoking more crack—permitted D.C. to accept this major life stressor. He left detoxification with a referral to outpatient treatment and a determination to gain visitation rights so he could see his children.

Analysis from a Biopsychosocial Theoretical Perspective

Sudden financial difficulties or poverty may cause narcissistic injuries to a young child forced to make uncomfortable adjustments. This childhood trauma may have predisposed D.C. to a reaction of anxiety and depression when adult financial difficulties and uncertainties about future income arose and triggered old feelings of anxiety. Chemical use served to self-medicate anxiety and dysphoric feelings. The availability of crack and crack's pharmacological imperative permitted D.C. to escalate to a high-dose ($100–150), daily crack-smoking pattern. Again, a biopsychosocial theory of the etiology of crack dependence receives support.

Case of L.A.

L.A., a 19-year-old white male, dropped out of high school but received his equivalency diploma. He decided to run away from his father's home because he was tired of "causing him pain" by stealing items from the home to support his crack habit. He had been living back in his home with his father only a couple of months. His father had asked him to leave because of his prior stealing behavior. L.A. entered treatment feeling guilty, ashamed, and depressed about his stealing and anxious over how his father probably reacted when he discovered that both valued possessions and L.A. had disappeared. L.A. ended up in New York City's Covenant House for runaway young people; after spending three days there, he accepted a referral to our inpatient detoxification program.

L.A.'s drug history began at age 16 with the smoking of just a "little marijuana," never establishing a regular marijuana-smoking pattern. At age 17, L.A. similarly drank "a little." At age 18, one year prior to entering detoxification, he began snorting half a gram of cocaine once a week, gradually increasing his use to 1 gram of cocaine on a daily basis. L.A. tried to stop intranasal use of cocaine at various times, but the longest he was able to do so was for a month, and he always returned to intranasal cocaine use "because of desire." Six months before entering detoxification, L.A. began smoking crack, using $5–10 of crack per day in addition to intranasal cocaine. He now uses $50 of crack per day, having discontinued intranasal cocaine use a couple of months ago.

L.A., the youngest of three children, had been exposed to an alcoholic mother. L.A.'s father told him that his mother had been an alcoholic all of L.A.'s life. L.A. became aware of just how heavy his mother's drinking was when, at the age of 15, he began finding vodka bottles hidden all over the house. His mother was always "smashed" by the time she was cooking dinner. However, she was the parent who was always there whenever L.A. got into trouble. During treatment on the detoxification unit, L.A. accepted the interpretation that his rebelliousness and "trouble-making" in school may have been a way to get his mother's "full" attention and elicit her concern. L.A. was referred to a psychiatrist when he was 12 because he was "a brat at school," always "creating a nuisance." Treatment stopped because there was no real problem. His mother died when L.A. was 16. He states that he felt empty and alone when she died, that he started "messing up" and her death was the reason he turned to drugs.

Interventions during detoxification assisted L.A. in managing intense levels of anxiety and shame. L.A. wondered if his father had discovered all the missing items, but seemed less concerned as to whether or not his father was worried about where L.A. was staying at this point. He accepted a referral to a TC postdetoxification.

Analysis from a Biopsychosocial Theoretical Perspective

From the perspective of a biopsychosocial theory of crack addiction, the case supports the role of numerous interacting factors in the development and maintenance of crack addiction. The depression following the death of his mother contributed to a pattern of seeking the relief chemicals afforded him from dysphoria and feelings of emptiness and aloneness. A history of dysfunctional family dynamics (mother's alcoholism) and his reaction of rebelliousness to these dynamics also predisposed L.A. to a pattern of chemical use. The introduction into the social environment of a drug that was so inexpensive that a teenager with as little as $5 could purchase this exciting "high" presented innumerable opportunities for adolescents such as L.A. to experiment with crack.

In L.A.'s case, intranasal cocaine use had already reached considerable levels and he was unable to discontinue it. However, the pharmacological imperative to use more and more cocaine is incredibly more intense after smoking crack, as a result of the even more deleterious disruption of brain functioning produced by the crack. Replacement of an intranasal cocaine-use pattern with exclusive crack smoking occurred as an increase in the frequency and dose of crack smoked followed from crack's pharmacological actions. Crack use also was so compulsive that it led to stealing, conflicts with his father, and his running away from home.

CONCLUSION

These cases support the contention that, in addition to biological and social factors, psychosocial variables also play an important role in the development of crack addiction. From the perspective of a biopsychosocial theory of crack addiction, clinicians, researchers, and policy makers must appreciate the "multiplicity of interacting variables that contribute to the individual's uniqueness and general level of function, as well as to the person's attraction toward and susceptibility to an addictive behavior" (Peele, 1985; Donovan, 1988, p. 14).

The cases also reflect the diversity to be found within a sample (Wallace, 1990b) of inner-city crack-cocaine smokers. The 12 cases—including five African-American males, four African-American females, one Hispanic female, one Hispanic male, and one white male—are representative of the patients in Wallace's (1990b) sample, which is 92.2% African-American, 5.3% Hispanic, and 2% white. Diversity in the frequency and dose of crack smoking, as well as in the degree of psychosocial functioning maintained at the time of entering treatment, also can be seen in the cases.

The analysis of cases reveals the necessity of drawing on a biopsychosocial theory in order adequately to account for the multiple, interacting etiological factors that lie behind crack addiction. What kind of treatment works in promoting the successful recovery of crack patients with these kinds of high-dose, high-frequency crack-smoking patterns, childhood histories in dysfunctional families, and living in a social environment where peer influence and a crack-saturated environment promote relapse?

III

CRACK-TREATMENT MODELS

8

What Works for
Crack-Cocaine Smokers
in Treatment?

Through a review and analysis of outcome-evaluation research studies, this chapter will attempt to answer the question, "What works for crack smokers in treatment?" What constitutes a state-of-the-art treatment for crack addiction, in this author's opinion, is a treatment that appreciates the role of biological, psychological, and social factors, as in a biopsychosocial model; recognizes the type of patient for whom the treatment works; acknowledges the phase of treatment or recovery when the treatment should be administered; and includes relapse prevention. A treatment that "works" produces, on follow-up, relatively high rates of abstinence from crack or cocaine.

Certain limitations are placed on the discussion and our ability definitively to answer the question of what works with crack smokers because of the dearth of outcome-evaluation research on actual crack-smoking populations. As a result, an analysis of what works with mostly white, middle-class, intranasal cocaine users will direct our attempt to ascertain what should work with crack smokers possessing diverse demographics and characteristics.

COMPREHENSIVE, INTENSIVE, MULTIFACETED
OUTPATIENT TREATMENT

An outpatient-treatment program that can be described as providing comprehensive and intensive services, while clinicians use multifaceted clinical interventions, appears to work. A comprehensive treatment addresses the drug problem through a number of interventions, such as education, urine testing, individual sessions, family/couples sessions, group sessions, and relapse prevention. An intensive treatment requires patients to participate at a level that involves contacts several times per week with the treatment program. Use of a multifaceted clinical technique means that professionals utilize educational, cognitive, behavioral, and psychodynamic interventions, or techniques derived from a rationale that involves cognitive, behavioral, or psychodynamic theory. Research studies support this characterization of the kind of outpatient treatment that works.

An Exemplary Treatment Model

Washton, Gold, and Pottash (1986) present treatment outcome data on 63 chronic cocaine abusers consecutively admitted to the Regents Hospital outpatient program during a six-month period. Their largely white, employed sample included a majority of patients who did not have a prior inpatient hospital stay. Another quarter of their patients (25%) did enter outpatient treatment from inpatient treatment. In their sample, a third (33%) engaged in free-base smoking, a minority (5%) presented intravenous use, and the majority (62%) were intranasal users. Compulsive use for six months preceded treatment. The actual treatment included the use of contracting (an agreement to stay in treatment for six months), drug education, urine monitoring, problem-oriented counseling, cocaine recovery groups, individual psychotherapy mixed with couples and/or family sessions where indicated, and relapse-prevention strategies. The program included flexibility in responding to individual patient needs. Follow-up status was determined by supervised urine testing and clinical assessment interviews. What kind of follow-up results does this kind of comprehensive and intensive outpatient treatment produce?

Washton et al.'s (1986) findings show that of the original 63 patients, the majority (94%, n = 59) completed at least three months of treatment and (67%, n = 42) completed at least six months of treatment. Average time of retention in treatment was 26.5 weeks, with a large proportion (49%) continuing treatment beyond seven months at the time of follow-up investigation. At the seven- to 19-month follow-up, 81% (n = 51) of the original 63 patients were still abstinent and 12 patients had dropped out of treatment and relapsed to cocaine use. Among the 51 (81%) who were still abstinent, approximately half had experienced at least one or two returns to cocaine use without a full-blown relapse to chronic or compulsive use. Success rates were directly related to length of time in treatment. A longer time in treatment related to more successful abstinence (pp. 382–383).

Patient and Program Characteristics as Keys to Outpatient Success

Washton et al. (1986) attribute their high success rates to patient characteristics (successfully employed in professional or highly skilled jobs, history of good functioning before cocaine use, willingness to enter a program that required complete abstinence, motivation out of fear of losing valued rewards—job, marriage). However, success rates were also attributed to characteristics of their program (addressed drug-abuse problem immediately, held high expectations, and placed a strong emphasis on abstinence, as well as recovery and relapse prevention). The researchers also note their use of a wide range of interventions, including cognitive, behavioral, and supportive techniques (peer support groups).

Good reason exists for speculating that active focus on the drug problem, conveyance of high and positive expectations of a good prognosis, emphasis on relapse prevention, and use of a wide range of interventions (individual, family/couples counseling, recovery groups, urine testing) with a multifaceted clinical technique might produce substantial success rates with crack smokers.

Inpatient Plus Outpatient Treatment for High-Severity Patients

Within the Washton et al. (1986) study, those with the most severe cocaine problems (25%) had inpatient treatment first and experienced a structured environment in which to undergo withdrawal from cocaine. "The hospitalized patients were using larger doses of cocaine and were more likely to show medical and psychiatric complications related to drug use" (Washton, Gold, & Pottash, 1986, p. 383). Washton and colleagues emphasize that, without initial hospitalization, these patients probably would have had little chance of succeeding in outpatient treatment. They assert that the treatment sequence of inpatient followed by outpatient treatment was an effective intervention strategy for these high-severity patients (pp. 383–384).

Charles P. O'Brien of the University of Pennsylvania in Philadelphia reports that two thirds of crack addicts who have enrolled in his outpatient-treatment program drop out within the first month. Bernard Bihari of Kings County Hospital in Brooklyn, N.Y., reports that only 15% of crack users showed up for the second day of an outpatient-treatment program he administered. The problems noted as accounting for the high failure rates of these outpatient programs relate to the fact that crack users must return to the same surroundings, have few social supports to help them stay in treatment, and usually lack employment. Herbert Kleber suggests that the institution of more programs that house addicts should be considered despite the greater expense (Kolata, 1989, Aug. 24, p. B7).

Crack-cocaine smokers require the kind of thorough assessment that determines whether they should be matched to inpatient treatment before direct entrance into outpatient treatment. Separation from the environment during a phase of withdrawal may be crucial if crack smokers experiencing intense neurochemically based cravings for more crack are to avoid conditioned stimuli in the environment and easy access to crack. Washton et al. (1986) conclude by emphasizing that no single treatment modality will be optimal for all cocaine abusers, and that research is needed to identify the essential ingredients of the most effective approaches.

The treatment model Washton and colleagues investigated emerges as a state-of-the-art treatment that includes carefully assessing patients for individual needs, matching patients to treatments (either inpatient followed by outpatient or direct entrance into outpatient), and educating for relapse prevention. It can be assumed that the need for biological interventions is inherent in an approach that recognizes that the high-severity, high-dosage cocaine user, or the user with psychiatric complications, requires inpatient interventions that probably include biological or pharmacological interventions. For cocaine users who are screened, assessed, and deemed appropriate for direct entrance into outpatient treatment, such treatment can work when it includes an intense and comprehensive program with the kind of elements Washton et al. include.

The Intensive Outpatient Rehabilitation Program

Washton's treatment approach (Washton, 1987, 1989a; Washton, Stone, & Hendrickson, 1988) has evolved toward an even more intensive and comprehensive outpatient program than the one evaluated by Washton et al. (1986). Washton (1989a) cites crucial elements of an intensive outpatient-rehabilitation program that may be capable of producing substantially higher long-term success rates than traditional inpatient care. The intensive out-patient-rehabilitation program has an intensive component that lasts two months and a relapse-prevention program that lasts six months. In the first intensive program, patients attend group-therapy sessions, educational lectures, and self-help meetings four evenings a week; this program usually lasts three hours each evening. Patients receive, in addition, individual, marital, and family counseling at least once per week, and family members attend an eight-week family education and counseling program. In the relapse-prevention program, patients attend group-therapy meetings, educational lectures, and self-help meetings three evenings a week, and receive individual and/or marital/family counseling once a week. Family members also continue in ongoing family recovery groups (Washton, 1989a, pp. 76–77).

Clearly, this program of interventions constitutes the very best in comprehensive and intensive outpatient treatment. Evaluation of the intensive outpatient-rehabilitation program shows that over 80% of patients admitted to the program successfully complete treatment; long-term follow-up studies have yet to be completed (Washton, 1989a). However, when this kind of nearly daily, intense involvement in a comprehensive treatment program takes place, Washton reports finding referrals to inpatient treatment decreasing. According to Washton, prior to implementing the intensive program, 35% of all treatment applicants were referred to residential care; however, now fewer than 15% require inpatient treatment (p. 77). Hence, Washton anticipates that utilization of an intensive outpatient-rehabilitation treatment model may be capable of producing substantially higher long-term success rates than traditional inpatient care (p. 77).

Still, Washton continues to recognize that some patients will require inpatient care—severely dysfunctional, debilitated patients, those with serious medical and psychiatric complications, and those for whom outpatient treatment has not worked (p. 77). Yet, here, inpatient treatment must serve as a "launching pad" for involvement in continuing treatment posthospitalization (p. 78).

More recent findings support the efficacy of treating employed cocaine and crack addicts in inpatient or outpatient rehabilitation programs that are combined with intensive aftercare treatment emphasizing relapse prevention; at 6-to-18 month followup, according to urine tests and clinical interviews, 68% of outpatients (n = 40) and 64% of inpatients (n = 20) were abstinent. Among these patients, 33% experienced a slip at least once to their drug of choice, 23% used alcohol or marijuana, and 46% experienced no slip or relapse to chemical use (Washton, 1989c). Again, individualized assessment of patients will likely reveal that substantial numbers of crack smokers will require not only some period of hospitalization or separation from the environment, but also the kind of intensive and comprehensive outpatient services following an inpatient stay that Washton (1989a) has refined.

Further Support for Comprehensive Outpatient Treatment

Rawson, Obert, McCann, and Mann (1986) provide further evidence that an outpatient program with certain key elements can indeed work. They examined treatment outcome following inpatient, outpatient, and no treatment among a group of 83 subjects who presented themselves at an information and education session regarding cocaine use and available treatment. Subjects were recruited from those calling a 24-hour cocaine hotline. After the educational session, subjects could choose inpatient hospital treatment, structured outpatient treatment, participation in anonymous self-help groups, or no treatment. Despite the limitations of no random assignment, findings showed there were no differences in subject characteristics prior to entering treatment. Among subjects, fee-base smokers accounted for 43% of those who chose no treatment, 40% of those who chose outpatient treatment, and 30% of those who chose hospital treatment. Results showed a return to cocaine use by 13% of those undergoing approximately six months of outpatient treatment, 43% of those completing a 28-day hospital stay and being interviewed some seven months after hospitalization, and 47% of those who received no formal treatment.

It should be noted that those in outpatient treatment in the Rawson et al. (1986) study were questioned fairly soon after completion of outpatient treatment, whereas those in the inpatient group were questioned nearly seven months posttreatment. Wallace (1989a) reports that of those who relapse, 76% do so within three months posttreatment and 94% before six months expire. Hence, for the inpatient group questioned seven months posthospitalization, more time had expired since treatment, and so this group was likely to include more patients who had relapsed. Another criticism of the study is that those who participated in outpatient treatment received the key elements of a state-of-the-art treatment—individual sessions, relapse prevention, family and couples counseling, and urine testing. However, the hospital model lacked relapse prevention and direct entrance into outpatient treatment did not occur for the majority of patients. The provision of relapse prevention during inpatient treatment and direct entrance into aftercare treatment after an inpatient stay are critical in order to reduce the chances of relapse (Wallace, 1989b). Thus, these factors deserve consideration when analyzing the conclusions of Rawson et al.

Rawson et al. (1986) conclude that their preliminary outcome data suggest that outpatient treatment may result in a lower relapse rate than hospital treatment or no treatment. The limitations of the study's design, however, and of the particular hospital model utilized must not be overlooked. In fact, the researchers acknowledge that the current hospital aftercare program may not be appropriately oriented to the needs of cocaine patients, since most patients did not attend the aftercare-treatment component. The deficits of the hospital program prevented its emergence as a treatment that works. What does emerge as something that works is an outpatient program that includes individual counseling, family and couples counseling, relapse prevention, and urine testing. This study reinforces the notion that outpatient treatment works when it has certain crucial elements that produce, in effect, a comprehensive and intensive treatment model.

Even within the most successful group of outpatients in the Rawson et al. (1986) study, a full 13% relapsed to at least monthly cocaine use. And some may have had just one or two episodes of cocaine use that did not qualify as monthly use. A report of 13% returning to monthly cocaine use highlights the risk of relapse that challenges clinicians and researchers to strive to improve even successful program models to better meet the needs of patients. Since within this study a considerable percentage of patients were free-base-cocaine smokers, it may be assumed that motivated crack smokers who would call a hotline and attend an informational session would probably do as well in recovery as did those patients who received no treatment, inpatient treatment, or outpatient treatment of the kind provided in the Rawson et al. study. Instead of having patients prone to a denial of the severity of their addiction select their own treatment, professional consultation might have better matched patients to treatments of appropriate intensity according to the severity of their addiction, perhaps further reducing relapse rates.

The Neurobehavioral Model of Cocaine Outpatient Treatment

In view of their earlier findings in the Rawson et al. (1986) study, Rawson began in January 1990 a study of 100 cocaine-addict volunteers randomly assigned to either what they now label the neurobehavioral treatment program or to a comparison situation consisting of referral to available community resources. Rawson has further articulated the components of the neurobehavioral model, which, he feels, works with cocaine and crack patients, outlining even more explicitly the elements of an effective outpatient treatment. Treatment focuses on behavioral, cognitive, emotional, and relationship problems that typically characterize different phases of recovery from cocaine addiction. The program lasts 12 months and strives to ensure that clients complete treatment, learn about issues critical to addiction and relapse, receive direction and support from a trained therapist (master's-degree level with 60 hours of specialized training), receive education for family members, and be monitored by urine testing. The actual treatment includes 52 individual 45-minute sessions in the first six months, a 12-week educational group, a four-week group focusing on structuring weekends and leisure time, a 20-week relapse-prevention group, seven conjoint/couples sessions in the first six months, weekly random urine tests, analysis of relapse episodes in individual sessions, and AA meetings. In months 7–12 of recovery, a weekly same-sex group is held, while individual and couples sessions continue for patients desiring to remain in ongoing therapy (Rawson, Obert, McCann, Smith, & Ling, 1990).

Rawson (1990) admits that this program is fairly expensive by outpatient standards, ranging in cost from $1,500 to $6,000 (p. 11). His treatment costs "$4,500 for patients whose health insurance covers treatment or who can easily afford it" (p. 12). In one facility, a sliding scale exists, and for those at the bottom of the scale, treatment costs $25 a month (p. 12).

The evolution and refinement of Rawson's neurobehavioral model have benefited from the assistance, recommendations, research, and experience of the best chemical-dependency-treatment professionals across the nation (Kleber, Gawin, O'Brien, McLellan, Washton, Marlatt, Gorski, Smith, Zweben, and Resnick and Resnick; see references). The resulting state-of-the-art treatment provides for the kind of structure, intensive level of participation, and availability of comprehensive services necessary to produce an effective outpatient program. Patients receiving these kind of supportive services "every day in the first weeks and at least several times per week for six months thereafter" (Rawson, 1990, p. 11) are likely to benefit in terms of a successful recovery from cocaine addiction. Rawson views his yearlong outpatient approach as preferable to inpatient treatment, which is "excessively expensive and often unnecessary for recovery" (p. 11). On the other hand, hard-core crack users who have been on a binge in the streets for a long time are placed in the hospital by Rawson for three to five days. He acknowledges that unless they have respite from cocaine, are able to sleep, and receive nutritious food, such patients are not coherent enough "to even hear the therapist" (p. 11). Thus, crack-cocaine smokers may require some period of inpatient care prior to entrance into the kind of quality outpatient treatment Rawson describes.

Individual Psychotherapy in an Inpatient Plus an Outpatient Treatment Model

Although based on a rather small sample size, suggestive findings support the assertion that a well-structured hospital program that includes aftercare treatment with certain crucial elements can also work in producing a successful treatment outcome. Schiffer (1988) reports that he successfully treated nine cocaine abusers with long-term in-depth dynamic psychotherapy that began on an inpatient drug-abuse unit and continued on an outpatient basis as aftercare treatment. After at least a year posthospitalization, Schiffer notes that these mostly white, male, employed patients, who for the most part used intranasal cocaine, were drug-free. Only two patients (22.2%) had a brief relapse a few months after hospitalization, but reestablished their abstinence and have been drug-free for over three years. While in the hospital, patients were seen three times a week in individual psychotherapy, and after discharge were seen as outpatients on a twice-a-week basis for one month. Patients were then seen individually once a week for an average of 22 months. The length of treatment ranged from ten months to 37 months.

Schiffer's rationale for individual psychotherapy rests on the fact that all patients suffered some form of trauma or psychological abuse in childhood that necessitates that the therapist do the following: (1) look for the traumatic or abusive condition; (2) establish empathic emotional contact with the patient involving appreciation of why cocaine abuse occurred; (3) help the patient appreciate the covert trauma (narcissistic injuries, neglect, rejection, humiliation, intimidation) suffered in childhood and its impact on his or her development; and (4) help the patient master traumatic experiences. A result of impaired psychological development may be depression and anxiety, which can be addressed in psychotherapy, according to Schiffer. He feels that supportive therapy aimed at enhancing abstinence is necessary as others have suggested; however, he argues that "supportive therapy without working successfully on the deeper issues would have been insufficient for a good long-term outcome" (p. 136).

Random urine-testing results and signed statements of abstinence by patients and their family contributed to the efficacy of the approach. Schiffer views the hospital environment as facilitating a decathexis from the life of drugs by providing firm limits, structure, and education. While psychotropic medication is often recommended based on clinical assessments, none in the sample received it. Beyond provision of in-depth dynamic individual psychotherapy, the hospital treatment also offered psychotherapy groups, drug-education groups, discussions of stress-coping techniques, and frequent staff talks. All of these elements emerge as important dimensions of a sufficiently intense and comprehensive inpatient program that works in contrast to the inpatient model in the Rawson et al. (1986) study.

Long-term Individual Psychotherapy as Relapse Prevention

Despite the weakness inherent in Schiffer's (1988) small sample size, the study highlights the role of long-term, in-depth individual psychotherapy as relapse prevention. In the process, the study reinforces the assertion of Washton et al. (1986) that where intensive aftercare treatment follows inpatient treatment, we effectively have a state-of-the-art treatment that works. While some patients attended a combination of group therapy and individual psychotherapy or self-help groups plus individual psychotherapy, aftercare treatment that addresses deeper psychological issues emerges as an element of treatment that may be crucial for successful recovery.

Kleber (1988) points out that cocaine use is extremely compelling in itself and may not require predisposition for abuse to develop (p. 1364). However, evidence that all patients in Schiffer's sample had traumatic childhood experiences and other data showing that 91% of crack smokers similarly experience trauma in dysfunctional families in childhood (Wallace, 1989c) argues for interventions that address this possibly predisposing risk factor for the development of addiction. Treatments that address these underlying emotional and psychological issues may provide an essential kind of relapse prevention or risk reduction for reinvolvement in any kind of addictive behavior and work in the long term as Schiffer's data suggest. Perhaps Schiffer correctly emphasizes that a good long-term outcome may depend on addressing these underlying traumatic events in a cocaine abuser's childhood.

Even though Schiffer's sample included mostly white, employed, intranasal-cocaine users, the fact that they, too, experienced childhood trauma argues strongly for the kind of vulnerabilities cocaine and crack users possess for the development of dependence regardless of race or demographics. It, therefore, logically follows that crack-cocaine smokers may also benefit from long-term individual psychotherapy that addresses the impact of childhood trauma and its relationship to the development of chemical dependency. The distinct advantage of individual psychotherapy that begins on an inpatient unit and continues with the same therapist on an outpatient basis also arises from Schiffer's work.

Outpatient Treatment for Pregnant Crack Smokers and Mothers

Regarding treatments that work for special populations, evidence suggests the efficacy of the treatment provided at the Center for Perinatal Addiction at Northwestern Hospital in Chicago under the initiative of Ira Chasnoff. The components of this "model program" are prenatal medical care, pediatric follow-up, social-service case management, chemical-dependency treatment on-site, an interdisciplinary staff, parent education, support groups, and the use of community outreach (Kronstadt, 1989). According to Kronstadt, the importance of these components arises from the fact that pregnant cocaine abusers present a typical profile of a history of physical/sexual/emotional abuse, present with chemical dependency, likely live with a drug-using partner, often come from poor and chaotic environments, feel guilty and responsible for their plight, and have low self-esteem. Kronstadt goes on to explain that once cocaine/crack babies are born, mothers face the challenge of caring for a difficult baby who will be jittery and have tremors; be irritable, overexcitable, and very sensitive to the mildest environmental stimulation; cry a lot; and be unable to calm itself. Even experienced caregivers find it difficult to care for cocaine/crack babies. Thus, treatment and support of mothers for their addiction and parent education are critical components of a model program (Kronstadt, 1989).

In the Northwestern outpatient program for pregnant crack mothers, 79% are still off drugs one year after giving birth (New York Times, p. A14, Aug. 7, 1989). However, Chandler (1989) concedes that while pregnant women are able to maintain abstinence while pregnant and shortly after giving birth within this outpatient program, they are still plagued by the problem of relapse. This author notes that this program may require a more intensive relapse prevention education component. Chandler reports that a study that was to begin in early 1990 will compare the treatment outcomes of 30 women treated in an inpatient setting and 30 women in an outpatient setting.

Halfon (1989) characterizes the kind of treatment models that need to be created for pregnant crack users and their babies as having to provide a continuum of care. Patients need linked services at every step of the treatment process. Halfon points out that "turf issues" among different social-service agencies must be resolved and that few good models exist. He suggests that the kind of continuity of care utilized with the elderly might provide a model for the kind of services he envisions as critical for pregnant women and cocaine babies.

Kronstadt's (1989) survey of experts across the nation indicates that programs for pregnant crack mothers must be comprehensive, offering as many services as possible at one site, such as prenatal medical care, pediatric care of the infant, chemical-dependency treatment, and coordination of social services. In addition, treatment interventions must be intensive, providing frequent contacts with clients over a long period, even home visits, a drop-in center, and a 24-hour crisis phone line. Upon treatment experts' strong recommendations, Kronstadt highlights the need for residential treatment programs for those most severely dependent, as well as drug-free housing for all other clients, which includes provisions for children to remain with their mothers. Most important, national treatment experts stressed the critical need for more treatment programs to serve the increasing numbers of pregnant women and their children, according to Kronstadt.

Northwestern's program emerges as a model comprehensive and intensive program, while exploration of the efficacy of inpatient care represents an appropriate direction for continuing research efforts. However, the kind of models that provide a continuity of care, and recognize that some mothers require inpatient treatment; others, outpatient treatment alone or after inpatient treatment; and still others, long-term residential treatment, have yet to be created in adequate numbers to meet the critical needs of this special population.

IMPLICATIONS FOR DESIGNING COST-EFFECTIVE TREATMENT

Marlatt (1988) cautions against uniformity myths where the same treatment is recommended for everyone exhibiting signs of the particular addiction problem. In this regard, he suggests that one alternative is the "notion that treatment for addiction problems should be graded in intensity, relevant to the magnitude of the presenting problem" (p. 480). This graded series of interventions would include first asking clients to make efforts to change on their own or with minimal intervention, such as attending a self-help group (AA/NA/CA). If progress is not made, a "more intensive form of treatment (e.g., outpatient professional treatment coupled with a self-help group) can be tried. Finally, if all else fails, the use of long-term inpatient treatment programs can be implemented as a last resort" (p. 481). Marlatt also explains that careful assessment must determine the nature and severity of the addictive behavior and must be carried out at each stage of the graded intervention process to monitor progress and select a matched treatment strategy (p. 481).

The Need for a Graded Series of Interventions

The research reviewed in this chapter suggests that such a graded series of interventions must be applied in the treatment of crack smokers. Individualized assessment of patients remains critical in matching patients to treatments of appropriate intensity. Rawson (1990) states that many "of these cocaine abusers won't be able to get off the drug no matter what treatment they receive. These hard-core abusers may be mentally ill, are often heavily involved in criminal activity, and generally suffer severe societal problems such as chronic unemployment" (p. 10). However, if we consider the wisdom of Marlatt (1988), upon failure in even the best outpatient treatment program, clinical assessment turns toward consideration of placing patients in even more intensive inpatient and long-term residential programs.

The Need for Modifications in Hospital Treatment

Marlatt (1988) notes that too many experts have erred by recommending the ubiquitous 30-day inpatient treatment followed by lifelong participation in AA. Changes in clinicians' strategies of assessing patients and matching them to treatments may be necessary considering the crack epidemic and what is likely to work with crack smokers characterized by diverse demographics and varied crack-smoking patterns. Improvements in hospital programs may be needed to increase their efficacy with crack smokers and ensure that they match patients to appropriate aftercare treatment. Instead of a 28- or 30-day hospital stay, a variable-length inpatient detoxification schedule may be a viable alternative, to be determined by patient assessments. The utility and benefits of a 14-day inpatient detoxification for the cocaine and crack dependent have been described (Wallace, 1987). Special programs should be designed for crack patients or existing programs modified to increase treatment outcome with challenging and difficult populations. Inpatient treatment programs need to include relapse prevention and other elements that make model programs sufficiently intense and comprehensive.

The Need for Funding Cost-effective Hospital Care

A conclusion that inpatient treatment has no role in the recovery process can have damaging consequences for those crack smokers desperately needing separation from crack-saturated environments during a period of withdrawal or when most vulnerable to relapse to chronic crack use. Policymakers must not conclude that funding need not support inpatient detoxification as a treatment option. On the contrary, they must act to ensure the availability of both comprehensive and intensive inpatient and outpatient treatment programs, as must those who design or modify crack-treatment models.

In view of "the current trend toward developing more cost-effective treatment approaches and the resulting emergence of a new treatment modality, namely, the intensive outpatient rehabilitation program" (Washton, 1989a, p. 75), it is imperative to underscore further the needs of many crack smokers. In further support of the specific importance of inpatient detoxification, policymakers and administrators must understand that the high-dose and high-frequency crack smoker must be separated from a crack-saturated environment during a withdrawal period when neurochemically based cravings (Rosecan & Spitz, 1987) and a compulsion to smoke more crack (Cohen, 1987; Herridge & Gold, 1988) may lead to immediate relapse. The characterization as a hard-core crack abuser (Rawson, 1990) arises from being driven by a pharmacological imperative (Cohen, 1987) to smoke more and more crack. Crack smokers *become*, as a result of this compulsion, unemployed and resort to crime to support daily or nearly daily $100–500 crack habits. These severely debilitated and dysfunctional crack patients must be able to enter inpatient detoxification programs in order to achieve initial abstinence and negotiate outpatient-treatment requirements.

Policymakers must strive to understand the complexities arising from the fact that cocaine and crack smokers have diverse crack-smoking patterns and addictions that vary in severity. The cost-effective option of a variable-length inpatient detoxification stay, perhaps ranging from five to 14 days, must be available as a treatment alternative that saves money in comparison with a 28- to 30-day inpatient rehabilitation period. On the other hand, assessment of some patients may still justify some intensive and comprehensive 28- and 30-day inpatient programs.

Toward a Continuum of Care for Crack Patients

Our policymakers must realize the importance of funding comprehensive and intensive outpatient programs into which patients can enter directly upon leaving inpatient detoxification. Without direct entrance into an outpatient phase of treatment, vulnerable crack patients suffering from recurrent cravings and anhedonia, and trying to avoid conditioned stimuli in the environment, will likely relapse to chronic crack use. Hence, policymakers cannot simply ask professionals, "What works?" They must ask, "What works for whom?" In this way, they may acknowledge responses that denote what works for patients with certain characteristics, and during specific phases of recovery (a first period of withdrawal or early abstinence, a second period of prolonging abstinence characterized by cravings and anhedonia, and a third period of one to several years to a lifetime of recovery). A continuum of care is needed that directly links inpatients completing hospital treatment (appropriate for a withdrawal or early abstinence phase) to outpatient services that can permit them to prolong abstinence and avoid relapse.

While the issues are somewhat complex, policymakers must comprehend the dimensions of the crack-treatment challenge and the kind of programs that need to be created and funded. Unless we concentrate efforts on constructing a service-delivery system providing a continuum of quality care, society will have to pay the price of crack smokers further deteriorating because no treatment is available, and relapsing to chronic use after they finally receive treatment.

Deficits in our national treatment strategy, flaws in currently inadequate programs, and errors by clinicians in matching patients to treatment must be examined before we conclude that some cocaine patients, or hard-core crack abusers, may not recover regardless of the treatment they receive. Professionals must analyze how we set patients up for failure when we mismatch them to inappropriate treatment that fails to meet their needs. Policymakers and program administrators collude in preordaining failure when they do not ensure the availability of a range of treatment options that provide a continuity of care. A cost-effective response to the needs of the crack-using population can result in the establishment of an artillery of treatment weaponry sufficiently potent to win the crack war.

CONCLUSION

This chapter has articulated a standard against which crack treatments should be judged. State-of-the-art crack treatments should attend to biological, psychological, and social factors underlying crack dependence, following a biopsychosocial model. In addition, model treatments should recognize the circumscribed population or type of patient for whom the treatment works, acknowledge the phase of treatment or recovery when it should be administered, and include relapse prevention. Despite the limitations of the available research, which is lacking random assignment and controls and is marked by a dearth of outcome-evaluation studies specifically with crack-smoking populations, a review of research with mostly white, middle-class intranasal-cocaine, intravenous-cocaine, and free-base-cocaine smokers has identified effective crack treatments.

Long-term outpatient treatment (six to 12 months), which is comprehensive and intensive (providing nearly daily contact with patients) and includes urine testing, individual sessions, family/couples sessions, group sessions, and relapse prevention, affords an exemplary treatment model. Moreover, within these outpatient treatments, well-trained or professional therapists typically utilize a multifaceted clinical technique that includes educational, cognitive, behavioral, and psychodynamic interventions, or techniques that derive a rationale from cognitive-behavioral or psychodynamic theory.

The review also highlights how for high-severity patients—perhaps most comparable to compulsive high-frequency and high-dose crack smokers—the intervention of inpatient before outpatient treatment may be critical to patients' recovery. We saw that even where treatment is successful, a brief return to cocaine use often characterizes a pattern of recovery. Although research supports the superiority of outpatient treatment over inpatient treatment, deficits in inpatient programs may explain their higher relapse rates. Inpatient treatment works when well structured (groups, education, stress-coping techniques, staff talks) and when it includes intensive individual psychotherapy (three times per week); moreover, after the inpatient phase, individual psychotherapy continues during outpatient treatment for one to two years, in addition to urine testing and group involvement. Thus, when an inpatient program can be characterized as comprehensive and intensive, and includes an excellent outpatient component, it may also work. Crack patients require a continuum of care that ensures that treatments take place in the early phase of abstinence or withdrawal, a second phase of prolonging abstinence characterized by continued cravings and anhedonia, and a third phase of a one- to several-year or lifetime period of recovery. Chapter 9 examines other promising treatments that should also be considered as viable and necessary treatment options.

9

What Treatments Are Promising for Crack Smokers?

This chapter reviews promising treatments that may play an important role in the creation of the kind of care that crack patients need if they are to recover from their addiction. Some of these treatment models require further investigation and/or replication, while others lack any systematic outcome evaluation. A few potentially promising approaches have been investigated, with results suggesting the modifications necessary to improve their efficacy. The chapter also recommends modifications that might permit these treatments actually to meet the needs of crack smokers.

PHARMACOLOGICAL ADJUNCTS

Inpatient Programs

Blum and colleagues (1988) present findings that showed that the nutritional supplement or pharmacological adjunct called Tropamine (Matrix Technologies, Inc.) to patients (n = 54) in a 30-day hospital treatment program during an open trial reduced drug craving or drug hunger. In addition, it significantly reduced the AMA (departure-against-medical-advice) rate; only 4.2% of Tropamine patients left AMA compared with 37.5% among the control group (Blum et al., 1989). Tropamine-treated patients were compliant, cooperative, less agitated, and much less acting out. Overall, the severity of the cocaine crash was reduced, but most important, craving or drug hunger decreased significantly in comparison with controls (Blum, 1989b).

A Rationale for Using Tropamine

The rationale for the provision of Tropamine is based on the need for neurotransmitter replacement or augmentation because of the actions of cocaine.

Recognizing that numerous neurotransmitter systems are affected by cocaine, the approach goes beyond a dopamine-depletion hypothesis that focuses on only one neurotransmitter system. Chronic cocaine use may cause a supersensitivity of at least the dopamine, norepinephrine, and serotonin receptors, and both catecholamine and indolamine transmitters are also depleted (Blum, 1988). Tropamine includes precursors for each of the affected neurotransmitters, substances that inhibit destruction of neuropeptidyl opioids, and vitamins and minerals that are usually depleted in the drug dependent (Trachtenberg & Blum, 1988).

Blum et al. (1988) argue that the performance of Tropamine is all the more impressive because 92% of patients who received it were intravenous or free-base smokers. The researchers assert that Tropamine is a prototypical nutrient product that helps to realize the first goal of treatment, which is to keep the patient in the facility. Retention in the hospital is important in separating the user from the drug-using environment, allowing education during treatment, and helping a patient to make the first steps toward abstinence from cocaine (Blum et al., 1988).

Hence, Blum et al. present important data on a pharmacological adjunct that recognizes the biological factor of depletion of neurotransmitters and addresses this phenomenon. Tropamine, however, represents only an adjunct or one part of an overall inpatient-treatment approach. Blum et al. emphasize that Tropamine is important in the early phase of treatment or recovery and for chronic users who need to be separated from the drug-using environment. Assessment of patients and matching to treatment with Tropamine is implied in selecting these users. Tropamine appears to be a very promising pharmacological adjunct insofar as it permits 95.8% of patients to manage drug hunger and complete inpatient detoxification, compared with 62.5% of controls. However, the weakness of this study lies in the fact that it was an open trial, in which only 24 patients were given Tropamine. As Blum et al. state, the data from this clinical trial warrant further investigation in double-blind, placebo-controlled studies.

Bromocriptine

Evidence suggests that bromocriptine also works in alleviating withdrawal symptoms. Following a dopamine-depletion hypothesis, Herridge and Gold (1988) have administered the dopaminergic agonist to cocaine abusers in a randomized, double-blind, placebo-controlled study in an inpatient hospital setting. In the study, bromocriptine reduced craving significantly more than did placebo. In an additional open trial with 40 patients, bromocriptine reduced craving for cocaine, and also reversed the typical withdrawal symptoms of depression, irritability, anergia, and sleep disturbance. Herridge and Gold also recognize that a brain-driven craving could result in outpatients' relapsing to cocaine use and in inpatients signing out of the hospital. They explain that patients may remain in treatment and avoid relapse if immediate withdrawal symptoms can be reduced. They believe that bromocriptine is also phase specific for the first period of initial abstinence or withdrawal. Targets of this treatment are chronic cocaine users suffering cravings and requiring an inpatient setting.

Herridge and Gold also compared the efficacy of bromocriptine and the noradrenergic tricyclic antidepressant desipramine in a small sample ($n = 12$) of predominantly crack patients meeting the criteria for dependence. Utilizing a double-blind, random-assignment, crossover design with these newly admitted inpatients, they found that bromocriptine reduced craving, improved depressed mood, and increased energy. Desipramine was somewhat less effective in reducing craving, had no effect on mood, and reduced already low energy.

Trachtenberg and Blum (1988) point out that bromocriptine's disadvantages include the fact that it fosters dependence, alters the sensitivity of postsynaptic dopamine receptors, and has side effects such as headache, sedation, tremor, vertigo, syncope, and dry mouth. They also note that Tennant and Sagherian (1987) found decreased compliance in those taking bromocriptine.

Despite the need for further confirmatory research, the work of Blum et al. (1988) with Tropamine and that of Herridge and Gold (1988) with bromocriptine support the critical role of pharmacological adjuncts during inpatient treatment as a form of relapse prevention. Their clinical observations and expertise reveal the difficult challenge of retaining high-severity chronic crack smokers who suffer such intense cravings in inpatient treatment and the promise that pharmacological adjuncts hold for helping to keep them in the hospital as well as aiding in their ultimate recovery.

Outpatient Programs

For patients matched to outpatient treatment, or for patients who need, prefer, or select outpatient treatment, pharmacological adjuncts may be a crucial element in the success of the treatment. The work of Gawin and Kleber has been most informative in highlighting the potential value of the antidepressant desipramine as one outpatient-treatment component.

Gawin (1989) recognizes the value of chemotherapeutic approaches with cocaine and crack smokers, but cautions that this biological approach offers no panacea. Within this approach, the phases that Gawin recognizes (in contradistinction to the work of Herridge and Gold, 1988) include a "crash" that lasts from nine hours to four days, followed by a second period of withdrawal lasting from one to ten weeks. (For an explanation of the term "withdrawal phase" and other phases of recovery, see Chapter 4.) According to Gawin, a third period of extinction to conditioned cues that may trigger craving lasts indefinitely. He likens the crash to a hangover, explaining that with daily crack smokers, a typical pattern is a nightly three- to four-hour binge followed by a crash. During the second period of a one- to ten-week withdrawal, anhedonia appears, along with the craving phenomenon. Peaks of craving occur in response to conditioned cues, which can lead to relapse. Anhedonia is an inability to experience pleasure; life seems empty and shallow, and feelings of boredom prevail. Gawin points out that in this way, this second period is characterized by an interaction of internal/environmental factors (cravings in response to conditioned cues) and the biologically based withdrawal.

Moreover, Gawin emphasizes that the logic of administering desipramine follows from studies with rats that suggest that use of antidepressants can help normalize the brain reward center. He views the use of antidepressants during withdrawal as facilitating discontinuation of cocaine use. He conceives of the use of desipramine as abstinence induction; once abstinence has been achieved, the standard treatment, psychotherapy, may have the opportunity to "take hold."

In working with crack outpatients, Gawin recognizes that with crack outpatients compliance is poor; some patients sell desipramine to acquire money. Another problem is that the oral antidesipramine regimen takes two weeks to take effect (Gawin, 1989). More recent work supports previous open trials of desipramine in combination with psychotherapy by Gawin and Kleber (1986) that the technique reduced, and eventually stopped, cocaine use, in addition to reducing craving. In a controlled study, the researchers found that desipramine doubled the number of crack smokers who were able to remain abstinent for the first three to four weeks of an outpatient-treatment program—59% were able to stay off crack in contrast to the extraordinarily high relapse rates that normally characterize crack smokers in outpatient treatment (Kolata, 1989, Aug. 24, pp. A1–B7). However, the remaining 41% of crack smokers in this outpatient program still relapsed despite the desipramine. Clearly, desipramine helped to reduce relapse rates, but this seems to be indicative that some patients may require an inpatient setting in order to achieve abstinence.

Gawin (1989) reports that in administering desipramine to cocaine patients during withdrawal suggests that the best predictor ($r = .8$) of initial abstinence being maintained is the 24-hour desipramine level a patient presents. Patients whose desipramine level was high did poorly, and they should be placed in an inpatient hospital setting. Such individuals seem unable to become abstinent as outpatients, and high levels of desipramine seem to fail for them as a form of abstinence induction. On the other hand, individuals with a lower 24-hour desipramine level did well, and the achievement of abstinence seemed to be facilitated by the taking of desipramine. Unclear as to the significance of the 24-hour desipramine level, Gawin (1989) wonders whether it is a matter of metabolism. However, these findings suggest that it is essential carefully to examine early desipramine levels, while the question "What does it mean?" remains unanswered, as Gawin stresses. A definite implication of early desipramine-level results is that they can predict which patients will require inpatient treatment in order to become abstinent.

Gawin (1989) also reports preliminary work with flupentixol—an injectable, slow-release antidepressant—in an open trial. Findings suggest that cravings decrease dramatically. Flupentixol is the first specific treatment for crack abuse with which Gawin reports having worked. Nine of ten patients reported that their cravings for crack were ameliorated within three days and their depression lessened; Gawin plans to expand this research (Kolata, 1989, Aug. 24, pp. A1–B7). According to Gawin, an additional consideration when working with crack smokers is the possibility that there may be no substrate left for desipramine to work, which may suggest the need for early intervention before the destruction of substrates.

In order to balance the enthusiasm over Gawin and Kleber's advocacy on behalf of desipramine, other research should be noted. A double-blind, placebo-controlled study by Tennant and Sagerhian (1987) showed desipramine to be no more effective than placebo. Also, Trachtenberg and Blum (1988) point out that a disadvantage of desipramine is that it typically takes three weeks to begin to take effect, and Gawin (1989) recognizes a two-week period for its action. Yet there are reports that the administration of desipramine on days 7 through 11 of treatment ameliorated the postcocaine dysphoria and hypersomnolence (Tennant & Rawson, 1983). Gawin's work suggests progress in determining the optimal dose of desipramine. Another problem with desipramine, which Trachtenberg and Blum note, is that it produces the side effect of a dry mouth and does not appear to be effective if cocaine is in the patient's plasma at the time of administration (Tennant, Tarver, & Seecof, 1986). Regarding the efficacy of antidepressants with cocaine patients, Rosecan (1983) reports that abstinence was prolonged or cocaine use substantially reduced in 20 of 25 patients receiving imipramine (another antidepressant), as well as tyrosine and tryptophan (amino acids that are precursors of depleted neurotransmitters). Craving or drug hunger was not controlled by imipramine alone, but when supplemented with tyrosine and tryptophan, it dramatically disappeared. Trachtenberg and Blum (1988) note that the combined use of amino acids and imipramine appears to be more effective than an antidepressant such as desipramine alone.

Kleber (1988) recognizes the lack of consensus regarding the use of pharmacological adjuncts such as desipramine. In addition. he summarizes the use of such agents by reminding us that each pharmacological adjunct has a different rationale for its use and that some are suited only for subgroups of patients. Desipramine seems effective in decreasing craving and promoting abstinence and is appropriate for patients presenting with chronic cocaine abuse regardless of whether there is a diagnosis of depression. Kleber characterizes the literature on pharmacotherapy by pointing out that while many positive clinical reports exist, most of them are anecdotal and uncontrolled. He emphasizes the need, as research progresses, to elucidate the differences between treatments, and to specify the target populations and the optimal dosages and duration (p. 1366). Gawin's specification of early desipramine level as predicting who can benefit from desipramine as a pharmacological adjunct—which assists cocaine and crack users in the achievement of abstinence—moves this nascent field toward this goal.

Kleber's position, therefore, focuses on the value of desipramine for chronic cocaine users. He advocates its use as a promising pharmacotherapy, but correctly emphasizes that it should represent only one part of a treatment approach that includes a careful assessment of patients for individual needs. Kleber cites the other crucial components of what again emerges as the preferred comprehensive, intensive, and multifaceted treatment approach for cocaine and crack users: individual, group, and family therapy to address psychological issues, relapse prevention, self-control strategies, ways to resist craving, and changes in life-style (p. 1367). Kleber's (1988) and Gawin's (1989) approaches adequately measure up to the standard set forth here. Pharmacological adjuncts represent one dimension of a much more comprehensive treatment approach that addresses psychosocial variables, in addition to the biological variable of withdrawal.

OTHER TREATMENT COMPONENTS

Anonymous Self-help Groups

In view of the long waiting lists for most programs and the unavailability of vitally needed treatment, the use of anonymous self-help groups must be seen as promising, since these groups are free, open to anyone, and meet daily, at all hours of the day, in virtually every neighborhood or community. Currently, they hold the only promise for homeless crack smokers, some prison populations, those without private insurance, and persons lacking Medicaid. Many newly unemployed crack smokers have lost medical benefits after a few months of unemployment but may still not qualify for Medicaid. Thus, a large group of patients may be forced to utilize self-help groups as the only treatment intervention to which they can gain access. Others use these groups as an essential component of inpatient, outpatient, and residential TC programs.

Narcotics Anonymous (NA) has grown tremendously. In 1982, there were 2,000 active groups in 50 states. Current estimates are that there are 14,000 groups with at least one group in every county in the United States and 2,000 groups in 50 other countries. (Malcolm, 1989, Oct. 2, p. B 10). The cocaine and crack epidemic of the 1980s must certainly be viewed as a major factor in this growth. Attendance at an NA meeting reveals that crack dependents account for the majority of drug users at such meetings.

Some key elements of a self-help group's effectiveness in promoting the recovery of crack smokers are the group's longevity and the presence of sponsors who themselves have been abstinent for a considerable length of time. Sponsors are typically self-help group members who have been abstinent for at least one year and are viewed as capable of providing the guidance, support, and assistance a new member requires. They are available by phone 24 hours a day and can be relied on to help members maintain abstinence. However, many of the groups are new, with less "old" leadership, and so could be less effective now than they will be when they have been in existence longer. Still, for many drug addicts, NA groups hold the only promise of treatment and recovery to which they have ready access.

Other individuals find that the even newer, fewer in number, and less widely available Cocaine Anonymous (CA) groups more specifically address their cocaine-use problems. Even Drugs Anonymous (DA) groups are available in some parts of the country. Other patients with chemical-dependency problems turn to Alcoholics Anonymous (AA), and its stronger, more stable 12-step tradition. AA groups usually have a longer history and a greater number of mature and seasoned sponsors. Issues of placing emphasis on one's alcohol use instead of cocaine use, of feeling a need to misrepresent a drug problem as an alcohol problem, and of rejection by some AA groups when only a drug problem is described complicate the use of AA by cocaine and crack smokers. However, many drug addicts consider encounters with recovering alcoholics who reject them for not being alcoholics as far outweighed by the positive, supportive, and nurturant environment provided by AA.

There are also other problems characterizing many NA and CA groups. Particularly in group meetings lacking skilled group leaders or members without several years of abstinence, discussion often wanders into a graphic description of getting high. For many vulnerable patients, this kind of prolonged discussion can trigger cravings and may lead to a relapse. Professionally led recovery groups in outpatient programs are sometimes preferable to groups where exposure to this kind of discussion might occur. On the other hand, patients who have had a negative experience with a particular group meeting must be encouraged to try other meetings, perhaps with a different group with leadership with a longer history of abstinence.

The testimonies of those who have recovered in anonymous self-help groups argue for the efficacy of these groups. However, the kind of outcome-evaluation research that could establish NA or CA as something that in and of itself "works" for crack-cocaine smokers is not available. Among important factors that permit AA/NA/CA to be potentially helpful to recovering crack smokers are the support that individuals find when they experience a relapse, the critical role of a sponsor, the emphasis on connecting with one's higher power, the 12 steps, and the traditions of these groups. Thus, the use of AA/NA/CA is another essential element of inpatient, outpatient, and TC programs that may help them to provide more intensive and comprehensive interventions.

Acupuncture as Part of an Intensive Approach

Acupuncture represents another very promising treatment that requires completion of major research studies to place it among those treatments that work with crack smokers. The use of acupuncture with recidivist alcoholics (Bullock, Umen, Culliton, & Olander, 1987) suggests the value of this approach with severe addictions where relapse is a problem. According to Smith (1989a), acupuncture provides a foundation for psychosocial rehabilitation and should be a part of a program that includes counseling, drug-free contracts, educational and employment referrals, and group involvement. Smith further explains that acupuncture controls withdrawal symptoms and craving; it also reduces fears and hostilities that tend to disrupt drug-treatment settings. Acupuncture has a balancing effect on the autonomic and neurotransmitter systems, as well as a rejuvenating effect. In New York State, in association with proper training and supervision, acupuncture can be taught to staff members who can easily learn how to insert three to five acupuncture needles under the skin or surface of the external ear (Smith, 1989a, pp. 1–2).

Utility with Special and Difficult Populations

Smith (1989b) emphasizes the availability of this treatment (at Lincoln Hospital in New York's South Bronx, a largely Hispanic and African-American community) to unscreened clients, and its utility in difficult socioeconomic settings and with difficult populations. He asserts that, in contrast, many patients in outpatient and inpatient settings are screened so as to eliminate problem or difficult patients, which increases such programs' success rates. For example, the fact that patients must have the perseverance to call intake workers perhaps several times a week in order to get an appointment, must remain on a waiting list, or must have insurance effectively eliminates some of the most difficult groups of patients. Smith describes how acupuncture instead has been given to unscreened court-mandated clients on probation. Also, a client walking into the clinic off the street will receive an intake interview and be given an acupuncture treatment on that very day. Instead of frustration and delay, the relaxation acupuncture provides and its other positive effects usually encourage patients to return for subsequent treatments (Smith, 1989b).

Also, a policy whereby clients can "drop in" during clinic hours without an appointment enables mothers who must contend with infants' and children's sometimes variable schedules to avoid worrying about being late or missing an appointment. These mothers can keep children with them in an accommodating atmosphere, thus permitting many to participate in treatment who would fail to meet the strict demands of many other outpatient programs, as Smith (1989b) explains. However, he cautions that what could be promising success rates with mothers and other women who use crack are compromised by harsh realities that often do not affect the success rates of other programs where the staff works with people with fewer psychosocial problems. Smith attempts to sensitize others to the reality that a woman returning to a spouse or partner who continues to use drugs, and living in a city where housing options are few, frequently relapses because of pressure to use drugs with the spouse/partner or because of the overall influence of this environment. When evaluating outcome data, Smith feels such psychosocial factors must be considered.

In terms of outcome data, Smith (1989a) reports on 55 clients referred from the probation department. Of these, 20% attended treatment only once or dropped out very early; 30 of the remaining 40 (68%) have provided consistently negative urines, and these successful patients have stayed in treatment for an average of nine consecutive weeks. Also, utilizing Dr. Michael Smith's acupuncture protocol at Lincoln Hospital, Chao (1989) reports that acupuncture seems to reduce craving and permits crack mothers to yield urines negative for cocaine. Mothers requiring treatment in order to regain or maintain custody of children could certainly benefit from acupuncture as one component of a treatment program. Parenting groups are another important component necessary for effective treatment of women with infants and children (Smith, 1989b).

Importance of Daily Urines

One interesting aspect of Smith's outpatient program is the provision of daily urine samples, which serve the function of a daily monitoring similar to that for dieters, who know they must get on the scale every morning and must report their weight. Smith argues for programs' leasing urine-testing equipment and computerizing findings so that on-site results are available almost immediately. He describes the ease with which a computer printout can display daily urine results over the course of a month or two. To a judge deciding the fate of a person on probation or of an infant in foster care, such a printout can tell a compelling tale of abstinence efforts, and even of the occasional relapse on a weekend, for example. Smith further explains that daily urines and the resulting printout prevent therapists from having to play the "bad cop" role—suspecting drug use or confronting patients without firm evidence or in anticipation of urine results expected from an outside laboratory in several days or weeks. Daily urine results speak for themselves.

Smith argues for reduced sentences for those whose urine computer print-outs support their attainment of abstinence with the help of acupuncture. His acupuncture protocol is being applied in prison settings in Florida and New York as a promising and cost-effective treatment intervention for the growing ranks of crack smokers there. However, as he explains, acupuncture should remain a part of a comprehensive treatment program that also includes such techniques as daily urine testing, counseling that addresses psychosocial problems, NA groups, and parenting groups for mothers.

Policymakers jumping on the acupuncture bandwagon and recommending the utilization of this very inexpensive, cost-effective intervention must comprehend the complex treatment needs of crack smokers. Acupuncture may function as an important part of an outpatient program that is intensive and comprehensive. Daily contacts, daily urine monitoring, NA involvement, and psychosocial interventions by counselors must not be overlooked as elements of an effective treatment that helps patients through a withdrawal phase and enables them to enter a second phase of prolonging abstinence. The role and value of other interventions, such as TCs and inpatient treatment, also must not be neglected, particularly in light of the needs and characteristics of many high-severity crack patients.

A placebo-controlled study (placement of needles in wrong position versus the correct acupuncture points) is currently under way at Lincoln Hospital utilizing Dr. Smith's protocol. Preliminary findings in the summer of 1989 suggested that acupuncture is indeed a promising treatment (Brewington, 1989). Final results of a placebo-controlled study may indicate that there are many inherent advantages to acupuncture as utilized by Smith (1989a).

Use of Contingency Contracting

Initial reports on the use of contingency contracting with well-motivated, well-educated outpatients for whom relapse resulted in severe consequences, such as resignation of professional license or notification of cocaine use sent to employers, were very promising (Anker & Crowley, 1982). Anker and Crowley report that 48% of patients (32 of 67) were willing to engage in contingency contracting—where receipt of a positive urine for cocaine would result in the severe negative consequence specified in their contract. Of those patients willing to engage in contingency contracting, over 80% were able to remain abstinent from cocaine for the duration of the contract, which was typically three months. However, later findings have diminished enthusiasm about this method. Crowley later reported that over 50% of patients who are willing to engage in such treatment relapse after their contract ends.

Cocaine abusers with severe craving and problems of control may not enter into such agreements because they recognize their inability to comply with its terms; also, those with nothing to lose may not have any negative contingencies (Kleber, 1988)—which is probably the case with a significant percentage of crack smokers. However, we must still acknowledge that contingency contracting does seem to work for some patients as a method of achieving initial abstinence (Kleber, 1988, p. 1367). Kleber and Gawin (1984) recommend a number of possible modifications in the contract that might improve compliance, such as the use of a positive contingency, where clean urines result in a reward; for example, the person deposits a large sum of money with the program and gets a small amount back with each clean urine (Rawson, 1990). An obvious problem with this approach that Rawson points out is the risk that possession of a large amount of money might trigger cravings.

Contingency Contracting in a Comprehensive Outpatient Approach

The use of contingency contracts in combination with urine testing has been reported as beneficial (Resnick & Resnick, 1986). Resnick and Resnick have found contingency contracting to be a very valuable therapeutic adjunct when patients are ambivalent about giving up cocaine use. What remains essential is checking urines several times a week if the contracts are to be effective. Even without a contract, Resnick and Resnick emphasize, urine testing remains crucial to undercut denial. They also utilize the elicitation of conditioned abstinence in response to a powder that looks like cocaine, while behavioral techniques of deep relaxation are taught to the patients to help extinguish the conditioned responses. Cognitive relabeling that helps the patient to integrate memories of the dysphoria following cocaine use, including family members in the treatment process, and administering psychotropic medications for symptoms of depression also are part of their treatment approach. In addition, Resnick and Resnick provide treatment that addresses patients' borderline and narcissistic personality disorders and problems. Breathing techniques help patients cope with internal tension. The use of contingency contracts may hold promise when utilized with patients as a part of the kind of comprehensive and intensive outpatient approach Resnick and Resnick describe. However, for those with nothing to lose, they may lack value, and alone they are insufficient.

Contracts with No Contingency

Other programs merely utilize contracts with no negative contingencies. Such a contract might include an agreement to pay regularly, arrive on time for appointments, provide urine samples, and openly discuss drug use (Rawson, 1990). The avoidance of contingency contracts by professionals or failure actually to send a letter regarding drug use to a patient's licensing board, for example, involves the recognition of the high risk of relapse attending cocaine and crack use (Rawson, 1990).

Washton et al., (1986) similarly endorses the use of written contracts, stressing that they should specify that patients immediately discontinue use of all mood-altering substances, remain in treatment no less than six to 12 months, provide random urine samples, accept immediate hospitalization in the event of a severe relapse, and designate persons to contact in the event of relapse or premature termination from treatment or for progress reports (p. 266).

Inpatient Detoxification

An approach to inpatient detoxification that is promising has been described by Wallace (1987, 1989a, 1989b). In Chapter 8 and earlier in this chapter, we described inpatient treatment programs typically lasting 28 to 30 days involving largely white, middle-class clients who had insurance. Interfaith Medical Center in Brooklyn, N. Y. treats a mostly low- and lower-middle-income African-American population, utilizing Medicaid or private insurance benefits. The inpatient hospital detoxification model attempts to provide a safe, medically supervised detoxification, together with psychological interventions. In response to the crack epidemic and in recognition of the needs of compulsive crack smokers, the length of the detoxification stay for the cocaine dependent was lengthened from seven to 14 days in October 1986, when a specialized "crack unit" was opened.

A Model 14-Day Inpatient Detoxification Program

The treatment includes the use of pharmacological adjuncts (L-tyrosine, L-tryptophan, lecithin, choline chloride, vitamins, pyridoxin) consistent with Trachtenberg and Blum's (1988) argument that adjuncts address more than just one neurotransmitter system depleted by chronic cocaine use and should include vitamins. The treatment approach also includes assessment of patients in order to determine the need for psychiatric medications for cocaine-induced psychosis, depression, or underlying psychiatric problems (schizophrenia, manic-depressive disorder, and the like). Clinical psychologists assess patients to determine short- and long-term treatment goals, and also conduct individual psychotherapy, group psychotherapy, relapse-prevention education, community meetings, and individual patient–staff talks to manage behavioral problems and prevent early departures against medical advice. The program strongly emphasizes, and psychologists arrange, referral of all patients to an aftercare treatment placement that meets individual patient needs. Clinicians repeatedly stress the need for aftercare treatment in order to avoid the high risk of relapse. Within individual and group psychotherapy, psychologists employ a multifaceted clinical technique that draws on psychodynamic, cognitive-behavioral, and educational elements (Wallace, 1989a, 1989b; also see Chapter 13).

A multidisciplinary staff strives to provide a therapeutic milieu in addition to a safe drug-free environment. The rather intensive and comprehensive inpatient model also includes groups run by activity/art therapists. Patients experience NA meetings through visiting NA representatives who run a weekly meeting on the unit and encourage continuing NA involvement after detoxification. Similarly, representatives of two residential TCs visit the unit and run two separate groups showing what their treatment encompasses, educating patients to the importance of long-term TC care for many crack patients. Other staff members conduct educational groups on the prevention of the acquired immune deficiency syndrome (AIDS) and on safe-sex practices. Special populations treated on the inpatient detoxification unit include those who test positive for the AIDS virus, pregnant women, adolescents at least 18 years of age, and patients referred by probation.

Program Modifications in Light of Research Findings

Although no outcome-evaluation research is available to document the success of this rather comprehensive and intensive inpatient-detoxification approach, research findings did direct modifications and improvements in the treatment provided by psychologists, who realized the necessity of including relapse-prevention education that went beyond recommending direct entrance into aftercare treatment (Wallace, 1989a). This led to instituting within a psychoeducational group (Wallace, 1989b; see Chapter 13) explicit education on the common determinants of relapse for crack smokers and behavioral alternatives to avoid relapse, representing a substantial contribution to the overall treatment program. In light of research highlighting crack smokers' characteristic experience of trauma in childhood (Wallace, 1987), clinicians realized the importance of identifying childhood trauma as an issue patients needed to be prepared to address in their individual and group psychotherapy in their aftercare treatment. To prepare patients for this process, group psychotherapy provides extensive education on the impact of childhood experiences and their probable connection to the development of crack addiction. Individual psychotherapy elaborates on the education received in group and explicitly explains how each patient's unique experience of childhood trauma probably affected his or her development and relates to the addiction; aftercare treatment recommendations and suggested issues that must be addressed in long-term treatment are tailored to an individual patient's needs.

Need for Long-term Dynamic Psychotherapy. Clinicians generally find that these African-American patients desperately need the kind of in-depth dynamic individual psychotherapy that Schiffer (1989) was able to initiate during his 30-day inpatient drug program and continue on an outpatient basis for one or more years (see Chapter 8). Having time for at most two to three individual psychotherapy sessions per week with patients during the two-week detoxification period, psychologists strive instead to provide patients with their first positive experience with an empathic therapist as a source of motivation to pursue the aftercare treatment these same therapists arrange and strongly urge patients to enter.

Heroic Efforts in Face of Service Deficits

The greatest limitation psychologists face in ensuring that patients have a continuum of care following inpatient detoxification is the problem of waiting lists (three days to three weeks for the homeless, and two weeks to eight weeks for domiciled patients) to enter residential TCs, the existence of only one TC for pregnant women or women with young children, and the lack of residential placements for patients with psychiatric problems. For the majority of crack patients who desperately need *direct* entrance into a TC, this task constitutes an impossible mission that can only sometimes be accomplished, depending on fluctuations in waiting lists and a TC program's occasional expansion.

The Interfaith Medical Center detoxification program represents a model treatment in its innovative and sensitive efforts to meet the needs of high-severity crack patients. In the ideal situation, a TC averages a two-week waiting list or prefers admitting our detoxified clients, sometimes juggling them to the top of the waiting list. During my stay at Interfaith, the hospital actually provided van transportation for these "lucky" patients for screening interviews at TCs during their two-week detoxification. For those with proper identification, no significant medical problems, and no significant psychiatric history, TCs accepted them for admission and tried to coordinate direct entrance into the TC program upon completion of inpatient detoxification. The hospital would again transport these "few and fortunate" to the TC program on the 14th day of their detoxification. In this way, our program attempted to address the extreme vulnerability of our crack patients, who often could not even safely negotiate a subway ride to a TC after leaving detoxification for fear that they might relapse.

This realistic fear of relapse after detoxification was reinforced for therapists (and patients remaining on the unit) who anguished over those few but unforgettable discharged patients who called for help after a three- or five-day binge following detoxification. These patients would beg for help in getting another TC appointment, another TC bed at another facility since they missed their entrance appointment, or reentrance into the inpatient detoxification unit. Clinicians are all too familiar with the vulnerability of crack patients who walk out of the hospital's doors into a crack-saturated environment, return to apartments where a spouse or siblings actively smoke crack, and must deal with the vast array of conditioned cues in the environment that may trigger relapse. Clinicians often feel as though they are literally throwing vulnerable patients to the wolves, as they're forced to match patients with TCs with long waiting lists—offering patients hope by stressing attendance at daily NA meetings until they are able to enter a TC. The majority of unlucky patients, who are initially motivated to enter a TC and do protect themselves from high-risk situations they learned about during treatment, often "lose steam" as they must call some programs daily for one to two months after detoxification, only to face persistent rejection and delays.

Also, outpatient clinics to which patients are referred usually lack the kind of comprehensive and intensive services that we identified in Chapter 8 as crucial components of an effective outpatient program. Most outpatient clinics to which clients are referred lack urine testing, relapse prevention, and psychotherapists with special training in treating the chemically dependent. Also, many of our patients who qualify for inpatient hospitalization for which Medicaid pays do not have outpatient Medicaid coverage. Many patients shun seeking welfare and associated Medicaid benefits, hoping to become gainfully reemployed once drug-free. Thus, patients are urged to combine intensive use of NA or CA groups (attending 90 meetings in 90 days) with outpatient clinic referrals, sometimes as the only outpatient treatment to which they have access. The program description highlights the kind of heroic efforts on the part of a progressive and empathic psychiatry department necessary in an inner-city hospital where a continuum of care for poor minority patients is an abstract concept, standing in contrast to the cold reality of the inadequate service-delivery system available to those lacking private health insurance.

Not all patients faced the nightmare of trying to secure quality aftercare treatment or needed our heroic efforts to do so. After leaving our inpatient detoxification program, a rather small percentage of our patients entered 30-day hospital rehabilitation programs and intensive and comprehensive outpatient programs for which their private insurance paid. On the other hand, another rather small percentage of our patients had *already* utilized their private insurance benefits for crack treatment during a previous period when still employed, having relapsed after this private treatment and further deteriorated into unemployment. Many of our patients with this prior private 30-day hospital treatment praised the Interfaith program for its emphasis on the impact of their childhood trauma on their development and its relationship to their chemical dependency—as well as for our emphasis on relapse prevention and aftercare treatment where they are told to address childhood trauma. Several of these patients articulated their preference for our approach over their prior private hospital treatment with its singular emphasis on AA principles and involvement at aftercare treatment. One patient was discharged from a private facility for becoming angry and disruptive in a group when told by a counselor, "That's your disease talking." This patient stated he preferred my approach, which utilized interpretations linking his rebelliousness and proclivity to set himself up for relapse to persisting and unresolved dysfunctional family dynamics that create substantial stress in his adult life and interpersonal relationships. Thus, despite the efforts required to arrange aftercare treatment for our crack patients, deployment of this treatment approach was gratifying overall.

A Model Detoxification Program

The Interfaith Medical Center 14-day inpatient detoxification program represents the kind of comprehensive and intensive program the crack dependent requires as a treatment during the first phase of withdrawal or early abstinence. Overall, this promising approach to inpatient detoxification deserves replication, particularly in states where inpatient detoxification is neither available nor funded as a treatment option. A grant-funded evaluation is also necessary to justify its replication. However, where inpatient detoxification programs exist, this approach is exemplary in attempting to maximize even a brief inpatient stay as an opportunity to educate patients on the impact of childhood trauma and introduce them to a positive experience of psychotherapy. More specifically, the treatment approach furnishes pharmacological adjuncts to address patients' intense neurochemically based cravings, individualized assessment of patients to match them to appropriate aftercare treatment, individual and group psychotherapy, relapse-prevention education, AIDS-education groups, and groups exposing them to NA and TCs. As a treatment for the first phase of withdrawal, inpatient detoxification of the kind described in this model deserves recognition as a promising approach striving to afford crack patients comprehensive and intensive services as a first-phase treatment. The department of psychiatry and psychologists worked very hard to forge a continuity of care where one did not exist, by trying to link patients directly to TCs, outpatient clinics, and NA/CA groups.

Providers of other inpatient-detoxification programs must not be harassed into feeling fortunate for even existing or experience the pressure of replacement by outpatient models. As the needs of crack patients suggest, the coordinators of many of these inpatient programs should consider extending their length beyond a typical five- or seven-day stay, while also striving to maximize whatever time they have to work with patients as an opportunity to furnish structured, intensive, and comprehensive interventions, as does the model Interfaith program. In particular, relapse-prevention education during this period of withdrawal or early abstinence is a novel element that other inpatient detoxification programs might incorporate to deal with the high risk of relapse crack patients face. In a second phase, the kind of comprehensive and intensive out-patient treatment described earlier (Washton et al., 1986) or residential TC treatment needs to follow inpatient detoxification.

The Therapeutic Community

What is a residential therapeutic community? DeLeon (1986b) asserts that the TC has established itself as a significant alternative approach to the treatment of drug abuse (p. 185). The TC uses self-help and positive peer pressure in a drug-free environment where members play a significant role in managing the facility and serving as role models for each other (Kerr, 1986). The TC emphasizes personal responsibility and provides a structure whereby members advance only through achievements (Kerr, 1986, p. 59). The TC structure also employs set behavioral limits, confrontation that affords members with social feedback on their actions, informal counseling by recovering addicts, organized recreation, and opportunities for education and formal skills training (Sugarman, 1986). DeLeon (1988) argues that the goals of a global change in life-style, abstinence from illicit substances, elimination of antisocial activity, achievement of prosocial attitudes and values and of social and psychological objectives, and overall rehabilitation are best met by the TC. The kind of severe psychosocial deterioration characterizing crack smokers suggests that their needs mesh with the TC's goals.

Before entering a TC, most patients in New York State undergo inpatient detoxification, suggesting the kind of continuum of care necessary successfully to rehabilitate crack smokers. However, research studies are not available that specifically examine outcome with populations of crack-cocaine smokers.

With crack users in particular, TCs are plagued by a high dropout rate, but treatment seems successful with the 50% who stay at least six months (Kolata, 1988, p. 30). Thus, crack patients who are TC residents present the problem of early departure from treatment, often in the first few days or weeks. TCs might consider including medical and psychiatric staff (Rainone et al., 1988) so that pharmacological adjuncts might be administered to crack smokers. Although most patients entering TCs have had a prior inpatient detoxification, sometimes a waiting list of two to eight weeks means that some have reengaged in crack use, frequently in a chronic binge pattern. Others may be taken in off the streets if a TC bed becomes available and the client is fortunate enough to be in the right place at the right time. Such clients may need pharmacological adjuncts to decrease neurochemically based cravings. Other patients in a second phase of recovery following initial withdrawal may experience the kind of anhedonia Gawin (1989) describes, which may justify use of antidepressants such as desipramine. Intense cravings or an anhedonia may compel crack users to leave a TC in order to smoke crack. Thus, crack smokers present a considerable treatment challenge to residential TC programs, as they do to all treatment modalities.

However, despite this challenge, long-term outcome-evaluation research specifically with crack smokers is likely to reveal that the TC can replicate with crack smokers success rates similar to those reported prior to the crack epidemic. Among findings with largely intravenous-drug-using populations, length of treatment is related to success in treatment (DeLeon, 1988). DeLeon reports that success rates (no crime and no drug use) among graduates exceeds 75% five to seven years after treatment. Among those who drop out, success rates average 31%. Approximately 50% of those who stay in treatment for one year or longer were successful compared with about 25% of those who stayed less than one year (DeLeon, 1988).

Recent Improvements in TCs

TCs have been plagued by the abuse of power and require the exercise of rational authority that remains ethical and curative (Bratter, Bratter, & Heimberg, 1986). The presence of mental-health specialists has reduced the incidence of "misuse of therapeutic authority and prerogatives by staff" (Carroll & Sobel, 1986, p. 217). However, Carroll and Sobel caution that those professionals need to have knowledge of and experience in working with addicted persons. In comparison with the utilization of master's-level and specially trained therapists (Rawson, 1990), which characterizes the clinical-skills level of therapists working in state-of-the-art outpatient programs, TCs rely heavily on recovered addicts as counselors. In this regard, DeLeon (1986) notes that the upgrading of the skills and practices of TC workers has been addressed by establishing credentialing and criteria to evaluate competence. DeLeon views this as a step toward strengthening the professionalization of addiction specialists (p. 188).

Carroll and Sobel trace the process by which mental-health professionals and their practices have been integrated into the TC structure and underscore the importance of blending the best from the TC and the mental-health fields. A key factor promoting the greater integration of the two fields relates to the greater demand for increased accountability and "proper" credentials (Carroll & Sobel, 1986, p. 215). One of the benefits of the greater presence of mental-health professionals in TCs that Carroll and Sobel emphasize is the ability to admit and manage patients with emotional and psychiatric problems. Despite the challenges they face in overcoming past abuses of power and authority, upgrading staff, and integrating mental-health professionals into their structure, TCs are a promising modality for helping to meet the treatment needs fostered by the crack epidemic.

Need for a Variable-Length TC Stay

Not all professionals concur in this assessment of the role of the TC. Rawson (1990) states that "for most addicts, they aren't appropriate" (p. 11). His views may reflect treatment of a population that includes many middle-class, intranasal-cocaine patients. On the other hand, Zweben (1986) recognizes that "(a)cross the U.S., therapeutic communities (TCs) have seen an increase in admissions for cocaine" (p. 239), and so have had to attempt a more complete integration of the middle-class client. Consequently, Zweben recommends changes in TCs that include "a continuum of care, with the possibility of a relatively short-term stay (30–60 days) and an *intensive* outpatient model either as a second phase or as a complete treatment" (p. 241). Others have also argued for this kind of variable and shorter-length TC stay (Rainone et al., 1988; Wallace, 1987) and the necessity for direct entrance into outpatient treatment from the TC. Patients who can return to employment and supportive families may only need a TC stay of one, two, three, six, or nine months. More debilitated patients may require the traditional 18- to 24-month TC stay. As Carroll (1989) reports, TCs have been forced to engage in more individualized assessment of patients' progress in treatment to determine the length of stay.

Patients' educational level, employment history, and job skills may also play a role in determining the length of a TC stay. At Phoenix House, a special program provides a shorter stay, which is paid for by insurance; employees participate in residential treatment followed by outpatient treatment (Schwabb, 1989). However, debilitated crack patients who once held lucrative jobs that included health insurance may still benefit from a shorter stay since they can reenter the job market. TCs have yet to institute such modifications.

One of the most exciting aspects of TC treatment in today's society relates to availability of training for jobs in the computer, word processing, and numerous other industries; this kind of training can ensure that, after two years in a TC, members typically can graduate to their own apartment, a well-paying job, and $3,000 in the bank (Scheintaub, 1990). Indeed, the TC remains a crucial factor in the recovery of severely debilitated crack smokers, including those who lacked substantial skills or employment histories prior to developing a crack problem.

Funding for TC programs thus must expand so that they can offer variable lengths of treatment and can attract more mental-health professionals. The presence of significant numbers of mental-health professionals would permit TCs to admit clients with histories of suicide attempts, for example, and allow assessment of individuals throughout the treatment process for a shorter (one, three, or six months), more cost-effective stay.

Need for Professional Therapy in the TC

Many patients in TCs may need to be matched to individual psychotherapy with professionals for psychological and emotional problems that become apparent through assessment. Signaling the need for individual psychotherapy for some TC patients, as well as for special supportive group approaches for others, are findings that 70% of residents at Odyssey House came from a home where one or both parents were alcoholic or had a drug problem; over two fifths had either been battered, sexually molested, or raped as children (Walker, 1988). Rohsenow, Corbett, and Devine (1988) argue that actual rates of molestation in substance abusers' childhoods may be much higher. They found that before they began to specifically ask about the problem, only 4% of men and 20% of women disclosed sexual abuse in childhood. However, after routine inquiries began, 42% of teenage boys, 75% of adult women, and 71–90% of teenage girls reported having been sexually abused as children. Rohsenow et al. (1988) assert that if such histories are a major factor contributing to the development of addiction and are not addressed in treatment programs, then this factor may contribute to early relapse.

Others—including Pinto of Samaritan Village (Kolata, 1989, p. A13)—report that some 44% of teenagers in TCs suffer PTSD, because of the severity of devastating drug-related experiences. Other TC staff members diagnose the persisting effects of childhood sexual abuse as PTSD (Carroll, 1989). This supports the need for individual assessment and professional treatment being made increasingly available in TCs. Treatment outcome may improve where individual psychotherapy or professionally led groups for special populations (sexually abused) are added to the TC regimen for those who need to resolve psychological and emotional issues that may have contributed to the development of an addiction, and that may contribute to relapse if left unresolved or untreated. Carroll agrees that, if funding permitted, the addition of enough mental-health professionals to provide individual psychotherapy to patients with these kinds of unresolved psychological and emotional issues would significantly augment the TC treatment model, thus, improving the chances of a long-term successful outcome and reducing the risk of relapse stemming from unresolved psychological trauma.

The TC's Utility with Special Populations

The TC represents a promising modality for adapting to meet the needs of crack smokers who are criminal offenders, adolescents, or dually diagnosed (having a psychiatric diagnosis in addition to the substance abuse). The TC accepts persons remanded from the criminal-justice system for treatment, with as many as 15% of residents having been convicted of crimes ranging from armed robbery and burglary to prostitution and drug sales (Phoenix House data, Marriot, 1989, Oct. 22, p. A36). Juvenile crack-smoking offenders may suffer in particular, since less than a third of Treatment Alternatives to Street Crime Programs (in the 28 states that have them) have made provisions for monitoring and referring juveniles (Brown, Rose, Weddington, & Jaffe, 1989). However, a number of TCs have special programs for adolescent crack smokers with and without juvenile records. Regarding the dually diagnosed, some TCs are accepting persons with suicidal histories and psychiatric problems as they add mental-health professionals to their staffs. Odyssey House reports that 25% of its residents have had a prior psychiatric hospitalization unrelated to their substance abuse (Walker, 1988). Others are using some TC principles as they establish halfway houses and day programs to meet the needs of the dually diagnosed or mentally ill chemical abuser. These programs are vitally needed, and promising as well (for example, the Weston United Program for Mentally Ill Chemical Abusers in New York City). Thus, with some modifications, the basic TC model can effectively meet the needs of today's crack smokers who are criminal offenders, adolescents, or dually diagnosed.

TC Programs for Homeless Crack Patients.   Program modifications may also include initiating special programs for homeless residents who have special needs. Many TCs have programs for homeless crack smokers—for whom, in fact, the TC remains the best available treatment choice. The New York State Division of Substance Abuse Service's Heart Program sends a mobile van to shelters and neighborhoods where homeless drug users can be assisted in being placed in TCs. TCs coordinate with this project by providing special beds for these clients that entail a shorter waiting list, although the reality of insufficient space still means waits of from three days to three weeks (based on the author's experience in making referrals to this promising project). However, for those homeless people who do not choose to enter a TC, intensive and comprehensive outpatient treatment and implementation of a halfway-house setting that follows TC principles and structure may assist them in pursuing a successful recovery. Outpatient treatment should continue after residents leave halfway house placement, achieve independent living, and are fully employed.

Model TC in a Prison Setting.   The TC model has also been implemented in prison settings for the large numbers of drug users who end up incarcerated. The "Stay 'N Out" TC model in New York State suggests the utility of prison-based drug treatment and of adapting the TC model to the needs of the criminal-justice system (Wexler, Falkin, & Lipton, 1990; Wexler & Williams, 1986). The crack epidemic has created a crisis measurable in terms of the increasing numbers of prisoners who use drugs, currently estimated at from 40 to 90%; moreover, never in U.S. history have so many of its citizens been imprisoned (Malcolm, 1989, Dec. 30, p. 1). Wexler acknowledges that there has been "a real explosion of drug use in prison" (Malcolm, 1989, Dec. 30, p. 1). Malcolm asserts that the explosion of drug use in this nation's prisons has created a new drug underworld and increased corruption as visitors, and even employees, smuggle drugs into prison, permitting some inmates to use drugs throughout their incarceration (p. 12).

The availability of drugs in prisons may undermine the effectiveness of a TC-based treatment model. Also, society must not mistakenly view crack dependence as a criminal activity, overemphasizing incarceration in lieu of treatment for those willing to be treated. When insufficient treatment exists, many crack smokers are forced to support their habit by increasingly engaging in criminal acts—stealing from family members, selling stolen goods, informal prostitution, and distributing drugs. Others respond to the compulsion to smoke crack by committing more serious crimes to secure money or goods that can be exchanged for the drug. Despite the debate over the effectiveness of treatment when crack smokers are remanded to treatment instead of to jail, clinical experience suggests that involvement in a long-term residential TC in the community can help criminals to recover from addiction. A prison environment is certainly much less likely to produce this outcome, but instituting a TC model in a prison setting still holds promise.

Model Programs for Pregnant Crack Smokers. The plight of pregnant crack smokers most dramatically highlights the need for TC programs to treat this special population. When pregnant women who are addicted to crack cocaine walk into a hospital seeking treatment and are refused admittance because they are pregnant (Johnson, 1989, Dec. 13, p. B10; Freitag, 1989, Dec. 12, p. B9), society must not resort to criminal penalties. Instead, treatment must be made available to this special population. Efforts to acquire funding for the treatment of pregnant crack smokers and adequate crack treatment for all must continue (Johnson, 1989, Dec. 13, p. B10). However, that funding must be adequate to ensure the comprehensive and intensive services required to produce successful treatment outcomes. The TC represents a promising treatment modality within a continuum of care that pregnant crack mothers desperately need.

Odyssey House in New York City and Mandela House in California are model long-term, residential TC programs for pregnant crack smokers and women with young children. Although a pregnant woman may only have to wait two weeks to a month to enter Odyssey House, if she has young children, they may not be able to join her until six months later—according to my experience in referring patients. This prospect frequently dissuades mothers with children from seeking this treatment option, increasing their chances of relapse and, if pregnant, the loss of their infants at birth.

The director and founder of Mandela House, Minnie Thomas, explains that she started her program in 1987 in response to her own experiences working in the criminal-justice system in an ex-offenders program. Thomas (1989) noticed that pregnant women were put out of the program and that those who were obviously pregnant were not admitted to the program. Also, taking infants away from their mothers at birth impressed her as "horrible," and she emerged from her experiences "wanting to do something about it" (Thomas, 1989). The resulting Mandela House represents a model program; however, it has facilities for fewer than a dozen women at present, and needs funding to ensure the program's expansion and replication.

Many more TCs are needed that can accommodate pregnant mothers and mothers with children, which may partly be realized by modifying current TC programs to permit them to do so. A halfway-house model could also be implemented that would afford adequate housing for the women and their children, while incorporating TC treatment principles and allowing patients to obtain comprehensive and intensive outpatient services.

Before entering a TC, however, pregnant women need inpatient detoxification—a first-phase treatment that remains largely unavailable to them. New York's North General Hospital, for example, refuses to admit pregnant women to its short-stay drug-detoxification programs (Freitag, 1989, Dec. 12, p. B9), and at Harlem Hospital, for over two years doctors have been unsuccessfully requesting funds to open a 20-bed unit to detoxify their pregnant, and often homeless, addicts (French, 1989, Sept. 29, pp. B1, B2). Interfaith Medical Center's two-week detoxification program, which accommodates pregnant crack smokers, again emerges as a model program worthy of replication; however, its experiences in fighting to establish continuing care for these women postdetoxification suggests inadequacies in our current service-delivery system when dealing with the crack population.

TCs No Longer Permitting Alcohol Use.   Another modification that TCs must institute is the discontinuation of a policy whereby members often were allowed drinking privileges. A number of clinicians have criticized this approach, recognizing the increased risk of relapse for those who use alcohol (Zweben, 1986; Wallace, 1987; Rawson, 1990). Many TCs have stopped condoning the use of alcohol. Rawson, Obert, McCann, and Mann (1986) provide evidence to support the commonly held belief that a return to alcohol or marijuana can lead to relapse. Relapse rates were higher among those who went back to using alcohol or marijuana. The disinhibiting influence of these substances or conditioned responses to chemicals, frequently paired with crack use, can contribute to a relapse episode (Wallace, 1989a).

TREATMENTS IN NEED OF MODIFICATION

A number of researchers and clinicians acknowledge that certain modifications in their treatment approaches are necessary if these interventions are to realize their promise as effective cocaine or crack treatments. These approaches merit review.

Extinction Trials as Relapse Prevention

Childress, Ehrman, McLellan, and O'Brien (1988) contribute important knowledge to our understanding of how classically conditioned stimuli, or reminders of cocaine, can trigger the conditioned response of craving that could lead to relapse. In an inpatient-detoxification hospital setting, they have begun a large-scale study in an attempt to understand and treat the causes of relapse. The present extinction protocol does not work in reducing or preventing relapse, although it does reduce craving—much like a pharmacological adjunct. Childress and colleagues report on a study with 29 male veterans presenting with cocaine dependence. During their hospitalization, subjects underwent 15 hour-long sessions of repeated, nonreinforced exposure to cocaine "reminders." It was found that craving was reduced gradually over the course of the 15 extinction sessions. All patients remained in the two-week inpatient-treatment phase and were compliant with the extinction regimen. However, though reduced, physiological arousal to cocaine reminders still occurred after the 15-session regimen, as well as in the real world. The current 15-session regimen does not work because of incomplete generalization to the real world, where subjective craving still arises; approximately two thirds of the subjects had at least one episode of cocaine use during the two months following the inpatient-treatment phase. The authors recognize that other behavioral techniques may need to be added, and that efforts to improve generalizability should be explored.

Childress et al.'s use of extinction may not work in sufficiently reducing relapse rates because they lack a relapse-prevention program that provides patients with knowledge of how to cope with determinants of relapse that go beyond classically conditioned reminders and involve painful emotional states and interpersonal stress, for example (Wallace, 1989a). This criticism of Childress et al.'s work is consistent with the view of DeLeon (1988), who acknowledge that in the early stages of detoxification, cravings are related to physiological cues, but later in recovery are more directly under the control of social and emotional cues. DeLeon points out that in the TC setting, cravings can occur after months of being drug-free in response to interpersonal stress or conversations about drugs. The training in cognitive and behavioral alternatives that Childress et al. are considering implementing may represent the modification needed in order for this treatment to realize its potential.

Outpatient Treatment for Cocaine and Crack Abusers

Kleinman, Woody, Todd, et al. (1990) report that low-intensity psychotherapy and family therapy as offered to clients in their study were insufficient to produce remission of cocaine use in most patients. The low-intensity psychotherapy they provided followed the supportive-expressive individual-therapy model of Luborsky et al. (1977), and the family therapy followed a structural strategic family-therapy model (Haley, 1980; Stanton & Todd, 1982; Todd et al., 1985). Most of the subjects in their sample were male (87%) and nonwhite (64% African-American, 18% Hispanic), had 12 years or less of education (66%), and had held a full-time job in the three years before they entered treatment (77%), mainly in blue-collar positions (69%).

Difficulties retaining clients in treatment characterized client participation. A full 42% of clients were seen for only one or two evaluations and did not return for therapy. Another 44% were seen for three or more sessions, and only one quarter (24%) of the sample stayed in treatment for six or more sessions, according to Kleinman et al. (1990). Kleinman, Kang, Lipton, et al. (1989) acknowledge that these dropout rates were high, but note that they fall within the broad range indicated as typical by Baekland and Lundwall (1975). However, approximately one fourth of patients did cease cocaine use during the period under study, suggesting that routine assignment of such patients to expensive 28-day inpatient programs may be unnecessary (Kleinman et al., 1990).

These authors conclude that more frequent contact on an outpatient basis may prove more effective, as might residential programs providing 30 days or more of treatment. (This supports the potential value of and need for variable-length-stay residential TCs.) In addition, Kleinman et al. (1989a) speculate that involvement in self-help groups such as CA might also be effective. Among the factors contributing to the lack of success of their treatment was the fact that the therapy they provided probably constituted the first treatment experience for 84% of their population. Kleinman and colleagues argue that this first failure in treatment might predispose these clients to be future successes in other programs, and cite evidence that heroin addicts with two or more treatment attempts are more likely to have a favorable treatment outcome (Brown et al., 1972; Kleinman & Lukoff, 1980; Williams & Johnston, 1972).

This study is important in underscoring the necessity for the kind of comprehensive and intensive outpatient programs that Washton (1989) and Rawson (1990) describe. Beyond just offering family therapy or low-intensity individual psychotherapy, treatment must also include the numerous interventions characteristic of the latest outpatient treatment. We saw that random urine testing on at least a weekly basis, individual and group sessions, educational and supportive services for family members, family/couples sessions, elaborate relapse prevention, and the use of contracts add up to the kind of comprehensive services necessary if an outpatient program is to be successful. The kind of intensive daily contact with a program in the early stages of abstinence that seem critical to the success of Washton's (1989) outpatient rehabilitation program and to Rawson's (1990) neurobehavioral approach needs to be replicated with the crack and cocaine patients in Kleinman et al.'s (1990) treatment.

To state it even more explicitly, Todd (1989) concludes from his involvement in the Kleinman et al. study that any form of treatment based on a once-a-week treatment model will fail. He explains that this model represents an intervention that is too low in intensity for crack and cocaine patients in the early stages of treatment. Acknowledging another weakness of the treatment approach of Kleinman et al. (1990), Todd suggests that chemotherapy in the early period of withdrawal might be helpful, as it would serve to ease the symptoms of withdrawal and help to engage clients in treatment. Based on their treatment experiences in the course of the study, Todd also suggests that both patients and their family members must be advised about the treatment during its early stages because many are naive about the treatment process. According to Todd, educating family members might help to retain patients in treatment, and also provide patients with a safety net. Without this education, cocaine patients become demoralized and spouses or other family members "bail out" after patients experience their first "slip" or relapse to cocaine use (Todd, 1989). Thus, Todd concludes that another lesson from this research involves the necessity of starting relapse prevention on day 1 of treatment, reinforcing the author's own position. As a consequence of his experience and research findings, Todd suggests modifications in the treatment approach studied that include a much more intensive program whose intensity diminishes over a 14-month period. He concludes by urging clinicians to remember that many cocaine and crack patients are new to treatment, and that although the first treatment effort may not work, it can potentiate the success of future treatment.

All of Todd's (1989) conclusions reinforce the value of the 14-day inpatient-detoxification model of treatment described earlier. This model program's provision of chemotherapies/pharmacological adjuncts during withdrawal, relapse-prevention education, the sensitive introduction of patients to an empathic therapist, and education on the process and format of psychotherapy would have well prepared crack patients for outpatient treatment. As we shall see in Chapter 13, the kind of psychoeducation in group therapy that Wallace (1989b) describes may be essential in preparing such patients for meaningful engagement in individual, group, and family therapy in aftercare treatment. However, the outpatient treatment needed by cocaine and crack patients must be of a certain intensity and provide a comprehensive range of interventions for patients (and their family/spouse). Most important, the Kleinman et al. (1990) research tells us that the characteristics of programs, and the degree to which they are adequately structured and are intensive and comprehensive, may be a better determinant of the success of patients in treatment than the characteristics of the patients themselves. Their largely African-American cocaine-dependent population likely needed the same kind of intensive and comprehensive treatment that has worked (Washton et al., 1986; Rawson et al., 1986) with cocaine patients representing diverse demographics.

Other Experimental Pharmacological Adjuncts

The use of other pharmacological adjuncts holds less promise than those reviewed earlier in this chapter. Another strategy designed to address the dopamine depletion characteristic of chronic cocaine users in general involves provision of the biosynthetic precursor of dopamine, L-tyrosine. L-tyrosine has shown some efficacy in one open study reported by Gold et al. (1983). Herridge and Gold (1988) recognize that amantadine, which causes the release of dopamine and norepinephrine from reward storage sites and slows reuptake, can also be effective in alleviating the symptoms of cocaine withdrawal during the first phase. Kleber (1988) reminds us, however, that adequate double-blind trials of amantadine are needed to delineate its spectrum of usefulness (p. 1366). Also, methylphenidate seems helpful, but only in cases of cocaine abuse where there is a clear diagnosis of ADD, residual type (Khantzian, Gawin, Kleber, & Riordan, 1984), while lithium is indicated for patients with a bipolar or cyclothymic disorder in addition to cocaine abuse (Kleber, 1988; Rosecan & Nunes, 1987).

Regarding available findings, Morgan, Kosten, Gawin, and Kleber (1988) report on a pilot trial with 12 patients presenting with cocaine abuse who were given amantadine for cocaine withdrawal during a 30-day trial. Patients were seen weekly on an outpatient basis and they reported daily craving ratings. Findings show that ten of 12 patients stayed in the study for 14 or more days. There was a 50% dropout rate between day 14 and day 23; only three stayed for the length of the study. Conditioned stimuli continued to trigger cravings, cravings fluctuated while patients were on amantadine, and patients on placebo and amantadine experienced a decrease in craving in comparison with baseline. Two patients complained that the medication did not work. The drug appeared to have no immediate anticraving effect, although a decreasing trend in cocaine use and craving was observed. The authors conclude that amantadine may be effective in treating the early phase of cocaine withdrawal, but recognize that its long-term administration could exacerbate an already dopamine-depleted state created by chronic cocaine use.

Trachtenberg and Blum (1988) also emphasize that releasers of dopamine and norepinephrine, such as amantadine, will not cure dopamine depletion, and if used alone, could exacerbate the chronic depletion of dopamine caused by crack and cocaine. Reported side effects of amantadine include possible kidney dysfunction, dizziness, sedation, dysphoria, and nausea (p, 324).

A Stepwise Withdrawal Procedure

In terms of a rather creative multidimensional pharmacological approach, Tennant and Tarver (1987) have investigated the efficacy of a stepwise withdrawal procedure utilizing amino acids, amantadine hydrochloride, levodopa, bromocriptine mesylate, and desipramine in 106 subjects withdrawing from co-caine dependence on an outpatient basis. Initially, amantadine, tyrosine, and tryptophan were given to subjects, and if, after one week of this treatment, craving, cocaine dreams, or withdrawal symptoms of agitation or depression persisted, bromocriptine was added to the regimen during the second week of treatment. During the third week of outpatient treatment, subjects who could not refrain from cocaine use were given desipramine. Group I ($n = 77$) was given a lower-dose regimen of this adjunct than was group II ($n = 29$). The higher-dose group had a lower dropout rate and more people in this group reported cessation of cocaine use. Although the difference was not statistically signifi-cant, group II subjects stayed slightly longer in treatment. Tennant and Tarver suggest that findings justify further investigation of this regimen (p. 317). Meanwhile, Kleber's (1988) assertion that we have yet to determine the appro-priate doses of these experimental pharmacological adjuncts receives further support.

CONCLUSION

This chapter has reviewed a number of promising treatments that either lack sufficient evaluation or require modifications in order to qualify as treatments capable of producing successful rates of recovery for crack patients. The chap-ter's analysis of these treatments suggests that within a continuum of care, the use of pharmacological adjuncts in inpatient and outpatient settings, anony-mous self-help groups (NA/CA/AA), inpatient detoxification, and TCs should all be recognized as playing a potentially critical role.

A review and analysis of available research findings suggest that the addition of pharmacological adjuncts to inpatient and outpatient programs, as well as to TCs, may enhance these programs' ability to retain patients in the early with-drawal phase, and even during the second phase of prolonging abstinence, when anhedonia and recurrent cravings may be intense. Clinicians must also assess patients for the severity of their addiction and match them to appropri-ate treatments, depending on a patient's phase of recovery. Specific treatments are appropriate for specific phases of recovery from cocaine and crack. For the first period of early abstinence or withdrawal, inpatient or outpatient treatment with or without the use of certain pharmacological adjuncts may be necessary, depending on assessment findings. During the second period of prolonging ab-stinence, outpatient treatment or residential TC treatment may be the treat-ment of choice, perhaps combining NA/CA/AA involvement; in the third phase of a one- to three-year or lifetime period of recovery, these same treat-ments may need to continue for at least one year, and for many patients for a longer time, according to individual patient needs and characteristics.

The chapter recommends modifications in a number of treatment approaches and in our service-delivery system that are crucial if we are successfully to meet the crack-treatment challenge that arises as a consequence of the crack war. The efficacy of the swords and shields we take into battle depends on our willingness to benefit from research findings and the experiences of "front line" clinicians who have treated the wounded and assessed the nature and magnitude of the injuries sustained. When front-line professionals recommend methods of constructing potent weapons capable of winning many small battles in the crack war and we neglect to refine our treatment weaponry, the cost to our society becomes astronomical. We shall inevitably face, in the 21st century, a maturing generation composed of crack babies and children abused and neglected by crack-using parents of all races and socioeconomic levels. All these children are at increased risk for learning disabilities, emotional and psychological problems, chemical dependency, criminal involvement, and poor employment prospects, depending on their access to adequate treatment. Meanwhile, in the 1990s, we see infants, children, adolescents, and adults of diverse demographics who desperately require care that is lacking, owing to the crisis in health care that has been exacerbated, if not created, by the crack epidemic.

Policymakers must consider the long-term and cumulative costs to society as they assimilate the best available knowledge to put in place the kind of treatment essential to ensure this nation's overall state of health. Having provided a review and analysis of proved (Chapter 8) and promising treatment weaponry that may help us win the crack war, let us consider the assessment process in more detail. Chapter 10 turns our attention to the clinician's task of utilizing a knowledge of patients' psychosocial functioning, history, and treatment preferences in formulating actual treatment plans.

IV

CLINICAL TECHNIQUE IN THE ASSESSMENT PHASE

10

The Clinical Interview

This chapter shows how the clinical interview operates as a powerful assessment tool and describes how clinicians can acquire the information they need to match patients to treatments. In order to perform an individualized assessment of a patient that highlights the unique features of that person's addiction and determines treatment needs, a clinical interview may be essential. Such an interview has the advantage, from the perspective of a biopsychosocial view of crack addiction, of permitting a search for the roots of a person's crack addiction. In addition, it allows an assessment of the level and severity of the addiction, the recent and current level of a patient's psychosocial functioning, and the extent of crack-related psychosocial deterioration. Within the context of a clinical interview, therapists may obtain information on which to base a formal diagnosis of crack-cocaine abuse or dependence, and also identify mental, personality, and mood disorders using DSM-III-R criteria. Observations of patients and their responses during the interview tell a great deal about the nature of their defensive functioning and their capacity for regulating their self-esteem, affective states, aggressive and sexual impulses, and overall behavior in interpersonal relationships. In this way, therapists begin to appreciate aspects of patients' emotional and psychological functioning that may be significant but too subtle to meet formal DSM III-R criteria.

A clinician can maximize the therapeutic impact of the clinical interview by utilizing the data acquired to increase a patient's awareness of information that is near consciousness. The clinician may also engage in the process of labeling and identifying feelings and affective states and their relationship to material discussed, and may offer interpretations or dynamic explanations of a patient's crack use and the range of the addiction's possible roots. A clinical interview can end by raising tentative hypotheses as interpretations or questions that the patient and clinician can hope to answer or confirm together. Also, the clinician should be able to provide professional recommendations on short- and long- term treatment goals.

For professionals who are experienced in conducting clinical interviews, this chapter prepares them for making effective assessments of those chemically dependent patients who present themselves for treatment in clinical settings in increasing numbers. For those clinicians who work with the chemically dependent, but who rely on the administration of questionnaires, this chapter can show them how to use the clinical interview as an alternative, and perhaps preferable, means of assessing patients in a thorough manner; where long questionnaires end, clinical observations may begin to provide information on subtle problems in a patient's ability to process, feel, or identify feelings, for example. Paraprofessionals, counselors, and other professionals who may need additional training or who wish further information about the clinical interview, diagnosis, and mental-status examination can refer to Othmer and Othmer (1989). However, paraprofessionals, counselors, and even concerned parents may begin to get a sense of what they need to know about a person's crack use and functioning before recommending a particular treatment. Thus, this chapter strives to provide a wide range of readers with a practical assessment aid in matching patients to treatments of appropriate intensity.

INFORMATION TO BE GATHERED

The information to be gathered in the clinical interview includes the typical information that is part of a psychosocial history and assessment in most hospital settings—the onset of the problem, drug history, psychiatric history, developmental history, family history, education, employment history, level of functioning over the past year, and the results of a mental-status examination. The interview permits arriving at an assessment of a patient's psychological and emotional functioning and any DSM-III-R diagnoses.

Rationale for Use

The inclusion of a clinical interview containing these elements as a standard part of the assessment process in settings beyond the hospital environment can certainly be justified. Marlatt (1988) critiques traditional treatment programs as providing little, if anything, in the way of detailed assessment for the process of treatment matching for addiction problems. He points out that many programs rely on "poorly trained personnel to administer some kind of 'Twenty Questions' screening test to determine the presence or absence of the addiction" (p. 481). Moreover, individual differences (age, gender, ethnic status, personality, cognitive functioning, socioeconomic status, social support, coping skills, and belief systems) are "too often overlooked or blended together under a single disease entity, or attributed largely to genetic predisposition or the unifying influence of physical dependency" (pp. 481–482). In contrast, Marlatt (Marlatt, 1988, Marlatt & Donovan, 1988) advocates assessment procedures "tailored to the development of unique, client-oriented methods of intervention" (p. 482) where assessment covers multiple dimensions.

The field of chemical dependency must utilize sensitive and progressive methods that can tailor cost-effective treatments to individual patient needs. The present approach follows Marlatt's (1988) standard in valuing the importance of a proper and thorough assessment on the part of the treatment practitioner. Since meeting the screening criteria automatically matches a patient to the treatment modality to which the patient has just gained entrance, a "20 questions" admissions screen may seem to some to be straightforward and sufficient. However, the process of patient treatment matching, both within the program and as aftercare, argues for the detailed information that a clinical interview can provide.

What Kinds of Questions Must Clinicians Ask

Within the clinical interview, clinicians ascertain data permitting a diagnosis of dependence or abuse according to the criteria covered in Chapter 2. However, they must also acquire sufficient information on which to base an informed decision as to which treatment seems best for a patient. Clinicians must ask detailed questions regarding the history of drug use and the dose and frequency of all drugs used. They must ascertain the time of first crack use, as well as the time course and pattern involved in the escalation from experimental use to the dependence syndrome. How much (the dose) and how often (the frequency) did patients smoke crack at each stage of their progression toward dependence?

This detailed information regarding drug-use history represents vital data a clinician needs to have in order to make informed treatment recommendations. This accords with the need to avoid assumptions (Marlatt, 1988) that a single treatment is appropriate for all patients. Recommendations are likely to vary depending on the dose, frequency, and nature of the progression to crack dependence. Whether crack dependence is mild, moderate, or severe (see Chapter 2) further informs decisions on treatment needed to facilitate recovery. Acquiring detailed information on just how much and how often the user smokes crack helps us to determine the severity of the addiction.

Whether a patient is a once-a-month crack smoker, a bimonthly smoker, or a weekly, biweekly, nearly daily, or daily crack smoker has meaning. The implications of this information are further clarified by whether or not one smokes a $5, $10, $20, $40, $100, or $500 dose of crack to get high. Given all of the possible combinations—a crack smoker who smokes only once a month, but uses $500 worth of crack, or one who smokes $5 daily or $100 daily—the problem can have unique features that have crucial implications for the kind of treatment needed. Thus, before a treatment professional can recommend treatment, information of this kind must be acquired as part of a thorough assessment.

As a part of a thorough and proper assessment, clinicians pursue data on the precrack level of functioning, as well as recent and current psychosocial functioning. This entails asking questions regarding a patient's educational and employment history, job skills, and training. Of primary importance for clinicians is the ascertaining of a patient's childhood history. Clinicians should ask who lived in the childhood household, what childhood was like for the patient, and what sibling and parent relationships were like, and should clarify the nature and effect of dysfunctional family dynamics or traumatic experiences. Clinicians empathically seek answers to the following questions: "Did anything traumatic happen to you when you were growing up?" "Were you molested as a child?" The clinical interview also seeks information on any developmental problems (head injuries, hyperactivity), as well as any psychiatric problems or symptoms (depression, anxiety, suicidal or homicidal feelings, hallucinations). A history of interpersonal relationships (marriage, recent partners) and the nature of current family relationships is also important. What kinds of crack-related problems have patients experienced? Is the loss of employment, family support, family trust, child custody, housing, or a spouse related to crack use? Also, patient preferences for specific treatment modalities must be sought.

Following Washton (1989b), clinicians also need to inquire systematically during intake procedures about drug-related sexual behavior (p. 32). Because cocaine acts as an aphrodisiac, many users experience increased sexual desire, prolonged sexual endurance, and reduced sexual inhibition, especially when users smoke crack. As a result, sexual acting-out behavior may be quite common. If left untreated, such behavior may lead to repeated relapses and the spread of AIDS (pp. 32–33).

All of this information serves to inform the clinician as to the dimensions of a patient's overall predicament—the unique features of the addiction, and the patient's unique skills, preferences, and pattern of psychosocial deterioration from a precrack level of functioning. As a consequence of obtaining all of these data during the clinical interview, clinicians can make treatment recommendations as truly knowledgeable consultants.

Clinicians should also ask for the same piece of information more than once in the interview—perhaps in a different way at different times—in order to check the consistency of a patient's answers. This is particularly important regarding dose and frequency of crack smoking, and sometimes also in the areas of housing and employment—areas where patients may tend to distort information, often out of feelings of shame and embarrassment or denial of the extent of their deterioration. When distortions or inaccuracies become apparent, clinicians may ask clarifying questions, make point-blank comments to which patients can respond either affirmatively or negatively, wait until patients develop more trust and explore these issues in a later session, or decide that the information is not important enough (for example, whether a woman sold her body for crack, a patient deals drugs, or a person actually has a job on the "books") to warrant increasing the patient's discomfort. While self-report information may include distortions, exaggerations, and misrepresentations, a clinician's skill in reasking key questions to provide a kind of internal consistency check can reduce the inaccuracy. At the same time, the gradual development of trust in a therapist who proves to be nonjudgmental, genuinely caring, helpful, and concerned permits clients devastated by and ashamed of the extent of their crack-related deterioration to admit that they are newly homeless, are unemployed, have lost family support, or are trying to escape the retributions of crack dealers.

MATCHING PATIENTS TO APPROPRIATELY INTENSIVE TREATMENT

The bottom line is that assessment findings need to be sufficiently detailed and accurate to play a part in treatment planning. Only by conducting this kind of a thorough assessment will the clinician be able to match a client to a treatment modality of appropriate intensity. In fact, the present approach expands on Marlatt's (1988) concept of a graded intensity approach, where a treatment of less intensity is attempted before one of greater intensity. Clinical diagnosis, as discussed in Chapter 2, inherently identifies those who have already attempted to stop by themselves, automatically discounting Marlatt's least intensive intervention of directing patients to quit on their own. Most patients meeting DSM-III-R criteria for cocaine dependence have already failed at such attempts, having experienced frequent relapses to crack smoking. Thus, by virtue of the diagnosis of cocaine or crack dependence, we must consider relatively intensive treatments. Inpatient treatment, sufficiently intensive and comprehensive outpatient treatment, or long-term residential treatment seems appropriate for those meeting the criteria for cocaine or crack dependence (or dependence on any psychoactive substance or designer chemical, for that matter).

Beyond a DSM-III-R diagnosis of crack dependence, information on dose and frequency also informs the process of matching patients to a treatment of appropriate intensity. For example, the typical recommendation to a patient leaving inpatient detoxification might be a residential TC referral. However, a bimonthly smoker of $5 or $40 worth of crack may not require an intervention of this intensity. On the other hand, other psychosocial information is a part of a thorough assessment. A pregnant woman who smokes such an amount may require a TC placement as an appropriate intervention. Reality and the kinds of treatments available also affect recommendations. A mother who smokes $100 nearly daily may not be able to leave her children and so may have to be referred to an outpatient clinic despite the fact that only a TC referral would be the appropriate treatment for her. Another mother in the same situation may recognize the need to leave her children with relatives, and even to lose an apartment, because she fears the ultimate disaster of losing child custody altogether if she relapses upon her return to a crack-saturated environment. Thus, patients' wishes and decisions as to what *they* want also inform recommendations on treatments needed. Clinicians must avoid projecting negative expectancies of poor prognosis and must maximize patients' motivation to engage in treatment that the clinicians may not consider ideal.

A diagnosis of cocaine or crack abuse tells the clinician a great deal about the kinds of treatments to which a patient should be matched. A diagnosis of cocaine abuse according to DSM-III-R criteria suggests the need for outpatient treatment within comprehensive and intensive models, although such patients might be able to recover without the kind of daily, highly intensive participation in a wide range of treatments (family, individual) that may be critical to a cocaine- or crack-dependent patient's recovery.

Those presenting with recreational or experimental chemical use may benefit most by education on the drug's actions and effects, and by a clinician's exploration of the role of chemical use in the patient's life. Also, clinical assessment of how chemical use likely interacts with a person's characteristic personality and affective functioning remains essential. Clinicians need to spell out the risk of continued chemical use in light of a patient's history and defensive functioning. Pointing out how being an adult child of an alcoholic or dysfunctional family or how tendencies to engage in splitting, symptoms of recurrent depression, or difficulties regulating self-esteem may all predispose patients to the development of a severe and intractable addiction may be effective. A clinician's knowledge of a patient's history and of the presence of multiple risk factors can provide fuel for even more persuasive arguments regarding the use of chemicals with the kind of high addiction potential that crack possesses. Utilizing a patient's unique array of predisposing risk factors (overreliance on splitting, weak ego, low self-esteem, being an adult child of an alcoholic), a clinician can present a compelling rationale for avoiding chemical use. Confronting patients with or educating them as to the kind of debilitated state they may enter, or to how they risk losing valued rewards and possessions, can also help to deter recreational chemical users from continuing the use of crack.

In this way, clinicians should immediately provide the following set of interventions to crack users when the clinical interview indicates recreational or experimental crack use. They should (1) explain the function a chemical is coming to serve in a person's life, (2) estimate the risk that the chemical may be experienced as increasingly extra-reinforcing in light of a person's affective and personality functioning, and (3) describe the dangers of escalating toward dependence in persuasive and graphic terms, perhaps by sharing real-life case histories of persons very much like the patient. This approach may prove much more effective than blanket exaggerations or scare tactics that patients find unbelievable in view of their own experiences. Depending on patients' responses to these interventions and our assessment of their determination to continue crack use, we may match them to individual psychotherapy or family therapy with therapists skilled in chemical-dependency treatment, or anonymous self-help groups (ACOA, Alateen).

MAXIMIZING CHANCES OF SUCCESSFUL RECOVERY

The systematic matching of patients to appropriate treatments theoretically may be carried out in such a way that chances are maximized that a recovery from crack addiction will be successful. However, many realities intervene and affect the patient–treatment matching process. These harsh and imposing realities include, for example, possible loss of child custody and fear of loss of an apartment in a city with a tight housing market, as well as patient preferences. Thus, an approach involving a graded series of interventions often becomes inevitable and reasonable to follow, with a least intensive treatment option being attempted before a more intensive option that requires more sacrifices (separation from child, loss of an apartment, loss of certain privileges in a TC environment) by a patient is pursued. However, in many cases, it is overwhelmingly clear as a result of assessment findings that treatment of a certain intensity seems absolutely necessary at a certain stage of treatment.

MAXIMIZING ONE'S THERAPEUTIC IMPACT

Treatment programs currently relying on detailed questionnaires may also find that information acquired through a more thorough assessment permits maximizing the therapeutic impact on patients. A very compelling therapeutic experience for the patient is coming to understand for the first time why he or she ended up in a hospital or treatment setting while peers still work and get high with no problem. By understanding what makes one uniquely at risk for the development of crack dependence and for a relapse to crack use, a patient is more likely to become engaged in the treatment and recovery process and less likely to return to chemical use with more functional drug-using peers. This understanding empowers patients to explain to others why they cannot get high anymore, or to state with the conviction that knowledge brings, "You go ahead, but *I can't* go with you."

Indeed, clinicians can maximize the therapeutic impact on patients by providing them with an individualized explanation of the unique features of their addiction and the kind of steps that need to be taken in order to recover. This explanation utilizes information acquired in the clinical interview and is the crucial element that clinicians extend to patients toward the end of the interview as tentative hypotheses, questions, or interpretations that the patient and clinician together can attempt to answer or explore.

The concept that patients receive from clinicians a "metaphoric key" that may unlock the door to further growth and understanding (Wallace, 1987) further clarifies what clinicians extend to patients at the end of the clinical interview as they maximize their therapeutic impact. They integrate material gathered in the interview in order to formulate the elements that can explain the development and maintenance of a patient's addiction.

Excerpt from the End of a Typical Clinical Interview

An example of how clinicians attempt to maximize their therapeutic impact may be seen through the following excerpt from the closing phase of a typical interview with a crack patient:

Clinician: Why do you think you started using crack?

Patient: I don't know, I guess it was just peer pressure, it was there.

Clinician: You said that six months before you started smoking crack your mother died.

Patient: Yeah.

Clinician: It sounds as though you had been very depressed for several months. You said you couldn't sleep, you lost weight from not eating.

Patient: That's true.

Clinician: Well, I wonder if your depression didn't have something to do with your continuing to use crack even after you tried it.

Patient: Crack was the only thing that could take me away from my problems. I could sit alone and cry or I could just feel better for awhile. But then it made my problems worse.

Clinician: It probably also made you feel even more depressed.

Patient: Yes, always the day after.

Clinician: The crash, or coming down from crack, includes depression, and probably made your depression worse. We'll talk in group about how crack causes changes in your brain's functioning. But I think you need to appreciate that there are several things you need to do, or begin to think about doing, in order to recover from your crack problem. I think your mother's death is something you still have not gotten over. [Patient starts crying, nods head in agreement; clinician pauses.] You still have a lot of pain inside of you and you need to do more of what you're doing right now [patient's still crying and is given box of tissues; clinician pauses]. But at some point, you're also going to have to begin to talk about your relationship with her and some of the things that happened to you as a child. [Patient listens intently.] I think her death brought up a lot of feelings in you from your childhood.

Patient: It sure did bring up a lot of feelings. And no one in my family wanted to hear about all the things my mom used to do. My aunts thought I was being disrespectful by even bringing the past up. My mother had been sober for the past five years before she died.

Clinician: It sounds as though your mother was a very frightening and violent alcoholic [as was described by the patient and cognitively reframed in terms of alcoholic behavior by the clinician when collecting family history earlier in the clinical interview]. There's a little girl inside of you who is still frightened, sad, and in pain from absolutely horrible physical and emotional abuse. The things that happened to you were never meant to happen to anyone, especially a child. You didn't deserve to be beaten. Nothing a child does could justify that kind of abuse. Do you understand that?

Patient: Yes.

Clinician: You have to begin to feel for that little girl inside of you. You have to learn to love her and take care of her the way your mother was not able to when she was drunk and violent [clinician pauses and proceeds slowly, evaluating patient's nonverbal responses to this material]. A part of what you have to do involves taking that little girl, or yourself, for treatment—not only for your crack problem, but for the bad feelings about yourself and low self-esteem that stem from your childhood. [Clinician tries to assess patient's response to this material and to increase her involvement at this point.] What impact do you think these things had on you? How do you feel now that you think about these things?

Patient: It's true. I don't love myself. People always tell me I don't care enough about myself, even before I started smoking crack. When I was angry and depressed after my mother's death, I knew I should've gotten some help, but I didn't go. Even when I'd be high and laughing and hanging out, I'd still be thinking about my mother and the things that happened to me. When I yell at my nieces, sometimes I get real ugly. It scares me out of wanting to have kids because I wonder if I'd be like my mother.

Clinician: Well, it's important that you appreciate that the pain and impact of that childhood are something that is still with you. Maybe if you hadn't felt so badly about yourself and been so depressed following your mother's death, crack wouldn't have been so appealing to you. So your low self-esteem, depression, and childhood abuse may have something to do with why you have ended up here in treatment for crack. These issues are something that you can't ignore for the rest of your life. We can bury our problems, but they remain with us. Do you know what I mean?

Patient: I sure do [smiles].

Clinician: These issues need to be addressed in your long-term treatment in order for you to feel better about yourself. You need to learn to love yourself. What kind of aftercare treatment are you thinking about?

Patient: I don't know. I'm not sure. I tried to stop before and I really want it to work this time.

Clinician: Well, I think that you have to realize that you've been smoking a great deal of crack nearly every day for over a year. That's a lot of crack! Returning to your apartment building, which, as you say, is full of crack, was essentially setting yourself up for relapse after your last detoxification at Hospital "X." Right after treatment you're especially vulnerable to relapse, plus you didn't go to outpatient treatment or NA meetings. Aftercare treatment is essential to avoid relapse. No wonder you relapsed. It sounds like you really need to consider a therapeutic community. How does that sound?

Patient: I'll think about it.

Clinician: We'll talk in more detail about therapeutic communities and other treatment options in group therapy. Also, two therapeutic community representatives will be here to talk about their programs. Okay, any other questions?

Patient: No.

Clinician: So, we'll talk later this week and will have group therapy tomorrow. If you have any problems or questions, or if you need to talk about any feelings about what we discussed today, just ask to speak to me. Otherwise, we will have another individual session on Wednesday. Okay?

Analysis of Excerpt

The sample excerpt from a typical clinical interview illustrates the utility of the kind of information acquired. It illustrates how information on the dose and frequency of crack smoking or the severity of crack addiction directly informs recommendations on short- and long-term treatment plans. It also illustrates how circumstances of a patient's current housing, life-style, and environment—or current level of psychosocial functioning—inform decisions on aftercare treatment that are ultimately the responsibility of the patient. The way in which the clinician acts as a consultant or expert with information and training that permits the evolution of an individualized explanation of a patient's addiction also emerges from the excerpt. In addition, the excerpt illustrates how psychiatric history and mental-status-examination findings suggest a major depressive episode after the patient's mother died. A childhood history revealing exposure to an alcoholic mother and the experience of physical and emotional abuse in a dysfunctional family provides material for the process of affect labeling, and empathically offering tentative interpretations.

After more education on dysfunctional family dynamics and their impact in group therapy, and additional individual-therapy sessions, this kind of treatment approach should permit patients to leave inpatient detoxification with an internalized "key" (Wallace, 1987) such as: "My mother was an alcoholic and I was physically abused as a child. I get depressed sometimes and get high to escape my depression." Patients understand that this internalized interpretation, or "metaphoric key," can unlock doors to growth and understanding and can be articulated by them in group therapy or individual therapy in TCs or in outpatient aftercare treatment as the meaningful point of initiation of therapeutic work.

CONCLUSION

The chapter describes the kind of information clinicians must acquire in order properly and thoroughly to assess patients, spelling out the actual kinds of detailed questions to which therapists seek answers. This chapter has held up the clinical interview as a potent assessment tool capable of replacing less sensitive questionnaire instruments as a way to effectively determine the treatment needs of patients. As a result, the clinical interview can facilitate the process of matching patients to treatments of appropriate intensity. The clinical interview can also permit clinicians to maximize the therapeutic impact they can have on patients by providing an individualized, dynamic explanation of the development of the chemical dependency and the risk an individual patient possesses for relapse. In this way, we provide patients with a cognitive and intellectual framework in which they can rationally understand why they are in treatment while their functional, resilient peers are still getting high; this may empower patients to prolong abstinence and pursue their recovery more successfully.

An excerpt from the end of a clinical interview illustrates the kind of empathic and sensitive approach that permits clinicians to maximize the therapeutic impact of the interview. However, one must not underestimate the technical skill required and the difficulty that rests in eliciting the participation of patients in the treatment process. Chapter 11 offers recommendations on how to handle difficult, ambivalent crack smokers through the use of specific techniques. A number of these techniques were actually suggested in the clinical excerpt and discussion in this chapter, but a more explicit description of appropriate clinical techniques in the assessment phase merits our attention at this time.

11

Clinical Techniques to Engage the Ambivalent Crack User in Treatment

In answer to a common dilemma among clinicians, this chapter suggests how they should go about the task of engaging the ambivalent crack smoker in the treatment process. The explanation of newly abstinent crack smokers' behavior and the techniques discussed in this chapter may be of value to those professionals, paraprofessionals, and counselors working in a variety of treatment modalities who may be faced with this kind of ambivalence. The chapter also describes practical clinical techniques that the author drew upon to meet the challenge of treating crack patients in an inpatient-detoxification setting. In effect, group interpretations in community meetings, empathic mirroring and attunement, affect labeling, cognitive reframing, and education combine to provide a short-term therapy approach of value in a 14-day detoxification setting. The multifaceted clinical technique described for use in the assessment phase should find extension to the work of professionals and paraprofessionals working with the chemically dependent in diverse treatment settings.

THE AMBIVALENT CRACK PATIENT IN THE ASSESSMENT PHASE

Frequently, a crisis—such as loss of a job, loss of family support, an arrest, or an encounter with violence associated with drug-using environments—awakens patients to the need for treatment. However, defenses are employed in response to the trauma of addiction (Bean-Bayog, 1986) or the narcissistic injury involved in having to admit a need for treatment, or being forced finally to reckon with crack-related problems. When grandiosity, inflation, arrogance, or aloofness sets in, this stance frequently replaces the initial desperation and willingness to participate in treatment. Patients may then openly deny a need for the very treatment they have entered. Clinicians must appreciate that this turnaround in commitment to treatment occurs when patients are in a state of defensive inflation against the pain, embarrassment, shame, and guilt associated with their crack use. The result is an ambivalent or potentially ambivalent patient who enters the initial phase of the treatment process—the assessment phase—and begins to interact with the treatment practitioner. Here, the very best of our clinical skill and capacity for empathy must be called on to manage this turning point in the early phase of treatment.

In order fully to ascertain a person's uniqueness and the nature and severity of the addiction, the patient must first of all become engaged in the assessment and treatment process. Particular difficulties are associated with the task of engaging ambivalent crack smokers in treatment, in the process of seriously assessing their own addiction, and in involving them in making decisions regarding their long-term treatment. Quite often, the narcissistic injuries crack smokers have incurred as a result of their personal deterioration result in arrogant, aloof patients presenting for assessment and treatment. Whether their narcissism reflects a regression in response to the trauma of their addiction or a prior fixation point (Levin, 1987), the utilization of defenses of grandiosity, inflation, and denial creates a difficult assessment and treatment challenge. Also, a characteristic aloofness and lack of emotional involvement in the treatment program combines with arrogance and tendencies toward denial of the severity of the addiction in fostering an overall ambivalence about the need for treatment.

THE DYNAMICS BETWEEN CLINICIAN AND CLIENT: A KEY FACTOR

It is possible to engage even the ambivalent crack smoker in the treatment process, but certain preconditions may need to exist in order to do so. These involve the clinician's affective tone, cognitive set and assumptions, and general behavior during the patient assessment. Depending on these clinical factors, which fall partly into the realms of clinical technique and countertransference phenomena, either the ambivalence of patients can be transformed into a genuine interest in and commitment to participating in treatment, or there may be a remaining ambivalence toward or rejection of important aspects of the treatment process. Specific clinical interventions in the assessment phase can facilitate the process of engaging the crack smoker in a serious assessment of the dimensions of the crack addiction and in the treatment process.

This view is consistent with that of Donovan (1988), who notes that, in addition to information acquisition, "the initial interaction of client and clinician during the course of the assessment may also serve important therapeutic functions. In particular, the process of assessment may contribute significantly to the individual's motivation for and commitment to change" (p. 26). Donovan also validates the high degree of ambivalence that characterizes the client just entering treatment, emphasizing the need "even while in the assessment process . . . to 'hook' the side of the client's ambivalence that is positively inclined toward change. It is necessary to tip the balance by strengthening the commitment and motivation for change . . ." (p. 26).

We also find support for our citing of countertransference reactions on the part of the treatment professional as playing a role in determining whether we successfully help patients resolve their ambivalence and become motivated participants in the treatment process. In this regard, Donovan discusses the treatment practitioner's possible view of addicted persons as unmotivated with the potential outcome that clinicians hold an expectancy of poor prognosis that may lead to a self-fulfilling prophecy. He further explains that, in particular, a patient's feelings of frustration and futility about changing may be based on past unsuccessful attempts to end the addictive behavior; the patient may also respond to clinical feedback or expectations of a poor prognosis. Donovan explains that these factors may subtly undermine treatment. In sum, clinicians must avoid projecting negative and low expectations for patients.

Support is forthcoming, as well, for our emphasis on clinicians' having fully to utilize their capacity for empathy in order to manage this potential turning point in the early phase of treatment with the ambivalent crack patient. Donovan warns us about the reduction in empathy that follows from viewing the addicted patient as inherently unmotivated. In addition to a reduced ability to empathize with the client, he explains how there may be increased suspiciousness on the part of the clinician, as well as hostility, moralizing, and power struggles that effectively undermine the clinician's attempts at intervention with the client. Following this analysis, Donovan feels that it is important to use an alternative approach (Miller, 1983, 1985) that views patient motivation as resulting from the interaction between the clinician and the client; the clinician can produce either the client response of motivation or of resistance, depending on how the clinician interacts affectively, cognitively, and behaviorally with the client regarding the client's addiction and ambivalence toward change (Donovan, 1988, pp 26–27).

Clinical experience also suggests that clinicians must convey respect for patients during all interactions with them. This attitude goes a long way toward eliciting the cooperation of patients and engaging them in the treatment process.

EDUCATION TO AVOID NEGATIVE COUNTERTRANSFERENCE REACTIONS

From this author's perspective, it is imperative that treatment professionals take responsibility for managing any negative countertransference reactions they may have in response to a crack smoker's reports of crack-related behaviors. This book has repeatedly emphasized how a brain-driven compulsion to smoke more and more crack, neurochemically based intense cravings for crack, conditioned stimuli that may trigger cravings, and the availability of crack in crack-saturated environments have combined in creating compulsive crack smokers who may do anything in order to smoke more crack. It is from this educated perspective that a treatment professional must empathically listen to histories of recent psychosocial functioning that may include graphic descriptions of unpleasant and humiliating experiences. The other piece of education that treatment staff must keep in mind is the fact that a crack smoker's arrogance, aloofness, and grandiosity represent a defense against painfully low self-esteem, shame, and guilt over crack-related deterioration and behavior.

If clinicians keep in mind these two dimensions of a crack smoker's state of being, education and knowledge may prevent the experience of negative countertransference reactions, judgmental or condemnatory attitudes, or nonverbal behaviors that are rejecting of patients. Instead, clinicians may utilize their knowledge and understanding about crack smokers' defensive functioning to relate to them empathically. Ironically, these arrogant, aloof, and grandiose patients require the very best of our clinical skill, capacity for comprehending the purpose of their defensive functioning, and ability to empathize with that part of them that is struggling to defend against overwhelming pain and narcissistic injury.

MANAGING PATIENTS' NEGATIVE TRANSFERENCE REACTIONS

Within any therapeutic milieu, patients who enter treatment in an arrogant, aloof, and devaluing state may also have negative transference reactions to the treatment staff. As Levin (1987) states, newly abstinent patients may utilize borderline defenses such as splitting, in addition to presenting a predominance of narcissism. Patients functioning on a borderline level, and even adult children of dysfunctional families who have only internalized memories of interacting with far-from-ideal parental figures, may project low and negative expectations onto therapists and staff. They may expect treatment staff to provide the kind of care that their inadequate and abusive parents did. This leads to negative transference reactions, with staff members the objects of the anger of demanding and frustrated patients. These dynamics can undermine the therapeutic milieu. Patients may find themselves wanting to leave treatment because they hate the staff, reactions that may prevent them from becoming engaged in the treatment process. Also, patients may see in some staff members the good parental object (good, loving mother from childhood) and in other staff members the bad parental object (inconsistent and abusive mother from childhood). When this occurs, patients can actually create tensions and discord that threaten to undermine the integrity of the unit as a therapeutic milieu.

Interpretations to the Group at Community Meetings

The use of community meetings as an opportunity to offer interpretations to the entire group of patients about such dynamics can resolve negative transference reactions toward staff members. The observations of Hamilton (1988) are relevant and informative in this regard. Hamilton recognizes the importance of confronting negative transference. This follows Kernberg (1975), who stressed the importance of interpreting transference early in treatment, especially with borderline patients. Here, the negative transference of which Hamilton speaks involves the projection of bad, devalued, abandoning, or at least disappointing or rejecting internal objects onto the person of the therapist (p. 216). In addition, this "bad" object-image "is usually associated with angry, hostile, or frightened feelings, which must be brought into the discussion so that they can be modulated and integrated" (p. 216). Hamilton makes the very important point that when these negative affects associated with specific self–object–affect units are left unattended, the feelings of anger or disappointment may lead to premature interruption of the treatment process.

Hamilton goes on to make the very excellent point that since well-timed confrontations have an empathic element, the current debate over whether therapists should confront (Kernberg, 1975) or empathize (Kohut, 1971) is often irrelevant (p. 217). Confrontation that points out how a negative transference or projection of a "bad" object-image upon the person of the therapist has just occurred can also serve as an empathic communication, as Hamilton emphasizes. With borderline patients who present such a negative transference very early in treatment, Hamilton feels that confrontation of negative transference usually diminishes hostile feelings.

In a similar vein, in drug-treatment settings, it is often important within the context of community meetings to offer the following kind of interpretation to the entire group of patients: "It's okay to hate me. I know some of you sit in your rooms and talk about how you can't stand Dr. Wallace. That's okay. I am here to do everything I can to make sure that this environment is safe and that you take the first steps toward overcoming your crack addiction. Some individuals hate me because they are reacting to me the same way they reacted to their mother or father. Maybe you know somebody who can't stand police, gym teachers, or any men in authority. Well, they probably had a horrible relationship with their father and relate to all men as though they were their father. It's not really the cop they hate, they hate their father. The cop just reminds them of their father. You know what I mean: It's called transference. You transfer feelings you have toward your father onto people who remind you of your father.

Or maybe you know how some people just can't stand women and can never get along with them. Well, usually they had a bad relationship with their mother." The interpretation also serves to educate patients, while resolving many patients' negative transference reactions.

Clinicians explain that everyone in treatment has some kind of emotional or psychological problem—many stemming from growing up in alcoholic homes or from depression resulting from crack-related problems. The importance of all patients having a safe environment and receiving the attention and treatment they need is also emphasized at this time. These kinds of comments, and the use of interpretations to the group, often have the effect of diminishing splitting on the unit, so that the projection of bad object-images upon the therapist can be decreased. These interpretations to the group can be very powerful in ensuring that the treatment milieu remains a therapeutic environment and that the projection of bad object-images does not threaten to undermine it. Many patients achieve tremendous insight into their own or other patients' behavior.

At community meetings, assurance should also be offered that the treatment environment must and will be kept safe and drug-free, and that certain behaviors will not be tolerated (verbal or physical abuse of staff or other patients). In this way, patients with poor impulse control who may have intense negative transference reactions to the staff become aware of firm limits that are placed on their behavior. When narcissistic patients experience group interpretations of this type, they are likely to assume that they are not being talked to and that the therapist must be powerful to know about conversations they have overheard involving such negative talk about the therapist. In individual sessions, they act as good patients deserving of a good therapist in contrast to those other devaluing patients, sometimes identifying problematic patients. These problematic patients, and indeed all patients, receive in individual sessions empathic responses that spell out how negative transference reactions are tolerated and understandable, while treatment goes on to address the needs of the patient. In fact, group interpretations in community meetings have empowered patients to understand and tolerate their own and other patients' negative-transference reactions. Meanwhile, the therapist's skill and empathy in relating to patients has begun to forge a positive therapeutic alliance and trust that staff members will be "good parents" who protect them and provide a safe environment during inpatient detoxification treatment.

THE TECHNIQUE OF EMPATHIC MIRRORING

The critical role of empathy in treatment, interpretations of Kohut's (1971, 1977) views on empathy/mirroring/clinical technique with narcissistic patients, and a host of clinical techniques derived from the schools of object-relations theory and self psychology have been discussed at length by numerous authors (Hamilton, 1988; Berger, 1987; Giovacchini, 1989; Rowe & MacIsaac, 1989; Rinsley, 1989). Others have dealt specifically with the kind of clinical technique appropriate with the chemically dependent (Wurmser, 1985; Levin, 1987). However, this chapter suggests techniques developed in direct response to the challenge of engaging ambivalent, arrogant, inflated crack patients in treatment on a 14-day inpatient-detoxification unit. The technique of empathic mirroring permits clinicians to engage patients in the treatment process. This section attempts to describe this practical and easily replicable approach; an analysis of this technique from the perspective of self psychology and object-relations theory is not elaborated on here in the interest of brevity.

The Rationale for Empathic Mirroring

Clinicians must find a way to reach that part of patients that is suffering from the trauma of addiction, and empathically mirror to the part that is in a state of defensive inflation the reality of an inner part suffering intense pain from the trauma of addiction. By empathically mirroring to patients the pain, shame, guilt, and disappointment they are harboring deep inside, we affirm a dimension of their experience that is very real. We gain their trust and admiration as credible professionals who validate the truth of their inner experience. Our empathic responses to patients' very fragile and vulnerable states, our labeling their pain for them, and our explaining how we understand their desire to escape this pain enable patients to begin to connect with and "own" their inner experience, instead of utilizing defenses that threaten to drive them out of treatment.

It becomes necessary to point out to patients, gently and empathically, the inner pain they harbor when defensive inflation and denial create a danger of leaving the treatment program. Even when these patients remain in our treatment programs, we need to help them connect with the inner part of themselves that is in pain over the trauma of their addiction. We must assist patients in beginning to process the painful feelings they hide; otherwise, they will "skate" through treatment, alternately devaluing the program through words and actions and failing to benefit from treatment because of their aloofness, grandiosity and lack of involvement. On the other hand, we must tolerate a considerable degree of narcissism in patients that they in fact need as a part of a necessary defensive stance. These patients cannot long tolerate the humiliation, shame, and guilt they feel when connecting with and processing painful affects. Painfully intense feelings emerge when they think about infants taken from them at birth, being raped in a crack house, losing a great job, losing a spouse/partner, running through financial resources, neglecting children, or stealing from family.

The feelings of shame, humiliation, and guilt are often followed by a state of manic laughter, high-energy antics and pranks, or grandiosity and inflation as a necessary defense. Or this defensive stance is relied on to prevent emergence of the underlying inner pain. We are sometimes forced to act by talking to patients and interpreting their manic or grandiose defenses when clown theatrics (Wallace, 1987), high-energy antics, or manic acting-out behavior threatens to destroy the therapeutic milieu.

Community meetings at which psychologists interpret group dynamics and recent events in the treatment program in terms of individuals' understandable need to defend against painful feelings and crack-related problems can be very effective. Interpretations to the group are followed by allowing patients to feel depressed, confused, and uncertain about regaining housing, a job, a spouse, or child custody. This is coupled with encouraging them to verbalize their depression, confusion, and problems in individual and group sessions, instead of defending against them with manic defenses. Such an approach can be very effective in restoring a therapeutic atmosphere to one's treatment program. Holding a community meeting at the end and beginning of each week (Monday and Friday), and a willingness to hold an emergency meeting, can permit preserving a therapeutic treatment atmosphere. Regular group and individual sessions also must afford patients an opportunity to express and process their depression, lessening anxiety and confusion as well. In addition, frequent talks between an acting-out or grandiose patient and the entire staff in private can help to assure a therapeutic milieu and prevent departures against medical advice or having to discharge disruptive patients.

What Does Empathic Mirroring Involve?

Essentially, the clinical technique of empathic mirroring involves reflecting back to patients the discrepancy between their denial of the severity of their addiction and the facts of their crack-related deterioration. A key piece of ammunition clinicians possess in working with these difficult and challenging patients rests in the information obtained in the clinical interview (see Chapter 10). Knowledge of those events in a patient's life that provide motivation for remaining in treatment and successfully recovering from the addiction arms clinicians with vital information that can be utilized when trying to retain patients in treatment. Also, knowledge of patients' precrack level of functioning (a wife, car, home, good job, family support, child custody) and the things they lost as they deteriorated provides clinicians with the material needed in designing effective interventions for inflated and grandiose crack patients.

All of this patient "data" are invaluable and permit treatment professionals empathically to point out the discrepancy between an inflated patient's denial of the need for treatment (or to attend a group, cooperate with staff, or complete inpatient detoxification) and the reality of the crack-related deterioration. At the same time, we empathically relate to the well-hidden inner experience of patients suffering pain as a result of crack-related problems and the trauma of their addiction. We also empathically mirror to the other external part of patients in a state of inflation as a defense against their well-hidden inner pain their own inner experience, or true state of their inner being. In this way, we affirm and validate a part of their own inner reality that they tend to deny. Also, clinicians can carefully and sensitively explain how we understand their desire to escape their pain, perhaps by setting themselves up for, or actively seeking out, an opportunity to get high. Through this process, clinicians may enable these difficult crack patients to complete treatment, become more meaningfully engaged in the treatment process, and increase their chances of avoiding a return to crack use and exacerbation of those crack-related problems causing so much internal pain.

Examples of Empathic Mirroring

The use of empathic mirroring with fragile, vulnerable patients—who may be experiencing painful affects without relying on self-medication with chemicals for the first time in days or months—actually represents a form of gentle confrontation. Patients are confronted with the facts of their psychosocial deterioration, but in an individual psychotherapy session where the clinician's empathy and creation of a holding environment support the patient's weak ego. The following are examples of this kind of empathic mirroring or gentle confrontation:

1. "I hear you saying that your crack problem isn't all that serious and you don't think you need to be here in inpatient treatment. On the other hand, you say that you've almost lost your wife and your job because of crack. You seem to be in a lot of pain."
2. "Do you realize that you nearly killed yourself the other night, as you hoped to smoke so much that you'd have a seizure? I can understand just how depressed you were when they took away your children. You need to do everything you can to get your life back together and to care for your children again. But now you say you don't think you need to be here in treatment. Is it easier to run away and get high instead of feeling the pain over separation from your children? Is that why you want to leave treatment?"
3. "It's very frightening to come so close to death; that crack dealer could've shot you in that hallway. You are an intelligent and sensitive person. Your life is very valuable. Your mother and husband love you. But here

you are coming so close to death in some dark hallway. What do you think you need to do about your crack problem?"

Analysis of Examples

The examples provide us with a better understanding of the kind of gentle confrontation involved in using empathic mirroring. We can interpret Hamilton's comments (1989) as providing support for such a technique. Let us first recall that we have explained in detail how crack patients present a predominance of narcissism because of either a fixation or a regression to a level of functioning characterized by pathological narcissism; crack-related trauma may add narcissistic injury to a fixation rooted in childhood trauma in a dysfunctional family (see Chapters 3 and 5). Hamilton makes the point that when children have experienced chronic failure on the part of parents to be empathic, this contributes to their development of narcissistic vulnerabilities. Hamilton stresses that, as a result, the therapist must help the patient overcome these vulnerabilities by providing empathic responses (p. 197). In terms of how narcissistic patients respond to the therapists' empathic responses, Hamilton notes that they "seem to flourish with empathy" and that long periods of "empathic paraphrasing" are often needed before narcissistic patients can accept even gentle confrontations and interpretations (p. 197). In fact, Hamilton makes the point—drawing upon the theory of Kohut (1971)—that empathic comments "apparently are as much confrontation as they can initially tolerate" (p. 218).

Typically, the kinds of interventions illustrated here permit patients to connect with their own inner feelings and experience. Once connected with the part of themselves that desperately seeks relief from their crack-related pain, patients increase their motivation to remain in treatment or become more involved in the treatment process. They flourish insofar as they become emotionally engaged with the therapist and the treatment program, and begin to benefit from a range of treatment interventions aimed at preventing a return to chemical use. The extent to which empathic mirroring—which points out the discrepancy between a denial of a need for treatment or the severity of the addiction and the facts of the crack-related deterioration—represent a form of gentle confrontation can also be seen from the examples.

Using Knowledge of a Patient's History to Increase Motivation

The examples show how, by pointing out the rewards patients hope to regain if they become abstinent, clinicians further increase patients' motivation to become engaged in treatment. Clinicians working with inflated crack patients also can use their knowledge of those factors that might motivate a patient to complete treatment or recover from crack addiction to increase motivation.

Once a clinician has empathically mirrored to a patient the discrepancy between the denial of the severity of the addiction and the facts of the crack-
related deterioration, the clinician should also do the following. The treatment
professional gently reminds the patient of just how important it is to regain the
trust of family members, reunite with a spouse, regain child custody, become
gainfully employed again, or avoid a relapse. Such an intervention can be very
powerful when we amaze patients with our recollection of the specific details of
their predicament, showing our genuine interest in them as individuals with
unique problems, concerns, and dreams. The power of this technique rests in
our having taken the time to individually and thoroughly assess the unique dimensions of a patient's addiction in our clinical interview (see Chapter 10). Instead of having an assessment procedure whereby questionnaires are
administered by poorly trained personnel who have no further contacts with
patients, we can ensure our ability to maintain a therapeutic milieu and retain
patients in treatment by having treatment staff members obtain detailed information in clinical interviews that will empower them to relate empathically to
crack patients.

How to Urge Patients to Enter Treatment

Even before a patient enters a formal treatment program, parents and other
laypeople, as well as professionals, may benefit from the success clinicians
achieve with crack patients in inpatient detoxification by utilizing these kinds
of interventions. An effective approach in helping patients overcome denial of
the severity of their addiction may mean gently pointing out to them the
things they may inadvertently have mentioned as having lost as a result of
their crack habit. By suggesting that these losses indicate that their crack use is
a problem, and then empathizing with that part of them that is hurting because of these losses, a concerned person may be able to provide an intervention that may motivate a crack user to enter treatment. Further motivation
may be afforded by pointing out all the things the person may be able to regain
by undergoing treatment.

Thus, any concerned person may be able to urge a crack smoker to enter
treatment by (1) pointing out (mirroring to or reflecting back to patients) the
discrepancy between a patient's denial of the severity of the addiction and the
facts of the crack-related deterioration; (2) empathically relating to the part of
the patient that feels shame, guilt, embarrassment, or sadness over crack-related
deterioration; and (3) further increasing motivation by underscoring what can
be regained.

However, the untrained person trying to intervene in a crack smoker's personal life must be very careful not to project low expectations or to be judgmental. But these techniques, if used sensitively by someone who is caring and

concerned, might at least get a crack user into a situation where he or she can be assessed and treated by a professional. Further, it is hoped, the professional will use such techniques to retain patients in treatment despite the wall of denial, grandiosity, and arrogance surrounding the inflated crack patient who may have gone to the treatment facility—as he or she believes—just to placate some concerned busybody.

Parallels with the Creation of Cognitive Dissonance

This approach bears some resemblance to the technique of creating cognitive dissonance. Donovan (1988) embraces the work of W. R. Miller (1983, 1985) in explaining how the clinician can help produce on the part of the client an appreciation of an inner inconsistency regarding how addictive behavior is discrepant with the client's personal beliefs, attitudes, values, and feelings. This results in a state of internal conflict on the part of the client that motivates a change in behavior that will bring about a greater degree of consistency. Donovan views the task of the clinician as involving the creation of an increase in the level of cognitive dissonance—or as increasing the discrepancy between the individual's personal beliefs and feelings and the addictive behavior. Also, the clinician must direct the motivational state or desire to change that results from this increase in dissonance so that it actually leads to changed behavior (Donovan, 1988, p. 27).

By sensitively guiding patients to become aware of the discrepancy between their denial of the severity of their addiction ("My problem isn't that bad" or "I don't need to be here in treatment") and the reality that they experience painful feelings (shame, guilt, embarrassment, and depression) about their crack-related deterioration, clinicians create cognitive dissonance. Patients move away from denial and become motivated for behavioral change and treatment of their addiction.

Achieving Empathic Attunement

Rowe and MacIsaac (1989) discuss empathic attunement as a technique of psychoanalytic self psychology that arises from an understanding of Kohut's (1971, 1977) work. The empathic attunement of which they speak involves clinicians' achieving understanding from the vantage point of the patient's experience. The present author discovered through clinical work with crack patients during a 14-day inpatient detoxification the importance of achieving empathic attunement to their inner feelings about their crack-related deterioration. As Rowe and MacIsaac point out, Kohut discovered many of his theoretical insights as a result of prolonged empathic immersion in the inner world of patients who were his most difficult cases (p. 9). No such lengthy encounters are possible with patients during a 14-day inpatient detoxification. Yet I, too, discovered—with these, the most difficult patients that I had ever encountered—that by becoming empathically attuned to their well-hidden and underlying feelings, or inner experience, I had found an invaluable point of entry for short-term clinical work.

The technique of empathic attunement, as this author conceptualizes and utilizes it, goes hand and hand with the use of empathic mirroring. Clinicians can only employ empathic mirroring if, in the course of collecting psychosocial data and interviewing patients, they become empathically attuned to their experiences and "hear" beyond the content of their answers (to questions posed in the clinical interview, see Chapter 10) the well-hidden low self-esteem and painful feelings against which crack smokers defend with characteristic grandiosity and denial. By being empathically attuned to patients' emotional responses to their crack-related personal deterioration, clinicians can sensitively convey their appreciation of the range of feelings associated with the patient's loss of control and the behavior associated with compulsive crack smoking.

Most important, clinicians must empathically grasp the effect of crack-related deterioration on patients and judge which issues need to be explored and which do not. Patients may not have negative or painful feelings about drug dealing, for example. We must not mistakenly articulate our own feelings about dealing in drugs and alienate patients because we failed to "hear" that their real pain was over not having given money for child support or not having visited a son in months as a consequence of compulsive crack smoking. This is why we ask in the clinical interview, "What crack-related problems have you experienced?" or "What impact has crack had upon your life?" The information we obtain requires our careful attunement to the feelings and emotional responses that may accompany patients' responses.

As a result of empathic attunement, clinical judgment might also dictate, for example, that it is not time for a woman to process feelings about engaging in prostitution during such an early phase of treatment. Feelings immediately available and experienced by such a woman could even include a new sense of power over or an ability to manipulate men; a clinician must not mistakenly focus upon his or her own feelings of horror as he or she imagines "walking in the patient's shoes." It is not the clinician's assumptions about what the patient might feel or knowledge of what the clinician would feel that should be called upon. Clinicians must attempt to sense instead the patient's feelings and which of the patient's crack-related experiences has had a profound impact on a deep emotional level. Empathic attunement to a patient's material elicited in the clinical interview permits us to discern the well-hidden painful feelings. For example, a woman who has engaged in prostitution to get money for crack or regularly exchanged sex for crack may need us to attune empathically to her pain and to mirror to her the pain over having been gang raped and frightened by the possibility of being killed. To be empathically attuned to a patient's experience and not held captive by negative stereotypes, low expectancies, or our own countertransference reactions is essential. In this way, we accurately appreciate the nature of an individual's inner pain and empathically sense what the person is feeling as a result of crack-related deterioration or the trauma of the addiction.

Clinicians thus have, in the patient's own words (obtained in the clinical interview), a description of crack-related psychosocial or personal deterioration. Metaphorically, the patient's psychosocial data and the evidence of crack-related psychosocial deterioration can be considered ammunition to be used empathically in the battle of engaging the crack patient in treatment and increasing the patient's motivation or investment in the treatment process. However, we only know how and when to wield these weapons if we have become empathically attuned to a patient's experience.

ERRONEOUS AND ON-TARGET EMPATHIC ATTUNEMENT

It is a very powerful experience to hear one's own description of crack-related problems mirrored or reflected back to oneself in a way that shows how a clinician has carefully listened to and appreciated the unique and individual aspects of one's addiction. When patients hear this, they feel gratified, are made whole, and have their inner experience validated by our ability to achieve empathic attunement. Patients even overlook or seemingly forgive us for countertransference mistakes when our earlier questions were "off target" in exploring the wrong material for its affective meaning. For example, the following dialogue illustrates both erroneous and on-target empathic attunement to psychosocial material elicited in the clinical interview.

Clinician: Okay, you said you smoked $200 per day of crack five times a week?
Patient: Yes.
Clinician: How did you support your habit?
Patient: I sold my body, my boyfriend gave me money, and I used what was left from my welfare check after I took care of my kids.

Erroneous Empathic Attunement

Clinician: How do you feel about having engaged in prostitution? [Clinician is most struck by this piece of data and pursues it as a line of inquiry.]
Patient: Not so great, I guess.
Clinician: What do you mean?
Patient: I did what I had to do. [Patient is put on the defensive, as the clini-

cian erred. But the clinical interview can still be salvaged if the therapist can achieve empathic attunement to the patient's inner experience and feelings.]

Correct Empathic Attunement

Clinician: What kind of problems have you had as a result of smoking crack?

Patient: Plenty of problems. I was beaten up by a "John" in a hallway three weeks ago. He tried to rape me.

Clinician: Did he?

Patient: [Nods head, begins to cry.]

Clinician: Did you tell anyone about it?

Patient: No, I couldn't. they would've asked me what I was doing there. It's a known crack location.

Clinician: You've been keeping this inside of you all of this time?

Patient: [Nods, crying softly.]

Clinician: Did this have something to do with your decision to come here?

Patient: [Nods.] After it happened, I started smoking even more crack. I was up (awake) for a week straight smoking crack. I couldn't stop thinking about it. I felt horrible. I was so angry I wanted to kill him.

Clinician: I can understand your anger and the pain you must have been in. [Clinician has permitted expression of affect without being too probing or intrusive. Later in this session, or later at a turning point in this early phase of treatment, the clinician can use this information to enhance the patient's motivation for the kind of long-term treatment necessary to ensure a successful recovery from crack dependence.]

Clinician: You have been out there smoking crack for over a year now. Look at the kind of situations you've been in. Anything could've happened in that hallway. You're lucky to be here.

Patient: I know. He had a knife.

Clinician: You have got to take care of yourself. Your children need you. As you said before, you don't want your neighbors to call the Bureau of Child Welfare. You don't want to risk losing your children. You have got to do everything you can to make sure you do not go back to smoking crack.

Patient: That's true.

Clinician: Have you thought about what kind of aftercare treatment you want?

Patient: I was thinking about Narcotics Anonymous.

Clinician: Well, I understand that there is no one you trust to care for your children, which rules out a residential therapeutic community. However, I think you need more than NA meetings. You still have a lot of feelings you need to process about your recent rape. I strongly recommend that you accept a referral for rape counseling. What do you think about that?

Patient: It sounds good. I'd thought about it before.

Clinician: I also think you could benefit by continuing in an outpatient program that provides individual and group psychotherapy. They also provide family therapy and could evaluate your children for any treatment they might need.

Patient: My son's teacher keeps asking me to come to the school. So I know there's a problem.

Clinician: Well, I think they could address his problem as well as your problems. Should we call and make an appointment for you now?

Patient: Sounds good.

Assessment of Clinical Interventions

In this way, a clinician's detailed knowledge of a patient's crack-related problems, family predicament, and concerns expressed in the clinical interview provides the kind of ammunition needed to "hook" the positive side of the patient's motivation inclined to change—as Donovan (1988) might describe the final outcome. The excerpt also shows how, through exploring crack-related deterioration and the patient's perception of the impact of crack-related problems, we can either ask the wrong or right kind of questions. The right kind of questions follow from our "hearing" or sensing patients' emotional responses to the questions we ask. When we ask the right kind of questions, we are traveling down the road that leads into a patient's inner emotional life, and we may then become empathically attuned to the patient's painful feelings and the trauma of the addiction. In effect, we engage patients emotionally in the treatment process. When a patient has become so engaged, we have effectively transformed an arrogant, aloof, grandiose patient, who may have devalued us and our treatment program and denied a need for treatment, into a willing, cooperative participant in the recovery.

We can also see through this excerpt how the information obtained in the clinical interview is employed to enhance a patient's motive   to take seriously treatment recommendations that must ultimately be t¹   :cision of the patient. But we must also strive to impress upon patient   .r need for the kind of treatment to which they should be matched a ,rding to our assessment findings.

AFFECT LABELING AND INTERPRETATION

By being empathically attuned to patients' experiences, and using empathic mirroring of their emotions and inner lives, clinicians can elicit responses that include beginning to verbalize and process some of the feelings that they escaped by continued crack smoking. By talking about, and perhaps crying about for the first time while not high on crack, the pain of separation from one's child, depression can begin to be felt, labeled, and processed by the container of the ego that gets stronger in the process, thereby decreasing the reliance on crack smoking to manage or regulate painful affective states. The therapist may have to engage in a process of identifying or labeling a patient's affects, and even offer interpretations that assist patients in the process of regulating and modulating their feelings, impulses, self-esteem, and behavior.

This is consistent with the view of Hamilton (1989), who would probably recognize in the use of empathic mirroring the kind of gentle confrontation of which he speaks. According to Hamilton, a gentle confrontation that provides external confirmation of the patient's experiences can make the patient aware of having just experienced a strong feeling, decreasing the chances that the tendency to have a strong emotional reaction and forget about it will not occur (p. 207). Clinicians who engage in affect labeling further ensure that patients begin to make progress in developing the ability to identify, label, process, and better regulate their feeling states or self-esteem.

Patients may actually rely on defenses of grandiosity and inflation because they lack self-regulatory capacities. Based on our psychoanalytic theoretical rationale for clinical interventions described in Chapter 5, it follows that many patients may possess deficits in the area of identifying, labeling, and processing feelings, as well as in the area of regulating and modulating painful feelings and self-esteem. So, even in the assessment phase, clinicians may perform an important therapeutic function by helping patients to identify, label, and begin to process painful feelings associated with crack-related psychosocial deterioration or problems. By beginning to process these feelings, patients realize the full emotional impact of crack on their lives, the implications of their crack use, and the importance of treatment and changing crack-use behavior. Not only do patients become emotionally engaged in the treatment process, but their apparent motivation for treatment and behavioral change seems to increase substantially.

Levin (1987) emphasizes that ego weakness results in a failure to modulate intense affects, which then threaten to fragment a tenuously cohesive self. He states that the very intensity with which long-anesthetized or repressed emotions are experienced constitutes a significant threat to sobriety in the period of early sobriety or abstinence. Feelings, therefore, can be experienced as overwhelming. Levin uses the metaphor that the container (the self) is too weak to contain the contents (primitive feelings) and the container is in jeopardy of disintegrating under the pressure. The patient thus may experience a panic that represents a response to the threat of annihilation of the self. As affects such as these may threaten sobriety, it is important to strengthen the ego's capacity for affect modulation through the exercise of verbalization, according to Levin. To recognize, name, and talk about a feeling, or to experience and talk about rather than repress, deny, somatize, or act out an affect, permits strengthening of the ego and the raising of self-esteem, he points out.

What Are You Feeling?

Levin (1987) identifies the clinical intervention—"What are you feeling?"—as an important one that must be used over and over again to facilitate the verbalization of affect and strengthening of the ego. In addition, the related task of "labeling the affects" permits feelings to be experienced as consciously owned aspects of the patient's self. Levin explains that initially affect labeling is done by the therapist ("You are angry") and involves actual interpretations of feelings that are "usually near the surface and are transparent to a trained and experienced therapist" (pp. 253–254).

While Levin feels that it is always the feelings that are close to consciousness that are interpreted, any feelings that threaten sobriety or the state of abstinence also need to be uncovered and worked through. He addresses the following important issue:

How can this strategy of uncovering feelings be reconciled with the principle of supporting the defenses in early sobriety? The answer is essentially a practical one. Functional defenses, which protect the recovering alcoholic from pain he cannot yet handle, whether such pain be the potential consequence of new knowledge or of new emotion, are supported. Dysfunctional defenses, which are threats to sobriety, are analyzed and interpreted. However, denial that is appropriately protective is supported, as is successful repression and obsessive-compulsive behavior that does not threaten sobriety. (p. 256)

Although Levin's remarks refer to the phase of early sobriety in the alcoholic, he emphasizes that his views extend to the treatment of other addictions. The period of initial abstinence or of early "sobriety" for the chemically dependent patient permits extension of these views to this phase of work with the crack patient. Levin's work reinforces and clarifies the use of the clinical technique of empathic mirroring, while also validating the importance of interpreting and labeling for patients painful affects that are close to consciousness and may jeopardize the treatment process, and lead to departure from treatment and relapse.

The response of self-medication and departure from treatment may easily occur if uninterpreted or unconscious feelings against which patients defend are acted out, or if the behavior of self-medication of these intense affects occurs with a return to chemical use. Empathic mirroring, labeling affects, and inter-

pretation of unconscious material not only may engage patients emotionally in
the treatment process, but may decrease chances of departure from treatment
by providing the ego with an opportunity to begin to master dysphoria by verbalization and processing of emotion. In this way, affect labeling and encouraging patients to feel and process the pain, for example, of loss of child custody or
of a spouse for the first time without getting high may thereby decrease the
need for reliance upon or a return to self-medication with chemicals.

Empathic mirroring also links the experience of painful feelings that clinicians may label to the patient's crack-related problems and psychosocial deterioration. In this way, patients receive through our interpretations a new
understanding of what may have been their feelings and experience. Levin
(1987) makes a related point, likening the process to new territory being gained
for the ego from the id (p. 254). Hamilton (1988) points out that interpretations
used to be thought of as making something unconscious conscious. However,
this may not be a technically correct description for patients who split off aspects of their experiential world instead of repressing them, according to Hamilton. Thus, "when a therapist interprets splitting, a link or association between
two events is created" (p. 208). By interpreting repression, the therapist is facilitating the memory of a previously existing association. Although we cannot
present a detailed theoretical interpretation of affect labeling and interpretation
here, they must be considered important techniques that, together with empathic mirroring and empathic attunement, begin to provide the clinician with
clinical tools to use with crack patients. Those interested in a theoretical analysis of clinical techniques of value with narcissistic patients can refer to the work
of numerous authors (Hamilton, 1988; Berger, 1987; Giovacchini, 1989; Rowe
& MacIsaac, 1989; Rinsley, 1989; Wurmser, 1985; Levin, 1987).

EDUCATIONAL INTERVENTIONS

Clinicians must balance their use of confrontation—even the gentle confrontation involved in empathic mirroring—that has the aim of impressing patients
with the severity of the addiction, or of persuading them seriously to consider
short- and long-term treatment plans, with respect for their free will. This involves recognition of the fact that crack smokers are autonomous individuals
who must take responsibility for their own treatment or healing. Often, the
therapist will sense that it is not the right time to challenge denial or interpret
defenses. In such cases, education in the context of group therapy may be more
effective in engaging patients in the treatment process. The experience of receiving a cognitive and intellectual framework in which to understand one's
crack addiction also occurs through the provision of education by the clinician

in individual sessions. An active clinician can offer education—as Levin (1987) also acknowledges—in either an individual or a group context.

Consistent with the perspective of Donovan (1988), the clinician can serve as a consultant, furnishing patients with alternative treatment recommendations and information that will help them choose among them, while respecting the fact that it is the patient's responsibility to make the final decision. Even where patient treatment decisions differ from professional assessments of what is best, clinicians must avoid the projection of prophecies of failure or expectations of a poor prognosis, while following their best clinical judgment as to the degree and kind of confrontation that is appropriate with a particular patient. As educators or consultants, clinicians actively impart information to patients. In group therapy, the clinician impartially describes in explicit terms the different types of treatment available postdetoxification—NA/CA groups alone or in combination with outpatient treatment, or residential TCs. They explain the kinds of treatments that patients might consider in light of the severity of the addiction. They may also offer case examples of patients who relapsed in an aftercare placement that was not sufficiently intensive and failed to afford the kind of support and structure they needed (e.g., not entering any treatment, attending NA/CA meetings too infrequently, failing to secure an NA/CA sponsor or to pursue outpatient treatment). Eliciting examples from patients in the group further amplifies the efficacy of education in motivating patients to become more engaged in treatment on the unit and to plan sufficiently intense aftercare.

Clinicians can describe to patients the pharmacological effects of substances and neurochemical disruptions in brain function and how these factors may explain aspects of their own experience, as well as how the administration of pharmacological adjuncts during detoxification attempts to restore their brain's neurochemical balance and to decrease cravings. Education can also cover the use of defenses (denial, mania, grandiosity) and the nature of one's emotional functioning and its origin in dysfunctional family dynamics. When the possible etiological roots of crack addiction or self-medication strategies are also explained, then clinicians essentially furnish patients with a new cognitive and intellectual framework in which to understand their addictive behavior. This education may alleviate feelings of self-blame or guilt and serve to motivate patients to accept treatment recommendations designed in recognition of the roots of the addiction. To cover the third, remaining base of the biopsychosocial model of crack addiction, education may also logically include the role of psychosocial or social factors in determining one's short- and long-term treatment goals. A spouse who smokes crack or a return to a crack-saturated environment may influence a decision to seek long-term residential treatment.

Education on the part that conditioned environmental stimuli play in triggering a possible return to crack smoking can impart vital information that a patient requires in taking seriously the rehearsal of alternative behaviors, or in appreciating the nature of the challenge of prolonging abstinence from crack and the importance of long-term involvement in treatment to receive support in negotiating numerous high-risk situations in the real world.

COGNITIVE REFRAMING

In the above, we suggested that education can provide patients with a cognitive and intellectual framework in which they can understand their addiction, cravings, vulnerability to relapse, and need for treatment. We might also think of this as somewhat similar to the use of cognitive restructuring (Lazarus, 1971; Meichenbaum, 1985) or the technique of reframing (Ellis, 1985; Ellis & Dryden, 1987; Ellis, McInerney, DiGiuseppe, & Yeager, 1989). However, the active provision of education may also be seen as involving the cognitive-behavioral technique of reframing crack addiction, or reframing the patient's view of treatment and the treatment challenge.

Patients commonly state: "I got high because of peer pressure." "I was weak and went back to getting high." "I have to be strong when I leave here." "After I clean my system out, I'll be able to resist drugs and go back to work." Without cognitively reframing their view of addiction—as involving multiple etiological roots, explaining their vulnerability in early abstinence, or specifying exactly how they can engage in alternative behaviors to avoid relapse, or the kind of aftercare treatment they must pursue to do so—patients remain naively capable of setting themselves up for relapse. Patients who believe they must only resist peer pressure, be strong, clean out their system, and go back to work will not enter aftercare treatment. If, on the other hand, they have a cognitive and intellectual framework within which to understand their addiction, they become empowered to engage in alternative behaviors, meaningfully engage in aftercare treatment, and successfully recover from their addiction. Because crack addiction may be so tenacious or intractable, and the risk of relapse so high, we must not overlook the importance of reframing for them the nature of their addiction and what they must do in order to recover or avoid relapse. Education or the reframing of patients' views in accordance with a biopsychosocial model of crack addiction may also serve to motivate them to make realistic decisions on their own treatment.

A very general and beneficial cognitive intervention that is appropriate in community meetings, group therapy, and individual sessions provides for an overall reframing of patient experience. Clinicians often state: "You are sensitive and intelligent." This is usually a true and accurate reflection of patients, but also conveys the respect patients so desperately require to boost low self-esteem and counter the effect of expectations of a poor prognosis. The need for treatment also can be reframed as: "You are vulnerable to the experience of a return to crack smoking, and must take responsibility for your own healing or treatment." This intervention attempts to convey the nature of a patient's vulnerability to relapse and can motivate patients to pursue treatment. It also reinforces their need to make decisions for themselves.

A therapist may cognitively reframe a patient's involvement in drug use and escalation to dependence on crack in terms of being an adult child of an alcoholic or dysfunctional family who had emotional and psychological problems that set the patient up for experiencing chemicals as extra-reinforcing. As we can see, the provision of education and the act of cognitively reframing that patient's experience go hand in hand. Education can give patients a new cognitive and intellectual framework in which they can understand their experience and addiction. Cognitive reframing can relieve them of feelings of low self-esteem, self-blame, or inadequacy, while empowering them to act constructively in pursuing their own recovery or healing.

CONCLUSION

In the assessment phase, treatment practitioners can enhance their skill and efficacy by utilizing a multifaceted clinical technique. This chapter has presented in some detail actual clinical interventions that they can employ in the early phases of treatment to increase ambivalent and grandiose crack patients' motivation to become engaged in the treatment. We have seen that clinicians must, first of all, assimilate education themselves so they do not project low or negative expectations of a poor prognosis upon crack patients; treatment practitioners must, instead, sufficiently understand the compulsive crack smoker's behavior so that they can empathize with crack patients in treatment. The chapter has also shown that a number of specific clinical techniques that the author developed in response to the treatment challenge of working with crack patients on an inpatient-detoxification unit may be extended to numerous treatment settings. The use of group interpretations in community meetings, empathic mirroring, empathic attunement, affect labeling, education, and cognitive reframing gives the clinician an effective arsenal of treatment techniques for work with crack patients in the assessment phase.

V

CLINICAL TECHNIQUE IN THE TREATMENT PHASE

12

Clearing Obstacles to Effective Treatment of the Chemically Dependent

This chapter attempts to identify and clear certain obstacles that may prevent the chemically dependent from experiencing empathic mirroring or empathic attunement, or might bar them from being matched to the kind of comprehensive and intensive treatment interventions that they need in order to recover from addiction. This necessitates addressing the negative countertransference reactions of the helping professionals, debunking certain myths, and ensuring that the projection of low and negative expectations upon patients does not block them from receiving the kind of effective treatment they so desperately require.

PROVIDING A POSITIVE TREATMENT EXPERIENCE

For the majority of crack-cocaine patients, treatment for their problem may be their first exposure to mental-health professionals. Todd (1989) recognizes this. Mental-health professionals therefore must appreciate how important it is that this first exposure to treatment be a positive one. If we maximize the experience as an opportunity to impress the patient with the role, purpose, and perspective of treatment professionals, then the chances of retaining the patient in the current treatment, and of successfully matching that patient to any subsequent treatments, will increase. Mental-health professionals can use an active educational technique to inform patients of helping professionals' roles and training as counselors, social workers, psychologists, and psychiatrists. We should state our goals and purpose in attempting to work with the chemically dependent. Helping professionals should share their perspective on treatment and recovery as it arises out of their own discipline and training.

By being empathic and genuine, and avoiding acting out negative countertransference feelings, treatment professionals can provide a positive learning environment within the context of individual, group, and family therapy. Patients learn that therapy is a unique and dynamic setting in which feelings can be safely examined, explored, and empathically mirrored back to them, while they gain knowledge about themselves and learn to function more effectively. Such intimate and positive knowledge of what treatment can and should be may establish the expectation that future and continuing treatment will similarly be a positive self-enhancing experience. This knowledge of what therapy is all about goes a long way toward combating community ambivalence about mental-health resources. It removes widespread misconceptions about what goes on between those "crazy" people and the "shrinks."

Role of Supervision and Personal Psychotherapy

Therapists can increase their capacity for accurate and appropriate empathic responses to patients. Patient responses to our interpretations and attempts to be empathic, reflection on the process of sessions, and supervision can guide us in learning how to attune ourselves to the material patients share with us. We must also learn how to avoid bringing our own assumptions and feelings into the act of interpreting patient material and experience. Treatment professionals require individual psychotherapy in order to work through their own experiences and traumas and to ensure that they empathically respond to patients' experiences without unconsciously identifying with the material and assuming that their internal affective state is the same as a patient is feeling. The predominance of "adult child of an alcoholic" and "adult child of a dysfunctional family" status among both recovering paraprofessional staff and professional practitioners necessitates their engaging in treatment themselves. Treatment practitioners must know how to discern "their stuff" from " a patient's stuff." A therapist can be genuine in attempting to engage patients in a positive treatment experience if negative countertransference feelings have been examined and worked out in supervision or in the context of a treatment professional's personal psychotherapy.

Danger of Projecting Low and Negative Expectations

One notion commonly held in the field of chemical dependency treatment involves the idea that it is very difficult to help people with their addictions until they are ready for help or can admit they have a problem. Characterizations of patients as resistant, unmotivated, or ambivalent may be accurate in some cases and based on assessment findings. However, our prejudgments that masses of people addicted to chemical substances "don't want treatment," as well as initial judgments of patients who are in treatment "as not serious about treatment," all too often reflect an expectation of poor prognoses. The projection of low or negative expectations by the clinician upon the client can doom patients' prospects of successfully engaging in the treatment process. The interaction between helping professionals and patients (or potential patients) must be free of the projection of low expectations that provides the basis for patients' actually fulfilling our negative prophecies. It is crucial that attitudes that "they're all sociopaths," that "they don't really want treatment," and that "they're all going to go back to drug use" are not dynamics prevailing in interactions between clinician and patients.

Our citation of the work of Donovan (1988) in Chapter 11 reinforces this view. When empathy is insufficient or reduced because of prejudgments of patients, it is no surprise that clinical suspiciousness, hostility, moralizing, and power struggles follow—as Donovan points out. In my clinical experience, subsequent to a reduction in empathy, treatment professionals see patients as "liars" and "the dregs of the earth," and a therapeutic milieu develops that is characterized by power struggles between the "good staff" and "those horrible patients."

When we consider the population of crack smokers in particular, and the kinds of behavior in which they have engaged to support their habits (stealing, lying, criminal activities, prostitution) and behaviors that may follow from crack-cocaine intoxication (paranoia, psychosis, irritability, violent or erratic behavior), even more negative and derogatory stereotypes may be internalized that could deleteriously affect the interaction between clinician and client. The projection of low and negative expectations upon patients may further hamper the recovery of already ambivalent clients.

Derogatory stereotypes that crack patients are all "criminals" and "prostitutes" may also be exacerbated by the fact that large numbers of women and minorities have gained access to the equal-opportunity drug crack—in comparison with intranasal cocaine, which belonged almost exclusively to middle- and upper-middle-class, white males. Therapist attitudes also arise from stereotypes that abound in our culture and are perpetuated through the media. Negative stereotypes reside within our collective unconscious (Fanon, 1968; Jung, 1969). Prevailing societal stereotypes can be unconsciously conveyed to patients and help contribute to a poor treatment outcome.

MYTHS THAT MUST BE DEBUNKED

Within the culture or community of treatment practitioners, there are a number of misconceptions that can prevent us from providing patients with a positive treatment experience, or matching them to treatments that may enable them to recover successfully. The following myths require debunking.

Myth 1

All Addicts Are Sociopaths

Although many substance abusers have met the criteria for antisocial personality disorders, have been engaged in criminal and antisocial behavior to secure drugs or money for drugs, and may possess psychopathology, this myth can be particularly damaging to the therapeutic process. It sets up the expectation that addiction is intractable, and that patients should be disdained and be kept at a distance. Treatment professionals with this attitude become functionaries who push paper to keep their jobs and avoid providing actual treatment that would not work anyway; when they do became involved in a treatment interaction with a patient, their low and negative expectations may be a relevant factor in the patient's failure to recover from addiction. Clinicians can and must engage in the diagnosis and assessment of patients and must adjust their clinical technique in light of any apparent psychopathology. However, when we hold negative stereotypes of patients that prevent our functioning as therapeutic agents who attempt to effect positive changes in patients' lives, we and the patients become the victim of negative prophecies that leave us both feeling bitter.

A predominance of narcissism may represent a more accurate observation of the newly abstinent. The trauma of addiction includes involvement in humiliating criminal acts. And an arrogance and aloofness, or even braggadocio, about one's exploits all reflect a defensive state of inflation against painfully low self-esteem and depression over the trauma of one's addiction. This kind of analysis permits therapists to understand what may appear as antisocial behavior. In this way, we cannot merely dismiss patients as hopeless "sociopaths" undeserving of our clinical interventions or empathy. The myth that all drug addicts are sociopaths must be debunked and replaced with clinical appreciation of the clinical skills that must be brought to bear in the treatment of the chemically dependent.

Myth 2

A Psychodynamic or Psychoanalytic Approach is Inappropriate with Drug Addicts

The notion that a psychodynamic or psychoanalytic approach is inappropriate with drug addicts and alcoholics has its roots in the experience of mental-health professionals who treated patients without recognizing the addiction or alcoholism, to the ire of self-help organizations such as AA. By itself, psychoanalysis as an approach to addiction remains an inappropriate treatment model, when modifications in technique are not made that recognize the phases of treatment and recovery that patients negotiate and how the role of the therapist should change in the course of recovery. The management of painful affective states and helping patients acquire the ability to regulate feelings and behavior are essential to successful recovery from addiction and for avoiding a relapse to drug use. Therefore, the psychodynamic/psychoanalytic approach and what it has to offer in this process must not be discarded because of myths. Instead, we must understand how a psychodynamic/psychoanalytic approach must be modified (depending on the phase of recovery). We must also remember that this is only one tool of use when treating addicts, particularly in the latter portion of the second phase of prolonging relapse and during one to several years or a lifetime of recovery (see Chapter 4).

Myth 3

A Psychodynamic or Psychoanalytic Approach is Inappropriate with Minority Patients

The concept that psychodynamic/psychoanalytic approaches are not appropriate for minority populations involves a similar issue of whether or not a set of clinical techniques and propositions that evolved in response to work with certain populations can be extended to other populations. Is there anything in psychoanalytic or psychodynamic formulations to suggest that human beings have certain psychological and emotional processes regardless of their race or ethnicity? The problem is that stereotypes interact with our perceptions of certain groups and prevent some of us from offering a resounding "yes" to this question. Members of minority groups experience the projection of a host of negative images and stereotypes from out of the collective psyche (Grier & Cobbs, 1980; Fanon, 1967), so that individual mental-health professionals may view these groups as inappropriate for the exercise of their analytic technique. Moreover, many authors suggest that race, ethnicity, and culture do affect a patient's world view and psychology (Jones, 1980; Nobles, 1980). However, the point to be made here is that a psychoanalytic technique may help the chemically dependent learn to identify, label, and process painful affective states and generally improve the regulation of self-esteem, impulses, and behavior. Unfortunate myths must not prevent utilization of these techniques with minority patients who are also chemically dependent.

Certain negative countertransference reactions or projections are closely related to the myth that a psychodynamic/psychoanalytic approach is not appropriate with minorities. Societal stereotypes that drug addicts are immoral and criminal are just as misguided as projections upon minorities that they are nonverbal and unintelligent; minority drug addicts suffer the double stigma that arises from these stereotypes. The treatment prospects for "immoral" and "criminal" drug addicts are bleak when patients unconsciously perceive and fulfill the negative expectations unconsciously projected by treatment professionals who assume that their clinical tools will not work with such patients. Sadder still are the bleaker treatment prospects for immoral, criminal, nonverbal, and unintelligent minority drug addicts who are even more disdained.

In debunking this myth, let us conclude by reasserting that many psychodynamic/psychoanalytic techniques and formulations are essential to the task of the long-term treatment and recovery of crack addicts and should not be discarded as inappropriate approaches with populations that are derided and devalued. At the same time, we must sensitively and intelligently analyze the need for modifications in techniques that may be necessary with the population of crack-cocaine smokers. Typical modifications are the utilization of an active technique, the provision of education, and the gradual implementation of a more analytic technique as treatment progresses. This is consistent with Levin's (1987) approach to treatment of the alcoholic.

Myth 4

When the Racial or Ethnic Background of Patient and Therapist Differ,
Understanding, Empathy, and Effective Treatment Cannot Take Place

Where the race, ethnic background, or socioeconomic class of the patient and treatment professional differ, clinicians must remain attuned to countertransference feelings that involve their own pejorative or negative conceptions of patients from a particular ethnic or racial group. Clinicians must strive to view the patients and their problems in terms of their unique and individual dimensions, and to achieve empathic attunement with the feeling content of a particular patient's experience. The bottom line is that clinicians must appreciate the uniqueness of individuals and their experience, and that tremendous diversity characterizes persons *within* a particular racial or ethnic group. This diversity often neutralizes the efficacy of preconceived notions or specific education acquired about the characteristics and functioning of a racial or ethnic group.

Clinicians must also be alert to and open to discussion about patient responses to the therapist's racial or ethnic background, welcoming the expression of the patient's feelings, thoughts, and beliefs. Often, African-American or Hispanic patients will feel it is impossible for a white therapist to understand their experiences, background, and feelings. However, in such cases, the best and most powerful response to such an articulated or inarticulated question clouding the therapeutic interaction is understanding on the part of the therapist. A doubting patient needs to experience a therapist as genuine, empathic, and "on target" in accurately mirroring back to the patient his or her experience and feelings in the "here and now." In the process, a therapeutic alliance is forged regardless of any differences in race and background.

Experience and observation on the inpatient-detoxification unit suggest that empathic and productive therapy did take place between minority patients and their white therapists. In fact, this positive treatment experience provided a kind of corrective emotional experience (Alexander, 1963); a positive interpersonal experience with a therapist begins to heal or compensate for the damage done through interactions with brutal police officers, devaluing schoolteachers, or other white societal authorities who projected damaging low and negative expectations upon patients in their past. So this positive reality is far from myths that must be debunked.

Treatment professionals need to acknowledge respectfully real differences between themselves and clients, express their belief in their own capacities to understand, and use their training in addressing the problem of drug use. They should articulate their willingness to try to understand a patient's problems throughout the therapeutic relationship. When the therapist achieves accurate empathic attunement, successfully articulates how a patient feels, and does not unconsciously project low or negative expectations rooted in stereotypes about drug addicts or minorities, a powerful experience serves to move both patient and therapist toward the establishment of a therapeutic alliance and good working relationship. Clinicians must also remain aware of material that may repeatedly come up in sessions that has its roots in differences in the patient's and therapist's racial or ethnic backgrounds. These issues probably arise with the same frequency as issues rooted in differences in the sex of patient and therapist. When they do arise, they may indeed be significant and real, but can be worked out. Supervision assists clinicians in remaining alert to the covert processes and dynamics that come out of these differences.

Myth 5

Clinicians Who Are Not Recovering from an Addiction Cannot Understand or Properly Treat Drug Patients

Differences in the background and experience between patient and therapist also involve the issue of past drug or alcohol use. Many support the myth that a therapist who has never experienced alcoholism or drug addiction cannot truly understand or help a patient with an addiction. Some proponents of this myth end up as victims of its corollary: an alcoholic cannot properly treat drug addicts, or an old-time heroin addict cannot understand the contemporary crack addict. This myth thinly veils its support for stereotypes about alcoholics, heroin addicts, and crack addicts as distinct and separate groups. The proliferation of new designer chemicals could also make the recovering alcoholic or drug counselor's experience and potential therapeutic impact obsolete, if we support this myth.

Often, this myth or assumption defies certain realities of the therapeutic situation. Many clinical psychologists, psychiatrists, or other professionals may be recovering from alcoholism, cocaine abuse-dependence, or some other chemical problem, or be struggling with workaholism, overeating, or other destructive compulsive behaviors. However, their training may dictate that self-disclosure is not always an appropriate technique. The solution for the predicament of a difference (or perceived or assumed difference) in the drug or alcohol experiences of patient and therapist lies in the respectful acknowledgment of a patient's point of view, and the welcoming of an open discussion of this issue (with or without self-disclosure). However, the most effective solution rests in the provision of the powerful experience of being listened to, empathically mirrored, and having one's feelings accurately heard and understood by a professional, while negative expectations or stereotypes arising from differences are not projected. Clinicians and recovering counselors limit their capacity for empathy and effectively working with an array of clients when they subscribe to the myth that differences in the drug/alcohol background between helping professional and client preclude understanding, empathy, and effective treatment.

Myth 6

Treatment Combining Anonymous Self-Help Groups (AA, NA, CA) and Long-term Dynamic Individual Psychotherapy Is Incompatible

This myth partly arises out of the negative outcomes many patients experienced when they spent years working in psychotherapy while their alcoholism was never discussed and just progressed further. It was not until such persons discovered AA that "the real" problem was addressed and managed. Much hostility toward those using psychodynamic/psychoanalytic approaches or offering long-term dynamic individual psychotherapy persists among proponents of AA, NA, and CA. Many treatment professionals must take responsibility for having failed to recognize the unique role and value of anonymous self-help groups in the overall treatment plan. Also, treatment professionals must become familiar with AA, NA, and CA, as well as with the availability and nature of these groups in their community, and should actually attend open meetings of these groups. The use of a combination of involvement in anonymous self-help groups and long-term in-depth dynamic psychotherapy must be recommended by both professionals and increasing numbers of AA/NA/CA sponsors if relapse rates are to decrease. At the same time, it should be remembered that this book endorses the use of a multifaceted clinical technique that includes psychodynamic/psychoanalytic elements, educational directives, cognitive-behavioral elements, and metaphor.

CONCLUSION

The chapter has offered clinicians an opportunity to consider the kinds of biases and stereotypes that are easily internalized in our larger cultural context and within the treatment community. Having possibly internalized these negative stereotypes and myths, treatment professionals must strive to work out countertransference problems in supervision and their own individual treatment. Also, professionals must recognize the need to get beyond destructive myths and to progress in their understanding of what kinds of interventions patients may need. Through this kind of rigorous self-examination and self-education, treatment professionals may emerge capable of empathic attunement with patients who need the very best of our clinical skill.

13

The Need for a Multifaceted
Technique To Address
Multideterminants of Relapse*

This chapter presents an approach to relapse prevention that arises out of re-search findings on the multideterminants of relapse for crack smokers. The chapter will review empirical findings on the multideterminants of relapse and explain how these data give treatment practitioners a strong rationale for utiliz-ing a multifaceted clinical technique with crack smokers as a part of their re-lapse-prevention efforts.

MARLATT'S CONTRIBUTION TO RELAPSE PREVENTION

Advances in clinical research on and treatment of the process of relapse largely came out of the pioneering work of Marlatt and his associates. Marlatt (1985) criticizes the standard practice in the addiction field to view relapse as an end state. He warns that these pessimistic approaches, if assimilated by patients while in treatment, set up a self-fulfilling prophecy where "any violation of ab-stinence will send the pendulum to the extreme of relapse" (p. 31). In addition, Marlatt criticizes the disease model's emphasis on internal causation. Here, the cause of relapse is usually attributed to internal factors associated with the dis-ease condition, and behaviors associated with relapse are equated with the emergence of symptoms signaling reactivation of the underlying disease. Ig-nored are the influence of situational and psychological factors as potential de-terminants in the relapse process (p. 31). Shaffer (1987) argues that just because "social scientists and drug treatment specialists are encouraging the application of the disease field label to various forms of substance abuse and dependence, that does not make it so" (p. 103).

In contrast to this disease-model perspective, microanalysis of relapse epi-

*Adapted, with permission, from *Journal of Substance Abuse Treatment*, Vol. 6, No. 4, 1989.

sodes reveals various determinants of relapse. Marlatt (1985) reports data on drinking, heroin, gambling, and overeating addictions. The most frequent determinants of relapse are (1) negative emotional states (35%), (2) direct or indirect social pressure (20%), and (3) interpersonal conflict (16%). These three primary high-risk situations are associated with almost three quarters of all the relapses reported (pp. 37–38).

For Marlatt, a lapse, or single slip, represents a metaphoric fork in the road that can lead to total collapse or toward positive change. Growth and positive change follow when a slip is used to provide important information about the causes of the slip and how to correct for its possible occurrence in the future (p. 35). Thus, Marlatt leads the way in inviting social scientists and drug-treatment specialists to utilize metaphor and to create relapse-prevention models that go beyond disease conceptualizations. The work of numerous authors continues to refine ways to address the problem of relapse (Allsop & Saunders, 1989; Shiffman, 1989; Heather & Stallard, 1989; Marlatt & Gordon, 1989). Other approaches to relapse have also evolved into excellent relapse-prevention models (Gorski & Miller, 1984, 1988a, 1988b; Gorski & Miller, 1986).

AN APPROACH TO RELAPSE WITH CRACK SMOKERS

The work of Wallace (1989a, 1989b) is unique, however, in that it constructs a model of relapse prevention that specifically arises from research results with a crack-smoking population. Curry, Marlatt, Peterson, and Lutton (1988) address the importance of analyzing relapse in changing addictive behaviors in order to shed light on the processes involved in relapse and abstinence over time. Wallace's (1989a) research is exemplary in following this research mandate and revealing the process of relapse in crack-cocaine smokers. With the rise in crack smoking across this nation, her research findings are vital in helping professionals develop and refine relapse-prevention strategies of specific value when working with the challenging population of crack patients who face such a high risk of relapse.

This approach to relapse prevention also receives reinforcement from the clinical work of treatment experts who pioneered treatment models specifically for cocaine patients. A careful review and analysis of these clinicians' approaches to relapse in the treatment of cocaine patients (Anker & Crowley, 1982; Kertzner, 1987; Stone, Fromme, & Kagan, 1984; Spitz, 1987; Spitz & Spitz, 1987; Washton 1987, 1989a; Smith & Wesson, 1985; Wesson & Smith, 1985; Gold, 1984) reveals certain commonalities. What emerges is a striking similarity in observations and technical interventions among the approaches reviewed. These clinicians validate the existence of a common mechanism underlying relapse since so many commonalities in technique emerge. Gold,

Washton, and Dackis (1985) state that their relapse-prevention strategies "incorporate a variety of behavioral, cognitive, educational, and self-control techniques aimed at reducing the potential for relapse . . ." (p. 140). Stone et al. (1984) and Kertzner (1987) directly address management of painful affect states from a psychodynamic perspective, while all the clinical approaches Wallace (1989a) carefully reviews combine behavioral, cognitive, educational, and self-control techniques.

These multifaceted clinical approaches implicitly suggest that multideterminants of relapse are being responded to as evidenced by the technical interventions chosen. Each clinician perceives and responds to the same part of a metaphoric "elephant," so to speak. Their common multifaceted clinical approaches affirm Marlatt's (1985) contention that "there is a common mechanism underlying the relapse process across different addictive behaviors" (p. 40). The clinicians' approaches (Anker & Crowley, 1982; Kertzner, 1987; Stone, Fromme, & Kagan, 1984; Spitz, 1987; Spitz & Spitz, 1987; Washton, 1987, 1989a: Smith & Wesson, 1985; Wesson & Smith, 1985; Gold, 1984), which Wallace (1989a) reviews, point toward the following factors as underlying the relapse process: (1) drug craving; (2) recurrent selective recall of cocaine euphoria; (3) the provocative power of drug-associated environmental cues; (4) processes of denial and addictive thinking that permit patients to set themselves up; (5) myths/delusions of being able to sell, use, or be around cocaine or other drugs; and (6) recurrent painful affect states previously self-medicated with cocaine. Wallace's research attempts to provide validation for these multideterminants of relapse, which she extracted from her review of the clinical literature. In addition, she strives to reveal the specific determinants of relapse for newly abstinent crack patients.

Psychological Vulnerability and Environmental Stimuli

Wallace's (1989a) approach to relapse is based on a rationale that appreciates the psychological vulnerability of patients who face conditioned environmental stimuli associated with prior cocaine usage. Psychological vulnerability in interaction with environmental stimuli represents a dynamic explanation of the high potential for relapse that cocaine-dependent patients possess after being detoxified. An additional central concept that explains the psychological vulnerability of patients is narcissism.

Kleber and Gawin (1984a) emphasize that cocaine serves narcissistic needs and helps patients to cope with boredom, inner emptiness, and the management of psychiatric disturbance. Pathological narcissism characterizes early stages of sobriety in the alcoholic and involves feelings of loneliness, boredom, and emptiness (Levin, 1987). Levin states that his views on the pathological narcissism of the newly sober alcoholic extend to other addictions. According to Levin, the patient is vulnerable, depressed, insecure, fragile, and perhaps exhilarated. Exhilaration represents euphoria and hope, but also the ego's response to escape from a life-threatening situation. Euphoria is a manic defense against underlying depression and fear. While this defense may be adaptive, it increases vulnerability to internal and external dangers (pp. 219–220).

Levin synthesizes the theory of Kohut (1971, 1977) and Kernberg (1975, 1976) in describing the self psychology and functioning of the newly sober alcoholic. Characteristic pathological narcissism in early sobriety involves a cohesive but insecure self. Therapists may observe grandiosity of less than psychotic proportions, arrogance, isolation, and unrealistic goals. Levin also observes feelings of entitlement, a need for omnipotent control, poor differentiation of self and object, and deficits in the self-regulating capacities of the ego. In addition, the ability to tolerate affect states is poor, while massive anxiety easily emerges. These manifestations of the grandiose self may be deeply repressed or denied; a resultant facade of pseudo-self-sufficiency, never smoothly integrated into a mature self, predominates (pp. 222–232).

Levin also discusses borderline phenomena related to the failure to securely integrate good and bad self and object representations into stable internal objects. This may also characterize psychological functioning during early stages of sobriety. The associated defenses of splitting, denial, primitive idealization, and projective identification are observed. However, narcissistic pathology predominates (pp. 233–234). Ritual, rigidity, and the need for omnipotent control are observed by Levin, as well. They are characteristic of the grandiose self and are seen in a compulsivity—which is a defense, a reaction formation, against the underlying impulsivity. Thus, obsessive-compulsive personality traits can characterize early sobriety (p. 240).

Wallace (1987) discusses overreliance on splitting, self-inflation, and grandiosity as defenses against inner pain. This suggests the presence in a crack population of the kind of psychopathology Levin describes in alcoholics. The predominance of narcissism in patients attempting abstinence reveals a not-at-all surprising difficulty in negotiating internal and external dangers. Massive anxiety and affect states represent internal dangers that are poorly managed. Thus, recurrent painful affect states are poorly regulated, contributing to self-medication strategies. A vulnerability to external dangers also results when facades of pseudo self-sufficiency and unrealistic goal-setting prevail.

The investigation's content analysis of actual patient relapse episodes attempts to document these processes. The way in which vulnerability to internal and external dangers plays a role in relapse may receive empirical verification, as Wallace's research reveals.

Procedure: The Clinical Relapse Interview

Out of 288 patients treated by Wallace during the specific period of her research, 12% (n = 35) returned for a second inpatient detoxification. (See Table 1 for sample demographics.) Marlatt's (1985) discussion of results of microanalysis of relapse episodes refers to data obtained from questionnaires completed by patients. However, Wallace (1989) engaged in a microanalysis of these 35 crack patients' relapse episodes via clinical interviews, which focused on the process of relapse and asked specific questions. Using the clinical relapse interview (CRI), data arise from (1) observation of patients during clinical interviews and individual psychotherapy sessions, and (2) patient responses to specific questions.

The CRI is suitable for use with all patients returning to treatment after a relapse episode—patients entering inpatient detoxification for a second time, or patients entering any treatment facility (outpatient or inpatient) after experiencing a relapse to chemical use (or possibly to any addictive disorder or compulsive behavior). The CRI focuses on several key issues through the following questions:

1. What happened postdetox (or after the last treatment for other addictive disorders)?
2. What were your aftercare treatment plans?
3. Did you enter aftercare treatment?
4. What was aftercare treatment like for you?
5. When was the first time that you used drugs postdetox (or returned to the problematic behavior)?
6. What were the circumstances surrounding relapse?
7. What happened after you used drugs (or after first engaging again in the problematic behavior)?
8. Why do you think you began using drugs again (or returned to the problematic behavior)?
9. What has been your pattern of drug use (or pattern of engaging in the problematic behavior)?
10. What made you decide to seek a second detox (or return to treatment)?
11. What kind of drug-related problems have you had (or problems related to the problematic behavior)?
12. What are your current aftercare treatment plans?

The CRI helps the patient to analyze the relapse event and to grow by understanding the determinants of relapse. Frequently, patients are able to utilize relapse education gained during the first detoxification (or treatment period) to analyze what happened themselves. Results of the CRI are utilized to formulate guidelines patients can follow for handling difficult circumstances in the future. Usually, the best management plan for potential relapse situations involves therapeutic support in negotiating internal and external dangers. Thus, the importance of using aftercare treatment is stressed and referrals are made for patients in light of their responses to question 12. Occasionally, confrontation,

TABLE 13.1
Demographics
N = 35

Background Data	N =	Percent	Mean Age
Patient race and sex:			
Black males	26	74.3	29.8
Black females	7	20	28.4
White males	1	2.85	25
Other	1	2.85	42
Level of education:			
College graduates	3	8.6	
Two years college	3	8.6	
One year college	3	8.6	
High-school/GED	11	31.4	
12th-grade dropout	2	5.7	
11th-grade dropout	6	17.1	
10th-grade dropout	5	14.3	
9th-grade dropout†	2	5.7	

Employment history:	Black males N =	Percent	Black females N =	Percent	Other N =	Percent
Unemployed	16	45.7	4	11.4	2	5.7
Worked past year	9	25.7	3	8.6	—	—
Past low/mid work	7	20	2	5.7	—	—
Currently employed	3	8.6	—	—	—	—
Current mid inc work	2	5.7				
Lost job past three mos	3	8.6	1	2.85	—	—
SSI disability	4	11.4	—	—	—	—
Welfare	3	8.6	2	5.7	—	—
Homeless past year	10	28.52				

*Adapted from Wallace (1989a). Reprinted by permission.
†Three learning disabled.

education, or interpretation of patient denial is necessary in directing patients into appropriate treatment. Responses to question 9 indicate severity of drug use (or of the addictive disorder), extent of loss of control, and nature of a patient's self-destructiveness; in combination with the mental-status examination, these factors determine final treatment recommendations.

The CRI also focuses on responses to questions 10 and 11 for feelings of guilt, shame, and depression attending the experience of relapse and further personal decline. Interventions stress the adaptive strengths of patients who seek help through a second detoxification (or treatment in general), and the fact that patients can acquire new knowledge about personal challenges to abstinence. Supportive psychotherapy throughout inpatient detoxification (or any treatment) should address painful issues such as loss of family support, employment, child custody, and housing, or problems associated with the addictive disorder. In addition, patients often discuss embarrassment on the unit, perceiving that staff members may be negatively evaluating them for having relapsed.

Patient responses in the CRI to question 5 are analyzed for the period of time it took to relapse. Responses to questions 1 through 8 (excluding question 5) are content analyzed for determinants of relapse. In addition, clinical observations of patients for use of defenses of denial and for narcissistic psychopathology are coded.

Thus, the value of the CRI goes beyond research purposes by actually helping patients understand the process of relapse and what the determinants of their personal experience of relapse were, and directs discussion on changes in behavior in the future to avoid another relapse episode. The CRI is, therefore, a vital instrument in addressing what is perhaps the most pressing problem facing clinicians and patients in the arena of chemical-dependency treatment: the task of relapse prevention. The research findings of interest arising from the use of the CRI with the specific sample ($n = 35$) Wallace (1989a) studied follow.

Time to Relapse

Results for time to relapse indicate that 31.4% relapse within a week, 24.3% relapse between two weeks to a month, 20% relapse between 60 and 90 days, 8.6% relapse between 3.5 and 4.5 months, and 5.7% relapse between six and seven months, totaling 94.3% before six months expire. Within the first 90 days postdetox, 76% relapse.

Psychological and Environmental Determinants of Relapse

Content analysis of patient responses and clinical observations reveals that the primary determinants of relapse fall into a psychological/personality domain and an environmental/interpersonal domain. Several categories within the psychological and environmental domains emerge. The relapse categories and results are shown in Table 13.2.

The Psychological/Personality Domain

The categories of the psychological/personality domain classify into five types the internal factors that relate to relapse. These internal factors may involve recurrent painful affect states (Khantzian, 1985), use of psychological defenses, and personality characteristics of individuals.

1. *Painful emotional state.* A painful emotional state can be a recurrent painful affect state, feelings of emptiness, boredom, loneliness, depression, frustra-

tion, or anger. In the sample, the majority (40%) of relapses in the psychological domain involve a painful emotional state.

2. *Narcissistic denial/denial.* This category reflects the use of a psychoanalytic approach (Wallace, 1987; Levin, 1987) in the microanalysis of relapse episodes. Narcissism exacerbates denial, as denial is more commonly understood. Accordingly, a "narcissistic denial" permits overconfidence, unrealistic goal setting, and naive courting of external danger. Primitive distortion of reality, where patients' behavior reflects assuming that impulses do not exist, is all the more dangerous where narcissism is also a factor. Reality testing is impaired and patients feel they can accomplish anything. Attitudes reflect a manic defense and exuberance (Levin, 1987).

More typically understood denial is also observed in patients. The category does not distinguish between narcissistic denial and commonly understood denial. However, 22% of relapses involve narcissistic denial and 5.7% involve denial, totaling 28.5%.

3. *Failure to Enter Arranged Aftercare Treatment.* Closely related to narcissistic denial/denial is a failure to enter arranged aftercare treatment. Usually a TC appointment or an outpatient treatment appointment is made for patients. Denial leads to the belief that they do not need to go, even though they agreed during detoxification. Overconfidence, manic defenses, and grandiosity fuel this and other unrealistic beliefs, affecting the formulation of poorly constructed goals. Patients frequently state, "I figured I could do it on my own" or "I decided I didn't need it." This is the second most common determinant of relapse (37.14%).

4. *Refusal of aftercare treatment.* This occurs during detoxification when a patient outrightly refuses aftercare-treatment plans. Grandiosity prevents assimilation of education. "It doesn't apply to me, my problem isn't that bad" is frequently heard, along with "I can do it on my own." Feelings of superiority over other patients and staff offering professional recommendations justify refusing aftercare treatment for some patients. This refusal is a factor in 11.42% of relapses.

5. *Drug craving.* Drug craving often follows vivid dreams or olfactory stimulation by cigarette smoke, or is recurrent as an internal event. As an internal experience often impulsively followed by a drive to seek drugs, it is a category within the psychological domain. Drug craving operates in 5.7% of relapses.

The Environmental/Interpersonal Domain

The environmental/interpersonal domain includes six categories classifying external determinants of relapse. External dangers are environmental and interpersonal stimuli that are poorly managed by psychologically vulnerable patients. The categories are as in the following.

1. *Environmental stimuli of people, places, drugs.* Patients encounter old conditioned stimuli in the environment and relapse. Stimuli repeatedly associated with drug use include people, places, and drugs. Compulsive cocaine use is easily triggered by reinforcing cues that become associated with the drug's rewarding effects (Stone et al., 1984, p. 36). These cues are external factors that constitute external dangers, given their power to evoke conditioned responses. Relapse episodes involve this factor 34.38% of the time. This is the most frequently cited category of the environmental/interpersonal domain.

2. *Interpersonal stress.* Interpersonal stress usually occurs with family or loved ones. It frequently involves the ambivalence others feel toward patients. These individuals, from whom patients have stolen, are disappointed and have lost trust in the patients. Patients are usually proud of completing detoxification and do not expect expressions of hostility, persisting suspiciousness, and lack of trust. Interpersonal stress, which is often followed by a painful emotional state, operates in 24.38% of relapses.

3. *Escalation to drug of choice.* Use of alcohol, marijuana, and intranasal cocaine led to compulsive use of crack cocaine in 14.28% of relapse episodes. This escalation to drug of choice occurred after celebrations (Christmas, New Year's Eve, and family celebrations) for three cases in the sample. Holidays are challenging external events that vulnerable patients may handle poorly, feeling pressure to sample alcohol. Escalation from just one sampling of alcohol or cocaine to compulsive crack-cocaine smoking is seen. One patient escalated from intranasal cocaine to compulsive free-base smoking.

4. *Hard test — Handling money.* Hard tests are situations that vulnerable patients have difficulty managing, with the most common involving handling sums of money. Because of the repeated association between having money and spending all, if not most, of it on drugs, possession of money is a hard test that vulnerable patients frequently fail; 11.42% of relapses are attributed to this factor.

5. *Homeless factor/no family support.* Being homeless usually follows loss of family support. Relatives and lovers eventually respond to theft and lose trust in patients, dismissing them from their homes. Homelessness and lack of family support are determinants of relapse in 14.28% of the relapse episodes.

Homelessness usually means use of the shelter system. Patients describe shelters as places where drugs are sold and rampantly used by residents and some staff. Also, returning to a shelter while waiting for a TC bed may mean automatic exposure to old conditioned stimuli in the environment or painful feelings such as depression. Homelessness and lack of family support dictate a TC as the only logical aftercare treatment, but a waiting list of a few days to a few weeks for the homeless can be too much of a challenge for vulnerable patients to manage. Thus, homelessness/no family support is frequently a determinant of relapse.

TABLE 13.2
Psychological and Environmental Determinants of Relapse

Typology and Multideterminants	N=	Percent
Psychological/Personality Domain		
Painful emotional state	14	40
Narcissistic denial/denial	10	28.5
Fails to enter arranged aftercare treatment	13	37.14
TC	3	8.57
Outpatient treatment clinic	10	28.57
Refused aftercare treatment	4	11.42
Drug craving	2	5.7
Environmmental/Interpersonal Domain		
Environmental stimuli	12	34.28
Interpersonal stress	12	24.38
Escalated to drug of choice	5	14.28
Hard test handling money	4	11.42
Homeless factor/no family support	5	14.28
TC shortcoming	7	20
Multideterminants of Relapse		
One factor only	5	14.28
Psychological only	3	8.57
Environmental only	6	17.14
Combination of two	13	37.13
Combination of three	14	40
Combination of four	3	8.57
Total involving multideterminants	30	85.7
Most Common Combinations		
Painful emotional state and interpersonal stress	7	20
Narciss. denial and fails enter/refuses aftcare	8	22.8

*Adapted from Wallace (1989a). Reprinted by permission.

6. *TC shortcomings.* A long waiting list or delay in entering a facility is one shortcoming of TCs. Domiciled patients can wait as long as four to eight weeks. Policies of refusing admittance to patients on psychiatric medication and with medical problems also represent disadvantages of TCs, as they generally lack adequate psychiatric and medical staffing and must turn many clients away. In the sample, three patients on antipsychotic medication, three with medical problems, and one on a waiting list experienced relapse in which TC shortcomings were a determining factor, totaling 20% of relapses.

Multideterminants of Relapse

Only 14.28% of relapses can be traced to only one factor; usually, both psychological/personality and environmental/interpersonal domains are involved.

However, for 8.57% of patients, only psychological determinants of relapse prevail, and for 17.14%, only environmental determinants operate. A combination of three determinants of relapse is most common (40%), while 85.7% of relapses have multideterminants.

The most common combination of determinants includes painful emotional states from the psychological domain and interpersonal stress from the environmental domain (20%). However, examining both failure to enter arranged aftercare treatment and refusal of aftercare treatment together, these occurred in combination with narcissistic denial 22.8% of the time. Thus, microanalysis of relapse episodes reveals the multideterminants of relapse. The psychological and environmental determinants of relapse highlight its complexity as an event involving the subtle interaction of a number of factors.

ILLUSTRATIVE CASE EXAMPLES

Case examples illuminate typical patient experiences of relapse after detoxification. The typology of psychological and environmental determinants arose from microanalysis of the kind of data presented in the case examples.

Case of U.S.

U.S. is a 35-year-old black female. She is a graduate of an elite northeastern university and has a work history in a municipal service industry, where she earned $25,000 annually. During her first detox, she primarily used defenses of intellectualization in interpersonal interactions with staff members and competed with the psychology rehabilitation therapist, who directs writing and drama workshops. During the first detox, she felt superior to the staff and to the lower-income patients. In the CRI, U.S. devalued this first detox as a "joke." She relapsed one week postdetoxification.

U.S. has two daughters, ages eight and ten, who were taken to distant relatives by a concerned family member three months prior to the second detox because of U.S.'s deterioration in functioning. At the same time, she was also asked to take a leave of absence from work after sleeping on the job as a result of crack-related exhaustion after all-night binges. She entered detox again one year after the first detoxification.

During the second detox, themes in therapy dealt with separation from her children. U.S. engaged in splitting between narcissistic rage at staff and relatives who pushed for her hospitalization and painful affects of depression and abandonment related to her children. Both states have long-standing roots in a history of less-than-ideal object relations. Separation from her children intensified her feelings of abandonment felt after her mother's death many years before. U.S. was very dependent on her mother, but split off all painful affect at the time of the death, describing a mask of control worn throughout her mother's funeral rites and never betrayed thereafter. Intranasal cocaine use characterized this former period of denial of grief. On the other hand, her denial and narcissism had roots in a dysfunctional family where the father's alcoholism was a hushed family affair that took place behind closed doors out of the sight of the children, while a close dependency on her mother was fostered. Separation from her husband several years ago buoyed her self-esteem and a sense of pseudo self-sufficiency. U.S. did not need him because she "did everything" herself anyway, reflecting her grandiosity.

The relapse interview indicated that U.S. failed to keep her arranged outpatient appointment. Grandiosity and feelings of superiority prevented her entrance into treatment. Narcissistic denial was evidenced by a failure to acknowledge the severity of her problem while dangers likely to lead to relapse were confidently courted. Relapse occurred upon resuming a relationship with a drug-using boyfriend, despite articulated plans to discontinue this relationship in response to education she received on this topic during the first detox. A visit to his apartment one week after detox led to resumption of regular crack usage.

Analysis of Case Example

The case illustrates the role of narcissistic traits in relapse and how narcissism exacerbates denial. Her denial of the severity of her addiction and a strong motive to continue self-medicating levels of pain and depression that kept rising—especially after her children were moved away from her—resulted in an entire year elapsing between the first and second detoxes. U.S. also utilized borderline phenomena of splitting between an enraged, independent, aloof, and grandiose state and a tearful, dependent, abandoned, anxious, and depressed state. The underlying painful affects and use of manic defenses contributed to her resuming drug use. The case illustrates the interactive nature of the multiple determinants of relapse. Narcissistic denial, failure to attend arranged aftercare treatment, and a return to environmental stimuli of people, places, and drugs serve as multideterminants of relapse.

U.S.'s psychological vulnerability contributed to her poor management of the challenge of encountering environmental stimuli of a drug-using boyfriend and his apartment where they previously had used drugs. Psychological vulnerability also contributed to poor regulation of internal recurrent painful affect states of depression and loneliness. Seeking out her boyfriend's company may have been a response to feelings of loneliness, although U.S. did not express this possibility.

After her second detox, U.S. entered a residential TC, for which she was on a waiting list for approximately eight weeks.

Case of E.J.

E.J. is a 30-year-old black male who dropped out of the 11th grade but had a $29,000-a-year job in a federal service industry. He entered his first detox depressed and dismayed over loss of his wife (also a crack user), his job, and his furnished apartment, and the dissolution of his family of five children. The Bureau of Child Welfare placed two children in a foster home, two children with a relative (also a crack user), and one child with another relative. E.J. lives alone in an apartment in a crack-infested tenement where he occasionally deals drugs. Numerous females narcissistically mirror E.J. They frequently visit him, get high, and take his freely offered advice on how to manage their affairs. E.J. recreates his large family with these women, acting as a central authority figure in their lives.

During both detoxes, E.J. was polite but similarly organized the patient community, recreating a family setting desperately missed. His efforts at community organization on the detox unit subtly implied grandiose superiority to the treatment structure offered on the unit.

E.J. did not directly refuse aftercare treatment during his first detox, stating he had his own (superior) plans to return to an outpatient clinic where an intake interview had already taken place. He was confident he would stay drug-free, having recently promised that one of his children would soon return to live with him. This pseudo-self-sufficiency contributed to his failure to enter aftercare treatment.

E.J. stayed drug-free for one month by staying in isolation in his apartment and working for himself in construction. Feelings of loneliness and social isolation were difficult to manage. Shame over his personal deterioration prevented contact with his mother and family of origin, whom he had not seen in over a year. E.J. began to smell crack rising from a downstairs apartment in his crack-infested tenement. In response to this stimulus, he soon resumed compulsive smoking. Shocked and dismayed by a relapse he felt sure would not occur, E.J. sought immediate treatment through a second detox six weeks after his first detox, after a long binge during which he lost all control.

Analysis of Case Example

E.J. exemplifies the manifestation of a facade of pseudo-self-sufficiency when the grandiose self is denied. His need for omnipotent control and setting of unrealistic goals betrayed a narcissistic personality disturbance. His overconfidence did not eliminate underlying depression and loneliness. He stated, "Things have snowballed, and everything is heading downhill." A compulsivity in recreating the structure and organization of his old family, where he was in charge, was seen in the tenement and in detox. Failure to attend aftercare treatment, painful emotional states (loneliness, depression), and environmental stimuli (crack smoke/fumes) combined as determinants of relapse.

DISCUSSION OF RESEARCH

Content analysis of relapse episodes establishes categories of the typology with psychological/personality and environmental/interpersonal domains. The research findings empirically validate the existence of a common mechanism underlying relapse for cocaine patients. Of the six factors that arise from analysis of clinicians' approaches to outpatient treatment of cocaine abuse (Washton 1987, 1989a; Smith & Wesson, 1985; Rosecan & Spitz, 1987; Stone et al., 1984), all but one were empirically validated. The roles of drug craving, environmental cues, denial, being around/using drugs, and painful affect states in determining relapse correspond to categories of the typology. Selective recall of cocaine euphoria was not a research finding in this sample. However, it may be an intervening variable following the dysphoria of a painful affect state or drug craving and actual use of drugs that remains undetectable in patient responses to the relapse-interview questions. Future research should refine questioning to detect action of the variable of recall of cocaine euphoria. Beyond the research sample, recall of cocaine euphoria does correspond to the author's clinical observation of patient experience.

By examining cocaine dependence in an inpatient hospital population, this research extends the body of literature on relapse phenomena. In addition, this empirical approach extends the data compiled by Marlatt (1985) on addiction to alcohol, heroin, gambling, and overeating by examining addiction to cocaine.

Time-to-relapse findings validate earlier research that two thirds of those who relapse do so within the first 90 days of attempted abstinence (Marlatt, 1985). In this study, time-to-relapse results show that 76% relapse within the first 90 days postdetoxification. In fact, these compulsive crack-cocaine smokers relapse at a higher rate than the alcoholics, heroin addicts, gamblers, and overeaters in Marlatt's sample. These findings validate clinical wisdom that the initial three- to six-month period of attempted abstinence is the time in which relapse is most likely to occur for cocaine abusers (Stone et al., 1984), since 94.3% of the relapses in the study take place before a six-month period expires. These results reveal the early stages of attempted abstinence to be a precarious period of vulnerability that must be carefully navigated by patients.

Microanalysis of relapse episodes supports the observations of Levin (1987). Narcissism, associated defensive functioning, and poor management of internal affect states are predominant factors in relapse in early stages of attempted ab-stinence. The psychological/personality domain covers these factors and re-sponses that are internal. Manic defenses and denial are, for example, internal defensive processes. On the other hand, the typology's environmental/inter-personal domain covers patient responses to external events. The two domains are intimately interrelated. For example, the use of defenses such as mania or denial affect reality testing and determine one's approach to environmental and interpersonal stimuli. Thus, the typology and findings are compelling in their support of the relapse-prevention model based on the dynamic interaction of psychological vulnerability with environmental stimuli.

Major findings are that relapse follows a painful emotional state (40%), fail-ure to enter arranged aftercare treatment (37%), and encounters with condi-tioned environmental stimuli (34%); 85% involve multideterminants. The category and finding of the prevalence of painful emotional states as determi-nants in relapse support Marlatt's finding that 35% of relapses involve a nega-tive emotion. Together, these findings empirically justify Khantzian's (1985) assertions that patients self-medicate recurrent painful affect states.

The finding that 37% of relapses include failure to enter arranged aftercare treatment reflects the importance of patients' receiving therapeutic support to address their psychological vulnerability. In treatment, patients can receive as-sistance in managing recurrent painful affect states, interpersonal stress, and challenging environmental stimuli.

Results showing that 34.28% of relapses involve encounters with environ-mental stimuli of people, places, and drugs are reminiscent of Marlatt's (1985) category of direct or indirect social pressures (20%). Encounters with these ex-ternal influences and factors are often too challenging for psychologically vul-nerable patients to manage successfully.

Another significant finding is that 24.38% of relapses involve interpersonal stress as a determinant. This is similar to Marlatt's finding that interpersonal conflict was a determinant in 16% of relapses.

Also of note is the finding that 14.28% of relapses involve escalation to drug of choice (crack) after use of alcohol or intranasal cocaine. This finding sup-ports clinical wisdom, warning against use of alcohol and marijuana and test-ing of control with cocaine (Smith & Wesson, 1985; Washton, 1987).

Another important finding is that TC shortcomings contribute to 20% of re-lapses. These shortcomings include long waiting lists and rejection of patients on psychiatric medication, or with medical problems. This finding directly re-lates to the research of Rainone et al. (1988), who report on the psychiatric and medical problems that characterize crack patients in drug-free residential pro-grams who were able to meet the stringent admission criteria. They recom-mend addition of medical and psychiatric staff to manage these patient problems. The presence of sufficient staff and modifications in TCs may permit the admission of patients on antipsychotic medication. Waiting lists can be remedied by creation of new, specialized crack residences.

The existence of long waiting lists highlights the special problems that patients who have lost jobs, insurance benefits, and financial resources face when seeking treatment postdetoxification. Compulsive crack-cocaine smokers readily deteriorate to such levels and are referred to TCs instead of private rehabilitation centers. However, long waiting times necessitate recommending that these patients attend NA or CA meetings daily until they can enter a residential program.

The role of psychological and environmental determinants, their interaction, and the complexity of relapse are illustrated through case examples. The finding that 85.7% of relapses involve multideterminants is dramatically illustrated in the examples, as is the predominance of narcissistic psychopathology in early stages of attempted abstinence by cocaine users.

Relapse of compulsive free-base cocaine smokers is empirically shown to be a complex process. The complexity of relapse and evidence of its multideterminants suggest the need for approaches that go beyond disease-model conceptualizations of internal causation and reactivation of an underlying disease state.

CONCLUSION

The approach of Wallace (1989a), which assesses through research the process of relapse in crack patients, provides important revelations on the multideterminants of relapse. By following Marlatt (1985) in a microanalysis of relapse episodes for 35 patients who return a second time to inpatient detoxification after experiencing a relapse, the research empirically validates the existence of a common mechanism underlying relapse in crack-cocaine patients. Results establish a typology of psychological/personality and environmental/interpersonal determinants of relapse. Case examples illustrate the kind of data content analyzed, the role of multideterminants, and the predominance of narcissistic psychopathology.

Research findings highlight the fact that the initial period of attempted abstinence is fraught with peril for psychologically vulnerable patients who face challenging environmental stimuli. Clinicians must recognize the nature of challenging internal and external dangers patients will encounter as they attempt abstinence from a seductive drug such as crack cocaine that has been smoked compulsively.

Perhaps of most importance is the finding that relapse is quite likely when patients fail to enter treatment after inpatient treatment. This highlights the necessity of being engaged in treatment as a strategy for maintaining abstinence from cocaine. Relapse-prevention models (Marlatt & Gordon, 1985; Miller & Pechacek, 1987; Wallace, 1989b) that appreciate and address the role of multideterminants of relapse—perhaps going beyond the disease model—may improve clinical efficacy and treatment outcomes.

An additional determinant of relapse not highlighted by this study may be an undiagnosed and untreated compulsive sexuality. According to Washton (1989b), "reciprocal relapse" occurs; this involves the tendency of addictions to cocaine and compulsive sexuality to coexist with a relapse to one leading to relapse to the other (p. 32).

The limitations of the research are that the sample was small ($n = 35$) and that no interrater reliability in content analysis of relapse episodes is available. Future research with the CRI could benefit by using a second rater for content analysis to provide interrater reliability for the categories that arose from microanalysis. Such future research must empirically assess relapse rates for all patients—not only those who return for a second detoxification. Efforts to document treatment outcomes (Washton, 1987, 1989c) must expand.

The results of the CRI should also be shared in case conferences and in staff rounds with all members of the multidisciplinary treatment staff. Continuing education for treatment staff needs to include information on the multideterminants and process of relapse. The use of Wallace's (1989a) typology and results of the CRI with those actual patients with which staff members work should enhance their appreciation of the relapse process. Staff members may therefore be more empathic with patients and avoid the decline in morale that occurs when patients return to a facility, perhaps suggesting a failure on the part of the treatment program staff or on the part of the patient. No one will feel this kind of disappointment and frustration if education clarifies the process and multideterminants of relapse.

The CRI may possess certain attributes as a research instrument, as well. An advantage over using questionnaires for microanalysis of relapse episodes (Marlatt, 1985) exists in the present approach, which employs clinical-interview data and incorporates clinical observations. Categories of narcissistic denial/denial arise from clinical observations, permitting documentation of the predominance of narcissistic psychopathology during early stages of attempted abstinence in the cocaine dependent.

In order to be able to work effectively with patients, the self psychology of patients and the role of narcissistic psychopathology must be appreciated by clinicians. Management of painful affect states, denial, and narcissistic psychopathology require psychodynamic techniques. The logic of utilizing multifaceted clinical approaches with cocaine patients is supported by the major findings of the study. Encounters with conditioned environmental stimuli and interpersonal stress require behavioral, cognitive, educational, and self-control techniques. Education must prepare patients "to anticipate the likelihood of relapse, so that they may engage in preventive alternative behavior" (Marlatt, 1985, p. 33).

The value of Wallace's (1989a) research lies in the creation of the typology of psychological and environmental determinants of relapse that validates a common mechanism underlying relapse and directs treatment interventions by predicting probable relapse situations. The typology is a key tool in the clinical work of preparing patients for successful management of various internal and external challenges that could lead to relapse. Beyond clinicians' preferences for particular treatment orientations and philosophies or disease models is a vital need for effective clinical interventions for a growing population of compulsive cocaine users (Siegel, 1985). Clinical appreciation of the subtle interaction of the multideterminants of relapse may prove an important element of successful treatment strategies. The research of Wallace, it is hoped, can assist in the development of a group of properly trained professionals who possess the integrated theory and multifaceted clinical techniques necessary for effective treatment of cocaine patients. Her research underscores the need for a multifaceted technique to address the multideterminants of relapse. Chapter 14 aspires to move the field of chemical dependency further toward this goal by describing in detail a multifaceted clinical technique and model of relapse prevention for use in psychoeducational groups that arises from her typology and research findings.

14

A Model of Relapse Prevention*

Marlatt (1988) asks how we are to handle clients who have "failed" to change or who experience setbacks and relapses in the posttreatment phase. He also asserts that "analysis of various determinants of relapse may provide clinicians and clients with a guide to changes that may be necessary" (p. 480). Wallace (1989a) follows Marlatt (1985, 1988) in an analysis and assessment of relapse episodes, producing invaluable insight into the multideterminants of relapse for crack smokers. Wallace states that clinicians can use the results of microanalysis of relapse episodes in guiding compulsive crack-cocaine smokers to make the changes that may be necessary to avoid a future relapse. Marlatt (1985) poses the question, "Is it possible to prepare persons in treatment to anticipate the likelihood of a relapse, so that they may engage in preventive alternative behavior?" (p. 33). Toward this end, this chapter offers a model of relapse prevention that does prepare patients to anticipate the likelihood of relapse while in inpatient treatment, so that they can engage in preventive alternative behavior. A detailed description of 29 interventions that make up an arsenal of relapse-prevention strategies permits treatment professionals to expand the range of their clinical tools.

The chapter will demonstrate the value of metaphor as a clinical tool and describe clinical interventions within a model of relapse prevention used in a form of group therapy that is psychoeducational. This work remains within the tradition of Curry, Marlatt, et al. (1988) in applying research findings on the multideterminants and process of relapse (Wallace, 1989a) to the development of treatment interventions with the aim of improving treatment outcome and reducing relapse rates.

The interventions that this chapter describes in substantial detail can be utilized in both individual and group psychotherapy with the chemically dependent. However, the author originally designed them for use in a form of group therapy that is psychoeducational. When the inpatient-detoxification unit became short-staffed, it was necessary to implement the most effective treatment interventions. This change in staffing patterns coincided with the completion

*Adapted, with permission, from *Journal of Substance Abuse Treatment*, Vol. 6, No. 2, 1989.

of the author's research findings (Wallace, 1989a) on the multideterminants of relapse. These two factors led to the development of a one-hour psychoeducational group held twice a week with 15 patients, which replaced twice-a-week group therapy with seven or eight patients. What resulted was an effective model of relapse prevention that should be replicated within a variety of treatment settings and within an array of treatment modalities (individual, group, family therapy).

This model of relapse prevention remains of specific value with crack patients and should be a part of any treatment program (inpatient, outpatient, residential TC) striving to increase treatment outcome with challenging crack patients. In fact, relapse prevention is the most important element of any treatment program. When program resources are limited, a relapse-prevention group should receive top billing as the essential ingredient of a chemical-dependency-treatment program. Also, this kind of relapse prevention should take place in all phases of treatment—early abstinence or withdrawal, the second period of prolonging abstinence, and a third period of one to several years or a lifetime of recovery. When Todd (1989) asserts that relapse prevention needs to begin on day 1 of treatment, he and other treatment practitioners may find in this chapter exactly the kind of practical and effective relapse-prevention strategies for which they search. They will also find that the 29 specific relapse-prevention interventions described in this chapter can find wide applicability in a clinical-interview, individual-therapy, group-therapy, or even family-therapy setting in any kind of treatment facility.

CLINICAL INTERVENTIONS: A MODEL OF RELAPSE PREVENTION

Given the challenge of combating relapse in compulsive crack-cocaine smokers, the clinician in psychoeducational groups must be an active educator, a motivational force, and inspirational, empathic, and frank in spelling out in detail patient vulnerability to internal and external dangers after detoxification. An active, multifaceted clinical technique incorporating metaphor, education, psychodynamic, and cognitive-behavioral elements is necessary in groups with newly abstinent patients.

Metaphorical forms of communication play an especially important role in relapse-prevention education for compulsive crack-cocaine smokers. Gordon (1978), Rosen (1982), and Marlatt (1985) recognize the value of metaphor as a clinical tool in treatment. Marlatt views metaphor as a vehicle for "communicating important elements of the big picture" and as a "powerful communicative tool"; he sees metaphoric imagery as something that both "brightens up" material and provides a "shorthand method of retaining important principles" (pp. 211–212). Barker (1985) recognizes several metaphorical forms that are of value, including stories, anecdotes, analogies, similes, and embedded statements. He stresses the distinct advantages of delivering messages in metaphorical form rather than in more direct ways when treating clients in therapy.

Often the use of a vivid metaphor engages patients and puts them in a receptive frame of mind. Once the clinician has an attentive and receptive audience, suggestions are made that otherwise might be rejected outside the context of a vivid and graphic metaphorical image. The clinician freely intersperses education throughout the group process, while also permitting patient involvement. The movement back and forth among stories, metaphoric examples, asking patients questions, permitting them to provide examples from personal experience, and providing a substantial piece of education on a "minitopic" constitutes the group process.

The overall psychoeducational group process freely indulges in the mixing of metaphors and the use of multiple metaphors in an attempt to maximize the utility of indirect forms of communication. The clinician's goal is to communicate as much information as possible in a one-hour group session. Groups serve to educate patients to the numerous psychological and emotional vulnerabilities they possess and how to cope with high-risk situations that may trigger relapse. The mixing of metaphors and the interspersing of educational directives between stories and analogies may seem esthetically displeasing and disjointed. However, clinicians must permit themselves the creative freedom of combining multiple elements within the group process to broaden the amount of information patients are able to absorb in light of defenses of denial and grandiosity. The description of clinical interventions shows how clinicians must draw upon their knowledge of psychodynamic theory and principles, as well as upon knowledge of cognitive-behavioral theory. The diversity of material presented and the combining of various kinds of clinical interventions keeps the group process enlivened.

The clinician encourages group participation by patients because, in the safe holding environment of the inpatient unit, they must begin to face depressing and frightening problems that may be unavoidable postdetoxification. A follow-up of the issues raised in group takes place in individual sessions. Aftercare treatment plans are "individually tailored" to patients' unique situations.

Psychoeducation also provides an in-depth description of the process and purpose of individual psychotherapy. Thus, after participating in psychoeducational groups, patients are prepared to engage more meaningfully in individual sessions on inpatient detoxification and in aftercare-treatment modalities after detoxification.

The provision of education on defensive functioning (denial, inflation) represents an important component of relapse prevention in psychoeducational groups. Metaphorical forms of communication also serve to circumvent the very defenses that are being described. Patients identify with the graphic description of a defensive activity they have utilized and are drawn into an appreciation of how it is dangerous and may lead to relapse, instead of immediately dismissing the information. Some patients laugh in group, as they identify with a story or graphic explanation of defensive functioning. Yet, at this point, they are also less rigid and more open to education on more adaptive behavioral alternatives. In addition, the provision of hope and educating patients on how they can take responsibility for their own healing constitute an important aspect of psychoeducation.

The following discussion attempts to furnish clinicians with an actual sense of what goes on in psychoeducational groups. Headings provide an encapsulated description of a specific clinical intervention. Some of the interventions are examples of metaphorical forms of communication. Others are best described as psychoeducation or as "educational directives." The essential text of what clinicians say to patients, ask patients, and explain to patients in psychoeducational groups in order to help patients avoid relapse postdetoxification follows.

Interventions in Psychoeducational Groups

Self-Medication

In group, the therapist asks patients to identify feelings they may have self-medicated or that precede drug use. Clinicians explain that patients have been their own doctors, using drugs as medicine to alleviate symptoms of emotional pain (Cinque, 1986). Many patients began this process with marijuana or alcohol in early adolescence, never learning to manage painful feelings without medicating themselves with drugs.

The therapist points out that many patients in detoxification may be experiencing feelings of depression, anger, fear, or anxiety for the first time in months or years, since that may be how long they self-medicated with drugs, often on a daily basis. Similarly, it may be the first time in months or years that patients have been drug-free for several days and are unable to get high to self-medicate.

Porcelain Vase

The therapist asks patients to imagine something as delicate as a porcelain vase. Just as one is careful and protects a porcelain vase from predictable dangerous situations, patients must learn to protect themselves from situations of danger that can trigger a relapse. The experience of painful feelings is a situation of danger patients must prepare themselves for by designing strategies of protection for their psychologically vulnerable and fragile selves. An effective strategy of protection is to learn how to experience and tolerate emotions in the context of individual or group therapy (in TCs).

Duffel-Bag Metaphor

Many patients have repressed, or buried, or stuffed all of their painful feelings into a large, overstuffed duffel bag that they carry with them (Cinque, 1986). Therapists ask, "How well can someone function in life carrying around this heavy duffel bag? Compared with someone who is not carrying around a duffel bag, how well can you climb a mountain or run a race?"

The therapist explains that in order to heal oneself or free oneself of the burden of carrying around this duffel bag, a process of self-healing must be undertaken in professional therapy. Clinicians stress that detoxification is a very brief period and is not the time to begin this process. However, it is important that patients become aware, perhaps for the first time, of the fact that they have emotional pain and traumatic memories that eventually must be worked out in psychotherapy in order to reduce their susceptibility to self-medication strategies and addiction. The time for this work is during one's aftercare treatment—after either developing a feeling of trust with a therapist, or becoming oriented to group therapy in a TC.

Bucket-of-Water Metaphor

The process of therapy is conveyed in the "bucket of water" metaphor. Unconscious memories and feelings that people carry around with them are like heavy buckets of water. In a single therapy session, patients sit and dip out one cupful of water and examine its contents. One cup represents a measure of the tears we cry in a single therapy session as we gradually heal ourselves by both describing traumatic memories and feeling the original affect we felt at the time of our traumas. This process may take some people two years and others may need four, five, or more years of therapy gradually to heal themselves, depending on the number of buckets they carry.

Dysfunctional Families

The clinician asks patients what a dysfunctional family is and for some examples. The idea that these families did not function properly is reinforced, while alcoholic homes, homes where domestic violence occurred, and families in which physical, sexual, or emotional abuse took place are all accepted as examples. Clinicians explain that inner pain and injuries to the self acquired in childhood may have left patients vulnerable to self-medication with drugs and escalation to addiction.

Concepts of the "responsible child" and the "rebellious child," common to alcoholic or dysfunctional homes, are explained (Woititz, 1983; Black, 1981). The clinician describes the responsible child through stories of children who are "31 at age 13." When a parent is alcoholic, these children act like adults. They get up early, cook breakfast, clean, and do laundry before going to school. The adult child of an alcoholic still has this child within, one who was overworked but very responsible all through childhood. The rebellious child who coped with dysfunctional family dynamics by getting into fights, being truant, and doing drugs is also described. Some responsible children become rebellious in adolescence or in later life, seeming to be exhausted and no longer able to cope. At age 31, they are like a 13-year-old, feeling a need to escape responsibility and "play" as they were unable to do as "responsible children." Other responsible children are still playing the role of the responsible parent with their grown siblings and their own children. As a result, they feel exhausted, justifying the feeling that they must get high.

Inevitably, at least one group member strongly identifies in such a way that he or she briefly shares a story from childhood. Usually, other patients sit enthralled as they also identify or achieve a sudden appreciation of key dynamics in their lives. Education covers ACOA groups—where members sit in groups and describe traumatic events that happened in their dysfunctional families, trying to reconnect with feelings and heal injuries to their selves.

The therapist describes a continuum of family life that progresses to the less traumatic. This is necessary because it frequently transpires at this point in group that a patient will articulate an inability to identify with the families thus described. Less traumatic but significant are homes where patients experienced an inconsistency in or actual lack of sufficient mirroring. Clinicians explain that parents may have been too busy to mirror patients when they were children. An example of proper mirroring is given in which a child falls and is picked up by a parent, who holds the child and says, "Oh, you just fell and hurt your knee. It hurts, doesn't it? You'll be okay. I'll put something on it and it will feel better." In this way, parents help children learn how to label, process, and integrate their feelings, while children internalize an ability to calm themselves down.

This is contrasted with a graphic traumatic scene of a parent in public who yells at a child who has just fallen, "Get up and hurry along," while perhaps hitting the child. Traumatic experiences such as this result in injuries to the self that stay with patients to adulthood. They result in low self-esteem and must be healed in therapy.

Also significant are those homes in which patients were overgratified or overstimulated. Childhoods during which patients were spoiled and given whatever they wanted did not prepare them for the reality that, in adulthood and in love relationships, they would not be presented with everything they want on a silver platter. Weekly childhood shopping sprees at Macy's may have been a parent's way of compensating for feelings of guilt about working long hours and never being home. These patients never learned how to manage feelings of frustration or anger, receiving easy and fast gratification from parents. Poor families may have provided too little gratification and tired, overworked parents may have provided too little stimulation. Therapists state that the point is not to blame parents, but to learn how to be a mother or father to oneself—how properly to love oneself, empathize or feel for that child within, and take oneself to treatment for healing and repair in psychotherapy.

For those patients who genuinely cannot identify with the experience of growing up in a dysfunctional family, the United States, or our society, is described as a dysfunctional family (Harris-Offutt, 1986). The clinician tells patients that self-medication with everything from tobacco, coffee, and aspirin to alcohol is widely prescribed by the media (Bernard & Wallace, 1986). Societally supported recreational drug use with a potent form of cocaine (crack) may explain their escalation to addiction.

Water-Faucet Metaphor

The need to learn how to connect with one's feelings, and to regulate and modulate one's expression of emotions, is explained via the image of a water faucet. Clinicians teach that children who grow up in chaotic dysfunctional families survive and adapt by disconnecting from their feelings. If friends saw one's parents arguing or intoxicated, they might have been frightened or shocked. However, the patients as children eventually adapted to typical chaotic scenes by disconnecting from their emotions. Children learned to "turn off" their anger, or fear, or pain as if their emotions were a water faucet. What was adaptive and a survival mechanism for a child in a dysfunctional family is now a maladaptive mode of functioning for an adult. Human beings must always know what they are feeling and when they are feeling an emotion.

Patients must learn how to turn on the water faucet for the first time in years and how to let the emotions drip slowly, or come out in moderate force, strong force, or full force. Some patients only express anger at full force, exploding after anger builds up over time. Closely related problems exist in relationships and involve an inability to express anger and other emotions to bosses, friends, or loved ones. Examples of appropriate verbal assertiveness with a boss who has irritated an employee is briefly role modeled by the therapist, illustrating appropriate regulation and expression of anger before it builds up to an explosive force.

Identifying, Labeling, and Processing Emotions

The therapist clarifies that adult children from dysfunctional homes (crack addicts, insider traders, famous actors) may function in life without knowing what they are feeling or how to process feelings. However, it is crucial to learn how to identify, label, actually feel, and process emotions.

Clinicians tell stories of patients who get very angry at their boss, or mother, or spouse, and say, "Forget it, I'm going to go and get high." Not knowing how to feel, or how to process strong feelings, these patients can only calm themselves down by self-medicating with drugs.

A process that must occur in individual or group therapy (in aftercare treatment) involves learning how to process emotions, which can then lead to a calm state. With the help of a therapist, patients will learn how to identify and label such feelings as loneliness, emptiness, boredom, anger, fear, anxiety, frustration, and depression.

How To Manage Painful Feelings

Emphasis is placed on the importance of patients not setting themselves up in situations likely to upset them or lead to strong or painful emotional reactions; patients may not yet be able to handle these feelings all alone after detoxification without resorting to self-medication. They have the responsibility to protect themselves by entering aftercare treatment immediately following detoxification and getting the support of a therapist in managing painful feelings (and healing old injuries to the self). In addition, patients must get an NA or CA sponsor (an NA/CA member who has been drug-free for at least a year) and learn how to seek out drug-free friends and relatives with whom they can talk about their feelings and avoid the painful emotional states that lead to relapse.

Back of My Mind

Clinicians ask patients what denial is, permitting group interaction. The clinician elaborates upon patients' abilities to tell "little white lies" to themselves, explaining denial as having an intention in the front of one's mind that is openly shared, while in the back of one's mind, a secret desire or fear is lurking. The therapist gives an example in which a patient states, "I'm going to the cleaners with this $20 bill to get the clothes I left there." Meanwhile, the person ends up going to get high, perhaps after running into a drug associate. Trying to recognize one's own processes of denial may involve this patient's admitting that all along, in the back of his mind, he felt like getting high, hoped to run into a drug-using friend, or actually was thinking, "I'm going to get high."

Clinicians teach that patients must learn to ask themselves, "What's in the back of my mind?" and to verbalize fears, feelings, and impulses that are lurking there. Regular contacts with therapists in aftercare treatment and seeking out NA/CA sponsors and drug-free friends or relatives permits talking about those desires, fears, and feelings in the back of their minds.

In group, patients talk about not knowing whether a spouse or mother will let them come home again, or whether they have really lost their job and have any chance of returning to it. Discussing these issues helps to clarify what kind of aftercare treatment is appropriate, given one's status as domiciled or undomiciled, or employed or unemployed. Clinicians stress that concerns in the back of one's mind must be verbalized so that denial does not undermine one's chances of successful recovery.

Balloon Metaphor

Imagine a balloon overinflated with air—all that is needed is a pin to pop the balloon. This metaphor depicts just how fragile and impermanent a patient's state of being overconfident, or inflated, or full of air can be. This state of inflation makes denial even worse. If one denies having a drug problem, or a need to avoid "people, places, and things," then an overconfidence, arrogance, and foolish daring can arise during an inflated state. Patients believe they can do anything, which leads to a relapse.

People who walk around as if "kings of the hill," "all puffed up," and superior secretly feel very bad—like a pile of feces—about themselves. Neither feeling very high (high in the sky like a balloon) nor feeling very low (deflated like a balloon that has lost all of its air) is a realistic assessment of one's self. Patients will learn in therapy how to have a healthy, balanced self-esteem, knowing their strengths and weaknesses based on realistic self-knowledge.

Looking-Good Syndrome

In this syndrome, patients feel they no longer have a serious drug problem because they now look good, having gained weight in inpatient detoxification. Therapists explain that looking good can be deceptive to the patient, as well as to others, such as employers and family. Unapparent problems—such as a serious drug problem that required inpatient hospitalization, underlying emotional problems, and injuries to the self—may all go unrecognized as crucial topics that patients need to address properly in aftercare treatment.

Clinicians state, "No one can tell you have a serious drug problem by looking at you." Therefore, it is the patients' responsibility to maintain their knowledge of hidden problems that must be attended to in aftercare treatment. The looking-good syndrome is a trap into which patients easily fall, particularly as their appearance improves.

Work and Workaholism

Depression, shame, and guilt over losing previous employment often drive patients to seek jobs. They are embarrassed about long periods of unemployment and want to find work as soon as possible so they can feel good about themselves and prove their worthiness to family and friends. Patients decide they do not need aftercare treatment, as it might interfere with time alloted to work. Employers cannot tell they have a serious drug problem, and readily hire them because they "look good."

Clinicians warn patients that they are vulnerable and may not be able to handle first paychecks. They tell stories of patients who fail to return to work after a several-day binge financed by their first paycheck. Work is not discouraged, but for compulsive crack-cocaine smokers who ideally require the environment of a TC for the first few months of heightened vulnerability postdetoxification (but choose outpatient treatment instead), many hazards are associated with working. Crack-cocaine users who have been getting high on a daily or nearly daily basis for from six months to several years got high every payday or whenever they had money, and for them regular paydays are dangerous high-risk situations for the one- to three-month period postdetoxification. Compulsive crack users often need residential treatment instead of jobs, money, and dangerous payday dates.

Warnings also cover the danger of patients' working too hard and risking "burnout" or a workaholic pattern. With poor concepts of a drug-free life-style, patients are frequently fearful of leisure time and view work as the only constructive activity in which they can engage. They work at more than one job, or seek overtime. A common result is the need for a reward after a period of work culminating in exhaustion. The need for a reward on payday usually leads to relapse.

To illustrate this danger, clinicians tell stories of patients who were counselors in TCs, became workaholics, and relapsed. They explain the need to develop drug-free leisure activities, and new networks of friends who are drug-free or also recovering (perhaps from NA/CA), and to avoid getting a job too soon or falling into a workaholic pattern.

A Slip vs a Fall

When walking down an icy pavement, it is possible to slip, but this is very different from a complete fall. Patients are prepared for the possibility of a slip, a brief return to drug use, and are told how to prevent a complete fall, or a return to compulsive drug use. They are told that the best way to avoid a slip or relapse is to enter their arranged aftercare treatment. A slip must not be responded to with feelings of failure, although disappointment may arise. Beating up on oneself or feeling like a failure may lead to depression and self-medicating these painful feelings with crack. In turn, this can easily lead to a long binge or a complete relapse. Clinicians teach patients that, in the event of a slip, they must assess why it occurred, or what may have contributed to getting high, asking themselves in what ways they may have set themselves up for a slip, or fall.

Depending on the analysis of the slip, it can be responded to by (1) increasing the frequency of attending NA/CA meetings, (2) securing an NA/CA sponsor (drug-free for one year) after initially neglecting to, (3) combining outpatient individual and/or group therapy with NA/CA (where a combination of the two had originally been rejected), (4) entering a more intense treatment intervention such as a TC, or (5) discussing in therapy stressful situations, feelings, or personal issues that were originally unforeseen but must be better managed in the future.

Aftercare Treatment

Education in group covers the fact that ideal outpatient treatment combines individual or group therapy with participation in NA or CA. Clinicians recommend daily NA/CA meetings immediately following detoxification (90 meetings in 90 days), since patients need support and people with whom to talk about feelings, fears, temptations, drug cravings, and challenges to their abstinence, while developing drug-free associations. The therapist elicits any patient experiences with NA/CA from group members. Daily meetings replace daily, compulsive crack use and serve to disrupt deeply ingrained daily habits. Clinicians teach that of those patients who relapse, most do so within the first 90 days following detoxification (Wallace, 1989), stressing attendance at 90 NA/CA meetings in those first 90 days. Clinicians emphasize the importance of securing a sponsor in NA/CA to maximize the benefits of participation.

Similarly, clinicians teach that nearly all patients who relapse do so within six months (Stone et al., 1984; Wallace, 1989), pointing out the need for continuing NA/CA involvement, and outpatient treatment (individual and/or group psychotherapy) for six months to up to one or two years. However, unemployed patients who are not covered by Medicaid for outpatient clinic referrals can only use NA/CA. They cannot engage in an "ideal outpatient treatment" combining individual therapy and NA/CA immediately postdetoxification.

The therapist explains that a TC is usually the treatment of choice for compulsive crack-cocaine smokers (without medical insurance for 28-day rehabilitation). Many patients relapse because of their decision to try outpatient treatment despite the therapist's descriptions of the odds against its success given the severity of their addiction. Clinicians tell stories of such patients or elicit stories from group members who have relapsed and plan to enter the more intensive and appropriate TC after their second detoxification. A pattern of further deterioration is possible if patients choose poor aftercare treatment plans now and end up relapsing in the future. It may be better to choose an intensive form of treatment (TC) than to risk court-enforced loss of child custody, incarceration, or an eventual decline into homelessness. The therapist honestly describes the weaknesses of TCs, NA/CA, and outpatient treatment. However, despite these weaknesses, and since nothing is perfect, a form of aftercare treatment should be chosen by patients from among the treatment options in order to reduce the chances of relapse.

Need a Plumber

Clinicians ask, "When do you need a plumber? If your car has broken down, do you ask a plumber to take a look at it? If your toilet is clogged up, do you ask your mechanic to fix it? If your electrical circuits need rewiring, do you ask your plumber to do the job?" The idea is that these people have all received specialized training to equip them to do a job. When you need a plumber, a plumber should be sought out. Similarly, there are people who are specially trained to treat people with emotional problems and drug problems (Cinque, 1986). The therapist explains the training and expertise of recovering drug addicts, counselors, social workers, clinical psychologists, and psychiatrists.

Little Red Corvette

The therapist asks patients to imagine driving a little red Corvette that lacks a muffler and an interior, but may look good from the outside. Patients may be able to drive for miles on a metal crate (having no seats in the car) and without a muffler; however, problems exist even though the driver may have been able to function and ignore them while "looking good" on the exterior. "'Failing inspection" or having to recognize a problem with crack is identified as similar to discovering that you cannot function forever at this level of "getting over." Patients did "get over" until they broke down (lost weight, neglected their appearance, became ill) and it became apparent upon closer "inspection" that they had a drug problem.

Free Will in America

Therapists declare (paradoxically) that the best thing about this country is that you can exercise your free will and do drugs until you die. Patients are urged to seriously consider professional recommendations, but are not given a negative prophecy that they will inevitably fail or relapse when they reject clinical recommendations. The therapist states that it may be possible to recover from crack addiction without any aftercare treatment. Clinicians tell resistant patients to use their free will and decide for themselves upon aftercare treatment plans, but ask the following: "Why risk a relapse and loss of child custody, a girlfriend, or job, and why risk incarceration or death, if aftercare treatment can reduce the chances that these things will happen?"

Explaining Drug Craving

Drug craving often follows dreams about crack. Crack dreams are explained as expectable. The clinician teaches that dreams about crack may change and give positive signs, such as dropping the pipe, deciding not to get high, or being ambivalent about wanting to get high. Patient dreams while in detoxification are elicited from group members and analyzed by group participants.

Clinicians prepare patients to expect a decline in the intensity of drug craving since they are given pharmacological adjuncts in detoxification to correct chemical imbalances in the brain caused by crack. Patients express relief in learning that drug cravings, thoughts of leaving detoxification to get high, dreams of getting high while on the unit, and awakening with either the sensation of being high or the frustration of not feeling high are all normal and expectable.

They also learn in group that cravings may reappear suddenly at any time, and may recur on anniversary dates of past heavy crack use, such as New Year's Eve or a weekend when they purchased a large amount of crack. The therapist tells patients that they may suddenly find themselves smelling cocaine, tasting cocaine, or experiencing sensations of a nasal drip (from snorting days) or jitters associated with the crack high. Drug craving may also follow smelling actual crack smoke or cigarette smoke reminiscent of crack. Such cravings decrease in frequency and intensity, but may suddenly get strong again after three or six months. When drug cravings do occur, clinicians reassure patients, they will go away and should not be responded to by getting high. Talking honestly about cravings (versus denial of their existence) is important. Calling NA/CA sponsors or drug-free relatives or friends can help during this period of drug craving, while avoiding drugs, drug-using associates, and drug environments is crucial.

In psychoeducational groups, clinicians openly interrupt patients who talk about the crack high or glorify crack. The therapist states, "Some patients are beginning to crave crack or will end up wanting to get high, so it's not a good idea to talk about getting high in group," refocusing the group on more therapeutic issues.

The Naked Body: Stimuli Response

The clinician asks patients to imagine a person's response to seeing a lover's naked body. Because of the repeated association between seeing his or her naked body and the sex that followed, just seeing the naked body may lead to a response of excitement or craving for sex. Similarly, because of the repeated association of the stimuli of certain people, certain places, and drugs, and the response of cocaine euphoria that followed, just seeing people, places, and drugs can trigger the conditioned response of craving crack.

To avoid triggering drug craving or getting excited and wanting to get high, all stimuli associated with past crack use must be avoided, particularly right after detoxification when patients are most vulnerable. Drug paraphernalia left in the home, old drug associates, and walking past a crack-dealing area can all serve as stimuli that can trigger drug craving. Patients are instructed to have the family throw out their drug paraphernalia before they return home, focusing on the power of these stimuli to trigger a slip or relapse and the importance of avoiding them.

The Fire Extinguisher: Extinction

Clinicians teach patients that one's love for an old lover can be extinguished or put out, as if someone were aiming a fire extinguisher and gradually putting out the fire of the love. As this takes place, the sight of the lover's naked body is less likely to be exciting as one falls out of love or the fires of the love are extinguished. As a user recovers from crack addiction, the "crack love" is extinguished or put out, like a fire extinguisher puts out a fire. As this happens, the sight of people, places, and drugs is less likely to excite a desire to get high, as the fires of one's crack love are extinguished. Because the fires of crack love are so strong, it takes about three months to a year for the fire extinguisher to put out these strong chemical fires. As time passes, anything associated with that past love will be easier to be around. A day will eventually come when old responses of excitement and craving are extinguished (or undergo extinction).

The Battle Metaphor

The therapist states, "Imagine that the enemy troops are approaching from Times Square and your troops are camped out on 34th Street. What are you going to do? You need a strategy and a battle plan in this crack war." Clinicians remind patients of how they had to look for the "lookout man," wait for the police to leave or drive around the corner, then get the nod from the "lookout man" to purchase drugs. After detoxification, patients must use the same kind of elaborate strategy to walk to the store, taking a zigzag route or going around the block to avoid the many crack houses that line some avenues. This kind of strategy is necessary to avoid people, places, and drugs at least initially after detoxification. Clinicians state, "We are giving you tools, a shield, and sword to use in battle when you return to the crack war."

Back-Injury Metaphor

Patients in detoxification are injured soldiers of the crack war. The therapist asks them to imagine the recovery process of a back-injury patient who is vul-

nerable to reinjury or pain and to compare it to their recovery as injured soldiers. There are easy tests and hard tests that recovering back-surgery patients
face. These tests are objects of various weights that can be picked up safely
gradually over time. Clinicians ask, "What kind of objects do you think a back-
injury patient can attempt to pick up after one month out of the hospital, after
three months, six months, nine months, and one year?" An easy test that
could be attempted in the first month of recovery is to pick up a relatively light
object such as a small bag. An intermediate test between three and six months
of recovery is picking up a bag of trash. However, not until nine months to a
year of back-injury recovery would one attempt to carry a light suitcase. Also, a
back-injury patient will probably never be able to carry a heavy suitcase or to
help carry something as heavy as a trunk.

For crack patients, carrying a large sum of money after leaving detoxification
is like a back-injury patient trying to carry a heavy suitcase right after leaving
the hospital. Clinicians urge crack patients to have the same awareness of their
personal weakness and vulnerability to relapse, choosing only easy tests in the
first 90 days postdetoxification and delaying harder tests until six, nine, or
twelve months of abstinence. Patients must acknowledge hard tests that they
may never be able to attempt, like sitting in a room full of people who are getting high on crack.

Anticipating Loss of Trust

Therapists tell stories of patients' offering to go to the store for someone and
being told, "No, that's okay." Similarly, relatives may decide not to go out at all
if it means leaving patients in the house alone, unsupervised. The bottom line
is that patients who have stolen from relatives, or failed to return from an er-
rand but instead spent the money on crack, are no longer trusted. They must
resist thinking, "If everyone thinks I'm going to get high, then I might as well
go and get high." Patients must not be offended, shocked, or surprised, but
must anticipate the likelihood that others will hold low expectations of them.
They usually find these vignettes humorous. Regaining trust will be a gradual
process. Patients must also protect themselves and be careful with whom they
share their history of drug addiction. Employers and others in society hold
negative stereotypes about drug users that could hurt patients.

Anticipating Ambivalence

While spouses, friends, and relatives may love patients and be proud that
they completed detoxification, they may also be very angry. Because of their
ambivalence, relatives may express anger to patients, directly or indirectly. Following detoxification and early in recovery, direct encounters with such people
must be avoided. Interpersonal stress and painful feelings follow such interac-

tions. Since interpersonal stress may be unavoidable, patients must seek out support following such interactions. Patients are given an example of a patient whose mother, whenever she sees him, reminds him of the Christmas gifts he stole in December, even though it might now be July, making the patient so angry that he feels like getting high.

Escalation to Drug of Choice

Therapists warn against the use of alcohol, marijuana or intranasal cocaine since such use can lead to escalation to the drug of choice—crack. They recount how one joint, one drink on Christmas, one snort of intranasal cocaine, or just one smoke of crack has led to a two- or three-day binge. Explanations stress that sampling a chemical substance can lead to escalation to one's drug of choice or drug of addiction. Patients may argue that marijuana or alcohol was never a problem for them, and that they can still have a drink or smoke marijuana. Therapists counter this with explanations of the disinhibiting effects of these substances. Alcohol, marijuana, or other chemical usage is particularly risky during the next 90-day period, six-month period, and first year of abstinence. Some TCs used to permit recovering drug addicts to use alcohol socially, but have changed this policy since clients either became alcoholic or ended up getting high from the disinhibiting effects of alcohol.

Hard Test—Handling Money

The clinician warns patients against handling large sums of money. Preparation for the "hard test" of handling money involves asking NA/CA sponsors or drug-free relatives to accompany patients when they cash checks or go shopping and carry a large sum of money. Stories of patients who relapse the first time they cash checks without a drug-free friend or relative or NA/CA sponsor with them (even though near their 90-day drug-free anniversary) underscore this point. Immediately following detoxification, patients may only be able to carry $5 or less safely. Refusal of money from relatives who are glad to see them "looking good" is encouraged; patients may thereby avoid being unwittingly "set up" for relapse or a slip by well-intentioned but ignorant people. Clinicians implore patients to attempt easy tests before hard tests. Carrying a small amount of money is a test that should be attempted early in recovery. After six months to a year, they can try a harder test of handling a larger sum of money.

Cold Bucket of Water

Compulsive crack-cocaine smokers frequently experience a pattern of decline that culminates in being homeless. They lose jobs and child custody, became involved with the criminal-justice system, lose family support, and eventually

are asked to leave relatives' and friends' homes. Each of these crises marking
the path of personal decline is likened to a "bucket of cold water" being thrown
in the patient's face. The shock tends to awaken patients to harsh realities that
processes of denial prevented them from fully appreciating, and they usually
enter detoxification after experiencing such a "cold bucket of water in the
face." The most effective of these is the shock of sudden homelessness. Therapists point out that one of the good things about experiencing a "cold bucket
of water in the face," or about a recent crisis, is that it finally awakens patients
(as a cold bucket of water tends to do) to the reality that their crack use must
be treated.

Some patients respond to these "cold buckets of water in the face" and the
pain that follows with more compulsive crack use to self-medicate painful feelings and escape unpleasant reality. It is usually such patients who end up
homeless, having used denial to cope with previous shock of losing jobs, child
custody, family support, and family trust.

Dangers of Shelters

Usually, being undomiciled means involvement in the shelter system. Shelters are infested with crack. Bathrooms in shelters are permeated with crack
smoke and drugs are sold in shelters. Patients share their experiences, validating such descriptions. The therapist warns that patients easily relapse when
they must leave detoxification and return to the shelter environment. In addition, feelings of depression are associated with having to stay in shelters and
contribute to relapse. Because of their heightened vulnerability postdetoxification, it is very dangerous for patients to return to shelters or the streets.

Homeless status dictates that patients be referred to TCs, and clinicians encourage them to contact family members who may be willing to provide temporary housing while they wait for up to three weeks to enter the facility. Staying
in a dangerous shelter for this length of time poses the risk of relapse. Therapists volunteer to describe the danger of patients' returning to the shelter to patients' families (by telephone or in family sessions during detoxification). They
caution patients, however, that many families may refuse to extend the level of
trust necessary to permit patients to remain in their homes, recalling past thiev-
ery, anxiety, and disruptions in family life created by the crack addict.

On the other hand, some families are willing and able to provide temporary
assistance, feeling relief upon learning that patients are alive, in detoxification,
and finally ready for treatment. Family and patients are told, however, that
having housing again is no reason to cancel plans for entering a TC. Frequently, regaining family support backfires, and patients end up reneging on
TC plans.

Coping with TC Shortcomings

TC shortcomings of long waiting lists are managed by instructing patients to attend NA or CA meetings every day while they continue to check in with TCs—daily if necessary—until they get a bed. Waiting times are one day to three weeks for homeless patients and four to eight weeks for domiciled patients in the New York metropolitan area. Patients who must return to shelters are also told to go to NA/CA meetings every day, or several times per day, until they get into a TC. Since TCs reject patients with a psychiatric history or with medical problems—lacking adequate psychiatric and medical staffs—these patients are told to go to outpatient treatment, and to attend 90 NA/CA meetings in 90 days.

EVALUATING THE RELAPSE-PREVENTION MODEL

The model provides the therapeutic benefits associated with the use of metaphorical forms of communication (Marlatt, 1985; Barker, 1985). Animated presentation of metaphorical forms in groups permits patients concretely to visualize and internalize graphic images that encapsulate complex psychological principles and knowledge of the multideterminants of relapse.

A multifaceted clinical technique using metaphor, education, and psychodynamic and cognitive-behavioral theory and principles permits explication of patients' emotional, behavioral, cognitive, and defensive functioning at a level comprehensible by the patients, given their varied levels of education. Patients are effectively taught about their own emotional processes, the impact of dysfunctional family dynamics on the patients as children, and current patient reliance on such defenses as denial and inflation. The model prepares patients to engage meaningfully in psychotherapy by explaining their deficits in self-esteem and affect regulation and the gradual process of therapy that will address these problems.

The strength of the model of relapse prevention lies in its detailed description of several things clinicians can say and do beyond warnings to "avoid people, places, and things." This actual text of one-hour-long psychoeducational group meetings considerably expands clinicians' options on how to entreat patients to avoid relapse. The relapse-prevention model maximizes detoxification as a time to affect patients' consciousness and to make them aware of their vulnerability to internal and external dangers.

Clinically, the interventions reliably opened patients' minds to the choices they had to contemplate, and eventually make, before and after leaving detoxification. The clinical interventions seemed to transform patients who were grandiose, resistant, and devaluing when they entered group therapy into questioning, open recipients of treatment recommendations upon leaving. Interventions sparked patient interest in psychotherapy, facilitating the making of aftercare treatment referrals. Psychoeducational groups also served to motivate initially naive patients, as well as those who had previously experienced relapse, to try their best to meet a difficult challenge of prolonging abstinence.

Limitations of the Model

A limitation of this model is the lack of treatment-outcome-evaluation research. While clinical knowledge of case histories of patients who successfully avoid relapse and meaningfully engage in aftercare treatment suggests the value of the relapse-prevention model, a systematic follow-up (Curry, Marlatt, et al., 1988) is necessary properly to assess the model's efficacy. An additional limitation of this work arises from the argument that these clinical interventions may represent the style of just one or two clinicians that might be difficult for other clinicians to emulate. A systematic evaluation of the model would involve the use of several clinicians and the follow-up of their patients, and could serve as part of a training manual for clinicians.

CONCLUSION

This chapter yields the results of applying research findings on the multideterminants and process of relapse (Wallace, 1989) to the development of treatment interventions with the aim of improving treatment outcome and reducing relapse rates. The chapter describes clinical interventions in a model of relapse prevention used in a form of group therapy that is psychoeducational. However, these techniques can be employed in individual, group, and family therapy settings in any treatment program. Clinical interventions communicate high-risk situations and internal and external dangers that may trigger relapse. The active, multifaceted clinical technique presented—combining metaphor, education, psychodynamic, and cognitive-behavioral elements—may be of value in treatment settings where clinicians work with newly abstinent compulsive crack-cocaine smokers, and the chemically dependent in general.

This detailed description of a model of relapse prevention meets an important and timely need in treatment programs striving to improve treatment efficacy with a growing population of compulsive crack-cocaine smokers. The author invites clinicians to emulate the flexible use of multiple metaphors, to mix metaphors, to include education, and to draw upon their knowledge of psychodynamic and cognitive-behavioral theory in order effectively to convey to patients the challenges involved in prolonging abstinence during the initial phases of recovery. The value of this work lies in the provision of a detailed description of what clinicians can actually say to prepare compulsive crack-cocaine smokers for the task of engaging in preventive alternative behaviors following inpatient treatment and avoiding relapse. It is hoped that the 29 interventions will enhance the effectiveness of other professionals and paraprofessionals, as it did for the author.

15

Conclusion

Having awakened wondering why I actually had a very long elaborate dream for the first time in days that did not involve editing and writing, I asked myself what it was all about. Eliciting from myself the same associations that I normally extract from my patients, I realized that, indeed, I did have yet another dream about my book!

In the dream, I had been at a party atop a luxury building in Manhattan, having a good time, taking pictures with a Polaroid camera, and making a home video. After the party, I noticed one bad Polaroid snapshot that, upon closer examination, showed in the distant background, just across the street from the party, three men trying to escape from the rooftop of a burning and collapsing building. With ropes wrapped around two of these men, the three men looked as though they had a small chance of escaping. Given the way they were entwined in the rope, the one falling could pull the other two down with him. The next day, there was a news report of a fire and a possible murder by two of the men I had captured in my snapshot—which might permit their identification by authorities, if only I could get the snapshot enlarged. I didn't know what to do with the picture, but I walked around with it in my pocket for a long time. Finally, the police came to me as a routine part of their investigation, and I enlarged my snapshot for them and excitedly began to share what I had figured out from a close examination of the photograph. This photograph permitted moving backward and forward as if it were video film, as I elaborated upon what these men had been involved in. The photograph showed that only two men escaped from the fire; the missing man either fell or was murdered by the two men who did escape.

Upon elicitation of my associations to the main elements of this long and elaborate dream, I discerned the following. The fire is the crack epidemic, the men are crack smokers, and the party represents the normal narcissistic indulgences we all pursue. The police who asked for my assistance represented the Smithers Alcoholism Treatment and Training Center in New York City, which had invited me to give three lectures on crack treatment in response to the staff's struggle with an increase in crack patients. The Polaroid snapshot was my view and experience in treating crack patients, which I have elaborated on and analyzed in journal articles and paper presentations. The building suggests the self structure and general life functioning of crack smokers, which are debilitated and in danger of collapse. And in all of our communities across the nation, there are crack smokers lurking in the background, struggling in a burning building, as we typically overlook or fail to see them. Only news reports tell us of recent small fires and deaths resulting from the ongoing crack epidemic.

Yes, another long dream about the book! However, if we further examine this dream and the set of symbols my unconscious offers, we see that we are all going about our business having a good time, while just across the street, no matter where we live, there are individuals trapped by crack addiction. The fires discussed in the news media continually tell us about a crack epidemic increasingly encroaching upon our lives—fueling our incessant social chatter with stories of crack-related murders, crack babies, dead fetuses, child abuse, and the unveiling of secret lives of crack smokers. However, we sometimes forget that what the media depict as "criminals" entangled in the crack war—or ropes depicted in the dream—are actually "human beings" struggling to escape from the collapsing buildings of their crack-ridden lives.

The look on their faces, the fact that they do not really see us, and the fragility of the unstable structure they inhabit reveal how my unconscious dream imagery powerfully conveys the predominance of narcissism observable in the newly abstinent. This imagery perhaps best describes what this book has emphasized—embracing the work of Levin (1987) and Bean-Bayog (1986)—as a fixation or regression to a state of narcissism as a consequence of the trauma of addiction. Many of these surviving soldiers of the crack war suffer varying degrees of narcissistic trauma (Chapters 2 and 3).

We, as a narcissistic culture (Lasch, 1979), are also having a good time on the roofs of luxury high-rise buildings, as we, too, are narcissists utilizing socially acceptable inflation to indulge ourselves with parties, Polaroid cameras, and home videos. The December holidays, for example, underscore the reality of our contemporary self-indulgences and excesses, which come back to haunt us in January. When will the reality of a war being waged in our midst come back to haunt us? The war-torn state of these patients, which reminds me of that of Vietnam veterans, forebodes an answer to this question. What will be the fate of patients who are injured survivors of the contemporary crack war that is being waged daily?

Perhaps even more so than the Vietnam war, the crack war has the potential to affect an even larger segment of our society, beyond just those who stand shell-shocked, fragile, vulnerable, and in need of help. Our youngest and most vulnerable adolescent soldiers returning from the crack war may even develop PTSD, as Pinto from Samaritan Village in New York City observes in his residential TC program. However, to this crack war, we have also sent women.

Many of these women (and men) already met qualifying criteria for or had the potential to develop PTSD symptoms as a consequence of childhood rape and physical abuse; Carroll of Project Return in New York City properly diagnoses these individuals in his TC program as suffering from PTSD. A strength of this book lies in the author's theoretical explanations of these phenomena in Chapter 5, better empowering clinicians to treat them.

In the crack war, it is not another culture's women who are sexually exploited as the spoils of war. It is not Amer-Asian infants who are born as the unfortunate victims of an unfortunate war. In our culture, crack babies of every color languish abandoned in hospitals across the nation, in addition to the cocaine and crack babies who are secretly born in private obstetrics practices. (Chapter 3).

As a society, we can remain like the majority of persons at the party I attended in my dream. Our new obsession with home videos and gazing narcissistically at ourselves in instant Polaroid snapshots, as we have a good time, promises to keep us preoccupied throughout the 1990s. But more and more, the crack war is not just the subject of news stories covering strategy, battle plans, and the death of victims. We can observe crack users all around us—the looks in their eyes and their desperate actions give them away. They sit at desks in corporate America, cruise in cars in New Jersey, ride the subways in New York, hang out on Main Street in Small Town, U.S.A., work on our police forces, and fly our airplanes. They are everywhere, trying with varying degrees of success to keep their secret or denying their crack use.

This book has suggested techniques and strategies that we may be able to utilize with our associates at work, friends, and family who seek, secure, and smoke crack once a month, on payday, during weekends, or on a nearly daily or daily basis. The detailed description of a biopsychosocial theory of crack addiction (Chapters 4–7), a multifaceted clinical technique (Chapters 10, 11, 14), and elaborate relapse-prevention strategies (Chapters 13, 14) are intended to enable treatment practitioners with diverse backgrounds and training to work effectively with crack patients once family, friends, and employers direct them to treatment. Other patients who search desperately for treatment—and have long since lost the support of their family, contact with friends, or jobs—cannot get quality treatment.

However, this book must not merely conclude with the graphic and potent imagery of a dream fresh from the author's unconscious. It must end with a clear, realistic vision of the kind of cost-effective service-delivery system that is absolutely essential if we are to preserve the health of our nation into the 21st century. A comprehensive and intensive service-delivery system must be set in place to address the needs of crack babies, children of dysfunctional crack families, pregnant crack addicts, and the diverse group of adolescent and adult crack smokers.

LIMITATIONS OF THE TREATMENT SAMPLE

What the author has to offer to the development of this treatment agenda can be likened to a snapshot view of crack or cocaine use in America. An excellent critique of my research and perspective involves recognition that I have treated the most severe and debilitated segment of cocaine and crack users who end up in an inpatient hospital setting (Chapter 3). These patients meet the criteria for crack-cocaine dependence, not for the less severe abuse or recreational use.

Many can justly point out that this snapshot view also includes experiences with a majority of African-American patients, and only a small percentage of Hispanic or white patients. A response to this criticism involves the explanation that the African-American population treated was extremely diverse, and included patients with private insurance who earned $30,000–50,000 annually. Although they represented only a small proportion of my patient population, these well-educated, white-collar employees, school teachers, transit workers, and supervisors in the Post Office system had experiences comparable to those of white, middle-class cocaine users. The lower-middle-income, low-income, poor, and welfare recipients among my diverse patient population are comparable to persons in rural communities and urban centers. The case examples in Chapter 7 reveal the diverse kinds of patients the author treated.

Diversity in my sample also is indicated by the various backgrounds of the patients. Some have always lived, as did preceding generations of family members, in New York. Others had migrated, or had parents who had migrated, from the South to northern urban areas, or from Jamaica, Trinidad, Barbados, Haiti, Cuba, Puerto Rico, Panama, and numerous other places. The generalizability of the author's data and experiences to other populations of cocaine and crack users may be significant. However, the limitations in generalizing my sample data and experiences must be recognized.

THE VANTAGE POINT OF A FRONT-LINE TREATMENT PRACTITIONER

An important strength of the book involves the fact that the author has indeed worked in the trenches of one of the most dangerous combat zones of the crack war. Treatment practitioners easily become burned out and move on to other, preferable work environments. Most clinicians still in the trenches are too busy handling casualties to have the time to sit back, write, and conceptualize, as I do, from the safe confines of academia. Thus, the vantage point I provide is crucial in validating what many other seasoned veterans are discovering about crack treatment, as they hone their clinical skills. It was the feedback and encouragement I received when I delivered three presentations at the Smithers Alcoholism Treatment and Training Center (spring 1989) that encouraged me to write this book. Many of these professionals said that I had clearly stated their sense of what works with the chemically dependent in a way that appealed to them. I, therefore, validate, writing from the province of academia (in Harlem actually), the kind of treatment experience and clinical technique that many professionals have developed and are utilizing in the trenches as front-line practitioners. Thus, my views are not only my own, but naturally arise as a perspective for many from the vantage point of committed and sustained work with this population. After all, clinicians ultimately learn from the patients what works and with whom.

ARTICULATION OF AN EFFECTIVE CLINICAL TECHNIQUE

A strength of the book is the articulation of an effective clinical technique developed for use with the most difficult patients presenting the most severe crack addictions. Of potential generalizability to other treatment settings is the fruit of my efforts in trying to figure out how to get beyond the emotionless and driven looks on crack smokers' faces (captured in the dream's Polaroid snapshot) who entered treatment with the hope of escaping their personal crack addiction. I have taken the time to describe, in substantial detail, clinical techniques that effectively transformed detached, aloof crack smokers into people who became emotionally engaged in the treatment process. A modified clinical technique is described that motivates ambivalent crack patients whose psychic functioning is very fragile and in danger of collapse by the time they enter treatment.

The Critical Role of Empathy

Although they appeared hardened and driven by their crack addiction, and utilized defenses to appear arrogant, aloof, and even bragadocious regarding their exploits in battle, they were actually the most fragile and vulnerable of souls needing my empathy and forcing me to further improve my clinical skills. I discovered that empathic mirroring and achieving accurate empathic attunement to their pain, shame, humiliation, and guilt afforded an essential treatment strategy (Chapter 11). The book has sought to prepare others to deploy this same technique with the chemically dependent.

A Multifaceted Clinical Technique

In addition, the book describes in detail other clinical techniques, such as the active provision of education, cognitive reframing, labeling of affective states, and interpretation elucidating the etiological roots of addiction (Chapter 11). Another critical clinical technique that considerably enhances the value of this book to treatment professionals working in individual, group, and family therapy in diverse settings is the use of metaphor. I provide numerous metaphors that others may use as a therapeutic tool (Chapter 14). As one metaphor seemed to be a particularly powerful treatment tool, I then stretched my imagination within group sessions, creating metaphor after metaphor as patients' eyes opened with interest and resistance decreased. These graphic visual metaphors soften patients' defensive stances and help them begin to work on the task of rebuilding their lives and avoiding relapse.

A Unique and Flexible Model of Relapse Prevention

The provision of an arsenal of 29 interventions as a model of relapse prevention considerably enhances the book's utility. These interventions are likely to prove their value with diverse treatment populations, going beyond the bounds of work with the chemically dependent. Those working with drug-free adult children of alcoholics and adult children of other kinds of dysfunctional families may find an effective treatment model in Chapter 14. Professionals working with populations presenting various addictive disorders may also find effective relapse-prevention strategies here. In this way, the book generally succeeds in providing clinical techniques of value in the assessment phase and treatment phase of clinical work not only with the chemically dependent in general, but with any person suffering from childhood trauma. Whether a treatment professional faces a smoker of "ice" or methamphetamine (Bishop, 1989, Sept. 16, pp. 1, 8), a pill popper in suburbia, or a user of the designer chemicals yet to be produced in chemical laboratories and garages, the book provides a biopsychosocial theory and practical clinical techniques applicable to these patients' addictive disorders.

The approach described is also novel in repeatedly emphasizing that our conceptualizations of relapse prevention must be extended to include pharmacological adjuncts (Chapters 4 and 9) and remediation of those underlying psychological and emotional problems the chemically dependent possess (Chapters 3, 5, 14). By remedying those deficits in self-regulatory capacities that may have left patients susceptible to the development of chemical dependency, the risk of relapse to chemical use or engagement in some other destructive compulsive behavior is substantially reduced. The pattern of an addict recovering from one addiction, only to become caught up in another addictive or compulsive behavior, can be avoided.

Patient Responsibility for Long-term Healing

Long-term engagement in the kind of in-depth dynamic psychotherapy that may be necessary (Chapter 8) to reduce the risk of this kind of symptom substitution may immediately impress policymakers and administrators as expensive. However, patients who have received intensive and comprehensive treatment for six to 12 months are likely to return to gainful employment and can take financial responsibility for their own long-term healing. Graduates of TCs who have spent 18–24 months thus may have acquired the skills necessary to qualify them for good jobs for the first time in their lives and they can pay for this treatment. Purchasing individual psychotherapy services represents a kind of insurance against relapse. Employed persons may also use insurance benefits to increase their chances of a successful long-term recovery. Minority communities generally underutilize available insurance, remaining distrustful of the mental-health system and its agents. However, the model of relapse prevention presented in Chapter 14 effectively educates those who are new to the treatment experience to the process and purpose of therapy, preparing patients to enter long-term treatment.

THE NEED FOR A CONTINUUM OF CARE

It pains clinicians to realize that deficits in our service-delivery system—which is plagued by long waiting lists, insufficient treatment slots, and outdated and outmoded treatments not yet sufficiently modified or updated to meet the needs of crack patients—actually contribute to patient relapse. Because of this, some patients literally fall through the cracks and die, as graphically depicted in my dream. But our purpose now is to clarify further the vision of the kind of continuum of care we must establish. Many patients who have access only to swords and shields to protect them as they attempt to recover from their addiction must gain access to the best available treatment weaponry.

This book's review of "What Works?" (Chapter 8) with crack patients in treatment and analysis of "What's Promising?" (Chapter 9) as a treatment modality can serve as a guide to policymakers whose funding of a service-delivery system must be adequate to meet the costs of providing continuity of care. The book has striven to present the kind of clear analysis that should be able to guide policymakers in allocating funding for a cost-effective service-delivery system for crack patients and their infants and children. The continuum of care recommended includes the provision of comprehensive and intensive treatment services in inpatient, outpatient, and residential TC programs.

A strategy whereby treatment professionals engage in a thorough and proper assessment of patients may ascertain their unique and individual treatment needs. The book has spelled out in detail the elements of such an assessment (Chapter 10) and the clinical techniques of value in drawing forth all of the information required to permit matching individual patients to specific treatment modalities. Patient–treatment matching in light of assessment findings permits recognizing the diversity of crack-smoking patterns and the severity of addictions. The book has also explained and described such a treatment-matching process (Chapter 10), representing a cost-effective strategy that should appeal to policymakers and administrators. Careful patient matching, together with utilizing a graded series of interventions, should permit a reduction in costs, in comparison with prevailing and historical practices of recommending the same treatment for everyone. Even with a sample of debilitated inpatients, I have tried to illustrate that they are not a monolithic group and have diverse long-term treatment needs. Many are even resilient and not very narcissistic or suffering much trauma from their addiction. Careful assessment may determine which patients would benefit from attempts to recover on their own or with anonymous self-help groups. Costs of treatment could be substantially reduced by not falling prey to uniformity myths that dictate placing all patients in the same kind of treatment.

Society must better distribute the wealth of treatment weaponry that has been proved effective in the cocaine and crack war, but has been deployed only with more fortunate middle-income patients who have adequate insurance (Chapter 8). The stress and frustration of being a front-line treatment professional and lacking sufficient treatment weapons involve knowing that you release wounded soldiers to negotiate their way through active combat zones without matching them to the treatment they need. Thus, policymakers and program administrators may find in this book a practical and cost-effective approach to treatment of the chemically dependent that resolves these deficits in our service-delivery system.

A SUGGESTION TO POLICYMAKERS

In fact, the crack epidemic provides society with an opportunity to set in place the kind of service-delivery system that was never created in the community mental-health movement of the 1960s. By finally establishing intensive and comprehensive service delivery in response to the immediate, critical needs of crack patients, we may solve the problem created by deinstitutionalization of psychiatric populations in the 1950s and 1960s. Also, the establishment of such a continuum of care within this service-delivery system can assist society with the problems of the homeless, the elderly, and persons with AIDS. The outpatient-treatment facility, hospital ward, or residential TC setting cannot, and will not, become obsolete for lack of potential clients, although the complaints in the 1990s or 21st century may no longer relate to crack addiction but to some unforeseen illness.

The crack epidemic has made us painfully aware of the fact that we lack an adequate service-delivery system. Policymakers can "strike while the iron is hot" and provide for this nation's improved health as we meet the challenges of the next century. Instead of planning the construction of more prisons as the main thrust of our national battle strategy (Weinraub, 1989, Sept. 6, pp. 1, B7), policymakers should establish the kind of health-service system that will insure that crack babies, who are at increased risk for many pathological and negative outcomes—and children of crack parents who are abandoned to foster care—do not end up in jail.

Why not recognize the need to establish the kind of health-service-delivery system that the United States has long needed instead of "proposing that we enlarge our criminal justice system across the board, at the local, state, and Federal level alike" (President Bush, quoted by Weinraub, 1989, Sept. 6, p. B7)? Why triple funding for military and law-enforcement in Colombia, Bolivia, and Peru (Weinraub, 1989, Sept. 6, p. B7) and plan interdiction strategies or destruction of cocaine crops in the Andean region when *America's demand* for chemicals guarantees the growth of clandestine labs (Bishop, 1989, Sept. 16, p. 1) that produce methamphetamine or ice? Why not prevent the likelihood that the smoking of ice will be our drug epidemic of the 1990s by making adequate treatment available to cocaine users or crack smokers whose continuing demand for a chemical high places them at risk for this next possible drug scourge? Only a continuum of care for today's crack smokers promises substantially to decrease America's demand for chemicals tomorrow. Receipt of comprehensive and intensive treatment services can reduce the chances that crack smokers will continue to seek out sources of cocaine, relapse to crack use, or substitute for their crack addiction reliance on some new designer chemical or engagement in other destructive compulsive behaviors. Why not establish for American citizens the health care they need?

It seems wiser to spend money on a service-delivery system that, in the 1990s, can adequately meet the needs of infants who are likely to grow up suffering from crack-induced learning disabilities, developmental delays (Rodning, 1989), and an increased risk of developing chemical dependency themselves. Why not incorporate into our national drug strategy the kind of comprehensive and intensive services needed *now* for pregnant crack addicts, abused and neglected children, first-offending adolescent crack addicts who should not be introduced to prison life, and newly homeless crack smokers, as well as for the diverse range of crack smokers across the nation without access to health care? It seems much less wise to plan prisons just because our present shortsightedness will assure them a plentiful supply of future inhabitants. Indeed, our tendencies to see the casualties of the crack war and devalued groups caught up in personal battles with addiction (women and minorities) as "criminals" blinds us to the realities of their plight, and prevents us from acting humanely.

As our nation mobilizes in the face of the continuing crack war, this book aspires to be of some aid to policymakers, treatment professionals, paraprofessionals, and anyone reaching out to the crack smoker lurking in the background of our Polaroid snapshots or home videos. At some point, we must also discard this "war and battle" metaphor and recognize that our very humanity is at stake—although, as a tool, the metaphor has been useful in trying to get beyond our society's narcissistic defenses. Perhaps we, as a society, can start "really seeing" what must be done today for the sake of our nation's future. Maybe the Polaroid snapshot I carried around for a long time, and which I have elaborated into a vision of a service-delivery system, will be adopted by others when they begin to "see" what should be done at this time of crisis. Although it may seem to be the worst of times, this crisis has the potential for transforming the darkness of the crack epidemic into a golden age of comprehensive and intensive health care for all of the country's citizens. The fires around us can either destroy us or provide the heat and energy that precede transforming a base mineral into bright, shining gold.

References

Ackerman, R. J. (1987). *Same house, different homes: Why adult children of alcoholics are not all the same*. Pompano Beach Fla.: Health Publications.

Ackerman, R. J. (1986). Alcoholism and the family. In R. J. Ackerman (Ed.), *Growing in the shadow: Children of Alcoholics*. Pompano Beach, Fla.: Health Publications.

Alexander, F. M. (1963). *Fundamentals of psychoanalysis*. New York: W. W. Norton.

Allen, M. H., & Frances, R. J. (1986). Varieties of psychopathology found in patients with addictive disorders: A review. In R. E. Meyers (Ed.), *Psychopathology and addictive disorders*. New York: Guilford Press.

Allsop, S., & Saunders, B. (1989). Relapse and alcohol problems. In M. Gossop (Ed.), *Relapse and addictive behavior*. New York: Routledge.

American Psychiatric Association. (1987). *Diagnostic and statistical manual of mental disorders* (rev., 3rd ed.). Washington, D.C.

Anderson, S. E. (1986). Working with black adult children of alcoholics. In R. J. Ackerman (Ed.), *Growing in the shadow: Children of alcoholics*. Pompano Beach, Fla.: Health Publications.

Anker, A. L., & Crowley, T. J. (1982). Use of contingency contracting in specialty clinics for cocaine abuse. In L. S. Harris (Ed.), *Problems of drug dependence 1981* (pp. 452–459). National Institute for Drug Abuse Research Monograph 41. Committee on Problems of Drug Dependence.

Banerjee, S. P., Sharma, V. K., Kung-Cheung, L. S., Chanda, S. K. & Riggi, S. J. (1979). Cocaine and d-amphetamine induce changes in central B-adrenoceptor sensitivity: Effects of acute and chronic drug treatment. *Brain Research. 175*, 119–130.

Baekeland, F., & Lundwall, L. (1975). Dropping out of treatment: A critical review. *Psychological Bulletin, 82*, 738–783.

Barclay-McLaughlin, G. (1989, December). Generations at risk to the nightmare of addiction. Paper presented at the Drug-Free Pregnancy Conference, San Mateo, Calif.

Barker, P. (1985). *Using metaphors in psychotherapy*. New York: Brunner/Mazel.

Bean-Bayog, M. (1986). Psychopathology produced by alcoholism. In R. E. Meyers (Ed.), *Psychopathology and addictive disorders*. New York: Guilford Press.

Berger, D. M. (1987). *Clinical empathy*. New Jersey: Jason Aronson.

Berke, R. L. (1989, August 1). Bennett asks tougher drug fight, declaring crack biggest problem. *The New York Times*, p. A14.

Bernard, G. A., & Wallace, B. C. (1986, August). Cigarette advertising, sales, and role model behavior. *Proceedings of the Division of Consumer Psychology, American Psychological Association.*

Bishop, K. (1989). Fear grows over effects of a new smokable drug. *New York Times*, September, 16, 1-8.

Black, C. (1981). *It will never happen to me: Children of alcoholics as youngsters, adolescents, adults.* Denver, Col.: M.A.C.

Black, C. (1985). *Repeat after me.* Denver, Col.: M.A.C.

Blakey, R., & Baker, R. (1980) An exposure approach to alcohol abuse. *Behavior Research and Therapy*, 18, 319-323.

Blum, K. (1988, May-June). The disease process in alcoholism. *Alcoholism and Addiction*, 1-3.

Blum, K., Allison, D., Trachtenberg, M. C., Williams, R. W., & Loeblich, L. A. (1988). Reduction of both drug hunger and withdrawal against advice rate of cocaine abusers in a 30 day inpatient treatment program by the neuronutrient tropamine. *Current Therapeutic Research*, 43(6), 1204-1214.

Blume, S. B. (1989). Dual diagnosis: Psychoactive substance dependence and the personality disorders. *Journal of Psychoactive Drugs*, 21(2), 139-144.

Borison, R. L., Hitri, A., Klawans, H. L., & Diamond, B. I. (1979). A new animal model for schizophrenia: Behavioral and receptor binding studies. In E. Usdin, I. J. Kopin, & J. Barchas (Eds.), *Catecholamines: basic and clinical frontiers.* New York: Pergamon.

Bratter, T. E., Bratter, E. P., & Heimberg, J. F. (1986). Uses and abuses of power and authority within the American self-help therapeutic community: A perversion or a necessity? In G. DeLeon and J. T. Ziegenfuss (Eds.), *Therapeutic communities for addictions.* Springfield, Ill.: Charles C. Thomas.

Brewington, V. (1989, August). Of Narcotic and Drug Research Inc., New York. Personal communication.

Brown, B. S., Rose, M. R., Weddington, W. W., & Jaffe, J. H. (1989). Kids and cocaine—a treatment dilemma. *Journal of Substance Abuse Treatment*, 6, 3-8.

Brown, S., & Beletsis, S. (1986). The development of family transference in groups for the adult children of alcoholics. *International Journal of Group Psychotherapy*, 36(1), 97-114.

Brown, B. S., Dupont, R. L., & Glendinning, S. T. (1972). Narcotics treatment and behavioral change. In *Proceedings of the Fourth National Conference on Methadone Treatment.* New York: NAPAN.

Bullock, M. L., Umen, A. J., Culliton, M. A., & Olander, R. T. (1987). Acupuncture treatment of alcoholic recidivism: A study pilot. *Alcoholism: Clinical and Experimental Research*, 11(3), 292-295.

Capaldi, E. J. (1967). A sequential hypothesis of instrumental learning. In K. W. Spence and J. T. Spence (Eds.), *The psychology of learning and motivation* (Vol.I). New York: Academic Press.

Carroll, J. F. (1989, August). Director of Project Return, interviewed by author.

Carroll, J. F., & Sobel, B. S. (1986), Integrating mental health personnel and practices into a therapeutic community. In G. DeLeon and J. T. Ziegenfuss (Eds.), *Therapeutic communities for addictions.* Springfield, Ill.: Charles C. Thomas.

Cermak, T. (1988). *A time to heal: The road to recovery for adult children of alcoholics.* J. P. Tarcher.

Cermak, T., & Brown, S. (1982). Interactional group therapy with the adult children of alcoholics. *International Journal of Group Psychotherapy, 32*(3), 375–389.

Chanda, S. K., Sharma, V. K., & Banerjee, S. P. (1979). B-Adrenoreceptor sensitivity following psychotropic drug treatment. In E. Usdin, I. J. Kopin, J. Barchas, (Eds.). *Catecholamines: basic and clinical frontiers.* New York: Pergamon.

Chandler, J. (1989, December). *Chemical dependency treatment for pregnant addicts.* Paper presented at the Drug-Free Pregnancy Conference, San Mateo, Calif.

Chao, C. E. (1989). *Evaluation of the effectiveness of acupuncture on maternal substance abuse clients.* New York City Department of Health Research Training Program. Prepublication copy. Supervised by Michael Smith & Ron Davidson.

Chasnoff, J., Burns, W. J., Schnoll, S. H., & Burns, K. A. (1985). Cocaine use in pregnancy. *New England Journal of Medicine, 313,* 666–669.

Chasnoff, I. J., & Schnoll, S. H. (1987). Consequences of cocaine and other drug use in pregnancy. In A. M. Washton & M. S. Gold (Eds.), *Cocaine: A clinician's handbook* New York: Guilford Press.

Chasnoff, I., & MacGregor, S. (1988). Cocaine in pregnancy: Trimester abuse pattern and perinatal outcome. *Pediatric Research, 4,* 403A.

Chasnoff, I. J., MacGregor, S., Dirkes, K., & Burns, K. (1989). Temporal patterns in cocaine use in pregnancy. *Journal of the American Medical Association, 261,* 1741–1744.

Childress, A., Ehrman, R., McLellan, A. T., & O'Brien, C. (1988a). Conditioned craving and arousal in cocaine addiction: A preliminary report. In L. S. Harris (Ed.), *Problems of drug dependence, 1987.* Proceedings of the 49th Annual Scientific Meeting, Committee on Problems of Drug Dependence. NIDA Research Monograph 81, National Institute on Drug Abuse, Rockville, Md.

Childress, A. R., McLellan, A. T., Ehrman, R., & O'Brien, C. P. (1988b). Classically conditioned responses in opioid and cocaine dependence: A role in relapse? In B. A. Ray (Ed.), *Learning factors in substance abuse.* NIDA Research Monograph 84. National Institute on Drug Abuse, Rockville, Md. Superintendent of Documents, U.S. Government Printing Office, Washington, D.C.

Cinque, J. (1986). Personal communication, Interfaith Medical Center, Brooklyn, N.Y.

Cinque, J., & Elberth, M. (1986). Personal communication, Interfaith Medical Center, Brooklyn, N.Y.

Clayton, R. R. (1985). Cocaine use in the United States: In a blizzard or just being snowed? In N. J. Kozel & E. H. Adams (Eds.), *Cocaine Use In America: Epidemiological & Clinical Perspectives.* NIDA Research Monograph 61. National Institute on Drub Abuse, Rockville, Md. Superintendent of Documents, U.S. Government Printing Office, Washington, D.C.

Cloninger, C. R. (1983). Genetic and environmental factors in the development of alcoholism. *Journal of Psychiatric Treatment and Evaluation, 5,* 487–496.

Cohen, S. (1987). Causes of the cocaine outbreak. In A. Washton and M. Gold (Eds.), *Cocaine: A clinician's handbook* (pp. 3–9). New York: Guilford Press.

Cregler, L. L., & Mark, H., Medical complications of cocaine abuse. *New England Journal of Medicine, 315,* 1495–1500.

Crowley, T. (1982, August 2). (Quoted in) Reinforcing drug free lifestyles, *ADAMHA News,* p. 2.

Curry, S., Marlatt, G. A., Peterson, A. V., & Lutton, J. (1988) Survival analysis and assessment of relapse rates. In D. M. Donovan and G. A. Marlatt (Eds.), *Assessment of addictive behaviors.* New York: Guilford Press.

Cutter, C. G., & Cutter, H. S. (1987). Experience and change in Al-Anon family groups: Adult children of alcoholics, *Journal of Studies on Alcohol, 48*(1), 29–32.

Daigle, R. D., Clark, W., & Landry, M. J. (1988). A primer on neurotransmitters and cocaine. *Journal of Psychoactive Drugs, 20*(3), 283-295.

DeLeon, G. (1986a). Therapeutic community research: Overview and implications. In G. DeLeon and J. T. Ziegenfuss (Eds.), Springfield, *Therapeutic communities for addictions.* Springfield, Ill: Charles C. Thomas.

DeLeon, G. (1986b). The therapeutic community: Looking ahead. In G. DeLeon and J. T. Ziegenfuss (Eds.), *Therapeutic communities for addictions.* Springfield, Ill: Charles C. Thomas.

DeLeon, G. (1988). The therapeutic community and behavioral science. NIDA Research Monograph 84, National Institute on Drug Abuse, Rockville, Md. Superintendent of Documents, U.S. Government Printing office, Washington, D.C.

DeLeon, G. (1989). Psychopathology and substance abuse: What is being learned from research in therapeutic communities? *Journal of Psychoactive Drugs, 21*(2), 177-188.

Donovan, D. M. (1988). Assessment of addictive behaviors: Implications of an emerging biopsychosocial model. In D. M. Donovan and G. A. Marlatt (Eds.), *Assessment of addictive behaviors.* New York: Guilford Press.

Donovan, D. M., & Chaney, E. F. (1985). Alcoholic relapse prevention and intervention: Models and methods. In G. A. Marlatt and J. R. Gordon (Eds.), *Relapse prevention.* New York: Guilford Press.

Donovan, D. M., & Marlatt, G. A. (Eds.). (1988). *Assessment of addictive behaviors.* New York: Guilford Press.

Dougherty, R. J., & Lesswing, N. J. (1989). Inpatient cocaine abusers: An analysis of psychological and demographic variables. *Journal of Substance Abuse Treatment, 6,* 45-47.

Downing, N. E., & Walker, M. E. (1987). A psychoeducational group for adult children of alcoholics. *Journal of Counseling and Development, 65*(8), 440-442.

Ellis, A. (1985). *Overcoming resistance: Rational-emotive therapy with difficult clients.* New York: Springer.

Ellis, A., & Dryden, W. (1987). *The practice of rational-emotive therapy.* New York: Springer.

Ellis, A., McInerney, M., DiGiuseppe, R., & Yeager, R. J. (1989). *Rational-emotive therapy with alcoholics and substance abusers.* Elmsford, N.Y.: Pergamon Press.

Elmer-DeWitt, P. (1989, November 6). A plague without boundaries. *Time,* pp. 95, 98.

Extein, I., & Dackis, C. A. (1987). Brain mechanisms in cocaine dependency. In A. Washton and M. Gold (Eds.), *Cocaine: A clinician's handbook* (pp. 73-84). New York: Guilford Press.

Fanon, F. (1967). *Black skin, white masks.* New York: Grove Press.

Flanzer, J. P. (1986). Double trouble: Alcoholism and family violence. In R. J. Ackerman (Ed.), *Growing in the shadow: Children of alcoholics.* Pompano Beach, Fla.: Health Publications.

Freud, S. (1974). *Cocaine papers.* Edited by R. Byck. N.Y.: Stonehill.

French, H. W. (1989, September 29). For pregnant addicts, a clinic of hope. *The New York Times,* pp. B1-B2.

Freitag, M. (1989, December 12). Hospital defends limiting of drug problem. *The New York Times,* p. B9.

Gawin, F. (1989, October). Treatment of crack and cocaine abusers. Paper presented at the "What Works" Conference, New York, N.Y.

Gawin, F. H., & Kleber, H. D. (1984). The spectrum of cocaine abuse and its treatment. *Journal of Clinical Psychiatry, 45,* 18-23.

Gawin, F. H., & Kleber, H. D. (1986). Abstinence symptomatology and psychiatric diagnosis in cocaine abusers. *Archives of General Psychiatry, 43*(2), 107-113.

Geary, N. (1987). Cocaine: Animal research studies. In H. I. Spitz & J. S. Rosecan (Eds.), *Cocaine abuse: New directions in treatment and research.* New York: Brunner/Mazel, Inc.

Giovacchini, P. L. (1989). *Countertransference triumphs and catastrophes.* New York: Jason Aronson.

Gold, M. S. (1984). *800-cocaine,* New York: Bantam Books.

Gold, M. S., Pottash, A. L. C., Annito, W. J., Verebey, K., & Sweeney, D. R. (1983). Cocaine withdrawal: Efficacy of tyrosine. *Society for Neuroscience Abstracts, 9,* 157.

Gold, M. S., Washton, A. M., & Dackis, C. A. (1985). Cocaine abuse: Neurochemistry, phenomenology, and treatment. In N. J. Kozel and E. H. Adams (Eds.), *Cocaine use in America: Epidemiological and clinical perspectives.* NIDA Research Monograph 61. National Institute on Drug Abuse, Rockville, Md. Superintendent of Documents, U.S. Government Printing Office, Washington, D.C.

Goodwin, D. W. (1976). *Is alcoholism hereditary?* New York: Oxford University Press.

Goodwin, D. W. (1979). Alcoholism and heredity: A review and hypothesis. *Archives of General Psychiatry, 36,* 57–61.

Goodwin, D. W., Schulsinger, F., Hermansen, L., Guze, S. B., & Winokur, G. (1973). Alcohol problems in adoptees raised apart from alcoholic biological parents. *Archives of General Psychiatry, 28,* 283–243.

Gordon, D. 1978 *Therapeutic metaphors: Helping others through the looking glass.* Cupertino, Calif.: Meta Publications.

Gorski, T. (1988a). *The staying sober workbook: A serious solution for the problem of relapse* (instruction manual). Independence, Mo.: Herald House/Independence Press.

Gorski, T. (1988b). *The staying sober workbook: A serious solution for the problem of relapse* (exercise manual). Independence, Mo.: Herald House/Independence Press.

Gorski, T., & Miller, M. (1984). *The phases and warning signs of relapse.* Independence, Mo: Herald House/Independence Press.

Gorski, T., & Miller, M. (1986). *Staying sober: A guide for relapse prevention.* Independence, Mo.: Herald House/Independence Press.

Gravitz, H. L., & Bowden, J. D. (1986). Therapeutic issues of adult children of alcoholics: A continuum of developmental stages. In R. J. Ackerman (Ed.), *Growing in the shadow: Children of alcoholics.* Pompano Beach, Fla.: Health Communications.

Grier, W. H., & Cobbs, P. M. (1989). *Black Rage.* New York: Basic Books.

Grinspoon, L., & Bakalar, J. B. (1985). *Cocaine: A drug and its social evolution.* New York: Basic Books.

Gross, J. (1989, August 6). Urban emergency rooms: An urban nightmare. *The New York Times.*, pp. L1, L20.

Haley, J. (1980). *Leaving home.* New York: McGraw-Hill.

Halfon, N. (1989, December). Intervention, treatment, and policy. Paper presented at the Drug-Free Pregnancy Conference, San Mateo, Calif.

Hamilton, N. G. (1988). *Self and others: Object relations theory in practice.* Northvale, N.J.: Jason Aronson.

Harris-Offutt, R. (1986). Personal communication.

Heather, N., & Stallard, A. (1989). Does the Marlatt model underestimate the importance of conditioned craving in the relapse process? In M. Gossop (Ed.). *Relapse and addictive behavior.* New York: Routledge.

Herridge, P., & Gold, M. (1988). Pharmacological adjuncts in the treatment of opioid and cocaine addicts. *Journal of Psychoactive Drugs, 20*(3), 233–242.

Hesselbrock, V. M. (1986a). Family history of psychopathology in alcoholics: A review and issues. In R. E. Meyers (Ed.), *Psychopathology and addictive disorders.* New York: Guilford Press.

Hesselbrock, V. M. (1986b). Childhood behavior problems and adult antisocial personality disorder in alcoholism. In R. E. Meyers (Ed.), *Psychopathology and addictive disorders*. New York: Guilford Press.

Holmes, S. A. (1989, January 24). A dealer finds many eager to launder his drug money. *The New York Times*, pp. 1, B4.

Hopkins, W. (1989, April). Street perspectives on drug abuse. Paper presented at a Conference on Substance Abuse Prevention, John Jay College of Criminal Justice, New York, N.Y.

Inciardi, J. A. (1987). Beyond cocaine: Basuco, crack, and other coca products. *Contemporary Drug Problems*. Fall 1987, pp. 461–492.

Inciardi, J. A. (1990). Trading sex for crack among juvenile drug users: A research note. *Contemporary Drug Problems*.

Inciardi, J. A., & Pottieger, A. E. (1990). Kids, crack, and crime. In press.

Jaffe, J. H., & Ciraulo, D. A., (1986). Alcoholism and depression. In R. E. Meyers (Ed.), *Psychopathology and addictive disorders*. New York: Guilford Press.

Johanson, C. E. (1984). Assessment of the dependence potential of cocaine in animals. In J. Grabowski (Ed.), *Cocaine: Pharmacology, effects, and treatment of abuse*. NIDA Research Monograph 50, Department of Health and Human Services. U.S. Government Printing Office, Washington, D.C.

Johnson, J. (1989, December 13). Dinkins, at Senate hearing, says drugs are overrunning New York. *The New York Times*, p. B10.

Johnson, J. (1989, August 4). Drug gangs and drug wars move into the rural states, U.S. warns. *The New York Times*, pp. A1, A10.

Jones, R. L. (Ed.). (1980). *Black psychology* (2nd ed.). New York: Harper & Row.

Jones, R. T. (1984). *The pharmacology of cocaine*.

Jones, R. T. (1987). Pharmacology of cocaine. In A. Washton & M. Gold (Eds.), *Cocaine: A clinician's handbook* (pp. 55–72). New York: Guilford Press.

Jung, C. G. (1969). *The structure and dynamics of the psyche* (2nd ed.). Princeton, N.J.: Princeton University Press.

Kalish, H. I. (1981). *From behavioral science to behavioral modification*. New York: McGraw-Hill.

Kernberg, O. (1975). *Borderline conditions and pathological narcissism*. New York: Jason Aronson.

Kernberg, O. (1976). *Object relations theory and clinical psychoanalysis*. New York: Jason Aronson.

Kernberg, O. (1986). *Severe personality disorders: Psychotherapeutic strategies*. New Haven, Conn.: Yale University Press.

Kerr, D. H. (1986). The therapeutic community: A codified concept for training and upgrading staff members working in a residential setting. In G. DeLeon and J. T. Ziegenfuss (Eds.), *Therapeutic communities for addictions*. Springfield, Ill.: Charles C. Thomas.

Kerr, P. (1988, September 30). Acupuncture seems to ease crack addiction, study says. *The New York Times*, p. B1, B4.

Kertzner, R. M. (1987). Individual psychotherapy of cocaine abuse. In H. I. Spitz and J. S. Rosecan. (Eds.), *Cocaine abuse: New directions in treatment and research*. New York: Brunner/Mazel.

Khantzian, E. J. (1985). On the psychological predisposition for opiate and stimulant dependence. *Psychiatry Letter, III*, 1.

Khantzian, E. J. (1987). Psychiatric and psychodynamic factors in cocaine dependence. In A. M. Washton and M. S. Gold (Eds.), *Cocaine: A clinician's handbook*. New York: Guilford Press.

Khantzian, E. J., Gawin, F., Kleber, H., & Riordan, C. (1984). Methylphenidate (Ritalin) treatment of cocaine dependence—a preliminary report. *Journal of Substance Abuse Treatment, 1,* 107–112.

Kleber, H. (1988). Epidemic cocaine abuse: America's present, Britain's future? *British Journal of Addiction, 83,* 1359–1371.

Kleber, H. D., & Gawin, F. H. (1984a). Cocaine abuse: A review of current and experimental treatments. In J. Grabowski (Ed.), *Cocaine: Pharmacology, effects, and treatment of abuse.* NIDA Research Monograph 50, Department of Health and Human Services. U.S. Government Printing Office, Washington, D.C.

Kleber, H. D., & Gawin, F. H. (1984b). The spectrum of cocaine abuse and its treatment. *Journal of Clinical Psychiatry, 45.* 18–23.

Kleinman, P. H., Kang, S. Y., Lipton, D., Woody, G., & Kemp, J. (1989). Retention of cocaine abusers in outpatient psychotherapy (unpublished paper).

Kleinman, P. H., Miller, A. B., Millman, R. B., Woody, G. E., Todd, T., Kemp, J., & Lipton, D. S. (1990). Psychopathology among cocaine abusers entering treatment. *Journal of Nervous and Mental Disease.* In press.

Kleinman, P. H., & Lukoff, I. F. (1980). The life cycle of treated heroin addicts. *Find report of the project on the life cycle of treated heroin addicts.* Unpublished report to the National Institute on Drug Abuse.

Kleinman, P. H., Woody, G. E., Todd, T., Millman, R. B., Yang, S. Y., Kemp, J., & Lipton, D. (1990). *Crack and cocaine abusers in outpatient psychotherapy.* (to appear in upcoming NIDA monograph)

Kohut, H. (1971). *The analysis of the self: A systematic approach to the psychoanalytic treatment of narcissistic personality disturbance.* New York: International Universities Press.

Kohut, H. (1977). *The restoration of the self.* New York: International Universities Press.

Kolata, G. (1989, August 11). In cities, poor families dying of crack. *The New York Times,* pp. A1, A13.

Kolata, G. (1989, August 24). Experts finding new hope on treating crack addicts. *The New York Times,* pp. A1, B7.

Kolata, G. (1989, November 26). Despite its promise of riches, the crack trade seldom pays. *The New York Times,* pp. A1, A42.

Kooyman, M. (1986). The psychodynamics of therapeutic communities for treatment of heroin addicts. In G. DeLeon and J. T. Ziegenfuss (Eds.), *Therapeutic communities for addictions,* Springfield, Ill.: Charles C. Thomas.

Kronstadt, D. (1989, March). Pregnancy and cocaine addiction: An overview of impact and treatment. Report presented at the Drug-Free Pregnancy Project, Far West Laboratory for Educational Research and Development, San Francisco, Calif.

Lasch, C. (1979) *The culture of narcissism.* New York: Warner.

Lazarus, A. A. (1971). *Behavior therapy and beyond.* New York: McGraw-Hill.

Levin, J. D. (1987). *Treatment of alcoholism and other addictions: A self-psychology approach.* New Jersey: Jason Aronson.

Louie, A. K., Lannon, R. A., & Ketter, T. A., (1989). Treatment of cocaine-induced panic disorder. *American Journal of Psychiatry, 146*(1), 40–44.

Luborsky, L., Woody, G. E., Hole, A., et al. (1977). *Treatment manual for supportive-expressive psychoanalytically oriented psychotherapy* (unpublished manuscript).

Maisto, S. A., and Connors, G. J. (1988). Assessment of treatment outcome. In D. M. Donovan and G. A. Marlatt (Eds.), *Assessment of addictive behaviors.* New York: Guilford Press.

Malcolm, A. H. (1989, October 1). Crack, bane of inner city, is now gripping suburbs. *The New York Times.* pp. A1, A24.

Malcolm, A. H. (1989, October 2). Affluent addicts' road back begins in a climb past denial. *The New York Times*, pp. A1, B10.

Malcolm, A. H. (1989, December 30). Explosive drug use creating new underworld in prisons. *New York Times*, pp. 1, 12.

Marlatt, G. A. (1980). Determinants of relapse: Implications for the maintenance of behavior change. In P. O. Davidson and S. M. Davidson (Eds.), *Behavioral medicine: Changing health lifestyles*. New York: Brunner/Mazel.

Marlatt, G. A. (1982). Relapse prevention: A self-control program for the treatment of addictive behaviors. In R. B. Stuart (Ed.), *Adherence, compliance, and generalization in behavioral medicine*. New York: Brunner/Mazel.

Marlatt, G. A. (1985). Relapse prevention: Theoretical rationale and overview of the model. In G. A. Marlatt and J. R. Gordon (Eds.), *Relapse prevention*. New York: Guilford Press.

Marlatt, G. A. (1988). Matching client to treatment: Treatment models and stages of change. In D. M. Donovan & G. A. Marlatt (Eds.), *Assessment of addictive behaviors*. New York: Guilford Press.

Marlatt, G. A., Curry, S., & Gordon, J. R. (1986). A comparison of treatment approaches in smoking cessation (unpublished manuscript).

Marlatt, G. A., & Gordon, J. R. (1985). *Relapse prevention*, New York: Guilford Press.

Marlatt, G. A., & Gordon, J. (1989). Relapse prevention: Future directions. In M. Gossop (Ed.), *Relapse and addictive behavior*. New York: Routledge.

Marriot, M. (1989, October 22). Struggle and hope from ashes of drugs. *The New York Times*, pp. A1, A36.

Martinez, J. (1989). In *Outlook on substance abuse in New York State* (Vol. 10, No. 2). New York State Division of Substance Abuse Services, Executive Park South, Albany, N.Y.

McCrady, B. S., Dean, L., Dubreuil, E., & Swanson, S. (1985). The problem drinkers' project: A programmatic application of social-learning based treatment. In G. A. Marlatt and J. R. Gordon (Eds.), *Relapse Prevention*. New York: Guilford Press.

McLellan, A. T. (1986). "Psychiatric severity" as a predictor of outcome from substance abuse treatments. In R. E. Meyers (Ed.), *Psychopathology and addictive disorders*. New York: Guilford Press.

Meichenbaum, D. (1985). *Stress-inoculation training*. New York: Pergamon Press.

Meyer, R. E. (1986). How to understand the relationship between psychopathology and addictive disorders: Another example of the chicken and the egg. In R. E. Meyer (Ed.), *Psychopathology and addictive disorders*. New York: Guilford Press.

Meyersburg, H. A., & Post, R. M. (1979). An holistic developmental view of neural and psychological processes: A neurobiologic-psychoanalytic integration. *British Journal of Psychiatry*, 135, 139–155.

Miller, N. S. (1987). A blood marker for pharmacodynamic tolerance to alcohol. *Journal of Substance Abuse Treatment*, 4, 93–102.

Miller, W. R. (1983). Motivational interviewing with problem drinkers. *Behavioural Psychotherapy*, 11, 147–172.

Miller, W. R. (1985). Motivation for treatment: A review with special emphasis on alcoholism. *Psychological Bulletin*, 98, 84–107.

Miller, W. R., & Pechacek, T. F. (1987). New roads: Assessing and treating psychological dependence. *Journal of Substance Abuse Treatment*, 4, 73–77.

Mirin, S. M., & Weiss, R. S. (1988). *Character pathology in substance abusers*. Paper presented at the American Psychiatric Association Annual Meeting, Montreal.

Mirin, S. M., Weiss, R. D., & Michael, J. (1986). Family pedigree of psychopathology in substance abusers. In R. E. Meyers (Ed.), *Psychopathology and addictive disorders*. New York: Guilford Press.

Morehouse, E. R. (1987). Treating adolescent cocaine abusers. In A. M. Washton and M. S. Gold (Eds.), *Cocaine: A clinician's handbook*. New York: Guilford Press.

Morgan, C., Kosten, T., Gawin, F., & Kleber, H. (1988). A pilot trial of amantadine for ambulatory withdrawal for cocaine dependence. NIDA Research Monograph 381. Rockville, Md.: NIDA.

Murphy, S. B., Reinarman, C., & Waldorf, D. (1989). An 11-year follow-up of a network of cocaine users. *British Journal of Addiction, 84*, 427–436.

New York Times, August 1, 1989. Casual drug use is sharply down. p. A14.

New York Times, August 7, 1989. Crack's smallest, costliest victims, p. A14.

New York Times, May 15, 1990. Medical emergencies for addicts are said to have dropped by 20%. p. A20.

New York Times, November 12, 1989. Rise in drug arrests is reported in New York. p. 46.

Nobles, W. W. (1980). African philosophy: Foundations for black psychology. In R. L. Jones (Ed.), *Black psychology* (2nd ed.). New York: Harper & Row.

Nunes, E. V., & Rosecan, J. S. (1987). Human neurobiology of cocaine. In H. I. Spitz and J. J. Rosecan (Eds.), *Cocaine abuse: New directions in treatment and research*. New York: Brunner/Mazel.

O'Brien, C., Childress, A., McLellan, A., Ehrman, R., & Ternes, J. (1988). Progress in understanding the conditioning aspects of drug dependence. NIDA Research Monograph 81. Rockville, Md.: NIDA.

O'Brien, C. P. (1976). Experimental analysis of conditioning factors in human narcotic addiction. *Pharmacology Review, 227*, 533–543.

O'Brien, C. P., Nace, E. P., Mintz, J., Meyers, A. L., & Ream, N. (1980). Follow-up of Vietnam veterans. 1. Relapse to drug use after Vietnam service. *Drug and Alcohol Dependence, 5*, 333–340.

Othmer, E., & Othmer, S. C. (1989). The clinical interview using DSM-III-R. Washington, D. C.: American Psychiatric Press.

Pavlov, I. P. (1927). *Conditioned reflexes* (G. V. Anrep, trans.). London: Oxford University Press.

Peele, S. (Ed.). (1985). *The meaning of addiction: A compulsive experience and its interpretation*. Lexington, Mass.: Lexington Books.

Rainone, G., Kott, A., & Maranda, M. (1988). Crack clients in treatment: Drug free residential programs. *Treatment Issues Report No. 64*, New York State Division of Substance Abuse Services, Bureau of Research and Evaluation.

Rawson, R. (1989, October). Treatment of crack and cocaine abusers. Paper presented at the Conference on "What Works: An International Perspective on Drug Abuse Treatment and Prevention Research," New York, N.Y.

Rawson, R. (1990, Winter). Cut the crack: The policymaker's guide to cocaine treatment. *Policy Review*, 10–19.

Rawson, R. A., Obert, J. L., McCann, M. J., & Mann, A. J. (1986). Cocaine treatment outcome: Cocaine use following inpatient, outpatient, and no treatment. NIDA Research Monograph 67. Rockville, Md: NIDA.

Rawson, R. A., Obert, J. L., McCann, M. J., Smith, M. S., & Ling, W. (1990). Neurobehavioral treatment for cocaine dependency. *Journal of Psycoactive Drugs* Vol. 22, No. 2.

Resnick, R. B., & Resnick, E. (1986). Psychological issues in the treatment of cocaine abuse. NIDA Research Monograph 67. Rockville, Md.: NIDA.

Rinsley, D. B. (1989). *Developmental pathogenesis and treatment of borderline and narcissistic personalities.* New Jersey: Jason Aronson.

Robins, L. N., Helzer, J. E., & Davis, D. H. (1975). Narcotic use in Southeast Asia and afterwards. *Archives of General Psychiatry, 32,* 955–961.

Rodning, C. (1989, December). The impact of drug exposure on the development of infants and toddlers. Paper presented at the Drug-Free Pregnancy Conference, San Mateo, Calif.

Rohsenow, D. J., Corbett, R., & Devine, D. (1988). Molested as children: A hidden contribution to substance abuse? *Journal of Substance Abuse Treatment, 5,* 13–18.

Rosecan, J. (1983, July). The treatment of cocaine abuse with imipramine, L-tyrosine, and L-tryptophan. Paper presented at the Seventh World Conference of Psychiatry. Vienna, Austria.

Rosecan, J. J., & Nunes, E. V. (1987). Psychopharmacological management of cocaine abuse. In H. I. Spitz and J. J. Rosecan (Eds.), *Cocaine abuse: New directions in treatment and research.* New York: Brunner/Mazel.

Rosecan, J. J., & Spitz, H. I. (Eds.). (1987). *Cocaine abuse: New directions in treatment and research,* New York: Brunner/Mazel.

Rosecan, J. J., Spitz, H. I., & Gross, B. (1987). Contemporary issues in the treatment of cocaine abuse. In H. I. Spitz and J. J. Rosecan (Eds.), *Cocaine abuse: New directions in treatment and research.* New York: Bruner/Mazel.

Rosen, S. (1982). *My voice will go with you: The teaching tales of Milton H. Erikson.* New York: W. W. Norton.

Roffman, R. A., & George, W. H. (1988). Cannabis abuse. In D. M. Donovan and G. A. Marlatt (Eds.), *Assessment of addictive behaviors.* New York: Guilford Press.

Rowe, C. E., & MacIsaac, D. S. (1989). *Empathic attunement: The technique of psychoanalytic self psychology.* New York: Jason Aronson.

Scheintaub, I. (1990, January). Executive director of Damon House, Brooklyn, N.Y.

Schiffer, F. (1988). Psychotherapy of nine successfully treated cocaine abusers: Techniques and dynamics. *Journal of Substance Abuse Treatment, 5,* 131–137.

Schwabb, E. (1989, August). Personal Communication.

Schwartz, G. E. (1982). Testing the biopsychosocial model: The ultimate challenge facing behavioral medicine. *Journal of Consulting and Clinical Psychology, 50,* 1040–1053.

Seixas, J., & Levitan, M. (1984). A supportive counseling group for adult children of alcoholics. *Alcoholism Treatment Quarterly, 1*(4), 123–132.

Shaffer, H. J. (1987). The epistemology of "addictive disease": The Lincoln–Douglas debate. *Journal of Substance Abuse Treatment, 4,* 103–113.

Shiffman, S. (1989). Conceptual issues in the study of relapse. In M. Gossop (Ed.), *Relapse and addictive behavior.* New York: Routledge.

Shore, M. F. (1989). The perversion of research and the paralysis of action. *American Journal of Orthopsychiatry, 59,* 482.

Siegel, R. K. (1984). Changing patterns of cocaine use: Longitudinal observations, consequences, and treatment. In J. Grabowski (Ed.), *Cocaine: Pharmacology, effects, and treatment of abuse.* NIDA Research Monograph 50, Department of Health and Human Services. U.S. Government Printing Office, Washington, D.C.

Siegel, R. K. (1985). New patterns of cocaine use: Changing doses and routes. In N. J. Kozel and E. H. Adams (Eds.), *Cocaine use in America: Epidemiologic and clinical perspectives.* (pp. 204–220). NIDA Research Monograph 61. U.S. Government Printing Office, Washington, D.C.

Siegel, R. K. (1987). Cocaine smoking: Nature and extent of coca paste and cocaine free-base abuse. In A. M. Washton and M. S. Gold (Eds.), *Cocaine: A clinicians' Handbook*. New York: Guilford Press.

Siegel, S. (1984). Pavlovian conditioning and heroin overdose: Reports by overdose victims. *Bulletin of the Psychonomic Society, 49*, 688–693.

Siegel, S. (1988). Drug anticipation and the treatment of dependence. In B. A. Ray (Ed.), *Learning factors in substance abuse*. NIDA Research Monograph 84, National Institute on Drug Abuse, Rockville, Md. Superintendent of Documents, U.S. Government Printing Office, Washington, D.C.

Siegel, S., & Ellsworth, D. W. (1986). Pavlovian conditioning and death from apparent overdose in medically prescribed morphine: A case report: *Bulletin of the Psychonomic Society, 24*, 278–280.

Skinner, B. F. (1953) *Science and human behavior*. New York: Macmillan.

Skinner, B. F. (1961). Cumulative record (3rd. ed.). Englewood Cliffs, NJ: Prentice-Hall.

Skodel, A. E. (1987). Diagnostic issues in cocaine abuse. In H. I. Spitz and J. J. Rosecran (Eds.), *Cocaine abuse: New directions in treatment and research*. New York: Brunner/Mazel.

Smith, D. E., & Wesson, D. R. (1985). Cocaine abuse and treatment: An overview. In D. E. Smith and D. R. Wesson, (Eds.), *Treating the cocaine abuser*. Center City, MN: Hazeldon Foundation.

Smith, M. (1989a, July 25). The Lincoln Hospital acupuncture drug abuse program. Testimony presented to the Select Committee on Narcotics of the House of Representatives.

Smith, M. (1989b, August). Interview by author at Lincoln Hospital Acupuncture Clinic, South Bronx, N.Y.

Spitz, H. I. (1987). Cocaine abuse: Therapeutic group approaches. In H. I. Spitz and J. J. Rosecan (Eds.), *Cocaine abuse: New directions in treatment and research*. New York: Brunner/Mazel.

Spitz, H. I., & Rosecan, J. J. (1987). Overview of cocaine abuse treatment. In H. I. Spitz and J. J. Rosecan, (Eds.), *Cocaine abuse: New directions in treatment and research*, New York: Brunner/Mazel.

Spitz, H. I., & Spitz, S. T. (1987). Family therapy of cocaine abuse. In H. I. Spitz and J. J. Rosecan (Eds.), *Cocaine abuse: New directions in treatment and research*. New York: Brunner/Mazel.

Spitzer, R., & Gibbon, M. (1987). *Instruction manual for the Structural Clinical Interview for DSM-III-R (SCID4/1/87 revision.)* NY, NY: New York State Psychiatric Institute.

Stanton, M. D., Todd, T. C., et al. (1982). *The family therapy of drug abuse and addiction*. New York: Guilford Press.

Steinglass, P., Bennett, L. A., Wolin, S. J., & Reiss, D. (1987). *The alcoholic family*. New York: Basic Books.

Stoffelmayr, B. E., Benishek, L. A., Humphreys, K., Lee, J. A., & Mavis, B. E. (1989). Substance Abuse prognosis with an additional psychiatric diagnosis: Understanding the relationship. *Journal of Psychoactive Drugs, 21*(2) 145–152.

Stone, N., Fromme, M., & Kagan, D. (1984). *Cocaine: Seduction and solution*. New York: Potter.

Sugarman, B. (1986). Structure, variations, and context: A sociological view of the therapeutic community. In G. DeLeon and J. T. Ziegenfuss (Eds.), *Therapeutic communities for addictions*. Springfield, Ill.: Charles C. Thomas.

Taylor, D. L., Ho, B. T., & Fagen, J. D. (1979). Increased dopamine receptor binding in rat brain by repeated cocaine injections. *Communications in Psychopharmacology, 3*, 81: 317.

Tennant, F. S., & Rawson, R. A. (1983). Cocaine and amphetamine dependence treated with desipramine. In L. S. Harris (Ed.)., *Problems of drug dependence, 1982.* NIDA Research Monograph 43. Rockville, Md.: NIDA.

Tennant, F. S., Rawson, R. A., & McCann, M. A. (1981). Withdrawal from chronic phencyclidine (PCP) dependence with desipramine. *American Journal of Psychiatry,* *138,* 845–847.

Tennant, F. S., & Sagheran, A. H. (1987). Double-blind comparison of amantadine and bromocriptine for ambulatory withdrawal from cocaine dependence. *Archives of Internal Medicine, 147,* 109–112.

Tennant, F., & Tarver, A. (1987). Stepwise withdrawal from cocaine dependence outcome of 106 consecutive cases. NIDA Research Monograph 81. Rockville Md.: NIDA.

Tennant, F. S., Tarver, A., & Seecof, R. (1986). Cocaine plasma concentrations in persons admitted to outpatient treatment: Relationship to treatment outcome. *Journal of Substance Abuse Treatment, 3,* 27–32.

Ternes, J. W. (1977). An opponent process theory of habitual behavior with special reference to smoking. In M. E. Jarvik and J. W. Cullen (Eds.), *Smoking behavior* (pp. 157–182). National Institute on Drug Abuse Research Monograph 17. DHEW Pub. No. (ADM) 78-581. Superintendent, of Documents, U.S. Government Print Office Washington, D.C..

Thomas, M. (1989, December). The Mandela House program: Testimonies From recovering mothers. Paper presented at the Drug-Free Pregnancy Conference, San Mateo, Calif.

Todd, T. (1989, October). Treatment of crack and cocaine abusers. Paper presented at the Conference on "What Works: An International Perspective on Drug Abuse Treatment and Prevention Research," New York, N.Y.

Todd, T.C., Stanton, M. D. & Carway, J. (1988). A manual for structural family therapy, unpublished manuscript.

Trachtenberg, M. C., & Blum, K. (1988). Improvement of cocaine-induced neuromodulator deficits by the neuronutrient tropamine. *Journal of Psychoactive Drugs, 20(3),* 315–331.

Tuchfeld, B. S. (1986). Adult children of alcoholics. *Hospital and Community Psychiatry,* *37(3),* 235–236.

Walker, B. (1988). Odyssey House, Inc., of New York. *Journal of Substance Abuse Treatment, 5,* 113–115.

Wallace, B. C. (1987). Cocaine dependence treatment on an inpatient detoxification unit. *Journal of Substance Abuse Treatment, 4,* 85–92.

Wallace, B. C. (1989a). Psychological and environmental determinants of relapse in crack cocaine smokers. *Journal of Substance Abuse Treatment, 6(2).* 95–106.

Wallace, B. C. (1989b). Relapse prevention in psychoeducational groups for crack cocaine smokers. *Journal of Substance Abuse Treatment, 6(4)* 229–239.

Wallace, B. C. (1990a). Crack cocaine smokers as adult children of alcoholics. *Journal of Substance Abuse Treatment,* VO1, pp. 89–100.

Wallace, B. C. (1990b). Crack addiction: Treatment and recovery issues, *Contemporary Drug Problems,* Spring 1990. *17(1),* 79–119.

Wanck, B. (1985) Treatment of adult children of alcoholics, *Carrier Foundation Letter,* *109,* 6.

Washton, A. M. (1986). Treatment of cocaine abuse. In NIDA Research Monograph 67. Rockville, Md.: NIDA.

Washton, A. M. (1987). Outpatient treatment techniques. In A. M. Washton and M. S. Gold (Eds.), *Cocaine: A clinicians' handbook*. New York: Guilford Press.

Washton, A. M. (1989a). *Cocaine addiction: Treatment, recovery, and relapse prevention.* New York: W. W. Norton.

Washton, A. M. (1989b) Cocaine Abuse and Compulsive Sexuality, *Medical Aspects of Human Sexuality*, pp. 32–39.

Washton, A. M. (1989c). Outpatient works, too, *The U. S. Journal of Drug and Alcohol Dependence*, *13*(12), 1.

Washton, A. M., and Gold, M. S. (Eds.). (1987). *A clinician's handbook*. New York: Guilford Press.

Washton, A. M., & Gold, M. S., & Pottash, A. C. (1986). Treatment outcome in cocaine abusers. In NIDA Research Monograph 67. Rockville, Md.: NIDA.

Washton, A. M., Stone, N. S., & Hendrickson, E. C. (1988). Cocaine abuse. In D. M. Donovan and G. A. Marlatt, (Eds.), *Assessment of addictive behaviors*. New York: Guilford Press.

Wegscheider-Cruse, S. (1986) From "reconstruction" to "restoration." In R. J. Ackerman (Ed.), *Growing in the shadow: Children of alcoholics*. Pompano Beach, Fla.: Health Communications.

Weidman, A. (1985). Engaging the families of substance abusing adolescents in family therapy. *Journal of Substance Abuse Treatment*, *2*, 97–105.

Weinraub, B. (1989, September 6). President offers strategy for U.S. on drug control. *The New York Times*, pp. 1, B7.

Weiss, R. D., & Mirin, S. M. (1986). Subtypes of cocaine abusers. *Psychiatric Clinics of North America*, *9*, 491–501.

Wesson, D. R., & Smith, D. E. (1985). Cocaine: Treatment perspectives. In N. J. Kozel; and E. H. Adams (Eds.), *Cocaine use in America: Epidemiologic and clinical perspectives*. NIDA Research Monograph 61, U.S. Government Printing Office, Washington, D.C.

Wetli, C. V. (1987). Fatal reactions to cocaine. In A. M. Washton and M. S. Gold (Eds.), *Cocaine: A clinicians' handbook*. New York: Guilford Press.

Wexler, H. K. (1987). Therapeutic communities within prisons. In G. DeLeon and J. T. Ziegenfuss (Eds.), *Therapeutic communities for addictions*. Springfield, Ill.: Charles C. Thomas.

Wexler, H. K., Lipton, D. S., & Johnson, B. D. (1988). A criminal justice strategy for treating cocaine-heroin abusing offenders in custody. *National Institute of Justice Issues and Practices*. U.S. Department of Justice, National Institute of Justice, Office of Communications Research.

Wexler, H. K., & Williams, R. (1986). The stay 'n out therapeutic community: Prison treatment for substance abusers. *Journal of Psychoactive Drugs*, *18*(3), 221–230.

Wexler, H. K., Falkin, G. P., & Lipton, D. S. (1990). Outcome evaluation of a prison therapeutic community for substance abuse treatment. *Criminal Justice and Behavior*, *17*(1), 71–92.

Wexler, H. K., & Williams, R. (1986). The stay 'n out therapeutic community: Prison treatment for substance abusers. *Journal of Psychoactive Drugs*, *18*(3), 221–230.

White, J. L., Parham, W. D., & Parham, T. A. (1980). In R. L. Jones, (Ed.), *Black/Psychology*. New York: Harper & Row.

Wikler, A. (1948). Recent progress in research on the neurophysiological basis of morphine addiction. *American Journal of Psychiatry*, *105*, 328–338.

Wikler, A. (1977). The search for the psyche in drug dependence: A 35-year retrospective survey. *Journal of Nervous and Mental Diseases*, *165*, 29–40.

Wise, R. A. (1984). Neural mechanisms of the reinforcing action of cocaine. In J. Gra-
    bowski (Ed.), *Cocaine: Pharmacology, effects, and treatment of abuse.* NIDA Research
    Monograph 50, Department of Health and Human Services, U.S. Government
    Printing Office, Washington, D.C.
Williams, H. R., & Johnston, B. A. (1972). Factors related to treatment retention in a
    methadone maintenance program. In *Proceedings of the Fourth National Conference
    on Methadone Treatment.* New York: NADAN.
Woititz, J. G. (1983). *Adult children of alcoholics.* Pompano Beach, Fla.: Health
    Communications.
Woititz, J. G. (1985). *Struggle for intimacy: Dedicated to adult children of alcoholics.* Pom-
    pano Beach, Fl.: Health Communications.
Woody, G. E., Luborsky, L., McLellan, A. T., & O'Brien, C. P. (1986). Psychotherapy
    as an adjunct to methadone treatment. In R. E. Meyers (Ed.), *Psychopathology and
    addictive disorders.* New York: Guilford Press.
Wurmser, L. (1974). Psychoanalytic considerations of the etiology of compulsive drug
    use. *Journal of the American Psychoanalytic Association, 22,* 820–843.
Wurmser, L. (1985). Denial and split identity: Timely issues in the psychoanalytic psy-
    chotherapy of compulsive drug users. *Journal of Substance Abuse Treatment, 2,* 89–
    96.
Yonekura, M. L. (1989, December). The impact of crack cocaine and other drugs on
    mothers and children. Paper presented at the Drug-Free Pregnancy Conference,
    San Mateo, Calif.
Zweben, J. E. (1986). Treating cocaine dependence: New challenges for the therapeutic
    community. *Journal of Psychoactive Drugs, 18*(3).

Author Index

Subject Index